Daring to Excel

The danger chiefly lies in acting well;
No crime's so great as daring to excel.

Charles Churchill,
Epistle to William Hogarth, 1763

Daring to Excel

THE STORY OF THE
NATIONAL YOUTH ORCHESTRA
OF GREAT BRITAIN

Ruth Railton

Secker & Warburg
LONDON

First published in Great Britain in 1992
by Martin Secker & Warburg Limited
Michelin House, 81 Fulham Road, London SW3 6RB

A CIP catalogue record for this book
is available from the British Library
ISBN 0 436 23359 2

Photoset in 12/14 Bembo by Wilmaset, Wirral
Printed and bound in Great Britain by
Mackays of Chatham PLC, Chatham, Kent

Contents

Illustrations

Photographs by the *News Chronicle* (2), the *Illustrated* (18), the *Irish Press* (34), Photo-Records ANP (35), John Dalby (42), the *Jerusalem Post* (43), Enomenon (44, 45), the *Daily Mirror* (3, 4, 6, 9, 11, 14, 15, 16, 17, 20, 21, 25, 26, 27, 31, 32, 33, 38, 40, 41, 46, 47).

Grateful acknowledgement is made to the *Daily Mirror* and the National Youth Orchestra for all their help in providing photographs, and to the *Mirror* for permission to reproduce them here.

Author's Note

This book, written by request, is the story of the National Youth Orchestra of Great Britain from its conception in 1946 through its birth and development to eventual international acclaim in 1965.

Its success was achieved by the hard work and devotion of hundreds of different people in all walks of life, many of whom are properly mentioned in the book. Alas, there are countless others whose names are not mentioned, through lack of space, loss of files, and perhaps worst of all loss of memory.

To all those people, and to all ex-members of the orchestra, whether it was the start of their musical career or just an unforgettable part of their general education, this book is dedicated.

Many people, to all of whom I am deeply grateful, have helped me with their memories, but all errors and mistakes, of which there are bound to be some, are mine alone.

Prologue

Off the coast of Scotland lies the tiny island of Lismore; one end is a short distance from the mainland shore and the road to Oban. It was Sunday, 3 September 1939, the morning we all heard on our radios Neville Chamberlain declaring war. Stunned into a silence that knows nothing will ever be the same again, we all set out on our respective plans. My task was to row over to Lismore with boxes of gas masks, one for every inhabitant of the island – men, women, children and even infants. It was an ominous-looking day, to fit the news, but the sea was not too rough for rowing. Arrangements had been made for the entire population to assemble in a large barn not too far from the landing stage, and sure enough, with Scottish reliability, we were met.

There was time to go to the morning service at the little Presbyterian church where I had sometimes played the 'harmoney' for the hymns: creaky and damp, its sound was regarded as a treat compared to no music at all, and 'O God our help in ages past' has never been more deeply felt. By two o'clock the entire population had assembled in or around the appointed barn, together with a few horses and carts and collie dogs, as there was no car on the island.

By now there was a strong gale and soon rain and approaching thunder, but we all huddled together for shelter while we continued fitting and distributing gas masks. As the waves got bigger and the lightning more frequent, there came a sudden roar of thunder; one whole side of the barn collapsed and the torrents poured in. The men shoved the women and children to the back in a protective barrier. The noise, the force, the flashing lightning were unforgettable. One young mother wept bitterly into her mask. 'Dinna fash yersel,' said the church elder, 'Hitler knows nothing of the winds and waves of the Lord. There'll be none of his gases here.' So we laughed and sang songs and hymns until all could return home. Walking back to the boat, wet through, I listened to the wisdom of the elder, who had been all through the Great War; as we untied the ropes to row away he said, 'We will not meet again, but remember, Hitler cannot kill music . . . *Never let your music go.*' The words fitted the rhythm of the oars, and when I reached the mainland I knew I'd never see Lismore again.

My whole family, especially my parents, loved the Western Highlands, and imbued us all from childhood with the wonders of nature – wild flowers, wild animals and birds, the power of the sea, the silence of the mountains – and for one month each year in August all the family came together on holiday. This August had stood in the shadow of inevitable war, through whose horrors my parents had been before. After only twenty years, the survivors of Ypres and Passchendaele must face it all again in their children. In 1939 my father was Rector of Liverpool, and decided to return early to be with his flock. On his last evening he spoke with courage and love to us all: 'This may be the last time we are all together.' (And so it was.) He knew we would stand by each other always, and spoke to each in turn about their special gifts. To me he said, 'You have your mother's gift of music. Try, *please try, never to let your music go*; you can do so much through music.'

I was at that time a student at the Royal Academy of Music in London. Nobody could possibly remain a student in wartime, so my first aim was to return to London and get permission to leave – without seeming ungrateful for a further exhibition recently awarded. The Principal, Sir Stanley Marchant, had been in the same regiment as my father in the Great War, and he looked at me over his glasses. 'Will you promise me not to rush into uniform? This is going to be a long war, and people will be needed for music. I will get in touch with you, and in the mean time *don't let your music go.*'

That hurdle over, my only thought was how to be within reach of my fiancé. Our engagement was only private: his RAF call-up had come in July, so I had spent August with my family. Now whatever I did was going to be close to wherever he was posted, on the spot for a sudden twenty-four- or forty-eight-hour pass.

In these first months of the war change was everywhere; the call-up left gaps to fill in every sphere. I learnt so much that was invaluable later: helping Lady Reading (then founding the WVS) fitting gas masks in the East End, the darkness cheered this time by Cockney humour; getting a student orchestra at the RAM in shape for Red Cross functions; taking over various choral-society rehearsals; helping to organise evacuating children from London. Then Sir Stanley sent for me: I was to go and see Dr Reginald Jacques, Music Director of the new Council for the Encouragement of Music and the Arts (later the Arts Council). He was auditioning for a team of musicians, from the most famous to postgraduate beginners like me, to keep music going in different areas of the country.

'What can you do?'

'Train choirs.'

'That may be important. Anything else?'

'Play the piano and organ a bit.'

'Sir Henry* says you can handle an orchestra.' I said that I couldn't really; I wasn't good enough yet. Jacques continued: 'I've just heard a marvellous young violinist, will you play with him now?' This was my first meeting with Yfrah Neaman (later Director of the Carl Flesch International Competition); next to appear was Kathleen Ferrier, whom I had met before when competing at music festivals. That afternoon three lifelong friendships were made.

Reginald Jacques was a sound musician and a remarkable person: Irish, in humour and charm; scholarly and sensitive. Badly wounded in both legs in the first war, he had difficulty

*I had been in Sir Henry Wood's conducting class at the RAM.

walking, but there was never a grumble and seldom a stick. I learnt much from him that I valued and needed later, particularly his judgement, his ability to assess what was good in our work and build on it with encouragement. I never once heard a negative criticism from him, and our professional association lasted for nearly twenty years.

And so 1940 dawned with my mind entirely with the RAF, and my living earned by rehearsing, playing and teaching before rushing back to the airfields. Spare time went to the Red Cross, twice helping out on the trainloads of wounded returning from Dunkirk. After that, the total loss of my flat and all my worldly possessions in a bombing raid was less of a shock. I learnt that to have health and strength and to live uncluttered by anything else, dependent on one's own work and character, was freedom. It was hard, and sometimes frightening, but it was freedom to serve; and a lesson in survival that I needed in the post-war world.

As the months went by and our skies were increasingly darkened by Hitler's Luftwaffe, more time was spent within reach of the Fighter Command airfield where my heart was. What a privilege – a heart-breaking privilege – to lie in the hedgerows through the summer days, and count the planes out . . . and back . . . or not back . . . May England never forget the few. By 15 September there were very few left. In our last month together my fiancé had said, 'If I fly on to Heaven, sing on, play on. *Don't let your music go.*' And music was all there was left.

Thus the war years went primarily to music; what a marvellous training it was. Wartime travelling involved long journeys standing, black-outs, air raids and nights spent on railway stations, but 'The show must go on', and we'd get there somehow. Choirs mattered most to me, and the choral societies of England – whether in small communities or big cities – would often have lost their conductors in the call-up. At Aldershot, for example, the choral society was joined by the friendly, disciplined Canadian troops stationed there; it cannot be often that such a society is suddenly overpowered by several hundred tenors and basses eager to join in the *Messiah* at Christmas away from home. The *Messiahs*, *Elijahs*, *Creations*, *Passions*, *Christmas Oratorios* and carols were ingrained in me from childhood, but experiencing the different personalities of choirs – the vitality of Yorkshire, the emotional power of Wales, the more practical attitude and enjoyment in the south – was revealing. I learnt from all this how different a conductor must be, both in rehearsal and performance, with different choirs if he is to use the gifts and temperament of the performers.

Orchestras, for me, were choirs with more varied voices and colours, all of which must breathe and *sing*, listen and blend. Malcolm Sargent showed me how to aim for security; Sir Henry Wood how to avoid too tight a rein and stifle the quality of sound – apparent opposites but both important. I needed to know all this, and later it enabled me to benefit from time spent with Toscanini and Bruno Walter.

At the many solo or ensemble recitals arranged by CEMA, I met great numbers of people who had never been to 'live' concerts before. With Kathleen Ferrier we always sang and played the greatest music: Bach, Handel, Mozart, Schubert and the marvellous tunes of our folk-song heritage. *Great* music never failed; Goethe said, 'If great art is not understood instantly by the simplest peasant it is not great art,' and here lay huge new future audiences, like sheep looking up to be fed.

On one occasion we were sent to the North-Western Approaches, where a Royal Navy battleship was based. Admiral Lockyer had a honky-tonk on board, so it was hymns for morning service and a sing-song in the evening. It was battle alert and mid-winter, at sea, but the happiness on the young men's faces is fixed in my mind for ever.

My work took me to Leicester. Although American troops occupied the race course and the Free French were not far away, it was considered a safe town in terms of bombing, having no heavy industry, and neither a port nor an airfield. The marvellous people were quiet, kind, courteous and responsive to new ideas. The children of Leicester, once given confidence, were especially memorable. Show them something, and they'd want more; start something new and they'd crowd in. Never before had I found so many marvellous voices; there was new talent everywhere. And the parents, though working overtime and in shifts, would give their last farthing if it was for their child's benefit. By far the majority of the nation's children live, learn and grow up in one place, unlike my own upbringing. I learnt so much from this that I needed later.

The work itself involved my first meeting with Harold Magnay, the Director of Education. He was very able, encouraging and full of enthusiasm. 'You go ahead and do all you can. You'll make mistakes, but that's my job to put them right. I'll support you.' And he did, then and after the war too. Then there was the exceptional Headmistress of the Wyggeston Girls' Grammar School, Nora Caress. She was herself tone-deaf, but had been at St Paul's with Gustav Holst, and knew the effect on a school of good music. She said, 'It's totally dead here; I want all the music you can create, to enliven my school,' and gave me a free hand. With what confidence doh-ray-me charts came off the music-room walls, and 'ta fe te fes' were gone with the wind. In came raw music: great tunes, great orchestral sounds, and singing. Then I bargained with the local impresario for a cheap price for all the seats behind the orchestra in the De Montfort Hall, and concert-going was introduced. In spite of transport problems and the black-out, the numbers grew and grew.

After a few months of children by day and various training-corps bands and choirs by night, I wrote to Cyril Winn, Her Majesty's Chief Inspector of Music, asking him to come for two days and help me. My tolerant headmistress could not contain her shock: 'The Chief Inspector? Here for two days?' What a lot I owe him though: his wealth of experience, his energy and enjoyment, his generosity with his time and advice. After the war he was the first person to whom I confided my plan for a national school for young musicians.

In a wild moment with Harold Magnay, we thought we'd start a Leicester children's orchestra. The newspapers announced that anyone who played an instrument was welcome on Saturday morning. Of course there was petrol-rationing and few cars; there were no grants and no free instrumental teaching or free instruments; there was a paper shortage and no copying machines. I'd prepared simple music and parts for about twenty, but sixty or more turned up, full of enthusiasm, as well as the orphanage brass band, stalwartly insisting on playing a tone higher than the rest of us. On the day, the local paper reported that 'the war effort in this city was seriously handicapped today due to scores of children, some of them with huge instruments, blocking available space in the morning trams'. (We only had two cellos.)

Around this time Myra Hess had started her lunch-hour recitals in the National Gallery. Of course we copied this in Leicester, in the museum, and through the fine performers that came from London week by week I made many new friends who supported me later. I also learnt that an excellent idea, if well organised and fulfilling a need, will be taken up all over the country.

For my second Christmas in Leicester I decided to attempt the Christmas part of the *Messiah*, performed entirely by schoolchildren. The orchestra was made up of local teachers and amateurs and a few children, and all the solos were sung by small groups; even Recitative was sung by four or five voices carefully blended to sound like one, as there were no solo voices ready to stand alone. Reginald Jacques came down to conduct the opening performance. Able to sit back and listen, I was moved by what could happen when potential young talent was led by so fine a musician. Perhaps it was then that the seed started to grow in my mind . . . the best talent from the whole country in the care of the greatest teachers.

Just before Christmas 1943 I went to call on Sir Henry. He

was not too well, and the tiredness of age was on him, but he was touched that I called. I told him about the young talent I had been discovering. I said that after the war I would form a very young symphony orchestra, all children of special talent. His eyes brightened, but he said, 'Now my dear, you look after your own special talent. You'll do something for music, but I'm not sure what.' And he gave me two of his batons, and two scores. I never saw him again as he died in 1944.

After my spell in Leicester I returned to London and considered how one musician might best serve the marvellous talent latent in British children, British amateurs, British audiences. *'Das Land ohne Musik'* was not true: it was just a lid on a newly bubbling cauldron. I was brought up to believe that talent was a gift not to be wasted, and I felt some responsibility for what I had discovered emerging all over the country. Obviously, we must start with the young, and find and teach the exceptionally talented.* Where? How? Whom could I find to believe in this wealth of hidden musical talent in Britain, which would undoubtedly bloom in the new era when at last peace was won?

*In 1977, I brought an eight-year-old cellist, whom I had spotted at six, to Slava Rostropovich. 'You and I have seen; therefore we are responsible,' he said, and he taught her free for four years.

Part One

THE FOUNDING YEARS

One

It was May 1945, and the end of the war was in sight. Based in London but travelling widely, I was constantly discovering marvellous talent, often where adequate teaching was not available. If only all the best could be put together in a boarding school, preferably in London, with day and evening help for those within reach, and Saturday and even weekend courses. I had no building; I had no money; I was unknown and unimportant. Surely the best start would be if it were attached to the Royal Academy or the Royal College of Music, which already had junior departments. I wanted a national music school for children, which must be headed by the nation's best musicians, so when I was not teaching I was asking to see the most important people in education and music. One evening at the fireside of Cyril Winn and his kindly wife we talked out the whole idea: boarding accommodation (full-time for a very few, but many more at weekends); about a hundred children for the symphony orchestra; that this could come together for ten days in the school holidays; a choir too; how these would go on tour; why it must be London-based but might have provincial branches. We listed conductors, and the great players who could also teach (not everyone can perform *and* teach). We thought of the cost. Cyril Winn genuinely believed it could work, but warned me of the barriers for a young person trying to start something new, especially a woman.

Next came Harold Magnay. He listened, asked about organisation, and finally said, 'If you do get started, and get in a jam, don't hesitate to come back to me in case I can help.' He mentioned that under the new 1944 Education Act, education authorities would be able to support children with grants. Finally he said, 'Go ahead: you have the talent, the ideas and the magnetic energy. I hope you're strong enough; I used to think a puff of wind would blow you over.'

Harold Craxton, the famous piano professor, was full of encouragement yet shocked to think I would contemplate giving up my own playing: 'Don't throw away one pearl for the possibility of a whole necklace.' Then Dr Armstrong Gibbs spent a whole evening discussing organisation; he thought it would be difficult and costly, but didn't dismiss it. Maurice Jacobson thought it was just what was needed, the talent was there, it was well worth an attempt. Dr Sydney Northcote, Director of Music for the Carnegie Trust, wanted to know every aspect of what I had in mind: he might be able to provide funding. At his request, I detailed my plans for the National School for Young Musicians and its Orchestra in writing. My first disastrous, naïve mistake.

In January 1946 Dr Northcote sent for me. He'd thought a lot about my idea, and decided that it would be best to start with a regional experiment. He suggested the Midlands, where I was known. While pleased at his renewed interest, I thought it much better to take the very best from the whole country from the start – if it succeeded then others could adapt the idea to suit their own areas; but pulling several area experiments together later would be too difficult. After much discussion, he persuaded me to try his suggestion. A base, a start, an experienced backer couldn't be turned down. I was to give up all my work and report to him on 1 March. He would have plans ready and finance for the scheme.

On 1 March I arrived as arranged, free of all commitments and ready to set off to pastures new. Dr Northcote simply said he was sorry to disappoint me, but he hadn't been able to 'get the education authorities to play'. I explained that I'd given up my work, on his express instructions. That, it seemed, was too bad.

I was set back, more because I'd been deceived, and by a well-known musician holding an important post, whose word I'd trusted, than because I had no means of earning my living.

While pondering what to do next, I was sent for by Sir Stanley Marchant again. How often I have found that when one door is slammed in your face another unexpectedly opens. It seemed he was considering letting me start my school, based at the RAM's junior department, but his time as Principal was almost over. So he wrote to Sir George Dyson, Director of the RCM, and asked him to see me.

I had never met Sir George before; he had very clear, penetrating blue eyes, a perceptive listener. 'When we are young we have these idealistic moods but we are not very practical. For instance, how do you think you could get children from all over the British Isles into one place to work?' I ventured to say that organisation seemed to be the least of my problems: it was the support of fine musicians that I most needed. 'You see, talent of the kind you are talking about doesn't often exist, it's very rare,' he said. Did he think I was mad to try? Another keen look at me. 'No. Too much faith and too few years.'

With no immediate work, there was time to go home to Scotland, to the family. This was the first plateau on which to pause and ponder after a long, dark war.

My father was a man of ideas. He had been all through the Great War as a chaplain, and after it thought up the idea of the Tomb of the Unknown Warrior in Westminster Abbey. It had not been easy for him to get that idea accepted, but it has been copied in most countries of the world. It was easy to talk to him about ideas, and I had many things I wanted to do apart from music. His view was, 'Always try; if you fail you can always come home, and then start again.' My mother was quite different. Pioneering was not her line: she was sensitive, a violinist. She had been a pupil of Eugène Ysaÿe in Brussels and a friend of Rachmaninov. Such were the social rules of the day that when Ysaÿe wanted her to give concerts, my grandmother brought her home instantly. There ended a musical career. She left home and took her broken heart to Liverpool, where she worked in the worst slums of Scotland Road in 1908. She would sometimes play the violin in the parish church, and the poor would come in, partly to keep warm, but also to listen entranced. Hers was a great love of music, shared with me from childhood. Now she said, 'Whatever you do next, *don't let your music go.*'

By the time I returned to London I had decided to go it alone; I wouldn't be happy if I hadn't tried. I knew this would mean sacrificing my own interests, and giving all my time and all I could earn to my cause. I wouldn't mind if after a huge effort it failed – I didn't mind being wrong – but I was consumed with the desire to find and help our outstanding musical children. I was convinced that even a hundred, properly taught and inspired, would over the years change the attitude of my country to musical performance, and raise its standards. It was the eternal amateur outlook in England that puzzled me. Everything was allowed as long as it was for fun and a good time was had by all, and the results didn't matter. I had never been able to understand why it was wrong to teach our young to do things as well as possible, why they should be denied the excitement and joy of achievement.

I decided to postpone the boarding-school idea for lack of funds, but thought I could borrow a boarding school in the holidays, three times a year, for three short ten-day terms of concentrated music. The children would then return to their own teachers and general education and come back for more professional help every holiday. When the time came to start, I would take about a hundred children from all parts of the British Isles, enough for a symphony orchestra – an experience not available to children in most places at the time – and a chamber orchestra, with superb teachers for all instruments. Most importantly, there must always be a public performance at the end of each term. There is no music until it is performed, and performance is quite different from practising and playing privately. Also, if the public saw and heard what I thought we could produce, they would believe and would support us.

A friend shared her garret amongst the bombed houses in Ebury Street near Victoria Station. There were three small rooms, a cooker on the landing, and a hole in the roof. She had a good library, which we would pile up against the driest wall as the autumn rains increased. It is surprising how little one needs to live. I had a bed, a chair, a table, piles of music and a variety of evening dresses for concerts, hanging in the least damp corner. I gave myself 10s. a week to live on, yet with the damp, the starvation diet and the long hours of work, I was never ill. Often I would sleep, exhausted, in trains, but somehow the energy and strength lasted.

While earning my living and putting aside every farthing for my orchestra, I had three special sources of happiness. I was a member of a small professional choir, the Cantata Singers, and with Reginald Jacques and his orchestra we rehearsed and recorded a Bach cantata for the BBC every Sunday. From my earliest childhood – Brandenburg 3 on the nursery gramophone – Bach has meant more to me than all other music. Now Bach on Sunday restored me each week. Then there was the Aldershot Choral Society. Elwyn Jones, the Secretary and leading tenor, had a small hotel near the station. I'd come off the rush-hour train and rest by their huge open fire and be fed with a home-made Welsh high tea. People came over from Fleet and Farnborough, many taking part for the first time in great oratorios. There was always laughter on Tuesday nights, and the joy of being among true friends. The third source, ingrained in my heart for ever, was the very special English village of Much Hadham. Its inhabitants included Walter de la Mare, Henry Moore, the Pasteur family, Mr Sporborg the banker, the Norman family of Bank of England fame, Sir Frank Lee and many other distinguished businessmen whose wives dragged them out to the Musical Society Choir on Thursday nights. It would be a night of 'home life' for me, with a different hostess each week. Much Hadham, and especially Moore Place and the Norman family, played its part in founding the National Youth Orchestra of Great Britain.

I was determined that my school would be in existence by 1 January 1947, and to that end I needed a secretary; the right VIPs in support; and the right title for the first printed statement of my aims and purpose. How would I find a secretary who was well educated, able to work on her own, full of energy and interested in music, all for the lowest wage? Then, at a Bach choir rehearsal in Westminster Cathedral Hall, I bumped into a former pupil.

'What are you doing in London?' I asked.

'I'm a secretary at the Conservative Party's headquarters.'

'If you hear of anybody interested in music, I'm looking for a secretary myself.'

'I'll come. I'd love to. I could start in a month,' she replied. I explained that she couldn't drop a good job and prospects for my wild scheme, that she'd often be working alone and it wasn't right for her; but nothing could shake her.

Philippa Ramsden was nineteen, radiantly attractive, full of laughter, independent, ready for a challenge, quick and intelligent. To have such a remarkable character at my side through the first two, tough founding years was a miracle. Her lovely youthful innocence overcame everything: disasters and setbacks were funny; ill-mannered replies to letters were contemptible; opposition was just stuffy or lacking in imagination; success for the NYO was inevitable!

It seemed to me that a national organisation must have a royal patron. So I wrote to the Queen (now Queen Elizabeth the Queen Mother), explaining what we were going to do and asking with the greatest humility for her to be our patron. Never will I forget the joy of the day we had the reply from Buckingham Palace. The fact that the answer was no was nothing compared with the interest, the encouragement, the warmth of the letter. It advised me that 'it is not the custom of the royal family to lend their patronage to ideas that are only in projection, and not yet in existence. But Her Majesty wishes you every success, and you are welcome to write again when your plans reach fruition.' From the day of this letter I was not going to fail. It kept me going at each major setback, and in due course I would write again.

Next I needed a president and vice-presidents. Sir Henry Wood's place (in charge of the Proms) at the BBC had been taken by Sir Adrian Boult. I asked him to be President; he accepted graciously, and asked to be kept in touch. Invited to be vice-presidents, Sir Malcolm Sargent replied enthusiastically, Reginald Jacques encouragingly, John Barbirolli (Conductor of the Hallé) with support and Sir Thomas Beecham amusingly – though he forgot to say if he'd be a vice-president or not, and I hadn't the nerve to write again and find out. With such an array of leading conductors behind us, we compiled a list of supporters. I went to see many famous musicians I knew, and wrote to others. I had known Vaughan Williams from my teenage years, when I used to help train village choirs for his Leith Hill Festival. Myra Hess, Boyd Neel and Arnold Bax were all keen. In any spare moments we wrote for financial support for this non-existent scheme. I remember a red-letter day when Jack Hylton, the dance-band leader of the day, sent us £5 and good luck. We were very grateful. To us £5 was a lot of money. Others who responded and sent gifts were Solomon, one of our great pianists; the Earl of Harewood; Viscount Kemsley; J. Arthur Rank; and Vic Oliver.

But suddenly there was no office. Returning home one evening in a heavy storm, I ran up the garret stairs and was met by a rush of water pouring in from the huge hole in the roof. After rescuing essentials – music, clothes and typewriter, in that order – and mopping up, I remember thinking, as the gas stove lit up, how lucky I was to have a dry bed, two hot-water bottles and hot tea; a human could survive on that.

The next morning I was teaching choirs in a private school in Bromley. Someone told the Headmistress my sad tale, and she insisted that I stayed at the school: a tiny room was allocated, with a telephone and a desk where Philippa could work. Because of one headmistress's belief in my idea, we were in action again. Not wishing to take advantage of my temporary rescuers, I made it a priority to find a London headquarters before going into print.

I thought of the music publishers and shops in London: perhaps they would help? I called on Augeners: they were kind and helpful and genuinely overcrowded. Next came Boosey & Hawkes, who supplied instruments to young players and bands and would stand to gain from any stimulus in instrumental work: a rather cold manager wasn't interested. This was lack of imagination, not lack of space. Then I remembered the publishers Curwens, and to my surprise the Chairman was Maurice Jacobson, the marvellous musician whom I'd known from schooldays through the Federation of Music Festivals; more recently he'd trained me as a judge for such competitions. I had already discussed the idea with him. So for a change there was a warm welcome, but for us to work in their small space was out of the question. He suggested Novello, who were near by; I trudged on.

Novello's premises were palatial. Here was huge empty space and a large unused pillared area from which a stylish staircase swept upwards. No doubt on the first floor much work proceeded apace, as they supplied the choirs of England with music. The gentleman I spoke to ignored my pleading – 'We couldn't possibly offer space to charity' – and as it was just about closing time escorted me down the stairs and shut the door firmly; from the pavement I heard the bolts clang behind me.

A new day, new hope: I set off again, looking at space in Steinway, Blüthner and OUP, before someone told me about Joseph Williams Ltd, who were in temporary premises after bomb-damage to their own. Once inside my heart fell: they were really overcrowded. There was just one floor of a prefabricated building, and a tiny space left for sales from the counter. I asked who the Chairman was, and got the reply, 'Would you like to see him?' I was taken to a tiny office at the back and greeted warmly by a smiling, grey-haired, blue-eyed gentleman.

Florian Williams was one of the most remarkable people I've

ever known. He built up the firm after the Great War for his sons, but they were not interested in it, and he carried on alone, through the bombing of the second war, rescuing it to this temporary storehouse. 'Sit down; it's nice of you to call on me. Nobody does these days because I'm stone deaf . . . Since the Great War – 1917 – I haven't heard a note of music. What can I do for you? Here's a slate, write to me.'

I remember so vividly scribbling about my ideas for helping young musicians, the best talent in the country, the National Youth Orchestra . . . handing him the slate, scribbling the answers to his questions. Did I want money? No, just a London address and office. I realised he was overcrowded already . . . His eyes shone at the thought of helping the young. Perhaps we could squash in where the customers came in, by the door. We went to the front, and he found a table and two chairs, and started organising for a telephone to be extended. My overflowing expressions of gratitude were halted with 'We look forward to seeing you in a fortnight.'

So on 2 January 1947 the National Youth Orchestra of Great Britain was in business: a London office, a president and vice-presidents, a long list of famous supporters, an ideal secretary and a bank account. I had saved £500 to open the first NYO account. Every Friday Philippa went to Lloyds in Baker Street to check the account and collect her wages – a mere £5 a week – and the clerk was always amused that the cheque was made out to her and signed by her, as I was often away. That £500, with occasional refills from my earnings and from small subscriptions, lasted us until after the first concert in April 1948.

Two

Our first morning's work in Joseph Williams was a red-letter day. Florian Williams greeted us with a pot of flowers, an envelope with a £10 cheque in it and introductions to all his staff. At the end of the first week I asked a rather suspicious elderly manager if all was well, and he asked if we could laugh a little less. It distracted his staff, especially if we shared the joke. (We had some very funny letters, often from children.)

The first main item of work was to produce a small leaflet stating our aims and purpose, and listing the names of our supporters. I wrote to directors of education, county music advisers, directors of music in schools, headteachers. I hope my letters were polite, explaining that we needed their interest and suggestions, but most of them went into the waste-paper basket. To several hundred letters, about eleven directors of education bothered to reply. The best of these was from the Shetland Isles: 'We have plenty of talent here, but no instrumental teachers. We wish you every success . . . you will always be welcome to help our young musicians.'

After a few months it was clear that the education authorities were not involved in the huge new growth of musical interest, and that the best talent in the country was not going to reach us via that route. So we spent a little on printing some black and white quarto posters, stating our exact aims and inviting any young musician who was interested to write to us direct at our office. My idea was to get every music shop in the British Isles to put one up in their window or showroom. Every manager was sent a persuasive letter and a poster. A majority must have put them up, because the results were stunning. Letters poured in by every post, over two thousand from children themselves.

They were often on scraps of paper, probably torn out of school exercise books.

> I love music, and want to play, I have a 'cello, but it has no strings on it – could you please help me.
>
> My father puts money aside every Friday from his wages, so that I can play the flute. I have to go by train to the city for this which costs money too. I want to do well, so please tell me how I can join you.
>
> I can play the trumpet in the Salvation Army band, but that's only hymns, I long for great big music of other kinds, what shall I do now?

There were formal letters too – some, full of enthusiasm, from parents – and most startling of all, people also called on us, sometimes travelling quite a long way, to make sure their pupils didn't get left out of this great opportunity. They must have been surprised to find our tiny 'headquarters' and two people coping with this avalanche of response. There were about five suspicious or antagonistic letters: it was a silly or impossible idea; we would be falsely raising the hopes of ambitious children. Every letter was answered, every address kept. We were now ready to plan a tour of the British Isles, and the first meeting of the NYO in August 1947.

How wrong I was. What the children had seen in the music shops, so had the adults who passed that way; these included teachers and trades unionists. It had not entered my head that anybody would want to oppose the idea of helping young musicians, particularly those who had not, previously, had any chance. I had after all approached so many important musicians in official positions and none had objected to the idea as such, only expressing doubts about organisation, money, or sufficient young talent. But now telephone messages and letters started to arrive, intimating that 'certain groups' wanted to stop me. If I asked friends why, the vague answers would be to the effect that a national scheme should be run by 'them', or if I succeeded, it might show 'them' up or do 'them' down. This was all so foreign to my idealism that it rather floated off me; but then came a telephone call from Sydney Northcote, asking me to come and see him. I agreed readily, thinking he'd decided to help us after all, and went round to his office where he and another man were waiting.

Dr Northcote's opening remark was, 'I hear you are trying to start a national youth orchestra, or am I mistaken?' Then: 'I thought I had told you that it was not possible, not even regionally . . . Are you telling me that you'd dare to try on your own what I've told you cannot succeed? The world of music in education will see to that . . . I have the power: I hold the money bags; the music advisers to the education authorities are paid by me . . . he who pays the piper calls the tune . . . Now, talking of money, I didn't know you were a millionaire . . . No? . . . I wonder where the large sums needed for a national youth orchestra come from? . . . Do you realise, a young woman alone . . . a word here and a word there and I can see to it that you will never get a job in the profession again . . .' After more threats came the emotional appeal: 'It would be such a pity to ruin your reputation so early . . . we all appreciate your talent, and only want to see your success . . . So I'm sure you'll agree to give it up . . . Now we don't want to hurry your decision . . . we'll leave you to think about it . . .'

When they rose to go to the door I intended to leave too, but they went through saying they'd come back presently. They shut the door, and then I heard the key turn. I waited until they were in the street, and tried the handle . . . *I was locked in.* (Years later, when I met my husband, he explained that all I had to do was to break a window and shout for help from the street below and I could have got plenty of money for the NYO by suing for wrongful imprisonment. Alas, I didn't know.)

In the next two hours I had time to think. Was it really no longer a free country? Was Britain now to be run by permission of trusts, associations and unions? Finally footsteps and voices announced the return of my captors. 'Of course, by now you will have accepted our advice and will give up.' I replied clearly that I thought it was a free country, and I wouldn't be happy if I didn't try.

Once outside I ran down Gloucester Place, and almost bumped into Philippa.

'What's happened? I was coming to meet you.'

'I think we've had it . . . he's out to kill.'

'He couldn't do that!'

'Yes he can . . . He *has* got the power . . .'

'What absolute nonsense! Look at all the power you've got, all those names on that piece of paper. He hasn't a hope.' Such was her total faith that I couldn't argue. I knew for certain that there was a nasty war ahead, and I had no tools for battle nor any desire to fight. But, with Philippa, I would go on.

As so often in life, a black cloud has a silver lining. Quite soon came a letter from the Music Masters' Association, inviting me to address their next meeting in London. These were the directors of music of all the great boys' public schools of England. They had seen the posters, and each school had had a letter from us asking for their views about the possible participation of their pupils. I had to accept, though I was expecting yet another attack. When the afternoon came I was so nervous, and so completely knocked out by the warm welcome and the courtesy of their President, Dr Hylton Stewart, that I had to ask to sit down to address them. They were very chivalrous, and simply asked me to tell them exactly what I was trying to do. I recounted the whole story to date, including being locked up by Sydney Northcote. I think they were a bit shocked by it all, and passed a motion promising me every support; they invited me to visit their schools, and expressed hope for the success of the NYO. When an NYO council was set up in 1948 it included an MMA representative and always has done.

Before the summer was over we had sent out over two thousand application forms. Sydney Northcote must have assumed he'd finished me off, as there was little opposition in the correspondence now. My mind was occupied with where we might meet first: which boarding school would have us? Where would be the best place for our first concert? I wanted to be in or near a small town, where our first experiment would attract no publicity, and this needed to be settled before I could embark on hearing the applicants.

After a short August holiday we returned to work with renewed vigour, only to discover that the summer conferences of various teaching and musical organisations had been discussing our plans, and now most, on the instructions of Sydney Northcote, regretted that 'on educational grounds' they would have to withdraw their support: some could not approve of children being allowed to perform in public; some said children would be used to further my own reputation; some thought I would give them false hope. In any case, musical education should remain in the hands of the established guardians thereof. The latter seemed to be the Music Teachers' Association and the Schools Music Association. At this time there were various summer schools for amateurs, students and teachers. The MTA may have been under the impression that I was intending some such summer school, as it was not long before they started on a campaign against me. The SMA, under its Secretary Mr Trethewy, behaved too badly to record. I refrain out of respect for a later secretary, Stephen Moore, who did all in his power to repair the personal damage, to serve the NYO and to clear this blot from the SMA's escutcheon.

By October we still had no premises for the first term, and were wondering what to do next, when the telephone went. It was one Ian Hunter, an impresario. Could I come and see him? Today? Yes. He was a newly demobbed young officer, embarking on his first important project, a new venture called the Bath Assembly. Bath was known for its mild climate, old ladies and the Pump Rooms; Ian Hunter wanted to revitalise its image, with the accent on youth and the future. He said he'd heard I had a youth orchestra.

'I haven't yet . . . I've got two thousand names on pieces of paper, and that doesn't mean anything.'

'Could you be ready to give the first concert in the first Bath Assembly?' I said I would need his help finding accommodation. 'Well, let's do it. April 21, 1948.' I accepted the challenge, but explained that as yet I could have no idea of the standard, and therefore no idea what programme to play, and there was opposition in my path. How could I promise to do this and then let him down? Ian Hunter was quick and imaginative:

'I will have other orchestras in Bath anyway, so why don't we agree that I will never hold it against you if you have to withdraw even at the last minute; and you will do all in your power to give the first concert of the National Youth Orchestra of Great Britain.'

I hurried back to the office. I had found enthusiasm, partnership, a goal to work for. Philippa declared this a red-letter day with such excitement that all the Joseph Williams staff joined in. The first NYO concert was to be the *first* concert in the *first* Bath Assembly and what was more on Princess Elizabeth's birthday, 21 April.

Late that night I began to ponder what those two thousand flat pieces of paper would actually sound like . . .

The next month went chiefly to planning a tour of the British Isles, to hear every child that had applied to join. I decided to go even to small places rather than expect children to travel. Travelling in 1947 was very different from now, and relatively inexpensive; there were far fewer cars. I had to work out the cheapest way to cover the whole country on our diminishing funds: night journeys instead of staying in hotels (sometimes I would have to spend most of the night in railway waiting-rooms); each Saturday night should be in an area where I had friends and could rest a bit on Sunday. I would be away from 1 January to almost the end of March, so a complete plan was worked out to co-ordinate the state schools and directors of education, the private schools, the music shops, the private teachers, my personal friends and individual musicians. I drafted standard letters for Philippa: 'Please can you arrange', 'Thank you for all you did' and 'Owing to emergency, we have changed our plans'. She had no previous experience, and was going to be in charge of the entire tour. In the event she was fully up to it, rising to each problem with charm and common sense.

Before the end of the year we had been to Bath, where accommodation in boarding schools and a day school with a big hall for rehearsals were willingly offered for the week preceding the concert. By the third week in December it was time to go home to the mountains and the sea and my family for Christmas. It was my last Christmas at home; a peaceful haven before the storm.

Three

On 1 January 1948 I crossed Scotland to start the first auditions in Aberdeen. I was setting off to find that *potential* talent that nobody would believe existed, although two thousand children had written to me. Apart from the actual playing, I looked for an elusive quality: a high sensitivity, a response, imagination and vitality, together with the qualities of character necessary to bring such gifts to fulfilment. To the outside world such children are usually called 'highly strung', almost as if it were a fault, but it is often a sign of some inner essence beyond the ordinary.

I hoped to discover up to 110 such children, aged from thirteen to eighteen, covering all instruments. I wanted to choose every child personally, and to meet their parents and teachers if possible, to see their school and gauge the atmosphere of their village or city. I would then create for them a family held together by love of music, but also by the desire to learn, by the discipline of work and relaxation. They would all need individual attention, all be at different stages, but would all help and learn from each other, to create together an artistic performance in an orchestral concert.

As the train moved through some of the finest scenery in the world and neared the granite city of Aberdeen, I began to wonder what talent I would find in one week in Scotland. With what nerve I had written to Aberdeen's Director of Education, saying I was coming to hear the candidates for the NYO on 1 January, inviting his music adviser and any teachers to meet me and asking if he could provide a suitable place and piano. The reply was most welcoming: the Superintendent of Music, John Dalby, would meet me in the main hotel. Only when I reached the deserted station did it dawn on me that it was the sacred New Year's Day in Scotland! But the sturdy Aberdonians had arranged everything without so much as an alternative suggestion. John Dalby wrote:

> I had not yet met Ruth Railton, but the powerful letters she wrote gave hints of a middle-aged, dragon-like woman of the tweedy type. On that fateful New Year's Day 1948 the lounge of Aberdeen's Caledonian Hotel looked dejectedly deserted as I entered it to make rendezvous with this enigmatic woman. Certainly the dragon of my imaginings was not present. True, a young lady sat demurely on a sofa but it was absurd to assume that such an elegant woman had written those forceful letters. Ruth Railton's expectation was of meeting a smartly dressed Superintendent of Aberdeen's music, but I lack talent in matters sartorial. So both of us sat and awaited the appearance of the person each of us envisaged.
>
> At long last I plucked up courage and approached the young lady. 'Do you, by any chance, happen to be Miss Railton?' I asked politely. 'Yes I am,' she said, adding with well-concealed surprise, 'And are you Mr Dalby?'

Once united, we went to his office and met three musicians from the university and schools; four candidates were duly presented. I still remember what nice people they all were, how seriously interested in their students and in the NYO, and a friendship with Aberdeen was established which has lasted to this day. There was also one possible member, John Reay, a violinist, whom I did select, so that the very first audition bore fruit.

John Dalby took me to the station for my train to Dundee, and already I was aware I had met a very unusual, able, kind and amusing person. He wrote that

> as the train was moving out of the station she called out, 'If we get to Bath, will you come and help?' Upon the spur of the moment, and in competition with the increasing rumblings of the train I yelled back, 'YES.' That yes proved to be the chief turning point in my life . . . It enabled me to participate in inspiring experiences and exciting adventures in company

with wonderful people, staff and students alike, and above all else the aura and leadership of Ruth Railton.

The next morning found me in Dundee's music shop with a very welcoming manager; a room and piano were provided and a few candidates turned up as instructed, including one good violinist, taught privately. But, understandably, culture was not a priority in Dundee. By lunch-time I was in the great capital city of Edinburgh.

This was memorable because of my first meeting with two remarkable people, the Doctors Waddell. Both were academic musicians, doctors of music of the famous university; both were also players and teachers (one a violinist, one a cellist). They welcomed me to their school; their pupils had a distinctive quality of playing and approach to music. Afterwards there was time to share ideas, so I left feeling that I had partners, and was no longer alone. As it happened, both Aberdeen and Edinburgh were to play a big part in the NYO's history, but at this stage all that existed were the first five names in my notebook. Years later I was often asked how I remembered all the people I heard each year. A good memory, aural and visual, was not enough. I wrote a fairly detailed report on every child, on a sheet attached to the application form which went back to the office; I also had a special notebook of my own in which I listed the most outstanding and impressive people. But a name was not enough, so I noted the room in which they played, often a description such as 'red hair and green dress', any unusual remark in our conversation and of course the music played. In this way I could recall months later the difference between a violinist in Aberdeen and one in Coventry or Exeter or Norwich. Each night I would refresh my memory and really hold each child's personality in my mind until the final decision was made. Looking for potential, a seed that will become a flower, is totally different from examining a performance on the day.

And so to Glasgow, only an hour by train but entirely

different in character from the east, with a large Irish element in the population. The Royal Scottish Academy of Music and Drama had responded kindly to my request for a centre for auditions. There was also my first meeting with the Misses Ommer, who had their own private music school doing excellent work on piano and violin, and they became and remained close supporters. While with them I sensed how seldom such private teachers met musicians from a wider field.

So my first audition tour of Scotland closed with a few names in my notebook, much latent enthusiasm uncovered and new friends made. Before I left Glasgow a letter arrived from Philippa to tell me where to go next. The old LNER and LMS railways had between them managed to give me a special cheap ticket which, provided I didn't go back on my tracks, would take me from Aberdeen through all the cities and small towns of England and Wales and back to London. While on tour I could not earn any money, and sometimes wondered if our tiny bank balance could possibly last until we got to Bath. Philippa reported that English schools were strangely unwelcoming, but on the positive side: 'Someone told me at a party that Lord Kemsley was very rich, so I wrote to him asking if he'd like to support us and he's sent a whole *TEN* pounds! So you needn't worry about money.'

My first stop in England was Carlisle, for a few candidates, then across to Newcastle's Royal Grammar School. The Musical Director, Arthur Milner, welcomed me to hear his pupils; but I sensed a certain stiffness towards me. He offered to accompany the performers, and afterwards I invited him to join me for dinner and, hesitantly, he accepted. During the evening it emerged that Sydney Northcote had written to all the education authorities' music advisers, warning them against me and my aims, and advising them to block any support. All the application forms had been signed by the child's parent, headteacher and instrumental teacher: I was very particular that both schools and private teachers should have agreed to the audition. Mr

Milner was interested in the idea, and as his was a partly independent school he did not withdraw his candidates, preferring to make up his own mind; Northumbrians are historically a proud, independent and poetic people, who think for themselves. Before the evening was over he had agreed to come to Bath and help with the chamber music group.

On I went to Sunderland and Durham. I saw the devastation, poverty and unemployment in these northern towns following the slump of the 1930s. Here the Salvation Army was active. If you were poor and wanted to play an instrument you joined the SA, and played emotional hymns. Without the use of SA instruments and its training, the profession would have lost much talent. I would often give auditions to young brass players and see that Railton was one of their names, and find they'd been called after the grandfather I never knew. Commissioner George Scott Railton introduced bands and singing into the SA, and it was he rather than General Booth who said, 'Why should the Devil have all the best tunes?' At brass auditions it was always easy to tell if young players had started in the works bands or the SA: the latter played musically, with shape, feeling and dynamics, the former with technique and efficiency.

The famous Darlington Grammar School had the highest standards so far. Its Director of Music was laden with letters asking for support in the fight against my wicked plans. We worked together for a whole day, while he struggled with conflicting loyalties: his links to the organised opposition, and wanting the best for his pupils. Some years later, after a few of his talented pupils were accepted and he saw the results, our association became friendly and lasted for many years.

At Sedbergh School in the Westmoreland hills, I was the guest of a remarkable headmaster, Mr Bruce Lockhart, and his wife. His clear independent mind plumbed the whole NYO concept, and he taught me much on the educational front and prepared me for the pettiness I would meet. It was here too that I first met Christopher Cowan, the Director of Music, later to move to Uppingham and then Winchester, who eventually had three of his own children in the orchestra. I left Sedbergh much strengthened.

Ripon unexpectedly – due to one private teacher, a Mr Higginbotham – produced some really lovely string-playing, and my notebook list grew by several names here. Harrogate and York were on my route to Hull, where I was welcomed, having judged at their music festival.

And so to Leeds, flourishing on the wool trade and allied industries. The education authority had supplied a large room and piano in the museum where for several days I worked alone. A sombre figure would often come in, walk around, then disappear. Each time he tended to stay longer and sit and listen. I presumed he was the curator, wishing we weren't in his museum. On the last afternoon he burst into life, and came up to me: 'I'm Dr Hooper, the Music Adviser for Leeds. I've had all the warning letters from Carnegie, and opposition from the MTA, but having seen you at work I've made up my own mind. Give me the music, let me accompany for you.' Later that evening he took me out to supper, and to the station for my next train. He remained a loyal friend of the NYO until he died.

But my most vivid memory of Leeds is owed to the charwoman at the museum. She thought it was grand for all these young people to play music. 'There's a little boy in our road, he plays lovely on the piano.' I asked her to go and get him, to tell him to come round *any* time, and I'd fit him in. In due course a tiny eight-year-old arrived, in a spotless white shirt and socks, and made his way to the piano. What a special moment it was: fine talent coupled with superb teaching, and something of rare beauty that only a child can touch. This was Allan Schiller. I asked, 'Who is your teacher? Go and ask her to come and see me; explain I'm leaving tonight.' Before I left, Fanny Waterman* and her supportive husband Dr de Keyser appeared. She always says that I was the first to give her real encouragement and appreciation; but for my part I'd found a

*Founder and Chairman of the Leeds International Pianoforte Competition.

gift for teaching that is very rare and special, and someone with whom to share standards as high as my own. Now, forty-four years later, we still keep in touch, and although we teach in quite different ways we still think alike regarding musical standards and performance.

After Leeds came many smaller towns like Halifax, Wakefield and Huddersfield, and then Bradford. I had lived there for four years, and childhood impressions of the hunger and poverty in the '30s were indelible: that ghastly tragedy on the top of the million dead in the First World War. I can still see the thick black smoke from the factory chimneys against the deep red sunset, the view from my bedroom window on the hill; I can hear the clogs on the paving stones, and the rattle and hiss of the trams in the rain. My first candidate was a tough-looking fourteen-year-old with a very fine trumpet. When we'd made friends I said, 'That's a very good instrument, where did you get it?'

'Ah lifted it.'

'Where from?'

'Where d'yer think? From t'band-room of t'band, for t'audition.' I asked him to promise me he would take it straight back. Trying to find out how much he knew technically and musically and how he would respond to teaching, I asked him to play some passage again a slightly different way, only to hear 'And wot d'yer know about t'trumpet?' After some years with the NYO and then college, he has had a very happy career in a great orchestra, and not long ago came to thank me.

Later the same day a small ten-year-old Jewish boy with shining eyes and an eager appealing expression was brought in by his father. Not only do the Jews have an inborn talent, but the violin is part of their nature. The most beautiful, musical sound emerged. His father explained that his boy was to be a soloist and play concertos, and offered, 'If you can help my boy, I could make you a beautiful suit.' He was a tailor, but the generosity was greater at this time of clothing coupons. I assured him there was no doubt about his son's talent and future career, but there was so much to learn on the way to being a soloist; I'd do all I could to help. He is now a famous violinist.

New instructions from Philippa sent me west, to the great cities of Liverpool and Manchester and the many small towns in their orbit. Civic pride was very strong through the black smoke, the endless rain and the winter fog. Although the rivalry is only humorous now, the difference in temperament between the Lancastrian and the Yorkshireman was still very marked. The Yorkshire child is extrovert and full of vitality; in Lancashire they move and speak much more slowly, are thoughtful and of quieter mood.

I started in Blackpool, and found an unexpected welcome from a little community of musicians; there was a lot of natural talent being fostered. To this day I remember hearing a clarinettist of fourteen: sensitive and poetic with that inner quality which matters most. His father had died, his mother went to work to help with the children's education, and he played the church organ on Sunday. He couldn't be left behind.*

In Preston and Blackburn, the convent schools were full of enthusiasm. The nuns know that spiritual qualities develop with the arts, and were eager to learn more about the NYO. And then came Liverpool. It had been my home for a few years when my father was Rector, and everybody remembered him. Philippa had reported that there seemed to be no opposition here, and how easy it had been to make the arrangements. It seemed a miracle that Harold Magnay, who knew my work in Leicester, was now the Director of Education for Liverpool. He gave me every support, and wrote to his friends and colleagues in other areas about the NYO. His faith in me allayed my worries, and his laughter restored my fatigue. Mr Rushworth of the famous music shop Rushworth & Dreaper lent his studios, even produced a cheque, and remained a devoted supporter for the next twenty years.

*Colin Bradbury, now principal clarinet of the BBCSO.

*

North Wales was a new area to me, and apart from the public-school pupils there were few candidates. The Welsh sing, of course, but instrumental work was not as strong. In the smaller places the MTA was at work, as people said to me, 'I hear you are going to exploit the young to fill your own pocket.'

The only way I was going to start work in Manchester at nine a.m. was via a dawn train from Crewe, where I arrived at one in the morning. The nearest hotel was about seven minutes' walk away, and I was frightened to risk it alone, in the dark; so I settled for the station waiting-room, and the lingering warmth from the embers of a coal fire. As clothes-rationing meant that if you took your hand or your eye off your suitcase it might disappear, I tied my luggage handles to my belt, and curled up to get some sleep. Not long afterwards, I heard heavy footsteps on the station platform, getting steadily nearer, and the door opened to reveal the ever-reliable British bobby. He started, 'Now, missy, you can't stay here . . . no lingering in railway stations . . .' Opening my briefcase, I displayed the large black type of our headed notepaper: THE NATIONAL YOUTH ORCHESTRA OF GREAT BRITAIN, and underneath this, *Sir Adrian Boult, John Barbirolli, Sir Malcolm Sargent*, etc. 'I work for this organisation and have to be in the *Royal* College of Music in Manchester at nine a.m. I'm waiting for the six a.m. milk train.' Faced with such an array of names his attitude changed: not only could I stay, but he'd complete his beat and come back this way to see that I was all right. At five-forty-five he returned with a porter and a cup of tea, and together they saw me into the train for Manchester.

The Royal Manchester College of Music had a long tradition of training professional musicians, and was closely connected with the Hallé Orchestra. The rain that ensured the success of the cotton trade was still pouring down. Lovely children with a wide variety of instruments appeared with wet shoes and wet hair; even the music seemed damp. After about two or three candidates I overheard from outside the door, 'She speaks London and that fast. I can't understand a word she says.' From then on I tried to remember to speak slowly. People no longer realise how very varied in pace, rhythm and pronunciation were the many dialects, and what a loss it is poetically and musically that the *quality* of the speaking voice is no longer noticed or valued.

Memorable too was a young violinist who, when I was playing for her or speaking to her, moved her head to one side to listen. Afterwards I asked to see her mother, and asked if the child was deaf. She had no idea, but was overjoyed at a possible solution to a problem: 'I know my daughter is intelligent and reads and does well in written work, but the school says she's stupid in class.' The child was found to be totally deaf in one ear, and the right medical help transformed her life. We never met again musically, but for many years she wrote to me every Christmas.

What impressed me most in Manchester was my first visit to Chetham's, the fourteenth-century college for the cathedral choirboys, and the modern school was still more interested in music than the average; but it was exceptionally so because of one teacher, the Art Master Gerard Littlewood. A naturally talented amateur and very gifted teacher, he lived for music-making. I was given an orchestral and choral concert. All this activity was backed and encouraged by the Headmaster Harry Vickers and his wife, who insisted I stayed the night. We talked into the early hours, sharing our views on musical education. He offered the loan of his school for the future, and from then on I was invited every year to Chetham's, and it almost always had members in the NYO.

Two violinists who were obviously professionally taught enabled me to meet Rudolph Botta; luckily I had time before my train to hear his story. He was a Czech who had escaped to England along with many others at the end of the war, and found himself in Manchester and unable to understand any English. He was interviewed by a committee as to what work he could do, and as he gesticulated as if bowing on a violin, the interviewer said, 'Ah yes, a window-cleaner.' So to his surprise he found his future was to be just that. He protected his hands with layers of gloves and worked away, grateful for any job. One day, cleaning the attic windows of a school, he saw a pile of musical instruments and broken-down violins, unused and wasted. So he went to the Headmaster and asked if he could repair them free, just for the love of it. After that he started to teach privately, and before long he was on the staff of the RMCM, now the Royal Northern College of Music.

From Manchester I went to Sheffield, whose Music Adviser (name forgotten, alas) looked after me most conscientiously. Before I left he told me of the propaganda – from Dr Northcote and from Mr Trethewy of the SMA – with which he had been bombarded; but he had decided to meet me himself rather than cancel the children's auditions. He added, 'Don't let that Mr Trethewy frighten you.' He didn't; but his followers could be a serious blockade. I asked why he could be against the best training for the best young talent, and he said that as an amateur musician he couldn't stand professionals who knew more than he did; and because if anybody was going to have a national school and orchestra for young musicians it should be the SMA.

The Music Adviser for Doncaster, William Appleby, was a warm, sensitive choir trainer. I sensed I was not very welcome and soon it was clear that within the BBC, where he did a weekly programme for schools, were friends of the MTA, who had tried to enlist his help to finish me off. We talked about the projected National Youth Choir and the part he could play, and over the years he became a friend and supporter.

I had completed Scotland and the north, and now I had forty-eight hours with friends in Lincoln, time for a much-needed rest. Lincoln Cathedral, one of the great works of art of all time, with the language of the 1662 Prayer Book, pure music in itself, and Bach on the great organ, was an inspiration. The heart of England still rests in its great cathedrals and in all the ancient village churches.

*

Alive again, I set off for the Midlands, Nottingham and Derby. It had proved difficult to find a place for auditions in Derby, and Philippa had turned to the local music shop. The friendly manager, enthusiastically displaying our original poster on the door, provided a studio; he hoped I'd be comfortable and lit up the gas fire. After about two hours I had to turn it off and open a window, as each candidate commented on the smell of gas, and I had become somewhat sleepy. Such was the friendship of the Derby music shop that for many years I came back for the annual auditions. On would go the gas fire, and after about two days my eyes were running and my throat was dry.

Leicester was like a welcome home – I was there for such a short time in the war, but apparently I had told the children in my Leicester Children's Orchestra (by now the Leicester Schools Orchestra) that I'd be back after the war to see their progress. Parents I had known some four years ago came with news and gifts: a leather worker brought a music case he'd made himself; others gave towels, pillowcases and warm underwear made locally, things that were very difficult to get during rationing. There was no opposition here.

There were several famous public schools in the Midlands – Oakham, Uppingham, Rugby and Repton – connected with the MMA, which had promised me its full support. At Uppingham I met the Director of Music Douglas Guest and his most kind and hospitable wife – they are among the nicest people I've ever met. He was so helpful that I enlisted his support for the future if we succeeded at Bath. Years later he became a key figure of the NYO.

In Northampton I came upon a school where chamber music was flourishing and met Ronald Harding. He was not keen on my idea for a symphony orchestra, and felt chamber music was much more important. But his experience of suitable music for early work in trios and quartets was exceptional, and I could see that we might have need of this. In the evening I asked if he'd come and join me in Bath; in the event he not only came, but generously brought a carload of music from his library, and became part of the team of devoted teachers.

I remember Birmingham for the mixture of people: Irish children, some refugees from Europe and some Indians. One Indian parent, though very courteous and grateful for help, would not shake my hand because of my 'blue aura'. I didn't understand, but when he bowed deeply for goodbye I joined the custom and did likewise. There was also a large and energetic amateur symphony orchestra run by a Mr Ludlow, who invited me to a rehearsal. His son was the most advanced violinist I had heard so far, and the most experienced orchestrally. John Ludlow became the first leader of the NYO, and eventually leader at Covent Garden. At Barrs Hill Grammar School in Coventry I found the viola player Margaret Major, now a leading performer, and Kathleen Hegan, a most musical violinist, who was in the front desk with John at the first NYO concert, and later married him.

Then followed the happiest part of the tour. The King's School Warwick encouraged string players; the cathedral cities of Three Choirs' Festival fame – Worcester, Gloucester and Hereford – were all welcoming; the great independent schools of the Malvern and Cheltenham area were keen and helpful; and Bristol was full of activity, the best standard coming from the private pupils of the famous Misses Garjulo.

It was time to pause in Bath to see the Director of Education and the headteachers who were being asked to accommodate us for the coming festival. I couldn't give them exact numbers until the tour was over, but I remember their surprise when I said I thought there would be about seventy boys to about thirty girls. More *boys* playing instruments? (Choosing purely on merit, the NYO nearly always had this proportion.) This involved a complete change of accommodation plans, and I cannot praise the city of Bath too highly for their co-operation.

There was still South Wales to cover; there were some candidates but also some very strong nationalistic opposition. The great talent of Wales lies in the voices of its people. There is a miraculous emotional power in their singing which can rise to a spiritual level. Who, having once heard a Welsh miners' choir, could ever forget the sound? One can only hope that changing times, and local populations moving away from native traditions, will not lessen this invaluable contribution to the world.

But in March 1948 instrumental work in Wales was at an early stage, and in Cardiff there was more promising playing than natural talent. Swansea was quite different, with a rugged native bite, more personality, more eagerness. I remember one little boy who kept trying to get into my room every time I went to the waiting-room for the next candidate. After about three attempts I brought him in to sit beside me and listen. When I was about to leave he managed to ask about his audition. He hadn't applied, but the local paper had reported the event, and he'd found his way in hope.

'What do you play?'

He raised a battered music case. 'Please miss, all my compositions.' We took out piles of manuscript, and his hands crawled about the keyboard playing different items.

'Play me your favourite piece.' Out came some crumpled pages.

'"Portrait of Sleep",' was all he said . . . I can still hear it.

He looked about nine years old. He had no access to a piano but the organist in the local chapel helped him. Before long I took him and helped him into a musical career; last time we met he was playing for the Royal Ballet School's rehearsals.

My extraordinary super-cheap zigzag ticket had now joined the Great Western, and delivered me to London on the night train from Swansea. I found Philippa still smiling, up to date with letters and with the tour of the south planned. Better still, while dealing every day with the railways for my tour, she had acquired a special form giving a cheap fare to every NYO member under eighteen coming to Bath. The railways had a cheap fare for groups travelling *together*, but the NYO members all started from different places. Philippa had found her way to a high enough official, and the red tape had thinned and snapped as she told him about the children, many of whom were really poor, and how they would be representing their country. This arrangement lasted for the next twenty years, and was a major contribution to our work. Throughout that time there was never an occasion when we appealed to British Railways – for special trains, extra luggage vans or just advice – when they failed to help.

It was March and time was running out: I still had several hundred candidates to hear in the entire southern area and London. I settled into a third-class seat for the night journey from Waterloo to Cornwall, the county of my paternal grandparents, with its beautiful sea shore and high-hedged flower-bordered lanes.

Spencer Toy, Headmaster of Launceston College, met me personally at the station, and took me to his house for a hot bath and a traditional breakfast. There was an air of excitement as the boys prepared to perform in orchestra, band or solo. The standard wasn't exceptional, but fresh and vigorous in character. Later the County Music Adviser, William Pearson, arrived and took me to other schools and areas, such as Plymouth where the terrible war damage was a shock. When we reached Exeter in the evening we had supper together. It was then that he told me of a letter from Sydney Northcote of the Carnegie Trust, which paid his salary. Having been told to have nothing to do with me or the NYO, he decided to find out for himself (having been a naval officer during the war, he was used to taking responsibility for his own judgement). I told him about being locked in at Northcote's office. Like Dr Hooper in Leeds, he pledged his full support, and gave it most loyally, as a member of the NYO Council, until his early death.

The south of England has a beautiful coastline, and wonderful cathedrals – Truro, Wells, Exeter, Winchester, Salisbury, Canterbury – around which grew up the historic public and grammar schools, and more recently many private boarding schools. As everywhere else, there was talent – not burgeoning forth from huge cities, but in one child here and there in small well-cared-for groups. With unfailing courtesy and hospitality, fifteen famous schools showed an open mind, helping me and answering my questions from their rich fund of experience.

In particular, I met Miss (later Dame) Diana Reader Harris, Headmistress of Sherborne Girls School, an outstanding, charming personality, the very antithesis of the prevailing picture of a headmistress. She encouraged me, and gave us active help later. Recently Dame Diana wrote:

> At Sherborne we always enjoyed Ruth's visits as she was a most stimulating and delightful guest. She took immense personal trouble selecting the musicians for the orchestra . . . every one she auditioned had individual and invaluable help from her whether or not they were chosen. She must have found these audition tours exhausting, but though often she looked frail and tired, her enthusiasm and spirit were indomitable.

At Bedales, the leading co-educational boarding school, Hector Jacks spent an evening teaching me all about co-education, and the different rates of development between adolescent boys and girls. He said the ideal balance in a residential school was two-thirds boys to one-third girls; one year the NYO was fifty-fifty and it was not so successful as a community.

My first visit to the King's School Canterbury was the start of another special friendship. The Headmaster, Canon Shirley, really wanted his school to have the highest standard in the country in everything. I was so often up against the amateur outlook that I found this encouraging. Over the years I was treated as a colleague and adviser; when they found an excellent director of music (Edred Wright) and team of teachers, it was true to say that the music at King's could not be surpassed by any other school.

The one exception to the small numbers of musicians I had been finding scattered through the countryside was the town of Bournemouth. Here I encountered several hundred children from eight to eighteen, the majority playing stringed instruments. As so often in new experiments, this was the work of one man, Noel Hale. He was a violinist himself, and his team of teachers, under the education authority, offered every child the chance to join strings classes and get a start in the world of instrumental work. While I was searching for the rare individual with exceptional gifts, he was firing hundreds of ordinary children with enthusiasm. We were philosophically oceans apart, but accepted each other's outlook.

So after many more stops at coastal schools and small towns in the home counties, it was back to London. I had purposely left the capital city to last, not just because there was a large number of candidates, but also because I expected more talent that was within reach of the fine teachers and opportunities there. There was a wider range of instruments; one child, William Waterhouse, even had his own bassoon. The best-taught were the 'junior exhibitioners' from all the schools of music.

The tour was over. For three months, through the crowded cities and the country villages, I had met nearly a thousand hopeful young musicians, often coming on their own initiative. Most of them had never played in an orchestra or any ensemble. For me it had been very concentrated work – sometimes lonely, sometimes enlightening, sometimes unfriendly – but always interesting with the children and their teachers and parents everywhere. Such differing people, yet throughout the British Isles the native custom of extending hospitality to the traveller in their midst had never failed.

Four

Now I had to choose. My special notebook had nearly two hundred names in it, the raw talent and the well-taught. I wrestled over the choice, putting first the most musical and those longing for help. I chose 110 (seventy-five boys and thirty-five girls as it happened). An individual letter was sent to each child saying, 'You have been chosen as a member of the National Youth Orchestra of Great Britain . . .' with an instruction sheet, clothes list, health-certificate form and cheap-train-fare form. We gave the date of the concert and the fee – six guineas per child – which we'd worked out should cover our board and keep and pay the professional staff. Philippa and I waited anxiously for the replies. Would they come? Would the opposition put them off, or prevent them? Was six guineas too expensive? Would they or their parents take fright?

We needn't have worried. Replies poured in by return of post, full of excitement and anticipation.

> Your letter has rendered me the happiest person in the world. Come hell, high water or anything short of fatality I will be with you on April 13th.

> I have been watching the post every day for weeks and weeks and now I am shaking all over. Thank you, THANK YOU. I kept waking up at night, and thinking it was a dream, so I fetched the letter and put it under my pillow. My Dad will send the money, and I have savings for my fare.

> I knew you wouldn't forget me by the look in your eye, but I prayed every night just in case.

> This is the most important thing that has ever happened in our family. I went to school early, and stood outside my Head Master's door, and when he saw me he said have you been

> misbehaving and I gave him the letter. He told the whole school, and he will send you the money, and my Dad will get a whip-round for the dark trousers and white shirt – so I can come. We have a lot of children in our family and only a little money . . .

There were the formal, educated letters too, but no refusals. What surprised me most was that only six parents wrote to ask how their child would be looked after, and about medical care. Two parents wrote to explain that their daughter had never left home before and was frightened of the long journey, and we were able to arrange for them to meet another member to travel with.

A few months earlier I had met a young trumpet player in the London Philharmonic Orchestra, Malcolm Arnold. He wanted to compose, and responded at once to the idea of a first performance at our first concert. His eyes shone, he radiated warmth and enthusiasm. When I explained that I hadn't yet got an orchestra, that the potential talent was only elementary in performance, that most members would never have played in a symphony orchestra, he laughed and said, 'All the better!' There was not much time, but he would write a suite,* would see to copying the parts and would come to Bath to help the young brass players. Rumour has it that he went back to the LPO, threw down his trumpet and left to be a composer.

I had spoken to some of the leading teachers of the day, concerned that each member should have their own professor: so many were self-taught, or had inadequate help. Douglas Cameron, a remarkable and experienced cello professor whom I knew from my RAM days, was the first to agree; then Henry Holst, Violin Professor at the RCM; and with what nerve I asked the great Lionel Tertis to teach my beginners on the viola. Then I went to Reginald Jacques to ask him to be the Conductor of this non-existent orchestra, to discuss a programme and to explain about the new unwritten work by Malcolm Arnold.

**Suite for Youth* Opus 1 Lengnick.

When CEMA became the Arts Council Dr Jacques was its first Director, and was also increasing his reputation as a conductor. He didn't want his image spoilt by being seen to conduct kids: he was suspicious as to why I didn't want to conduct them myself, but the purpose of this school for the best talent was to provide the *best* teachers and conductors. More important, I'd have to be free to stand back, assess and watch every individual child's progress; to plan the balance of the whole week's work, apart from the orchestra; and to be accessible to each child and each professor.

So with a team of fine musicians, a programme planned and a thirteen-year-old pianist ready for a Mozart concerto, I had just one week for the final preparations in Bath and to find volunteer friends, preferably with cars, to be our nurse and house staff.

It was time to see Ian Hunter again. I was able to tell him that the NYO now existed, in the raw; but I had stuck to potential talent rather than the most advanced players. Therefore we might not be able to perform as an orchestra in one week. We shook hands on our original agreement that with just two days' notice I could cancel.

Bath's Domestic Science College would provide meals, teaching-rooms and luxurious accommodation for the girls; the City of Bath Girls' Grammar School's main assembly hall would be used for full rehearsals; and the boys slept in Kingswood College, a boarding school some distance away. So I needed to organise transport; I'm glad to see from the press cuttings that in thanking the people of Bath I mentioned 'the good-humoured coach proprietor and his drivers who transported the players, their instruments and luggage between the stations, the hostels, and the college at different times each day without a hitch'.

Of course two or three cars were needed as well, for getting around and in case of emergency, but the owners had no petrol as it was still strictly rationed. Perhaps the MP for Bath would have the power to rescue us. Sir James Pitman was a most understanding man, and he cared about education too. He took me to the House of Commons and found the Minister of Transport, who signed a paper to allow us an extra supply for 'NYO needs during residential education'. This paper signed by the minister rescued us wherever we worked until rationing ended in May 1950. If somebody proved uncooperative we could always say, 'But the minister himself . . .' and all was well.

In the mean time I had written to John Dalby to confirm his 'Yes' as the train left Aberdeen Station on 1 January. With forty-eight hours to go, and Philippa with me in Bath, came the first emergency: the score and parts of Malcolm Arnold's new work were only just ready and were going to be left in the Albert Hall for us to collect. Would Mr Dalby fetch them and bring them with him to Bath? He wrote:

> My first duty for the NYO (apart from shepherding members from Aberdeen and Edinburgh on the night train to London) was to call at the Royal Albert Hall and there collect the original score and parts of the new work by Malcolm Arnold, and bring them to Bath. Next I was to gather members together at Paddington Station and bundle them aboard the so-called escort train for Bath. Picture my predicament. Nobody knew anybody else, and it was only too easy to shepherd into the fold a possible bassoonist who, upon close scrutiny, was identified as a young and indignant plumber on his way to Reading. Conversation on the train was interesting, each young player confessing to only mediocre ability. 'I'm only Grade VI,' 'I'm no good at all,' 'I've never taken any exams.' It was rumoured there was going to be a vast orchestra of 70 players. In the event it numbered 110, and playing standards were far in excess of those modest self-assessments.
>
> Upon arrival at Bath I was astonished to find I was to work alongside musicians of such eminence as Henry Holst and Lionel Tertis. I am not in that class, and in sheer fright I was sorely tempted to catch the next train home, but the immediate activity of that very first evening of the NYO quickly involved me.

*

By three p.m. on 13 April, Philippa and I sat down with pencil and paper to check that we had completed all the essentials before the exciting moment of the invasion was upon us.

As I stood on the steps of the college awaiting their arrival, I felt a certain tremor within me at the huge responsibility of looking after 110 of other people's children. They knew nobody but me, whom they had met just once, but they had seized this opportunity in total faith. Many of them had never left home before, two had never even been in a train. Yet on the given day, with courage and a spirit of adventure, from all over the British Isles, they had set off for the unknown. I wanted the atmosphere of the NYO to be one in which every individual mattered personally, so shook hands with each as they arrived. I had not expected so much excitement and warmth, with comments such as 'We're here . . . we're really here' or 'Thank you for choosing me' and a big hug . . . There were also the nervous and reserved, but it was easy to coax a smile. Finally came the last bus and my second meeting with John Dalby, carrying with pride the score and parts of Malcolm Arnold's first composition.

The first meal was important. As the food went down, the tiredness wore off and the talk increased, rising in pitch. The first, unexpected, problem was that the dialects were so different they couldn't all understand each other: some were a little bewildered, but mainly they found it funny. A girl from the south said to me, 'I've met a boy from Scotland who can't speak English. He goes out with his dad on trawlers in the North Sea. Would he be a Viking?' A child from Birmingham said, 'I've met a boy who lives by the sea, he actually touches it every day!' On that same first evening they all handed in their ration cards for one week, and one girl was in tears because she'd left hers behind. Instantly another girl came to me and said, 'I don't eat very much. If she could sit next to me at meals we could share our food.' It was easy to see in the first few hours how much loving care, reassurance and careful explanation would be needed for this highly strung family of sensitive children.

As soon as the meal was over they made for their instruments, and sounds of tuning emerged from all quarters. When told there was to be no playing till after breakfast, some were mystified: 'Our band works from eight to eleven p.m. Are we going to waste time?'

Soon they were all in the main hall for the first event of the week. Cyril Winn, recently retired Chief Inspector of Music, had come from London to welcome them and to tell them a little of how the NYO had come about, why they'd been chosen and what it might lead to if they proved worthy of the great teachers coming to help them. I then told them about Dr Jacques and all the professors and the plans for the next day. By nine we were all having cocoa and biscuits, and everybody met John Dalby, Philippa, the house staff and nurse for the first time.

And so to dormitory life. I had expected the girls to be shy at first and that the more gregarious males would be all right. On this occasion the girls were in single or double bedrooms, and there was some fear of sleeping in a room alone, or in one case in a bed alone. I had arranged the boys' dormitories in age groups, and mixed geographically and instrumentally. The boys were no problem, perhaps a little over-excited or over-tired; plenty of laughter and kindly help were required. The housemasters said the experienced boarding-school pupils were marvellous – without snobbery but ready to help the others and quicker to carry out instructions, and of course this was markedly so throughout the week.

While they slept Philippa, John Dalby and I went through the plans for the next day. My partnership with John began that night and lasted for the next nineteen years; our friendship until his death in 1989.

Five

The next morning I was relieved to see all present, refreshed, lively and talkative. There was much to be explained beyond a huge and detailed timetable on the noticeboard. It seemed to be of the very first importance that an atmosphere of courtesy and appreciation should be established, for the distinguished musicians who were coming to teach them. This led on to the importance of orderliness in the classrooms; I had named someone responsible for each instrument-room, and for meeting and escorting their professor round the strange building. Punctuality was paramount, and of course no running in corridors when carrying instruments. They quickly understood that a school of music has a style and life of its own; all the details, starting from the first morning, were to enable them all to do their best work. We stressed from this first week that the best behaviour alone was good enough if you were representing your country in a national school.

I had planned that every student would have help on their own instrument and the theoretical side of their work, and some ensemble experience or choral work; all would play in the full orchestra and take part in the end-of-term concert.

My next task was to meet Henry Holst, Douglas Cameron, Frank Probyn (Horn Professor at the RCM) and Lionel Tertis, and after a brief explanation to throw them in at the deep end. None of them had taught at this elementary level before, and by the eleven o'clock break in the staff-room I was quite nervous. Would they all feel insulted and go home? Far from it. Their first reaction was surprise. Douglas Cameron, a very experienced and gifted teacher, had no problems: 'They may be beginners but they're so quick, so keen.' Lionel Tertis was full of astonishment: 'All this young talent on the *viola*! But they all need individual lessons every day before they can play in an orchestra.' Frank Probyn was more concerned with the French horns they had, and their condition, with poor mouthpieces and loose or stiff valves, but said how well they managed. Henry Holst was at a loss as to where or how to begin, so I suggested an afternoon of basic technique, holding the instrument, etc. 'They want to know: tell them, show them, watch the results as the days go by.' I also reorganised his programme, moving the younger ones to Ronald Harding.

We were short of rooms and had only two pianos, but with careful planning and improvising everybody had one and a half hours free each afternoon for rest and fresh air away from musical sound. With the lovely energy of the young, several asked if they could practise instead, as they didn't need rest, but I explained that they would before the week was over.

From after tea till supper everybody was at work, thrilled with their marvellous teachers. I remember taking a 'class for clefs', having found the trombones busy putting their orchestral parts into the treble clef – the only one they understood.

Six hours' real work a day seemed to be enough and so after supper we would do something different. Mr Scott, Headmaster of the City of Bath Boys' School and later a staunch NYO supporter, organised an excellent speaker to talk about the history of his city, with many amusing stories.

So the first day ended with the pattern of work, rest and play very firmly set. When I went round to say good-night to all the girls, one fourteen-year-old, now a well-known musician, said, 'I love everybody here. I am so happy I could explode.'

On Sunday, to their amazement, there was to be no practising till noon. Ecumenism was hardly heard of in 1948, so the churchgoers gathered in groups – Catholic, C. of E., Methodist, Presbyterian, etc. They had to be back for a twelve-forty-five roll-call, and mustn't go about a strange city in groups of less than three. I expected 'Why threes?' but not 'Is there a musical reason?' The purely practical idea that they were responsible for each other was a great joke. But as the week went by the idea of the older helping the younger, the boys helping the girls, the natural leaders helping us all, established itself; and in the years to come it was part of the tradition of life in the NYO.

The afternoon was spent in individual and group lessons, but after supper this time we became a choral society. Copies of *Acis & Galatea* had been lent by the Organist of Bath Abbey and I discovered two outstanding young voices, both professional singers later; also that the girls were better readers than the boys; but never had there been a more vigorous, healthy, laughing 'monster Polypheme' than that produced by our seventy young men. At bedtime I said, 'Tomorrow we will become a symphony orchestra,' and the subsequent chatter reminded us how few of the children had ever played in an orchestra before.

The next morning an air of excitement reigned: today the conductor and more famous musicians would come. There was a chart on the noticeboard showing exactly where each member would sit, and the system of seating we would use. Everything had to be taught to the majority: how to sit, how to turn pages, nothing to be put on the floor. 'Sensitive musicians can't work in an untidy place,' I am reported to have said, and soon the 110 were in place and ready for tuning. I went to meet the conductor and others from the London train. The first was Richard Adeney, a fine flautist who would help the woodwind ensemble; then came Malcolm Arnold, full of enthusiasm; but no conductor: he couldn't be there till late afternoon. At such a moment the orchestra couldn't be disappointed, so Douglas Cameron agreed to conduct the first rehearsal. Henry Holst surveyed his thirty-six violins, Lionel Tertis sat amongst violas, Richard Adeney soothed the woodwind, Frank Probyn tended his horns, Malcolm Arnold made straight for the heavy brass; a quick message to John Dalby sent him to guide the percussion. John wrote:

> No one, at that moment, had any inkling of what the assemblage of young musicians would make of Weber's *Oberon* overture. We held our breath as Douglas Cameron raised the baton, and then heaved a sigh of relief when the principal horn, with the aplomb of a professional, floated the opening call.* The overture got into its stride, and the NYO's exciting sound was born.

The mood in the staff-room at lunch was one of astonishment. The speed of improvement shook them – 'So quick, so responsive.' By tea-time Reginald Jacques had arrived for the five o'clock rehearsal. He was charming, patient and full of amusing stories, just what was needed through the many odd things that happened as we embarked on a Beethoven symphony.

There had been enough playing and excitement for one day, so a quiet evening was needed. Richard Adeney offered to give a recital. The only music available was Bach sonatas, and one was rehearsed and duly performed, with Mr Dalby accompanying. The reception was such, however, that they played another. 'Never heard that lovely music before,' 'Never been to a recital,' they said. How hard it is now to remember life when very few had TV and no one had recording machines, and records were so expensive. From that day, recitals were part of NYO life.

With only four days left till the concert, Ian Hunter was eager to know if we were going to play. I said I thought so, but was not sure of the programme, which we might have to change to make it a little easier. He was full of encouragement and ready to help in any way, whereas most impresarios would have baulked at changing a programme at the eleventh hour. By lunch-time we discovered that Sibelius's *Karelia Suite* was too difficult, and decided that we'd replace it with Elgar if we could get the parts. Philippa worked a miracle on the music-hire firm of Goodwin

*Harry Brennand.

& Tabb. One of the housemistresses set off to London, got to Goodwins just before five-thirty and returned in triumph by nightfall.

After a mainly orchestral day, we relaxed with an evening of folk dancing and Scottish reels. Meanwhile the professors, who stayed in a nearby hotel, went off to the local pub and were asked what was 'going on' up there in the Domestic Science College. Knowing my desire to avoid publicity, they said they were all chefs on a special bakery course!

The next day was one I shall never forget, because it might have sounded the death-knell for the NYO almost before it was born.

The morning rehearsal started well, though it was soon apparent that the instruments were unused to being played on for six hours a day. Strings were breaking, pegs were uncontrollable, bridges were falling down and keys falling off, reeds were going soggy . . . An expert repairer would be needed. Miraculously a local member knew of one, and lured him to the next rehearsal. He danced attendance on us for the rest of the week, even lending instruments and bows, a most devoted craftsman whose name I have forgotten but whom I remember with grateful respect.

After the mid-morning break all was going splendidly when a sudden invasion appeared at the hall door, looking around and walking about, and they seemed to have cameras. One knocked over some percussion equipment, and the enraged conductor put down his baton. A few of us collected up the members of this gang, took them into the foyer and asked who they were. There were nine hefty toughs and as we spoke five more arrived.

'We're the press, the London press. We've been sent to get photographs and stories from the children.'

'Well I'm terribly sorry,' I replied, 'but we are a private school, and quite new, and we don't want any publicity at all.' I said I was sorry that I couldn't allow it, and it wasn't our fault that their journey had been in vain: we had no idea they were coming.

'But we're the *press*, the national press. We take pictures wherever *we* want to, whether you like it or not.'

I tried again. 'Do you mean you will enter private property by force, and against our wishes?' Luckily two of the men were of a different calibre, and explained that they had arrived in Bath, they went to the Domestic Science College, they were sent here, nobody met them, but could I help them get their pictures? I could see I had no choice. I went back to Jacques and arranged to stop ten minutes early and let everybody in for photos. They had to wait a bit, but quite a few said thank you.

I thought that episode was over, but I didn't know the press. Now they wanted individual stories. Seeing that we went back to the Domestic Science College for lunch and the afternoon, some of them hid in the grounds, and when the girls were resting on their beds in the afternoon they climbed the drain-pipes and got into the dormitories. One terrified the cook by hiding under a dining-room table; thinking he was a burglar, she made for her rolling pin and chased him out of the grounds.

Through all this I had been unable to see Lionel Tertis, who had some problem with his timetable. When he left at lunch-time he handed in a note. He thought I had ignored him that morning, and was only interested in the orchestra, so he was saying goodbye and wouldn't be coming back ever again. I was sorry, but had no time to let it upset me, and he sent an apology and flowers that evening. I was taking the woodwind but, realising I would have to be free for emergencies, I sought out Douglas Cameron. He would spread his wings over the violas as well as the cellos, and suggested his friend Frederick Thurston might come to my rescue for the woodwind. Thurston was principal clarinet with the BBCSO, which was stationed in Bristol for the war. I told him of my need for his help on the telephone, and heard a Gloucestershire voice say, 'Don't worry, my sweet, I'll come over as soon as I can.'

By tea-time Ian Hunter was on the phone, saying he'd sent

the press, as he had to have maximum publicity for the first Bath Assembly, and they hadn't felt welcome. 'Without any warning at all, *of course* they weren't welcome. They upset the conductor; Lionel Tertis has left; they picked on a violinist with no fingers; frightened our best cook; climbed drainpipes to get into the girls' bedroom . . . And worst of all every bit of publicity about us is ammunition for those who want to show us as wicked exploiters of the young.' Ian soothingly explained that we must fill the hall, but he would try to control the arrangements. Did we want to cancel the concert? Did *he* want to cancel the concert? No, we both wanted to make a success of it, if we could be allowed to work in peace.

The next phone call was from Bernard Shore, Cyril Winn's successor as Chief Inspector of Music, formerly principal viola of the BBCSO. He was in the area; could he come round and see us at work? The answer was, 'Yes please; you're needed to take over the violas at the five o'clock rehearsal.' He arrived in time and settled in as to the manner born, purring happily over his young team of beginners; from that day he became one of our most devoted supporters, and a major help to us in the world of education.

The evening rehearsal started with the first run-through of the Malcolm Arnold, with the composer conducting his first composition. I went to look after the woodwind, as it was important that the new work went well. Before long I was beckoned to the hall door. Frederick ('Jack') Thurston had arrived: a short man, with quick movements, firm handshake, bright sparkling eyes and an eager curiosity. He put his head round the door, his face lit up with the smile and mischievous look that I came to know well, and he made a bee-line for the woodwind. From that moment until his death in 1953, he belonged to the NYO, a friend to us all, a consummate artist and an authoritative teacher. A day that seemed all problems and clouds brought us also this diamond lining.

Bernard Shore volunteered to do a recital in the evening. He wrote to me a few years ago at the age of eighty-eight, saying he still remembered that evening in Bath, and how he'd hoped to stay as our viola professor in the future, but as HMI it was not thought appropriate. He always came to visit us, and always supported us until his retirement in 1961.

We were hardly through breakfast the next morning before the front page of a leading newspaper was thrust into my view. It had a close-up of the thirteen-year-old violinist with a crippled hand (this child was very talented and had devised his own way of holding the bow). I alone knew what this would mean to the opposition, and after such a fight to get started this might be a very damaging setback. I could have wept. These few days had already shown me that I could never desert these young musicians, but the road ahead would now be even tougher.

My chosen pianist for the Mozart concerto, Elizabeth Powell, was thirteen and beautifully taught by Madame Gombrich, whom I'd met in Oxford. Secure, musical, Viennese in style, she played with the natural purity of the pre-adolescent, a quality of beauty too good to miss on those rare occasions when it could be found. Elizabeth had no problems, but the orchestra found it more difficult than I had anticipated. My two little oboes were not really up to it; the two clarinets were better. Jack Thurston and I perpetrated a major artistic crime and transposed the parts. In the event it sounded very Mozartian, and there was no comment from the music critics. I remember especially my fourteen-year-old second clarinet, Colin Bradbury: eager, conscientious, very sensitive, his blue eyes looking up for help from Jack as to some archangel.

By this stage my new-found friends and colleagues, the professors, had become like shepherds, each guarding and guiding their own group with pride. The house staff, equally, were sharing and sorting the little anxieties and excitements. There were some notable leaders among the boys, such as Christopher Wellington, a viola player, and John Ludlow. The whole programme was under way, so after a day of playing and concentrating we embarked on a concert-uniform inspection, amid much laughter. Clothes-rationing was tough, as a pair of trousers used a lot of coupons and dark trousers were hard to find, grey being the utility model. There was much kind lending or swapping – a cellist with a pencil-slim skirt was in difficulties, and would a pair of Black Watch trousers from father's regiment pass? It was surprising how many buttons and safety pins, needles and thread were on our shopping list.

I remember this day as the one in which everyone seemed increasingly moved by the atmosphere, the day on which we first became one team in a cause, and one family in music.

Jack Thurston arrived the next morning with the news that the BBC wanted to come over from Bristol and record us as we rehearsed. Although this meant a big disturbance for our last day, it was an important experience for the children, and so had to be accepted. It also gave them a first taste of performance, so different from rehearsing. From this earliest moment, the music departments of the BBC in all the regions were alert and keenly enthusiastic about the NYO. I never approached them; they always found us. They caused as little disturbance as possible fixing their mikes, took the excerpts they wanted and rushed back to Bristol. We were then mentioned in their local news programme, and I am told that quite a lot of people came over from Bristol for the concert as a result.

The culmination of two years' thought, planning and hard work arrived on 21 April 1948, bringing the first public concert of the National Youth Orchestra of Great Britain, which was also the opening concert of the Bath Assembly. The Lord Mayor, many local dignitaries and the London press were going to be present for this exciting occasion.

But the mood of the performers at the morning rehearsal in the Pavilion was more restrained than usual, partly a controlled excitement, partly sensing an important event – and a slight nervousness was apparent. Most of them had never been on a concert platform or played in a concert, and they felt cramped for space. To give confidence we had learnt platform behaviour:

how to keep still, in a relaxed way; where to put bows when resting; page-turning; and tuning. Any manners we adopted were accepted as part of our style, in which we all took pride.

There were no artists' rooms behind the stage, so in the afternoon we arranged for our buses to come down a path on one side of the hall. Everybody got ready in the buses and lined up on the path outside. When all had instruments in hand, down came the rain! We had to assemble on the platform earlier than intended, and watch the audience arrive.

Weber. Overture. Oberon
Mozart. Piano Concerto K488. Soloist: Elizabeth Powell
Malcolm Arnold. Suite for Youth

Beethoven. Symphony No. 2 in D
Elgar. Pomp and Circumstance No. 4

The concert made a great impression. This was due to the atmosphere the orchestra created rather than the actual standard achieved by such young players in one week. There was enormous vitality, determination, concentration, and great love of the music. What struck me most as I sat back and listened for the first time was the way they held together, the strength of the sound as well as the sensitivity and beauty of some of the solo parts. Our principal horn Harry Brennand, principal flute Bernard Hermann, principal bassoon William Waterhouse, the leader John Ludlow, the solo pianist Elizabeth Powell (and many others) all made successful careers in the future.

After the Lord Mayor's speech, a stranger came up to me at the back of the hall. 'Are you the person responsible for this marvellous event? How do you manage? Do you want any help?' Yes I did. 'Have you got a committee?' I hadn't. 'I'll write to you.'

He did, revealing that he was the new Director of Education for Bristol, George Sylvester, and inviting us to his city. From the time our Constitution was established, he was our Hon. Secretary and held that post for forty years. He was a most able, kind person, with a quiet manner and a desire for 'the best education for *all* our children', not just for those who could afford it. A wise and loyal friend, he did great work on our behalf among his fellow directors of education.

But now suddenly it was all hands to packing up instruments and checking that suitcases were in buses, and a rush to the stations. Almost everybody could get home that night, or connect with the night trains from London or Crewe, and it was a hurried departure. Perhaps it was just as well, because the realisation that it was all over hadn't really dawned; the parting from new friends, the gratitude and the tears and the brave waving from bus windows was best not prolonged. From the pavement I called, 'Write to me, and we'll all meet again in August.' I thought intuitively that we would, but of course I had no idea how. When the buses had faded from sight, Philippa and I returned for a quiet tour of all the buildings we'd occupied, making sure everything was as we found it, and past complaint. Then a personal farewell to all the caretakers and cooks, and especially the owner and manager of the bus company. That firm had made not one mistake throughout the week, and the kindly West Country drivers almost became part of our staff.

As evening fell, the naked silence and emptiness, the music and the children's laughter so suddenly extinguished, caused us to relax; straight away we were so tired we decided to catch the next train home. I just about tottered into my flat and slept for thirty-six hours, woken only by the telephone announcing Monday morning. I came round as from a dream, but no, it was reality; it had all happened. The National Youth Orchestra of Great Britain was alive.

Six

In the office there was a delightful welcome. The Joseph Williams staff had come to feel part of the NYO, and they had all sorts of press cuttings and pictures, and the music critiques from the quality papers. I could see at a glance the opportunities given to our detractors, but I was genuinely grateful to *The Times*, which without condescension found 'the orchestra as a whole was able to do considerable justice to a typical symphony orchestra programme with Malcolm Arnold's first work cleverly scored', and gave credit to soloist and conductor.

I went in to see Florian Williams to thank him for the part he'd played in launching us. I knew we couldn't accept his hospitality much longer, and indeed in a most kindly way he explained he needed our space. So already there was a problem to tackle: how to find a new London office – rent-free.

The next important item was the bank. I crawled nervously along the road to Lloyds. There was just enough to pay Philippa, and when everything else was dealt with we had 11d. left. This was a bit worrying for the future of the NYO, so my immediate thought was to get work myself. The end of April was not a good time in the academic year or musical season, but miraculously a few choral societies and two schools were in need, and gradually I could see my way to keeping us alive until August, when somehow, somewhere, the NYO would meet again.

Quite soon a flood of letters came in. Philippa had sorted them into *Nasty*, *Nice*, *Parents & Children* and *General*. The *Nice* were very much so: encouragement, enjoyment of the concert, appreciation from the people of Bath; the *General* had some invitations to give concerts or lectures; *Parents & Children* I took home to digest and enjoy; *Nasty* was the infuriated opposition:

two anonymous death threats, one cutting from the *Musical Times* in which the MTA complained that the NYO had been called 'new', whilst they had been running a summer orchestral course for students and teachers for four years already. So it seemed their opposition stemmed from the misunderstanding that we were doing something similar, whereas in fact teaching exceptional *children*, three times a year over a period of years, was entirely different. A letter from my friend and adviser Maurice Jacobson asked me to come and see him about a piece in the *Music Teacher*, and there was one press cutting damning our performance of a programme we hadn't even played.

The *Music Teacher* was a monthly magazine edited by one Mr Tobin. Their main article had attacked us, and the closing paragraph was malicious and libellous. I knew nothing of libel, but apparently this was an open-and-shut case. Jacobson had frightened Tobin by saying I was going to sue, and arranged for the three of us to meet. It then emerged that, if I sued, the damages would bankrupt them; Tobin was very nervous indeed. I couldn't help imagining what all that lovely money could do for the NYO, but thought it was beneath my standards to finish off part of a man's livelihood and a teachers' magazine. So I let him off, bound over, as it were, for good behaviour to us in the future.

I also wrote to the music critic of the daily that had reviewed the wrong programme, saying that I was always prepared for just criticism of my concerts, but a damning report of works we didn't play indicated that he could not have been present; perhaps he could explain? It was a polite letter, without threat, but they never even answered. I thought that was so rude they weren't worth bothering with, and put the matter aside. (Years later my husband told me that they were probably pretending they hadn't had my letter, or were awaiting one from my solicitors, or just working out how much they'd have to pay. Apparently 'malicious damage' is quite pricey: it would have kept the NYO for some time, but I knew nothing about such matters.)

And so to the personal letters from the children themselves – the first NYO.

> You made us all feel important, as if we mattered. I don't think I had ever been noticed before . . . Now I can play and play until I get good at it.

> I liked the lessons and the evening recitals best, but the concert was a good idea because it was exciting and made a proper finish to everything.

> How long will it be before you can tell us when we can come back again?

(Several of these.)

> My teacher is so thrilled with my improvement I am going to take Grade VII before we meet again.

> I love music so very *very* much but I thought I would never get good and would just slowly drown, but now I know there are 100 others there is a lifeboat for us all.

> My friend who sat in the same desk with me is coming to stay in the summer, as he has never been in mountains and lakes in the country. He plays the violin *beautifully* but cannot milk a cow . . .

> The boy who was head of our Dorm talked posh, and I felt odd. But he knew what to do all the time, and was funny, and helped us all in everything. He is the best friend I have ever had – smashing at music too.

A parent wrote: 'J. has come home safely thank God. Before he was a quite boy, but he has never stopped talking since he came the door. Thank you for him so happy.' Most important of all, my new-found friend and colleague John Dalby said:

> I was astonished by the quality of teaching you provided, and the well-ordered way of work and life, the gradually emerging ideal and the wonder and astonishment of all that was happening: the vitality and energy of the young, with

> everybody doing a little more in one week than they'd ever done before, everybody getting more involved. What you provided led to quick and astonishingly good results. The astonishment everybody experienced was a major factor in establishing this school. How much we did and felt in this invigorating environment exceeded expectation. So astonishment is not far removed from inspiration . . . I love, above all, being at home, but on this occasion, like the children, I did not want the week at Bath to stop. It must continue, it will, for you have proved your point.

So Sir George Dyson's opinion that there was little native talent, which had once haunted me, was exorcised. Perhaps our tiny bubbling fountain of native talent would help to transform *das Land ohne Musik* into a flood of musical life worthy of our heritage.

But what was the use of planting the seed if it could not grow? Letters continued to flow in from all parts of the country: more applications to join, more teachers wanting information, more encouragement from headmasters, invitations to give concerts and of course a few threats, of the 'If you dare go on it will be worse for you; this is the last warning' type. But the most important letter was from Boris Ord, Musical Director of the Cambridge University Musical Society, who had heard us in Bath; he was supported by Patrick Hadley, Professor of Music. Would we come and work in Cambridge, and give a concert in the Guildhall in the summer? Here was the chance to continue for which we were hoping. This offer was of major importance in the NYO's history, not only for the immediate stimulus but also because of the link we would establish with the musical life of the university for our young musicians going to Cambridge, whatever subject they read. Many of today's famous performers and conductors cut their professional teeth in CUMS, such as David Atherton, Christopher Seaman, Derek Bourgeois, Mark Elder and Tony Pay.

The Headmaster of the Leys School, Dr Humphrey, agreed

to let us live and work there for a week. This was especially courageous and generous of him, as we were too new to have established a reputation for good behaviour. I could see him summing me up, wondering if I would be able to control a mob of wild musicians!

Somehow I would have to collect or earn a bit more money to keep us till August, to avoid raising the fees. We had written a few letters to wealthy people, and suddenly one morning a nice letter came from J. Arthur Rank with a cheque for £100. It is impossible to express the relief from anxiety and resultant happiness it brought. Now I could write to the children as promised, and back came the letters, all accepting and full of excitement. The shortest just said, 'I'm coming – OF COURSE I'M COMING – Lots of love. Peter.'

The morning of 2 August found the faithful Philippa, our nurse Bunty Neave and two housemasters putting the finishing touches to the excellent premises of the Leys School ready for the invasion of our musical family that evening. To me it was of the utmost importance that homely, feminine touches should abound: flowers on dining-room tables, a comfortable staff-room. Equally important was tidiness and order, with every classroom designed for its purpose. When the aim is creating beauty the atmosphere must play a part. The beds, chairs and desks can be of the simplest, but must be clean and polished; this helps promote calm assurance when arriving in a strange place. Clear labels and direction signs play a part too. Time-consuming though this was, I never stinted on the detailed preparations for the orchestra's welcome. As we worked on, the members were on their way to Cambridge Station.

What a different arrival scene! Everybody knew us, everybody was so happy to be reunited with their friends. To my surprise, they followed directions and settled into dormitories as if we were still in Bath. After a good meal we had a walk in the grounds, as only three had ever been to Cambridge, and they were very appreciative of the chance to see and know more of it; also that this time we were all together in *one* school for the week.

And what was new this term? Dr Jacques would conduct; Douglas Cameron and Jack Thurston would be coming. Malcolm Arnold would teach the brass and the composers, John the percussion and organists. There was one special new arrival, Manoug Parikian. He was young and handsome, a superb violinist, leader of the Philharmonia. He made a great contribution, demonstrating with authority what something should be like, and filling in details in class later.

There was one other newcomer to the NYO, one of the most remarkable characters I have ever known, Eugene Genin. He came to us at Cambridge and never left us for twenty years. A violinist and viola player, he was a totally dedicated teacher. In his care several hundred Liverpool children learnt to play and to work with enjoyment, gradually joining groups and orchestras. I invited him to join me partly because we needed his kind of expertise, partly because he was genuinely enthusiastic about the NYO and wanted the highest standards for his students, but mostly because he was an exceptionally nice person. He wanted to give all he had, to serve a cause, and from the first day at Cambridge this was exactly what he did. He was a most courteous gentleman by whom no task, however humble, was not readily undertaken with the greatest good humour. At work he appeared so serious, so conscientious, but you could not be in Genin's company for long without laughing. This was a major asset in our staff-room community, for in the various times of pressure or disappointment, no problem could descend on us without Genin seeing the funny side. I pay tribute to a fine teacher, a special friend and a most devoted member of the NYO voluntary staff.

At the first full orchestral rehearsal, the same players assembled as at Bath, but without the bewilderment of the unknown. The playing of the overture revealed an entirely different orchestra – in sound, in style, in accuracy, in so many ways unbelievably better. The staff-room at break buzzed with excitement. For me it was the proof of what until now had only been intuitive: that the best teaching, for even a short period, is of the first importance for young talent, and that the most gifted should be together in a sensitive atmosphere to share and stimulate each other. If the stunning change we had witnessed could take place in three months, what could happen in years?

The next shock was when I was rehearsing the choir. Interruptions to any rehearsal were not allowed, but Philippa appeared, somewhat flushed, saying some important-looking gentlemen had arrived, and one was a general. This was General Wilson, Director of King George's Jubilee Trust. Founded with money raised at the Jubilee of George V, its aims were to foster projects to help the young, and its policy to visit by surprise. We toured all the classes, the chamber music group and the choir, and later he watched the full orchestra assembling and going into action. He was very understanding, gracious and encouraging, and just before he left revealed that the trust might be interested in helping us. I never discovered who told them about us, but amid so much opposition we must have had good friends also.

I was studying the teaching, because in future I would have to discover gifted teachers and balance the qualities of a team. I observed Jacques's persuasion, Thurston's vitality, Cameron's experience and John Dalby's subtlety; but I learnt most from Malcolm Arnold: so talented, full of ideas, imagination and humour, with the warmest, most generous personality. He explained that the young know when things are wrong but can't always analyse why, and teachers are vague and don't *tell* them. They say, 'Do it again' or 'Practise it.'

'Tell them it's sharp,' said Malcolm, 'and they'll put it right; or that those actual notes were too slow, and they'll respond at once. Teaching is telling them what they don't know.' The experienced performer has often forgotten the obvious and the simple, and has to rediscover or remember what it is that young players don't yet know and don't yet hear.

The peace and calm of Cambridge helped them through so

many hours of concentration. It was essential to improve *listening*, as opposed to hearing, which could only be done in silence. Musical noise all day can deaden the ear, and take the edge off concentration: silence restores the balance. They must also understand that stillness was not stiffness, and that after a period of real work should come one of rest and relaxation. There is a certain amount of tension in playing instruments, and the majority were not used to playing for six hours a day, and this was an investment against physical tiredness. It was a very funny idea, particularly to our young men, that rest on beds for everyone for an hour each day was helpful. But before the week was out they were the first to admit its value, and this silent hour became an important part of our training, maintained through many adventures in the years to come.

The orchestral programme for the concert was far in advance of Bath, arranged to cover the various ages and stages of the players – not beyond the youngest, yet with plenty to challenge the most advanced. The *Nutcracker Suite* gave more work to the percussion and harp; the soloist in the Grieg concerto was a sixteen-year-old pianist from Clifton College, Nigel Coxe; the Delius was strange to them, and in some ways too difficult.* 'That man Delius seems a rather dreamy chap,' said a miner's son from the Midlands.

Boris Ord was with us in support throughout the week, and together with Professor Hadley must have worked hard to fill the Guildhall for our concert (promoted by the Cambridge Arts Theatre Trust), which was during the long vacation, when the city is half empty. Our standard of playing and sense of performance were so far in advance of Bath it was quite hard to believe. Once again *The Times* troubled to come, finding 'the quality of the orchestra was evident from the start', and foreseeing the impact of such training on the future standards of performance in England. The Lord Mayor was our chief guest, and fortunately for us was really impressed. When it came to

*See Appendix A.

paying the bills for the whole week I would have run short, but the Mayor and Council gave us the hall free, a spontaneous gesture which saved me from debt.

The week in Cambridge, away from all publicity, had been a great help. John Dalby summed it up when he wrote, 'I think Cambridge has set the seal on what was begun in April, showing us the value of our methods, discipline and orderliness, and establishing our ideals and high standards on a sure foundation.'

After such a stimulating week, we were now pondering our desk swamped with work, and acutely aware of our penniless condition. As we piled through the letters, one crested envelope looked important. It was from General Wilson: King George's Jubilee Trust had offered us a grant. Re-reading many times the letter bearing the news – the huge sum of £1,000 for the first year, £1,500 for the next, £500 for the third – it seemed unbelievable. How grateful I was for the support of such a fine organisation, but also for the relief from the perpetual strain of finding next week's money, and building future plans on faith and hope alone. I wouldn't like to be without that experience and all it taught me, but too long on the brink tires the mind. This generous gift brought the chance to plan on firm ground.

I have very little memory of how it came about, but this very month the NYO found itself with a council of distinguished musicians and educationists from all over Britain. We needed a constitution and a governing body in order to gain charitable status to enable us to accept the KGJT grant. As the only official of the NYO, I must have been consulted; but it was probably handled by George Sylvester, after his offer of help at Bath.

On 21 September 1948 the Council held its first meeting. I was amazed at the breadth of support represented by this gathering: all the heads of music colleges; Professor Hadley; Leslie Scott, Headmaster of the City of Bath Boys' School; Cyril Winn; Bernard Shore; Douglas Guest and Hector McCurrach, Directors of Music at Uppingham and Harrow respectively, representing the MMA; John Newsom, George Sylvester and John Dalby from the state educational system; John Denison, the new Music Director of CEMA; Sir Arnold Bax, Master of the King's Musick; Maurice Jacobson; two county music advisers, Dr Hooper and William Pearson – to name a few outstanding members.

I met John Newsom for the first time after this meeting. He was a wonderful personality, to whom the NYO owes a great deal, as do I for his friendship. Highly intelligent, witty, quick-tempered, charitable and sympathetic, he had an underlying intuition and spiritual faith which enabled him to separate the petty from the worthwhile. I valued most the mischievous sparkle and laughter with which he would demolish the many obstacles in our path.

So here we all were, our task to guide this infant school for young musicians, penniless and opposed as it was, into calmer waters. Sir Adrian Boult, as President of the NYO, was elected Chairman of the Council with Reginald Jacques as Vice-Chairman; an executive committee was soon selected, comprising seventeen Council members. They were to be responsible for the running of the NYO, while the whole Council would only meet annually. The grant from the KGJT was the main topic on our agenda, and John Newsom wasted no time in declaring that the orchestra must be self-supporting by 1951, when the grant would stop. He also suggested we could meet and work in state schools to keep down costs. George Sylvester explained that the 1944 Education Act would enable local education authorities to give grants to children from their areas.

Finally, opposition from the MTA was to be tackled by Sir Adrian and Dr Greenhouse Allt of Trinity College of Music. Then everybody went home, and I was back in the office to get on with the work as before.

As we could not overstay our welcome in Joseph Williams' shop, and we still had not found a rent-free office, I decided to call on Sir Robert Mayer. I had met him when he heard me play as a child, and he introduced me to Myra Hess. Sir Robert came from Vienna, and never lost his German accent. His claim to fame was that he started the Robert Mayer Concerts for Children, a great contribution to music in England. It was a marvellous idea to bring children in to the best orchestras, conductors and music – not to play down to them but to allow them that unforgettable impact. I remember going to one in the Queen's Hall in 1927 and still possess the photograph of Beethoven that every child was given to take home. That occasion was also my first live hearing of Beethoven 5 conducted by Sir Malcolm Sargent. I spent weeks thereafter trying to work out how the orchestra could come in together when not starting on beat 1. Over twenty years later Toscanini said to me, 'It is always the very simple things that are *so* difficult.'

Sir Robert was pleased to see me. He wanted to know what I was doing, and I told him all about the NYO, and mentioned I had no office. It so happened that a student organisation that he was chairing had rented a building whose basement room was empty as it was too damp. We went to investigate: the floor was very wet. Sir Robert said, 'If you can make that habitable you deserve it free.' He gave me, in writing, on the spot, my use of it till the lease ran out. Overflowing with gratitude, I rushed back to Philippa with the news. Now we could write letters on important-looking headed notepaper with the addition of *King George's Jubilee Trust* and a very good address – 59 Gloucester Place, London W1 – and nobody would know we were sitting with our feet in the Thames. A weekend spent in the junk shops and markets of the East End yielded an old wooden typing desk, a wooden table, three rickety chairs and some shelving. A parent soon got things fixed, including making rough wooden footstools to save us from pneumonia, or worse, with our feet being on the wet floor all day. I indulged in a small electric fire to help dry out the room.

Seven

Philippa and I could now be ambitious and plan our first full year. She sorted new applications and prepared the audition tour, while I worked on the possibility of Liverpool in January (invited by Harold Magnay), London in April and Leeds in August. Finding a concert hall in London was difficult: the Queen's Hall was bombed in the war and the Albert Hall was too big; boarding accommodation was even harder to find, but I pressed on. Leeds produced an unexpected response: a fine training college would be made available to us. It seemed just now that doors were opening and our perseverance was being rewarded.

Once again, from October to December, I embarked on a tour of the British Isles. As before, I chose not necessarily the most advanced players, with the most technique and the best teachers, but always those with that indefinable potential that would develop later if they were taught now. Over the next twenty years I was so often asked, when beginners hatched out quickly into beautiful players, 'How do you know?' It is an instant recognition in others of a special inner quality. It shines in movement, in voice, in sensitivity, even before the person plays and shows their love and need of music. My role in auditions was to discover the spiritual potential as well as the musical talent, and to reduce nervousness by being relaxed and informal.

On 26 December Philippa and I set off in the night train to Liverpool to prepare the Kirkby Emergency Training College for the invasion of our family of 112 musicians. Lime Street Station in heavy rain on a dark winter's dawn, following the Christmas holiday, was not impressive. 'And what would the likes of thee be doing in t'soldiers' camp?' asked our taxi driver as we drove past barbed-wire fences and military gates to the former camp. At the mention of our bringing over a hundred children to stay, he put down the luggage dumbfounded. 'Tha must be from London.'

Once inside, a Lancashire welcome awaited us, with every assistance for all the work involved. Few people realise how much luggage a full orchestra has: double-bass and cello boxes, harps, timpani and all the percussion cases, and so on. Once settled, furniture-removing was our task; over the years my colleagues and I became experts at doing this without injuring fingers, hands or backs: rhythm is the trick. Later on, we would find some local NYO members to help; on this occasion Mr Genin and some of his pupils called in the morning, and the cleaning ladies sent their husbands and sons round in the evenings.

Next day the orchestra, with thirty new members, would arrive. One extra member, a violinist, had not applied in time for the audition, but was recommended very warmly by Douglas Cameron. In a recent letter Angus Watson says of his arrival in the NYO, 'It was quite simply wonderful . . . you placed me in the second desk of the first violins just behind John Ludlow, from where I had a delightful view of the beautiful (but infant) Lesley White, who has remained a close friend of our family ever since.' Angus Watson became Master of Music at Winchester College, then Dean of Music at the Hong Kong Academy, 'where so many NYO traditions and your methods seem to flourish in the heat and humidity as well as they did in the cold and damp of England'.

The excellent administrator of the Kirkby College turned on the perimeter lights above the barbed wire to make the place more welcoming. Yet from the windows of a bus, on a dark December evening, all that could be seen was tired snow disintegrating in the rain, the network of wire fences and the endless rows of Nissen huts. I detected a certain apprehension as they alighted from the bus to greet our host, and a new member, our youngest, fresh from the glorious Devon countryside, said, 'Good-evening zur. Is this Belsen?' (Later in the staff-room the administrator told us that he had in fact been the first British officer to enter Belsen.)

A good meal worked wonders, and was followed by Mr Magnay welcoming them to Liverpool as representatives of the musical talent of the whole nation. In those days the young accepted the compliment, and the responsibility of being chosen for the NYO, and they were right. Twenty years later children were tending to expect privileges as of right, at somebody else's expense, regardless of whether they were earned or deserved. Now for everyone it was their first Christmastide away from home. The Nissen huts were warm but the rain beating down on the galvanised roofs was frightening; yet, tired from long journeys, they set off to bed with courage and smiling faces.

I had persuaded some new people to come as house staff. Colonel Liddell, a housemaster at Clifton College, was introduced to me by my brother-in-law. What a find for the NYO! He took the great responsibility for those boys off my shoulders. Strong and authoritative, unfussy but watchful, with the essential sense of humour, he made a great contribution for nearly two years.

On the musical side, I had kept the same conductor and much the same team of professors as at Bath. But now we could afford a double-bass teacher, in the shape of J. E. Merrett, and the famous flautist Gareth Morris came for two days to help our flutes. For the viola we added Keith Cummings,* who played in the same quartet as Douglas Cameron. And there was Leonard Hirsch, leader of the Philharmonia, then the best orchestra in London. I might never have dared to ask him, but my mother had encouraged him as a young violinist in the 1920s; she said, 'He is such an exceptionally nice man, he will be good for your children,' and she was right.

Leonard was warm and charming, radiating confidence and

*His two sons were with us later; one leads the LSO cellos and the other is a violinist for the RPO.

style to the whole orchestra: tired playing would sparkle; difficult problems were made amusing, often fed from a fund of anecdotes from his professional life. He had taken a great deal of persuading as he had never taught before and was adamant that he couldn't. Coming off the night train and arriving at 'Belsen', finding all kinds of musical sounds emerging from every room and forty violinists eagerly awaiting him in the main hall, somehow panicked him. Nothing would persuade him to face them. 'But I don't know what to do,' was all he could say. 'But you soon will,' from me, was no help. We agreed that I would take the rehearsal and he would sit behind me and listen. After about five minutes violin expertise was badly needed, and I turned to him: 'Could you take out your fiddle and show us . . .' Soon, almost imperceptibly, I slipped away. For the next sixteen years his teaching and his personality were treasured by the NYO.

One morning BBC Northern rang to ask if their Head of Music could visit us. Maurice Johnston and colleagues duly arrived from Manchester. He was both excited and very moved by what was going on and offered us a recording for *Children's Hour*. It was fixed; and then cancelled; and then restored. It emerged later that his bosses in London, evidently friends of the opposition, had objected very strongly. But Johnston was in charge of his local programmes and decided to follow his own judgement. He made a great success of this performance for us, but not long afterwards his promotion was diverted, and he thought it was the price he paid for believing in us. But he remained a good friend until his death.

Then came the first formal social invitation in our history: the Lord Mayor of Liverpool invited the NYO to an official reception with tea afterwards. The timetable was changed so that we could be free for this great honour in the afternoon, and rehearse after supper. We prepared for this event, as for concert day, with a uniform inspection, a rehearsal in how to speak clearly when giving your name (and not to laugh if it is announced incorrectly), how to walk rather than shuffle, how to shake hands and answer questions if spoken to and how to applaud an official speech. We had a hilarious evening with Colonel Liddell and John Dalby as Mayor and announcer, showing what can go wrong.

The Lord Mayor enjoyed young people, and had arranged for all the civic regalia to be on show, for the police band to play for us and for a marvellous sit-down tea. After our long procession of 120 had been individually received, the Mayor moved to the dining area where all were now seated at tables, and made a welcoming speech, explaining some of the historical treasures we had seen, ending, 'Now I'll say grace, and then you can enjoy your tea.' He glanced at the tables . . . every plate was empty. He laughed and said how glad he was that they had already enjoyed his hospitality, and tea was poured by waiters to complete the party. After eight years of sugar- and sweet-rationing, the sight of iced cakes and chocolate biscuits had been too tempting. That night I made a note: 'Rule for all future official receptions, Never start eating until you are told.' At bedtime the comments were revealing: 'I've never been near our City Hall; that was smashing'; and my youngest girl: 'Would it be like that at Buckingham Palace?'

The next invitation was to visit the Liverpool Philharmonic Orchestra in rehearsal, which I sadly turned down. We had only seven days for all the individual work, a more advanced orchestral programme than before and a BBC recording; and we could not afford the buses to and fro. I told them all about the invitation and why I'd turned it down, and there was great disappointment, but also immediate acceptance of where our duty lay, our own concert. British children at this time were more ready to sacrifice an individual pleasure for the good of the whole. And that evening we had our first New Year's Eve party.

But the main purpose of these precious seven days always came first. We worked hard to bring the new members up to the standards of those who had been with us in Bath and Cambridge. I would creep round in rehearsals to encourage and give confidence. We gave special attention to the Schumann with our young soloist, Sheila Randall; the percussion section flourished in the Elgar. The evening recitals and outside events played a part, but this week the orchestra itself developed a stronger sense of presentation and performance.

With an orchestra there are always minor crises – the harp breaks, a bridge collapses, keys fall off – and we were ill-equipped with reserve instruments and spare parts. This time as the players were setting off to the concert hall in a double-decker bus, it turned a corner out of 'Belsen' and the top got stuck in some overhead pipes and they were jammed. Twenty minutes ticked by until with a final push and swerve they were free and the concert was saved. I always insisted on arriving one hour early before concerts, so we had time in hand; how important this rule has been.

The lovely Philharmonic Hall was sold out on the great day; over two hundred were turned away, local enthusiasm having grown as the week went by. I remember myself being amazed at the improvement in standard – partly due to better technique and to better listening – and in expressive power, due to increased confidence. The Liverpool audience, so warm and appreciative, made the whole concert into a great occasion. At this concert Hugo Rignold, Conductor of the Liverpool Philharmonic Orchestra, was our guest. He had intended to come only to the first half but 'I could not tear myself away.'

The reviews showed an understanding of our aims which was gratifying, and the *Liverpool Post* of our playing:

> The high quality of the playing – the excellence of the ensemble, the delicacy of the shading, the feeling for style, the punctuality of the rhythm – are things of which they can afford to be proud . . . This orchestra is a phenomenon of the times. Let no one henceforth speak of '*das Land ohne Musik*' where such native talent stands revealed.

After the children had gone home I went to thank everyone involved in this term and concert. While I was in the Philharmonic Hall, I was accosted by three tough-looking men. There was tough talking too. They were from the Musicians' Union, upset and angry that I was 'training up young people to take away our jobs'. I explained that most of our players would not take up music professionally, but this did not pacify them. They had heard young players who *were* better than them, and I was setting out to show them up. Was I in the union? No.* Were the children? No, they were still at school, not old enough. Then came the threats: any more concerts and I'd regret it.

I had been brought up to believe I lived in a free country; we'd just finished a ghastly war to free others and ourselves from tyranny. What was this threat to my freedom to teach? It amazed me that in most employment people could not get a job unless they joined a gang called a union and remained in meek subjection to the gang. Yet no politician until Mrs Thatcher dared to set us free and allow the initiative and ideas of an inventive and independent people to light up the nation again.

Before we left Joseph Williams, there was one more event. We thought our members should have a pin-on badge, designed to include all instruments and with the title round the edge. One of the staff had a son studying commerical art; he came to see us, then two days later brought us his completed design – the right size and colour – and a specimen in enamel. It was exactly what we needed. He supervised our first order to make sure it was right and refused all personal remuneration. It is still the proud possession of all NYO members to this day.

At first every new member was given a badge. But later we decided only to award them when a member had achieved a certain stage of progress, usually after a year or so. It became a

*At the time all members of professional symphony orchestras had to belong to the union, but not conductors and soloists.

highly prized honour to get a badge, and a symbol of permanency. Members had to be invited to *every* term, which left me free, if I had chosen wrongly, to part with anyone – though in fact I never did.

Eight

With our first Christmas term happily completed, it was time for another Council meeting, arranged for 7 February 1949.*

The essentials covered were that General Wilson joined the Council; the KGJT grant was partly to be used to give me a salary of £750 a year, and the secretary £312. We needed a new treasurer, and the County Accountant of Hertfordshire, R. S. McDougall, was invited to take this role. Of course I gave a full account of our Christmas term. Then Bernard Shore reported that he had extracted a promise from Sydney Northcote not to deprecate the work of the NYO any more. John Newsom and George Sylvester were appalled by the damp conditions in our basement office, and I was authorised to spend up to £100 a year for better accommodation. Sir Adrian adjourned the meeting for a year, expressing pleasure at 'the progress being made by the orchestra in every way'.

My main concern at this time was that my beloved Philippa was heading for the altar and we had to say goodbye. How lucky I had been to have such a special personality at my side; how I would miss her. Thankfully her successor, Mrs Singer, was ready to endure long hours in tough conditions in the service of a cause.

After much pleading, the Methodist Church, owner of the Central Hall, Westminster, allowed us to have it for our first London concert on 29 April. Even more difficult was finding boarding-school accommodation within reach of London. Through John Newsom and the Hertfordshire Education Authority I had already been offered the Hitchin Girls'

*See Appendix B.

Grammar School for all our work, and it was perfect for us, with a big hall and ample rehearsal-rooms, but it had no residential arrangements. Without this we couldn't meet at all. No Easter term, no continuity, a hundred broken hearts . . . I worked out a plan and returned to Hitchin: only a remarkable head could have responded as calmly as Mary Badland. Could we possibly bring in 120 mattresses and pillows, and use her huge gymnasium as a boys' dormitory; then empty the class-rooms for the girls? She didn't say, 'Impossible', but raised all the practical problems. Soon, as in a wartime emergency, we had mapped out male and female parts of the school, leaving enough teaching-rooms, and some just-adequate washing facilities, but there would be no baths for a week! Hanging space for concert clothes was to be on the gym wall bars and on ledges above blackboards. The gracious Miss Badland even offered me her own office for my mattress, and very quiet and pleasant it was.

We owe to Mary Badland and John Newsom the success of this first mattress experiment. In the ensuing years, no matter how complicated or primitive the conditions, we used it whenever nothing better was available. It saved us much financially, and taught us all important things: closer co-operation, better discipline, maintaining standards in difficult conditions, and appreciation of luxury in its turn.

There were other matters to arrange before the term began. All the boys were called up at eighteen, but I had found a military contact able to grant a short deferment. Some of our members joined army bands; all hoped to be stationed in Germany or Vienna where there would certainly be good music and good teachers within reach.

All the children would have to bring sheets or sleeping bag, pillowcase and towels, all in one suitcase. But with the end of clothes-rationing in March I was looking forward to less crushable concert trousers and skirts.

On 21 April the entire NYO family arrived. There was amazement, then laughter, and varying reactions to the camp-life that faced them. After a good supper they tackled their new home in a spirit of adventure, but bedtime did take longer that night. Those from boarding schools and any boy scouts were in their element, and Colonel Liddell found happy ways of settling his young recruits.

We had been helping our members with scholarship exams to the RAM, RCM and universities. Some practical exams took place this month, some during this very week, so candidates would have extra rehearsals before an audience to build their confidence. We also took part in a short film for the British Council. How excited they were to be in it; and it was so good for them to learn how much detailed work was involved. As the week progressed, there was marked improvement in the woodwind, and John Dalby's percussion department had taken a big leap forward. A few years ago John wrote to me:

> You instructed me to introduce some artistry and precision and style into my department, which, to put it realistically, was in need of drastic reform. Let us not forget that in those days percussion playing in general was in a poor state – the 'Cinderella', if you like, of the orchestral world. It was at that point (not on the road to Damascus like St. Paul but in the suburbs of Hitchin) that I saw the light. Why shouldn't the percussion be highly skilled and artistic contributors to the symphony orchestra? From then on I, like others, did my bit. Today percussion departments are supreme.

At this time sweet-rationing ended, and partly to celebrate this important event for the young, and partly as it was the first anniversary of our first public concert, we had a short evening party. Instead of cocoa and biscuits before bed, the cooks produced a huge birthday cake, and the house staff scoured the town for 110 bars of ration-free chocolate. We laid these out on the floor to spell NYO, and then everybody took one.

The climax of this fourth term was our first London concert; it must be the best. We had kept what we knew to be important: the same conductor, the same professors, the recitals (this time a memorable one from Gareth Morris). We had advanced to our most difficult symphony so far, and another young pianist, Robin Wood, would play a Beethoven concerto. We repeated the Elgar to avoid overloading such a full week.

Excitement rose considerably on the last evening: we discovered that over thirty members had never been to London. As we were going to Westminster, they would see the Abbey and the great wartime signal, Big Ben. I can't remember how we managed to fill the hall, with no money spent on publicity – just a few posters, and of course some parents came. Yet it was fairly full, and the response very exhilarating.

Sir Adrian came as our President, and said afterwards to the press, 'I had been told how good they were, and I am not disappointed.' Two famous music critics thought us worthy of their columns, Eric Blom writing in the *Birmingham Post*, '. . . the NYO, from which frankly one expected the worst and got very nearly the best . . . what one heard was the sound of a professional orchestra and a very good one too . . . a concert uncommonly good by any standards,' and in *Time and Tide* Dr Mosco Carner wrote, 'Freshness, vigour and enthusiasm one did expect but not such a high degree of precision and attack, of ensemble and balance as these youthful players achieved . . .'

After such a successful London concert, invitations started to come in. No longer would I have to seek out places where we could work that also had a big concert hall. The City of Leeds offered to provide for us all that Liverpool had done, only better! Previously, every time I said goodbye to the orchestra I could only say, 'I *hope* to see you all again next holidays,' without any idea where or exactly when. But now I could fix Leeds in the summer and Bristol for Christmas; Aberdeen and Durham were in the queue, and most exciting, Paris.

There was so much to learn, so many contacts to make and keep. I knew nothing about printing but Vails were endlessly helpful and kind, helping me with posters and concert programmes. The post-war paper shortage meant a shortage of sheet music, parts and scores. Tape-recording and photocopying for everyday purposes did not exist, and the planning of orchestral programmes was dependent on what music could be obtained and on what parts could be hired at a given time in sufficient quantity. And I always needed more voluntary house staff; the headteachers and other educationists on the Executive Committee recommended many fine people over the years.

There was indeed unceasing work for such a small organisation (but with nation-wide tentacles): in the tiny damp basement, wooden tables creaked, damp paper was dried in front of the electric fire and the antique typewriter clattered on unceasingly.

By contrast with Hitchin, Leeds was luxurious perfection in a beautiful training college for teachers in Beckett Park, with ample grounds, a large hall, plenty of separate blocks for housing students of both sexes, and single rooms for our staff. The warmth of the Yorkshire welcome and the summer weather completed the happy atmosphere as our family arrived in busloads from the station. They had been together for a whole year: Christmas in Belsen, Easter in camp and now summer in a 'palace'. My own happiness on the first evening was seeing the joy with which they greeted each other, such marvellous friendships, as Brighton met Newcastle again, or Aberdeen met Cornwall. Many such contacts have lasted to this day, and not a few happy marriages emerged as the years went by, and their offspring play in the NYO today.

As far as possible I kept the same team of musicians, my essential colleagues-for-all-purposes being John Dalby and the faithful Mr Genin with his car. But the great event was the new conductor. I had met Walter Susskind, then conducting in Melbourne and Toronto, through Maurice Jacobson. I studied him in action when he was in London, and after a concert I sought him out; I explained what we did and invited him. He didn't hesitate or worry about his reputation, just said, 'That sounds to me interesting and quite important; yes, I will come.'

Walter was a strong and vibrant personality, with the added attraction of his accent and broken English. He was a first-class musician with a talent for drama and colour who never lacked energy. We had been working for three days before I let him arrive for his first rehearsal: the scaffolding had to be safe enough to withstand the whirlwind. The children, ready with Dvořák's *Carnival* overture, were nearly knocked out by the power and speed that hit them. They clung on, with determination to match his exuberance, and at the end the sudden relief gave way to laughter and expressions of shock. Not one child had ever experienced or imagined music-making of that level. After a pause for breath Walter just said, with a glowing smile, 'We made it.'

Coming from Prague, his Haydn was authentic and stylish; and his accompanying of our young Australian violinist was so understanding. At his suggestion we were tackling *The Young Person's Guide to the Orchestra* by Britten, technically beyond anything else we'd done so far. It was written for professionals to play to children, but we were reversing the intention, with children playing it to adults. Walter could teach and plan, but most important, he was ready to learn. There are things you can ask for and get right at once, things that can be achieved in a few days' time, and things that are not possible with limited technique and poor instruments. He learnt to save time and trust us as musicians to get the details right. He was never impatient, and musically he was a wonderful colleague. (His personal inclinations, however, could be a problem, so that the term at Leeds was a trial of wits and diplomacy. After the evening rehearsal, he would return to his hotel and the attractions of city night-life. What mood would he be in for the morning rehearsal?) John Dalby once wrote to me: 'Although I deplored his quixotic ways and his resort, at times, to unaccountably sulky moods, I grew to admire this remarkable man and to regard him as a close friend.' There is no doubt in my mind that the NYO came into its own in August 1949.

Two incidents stay in my memory, one of great joy and the

other a near-disaster. Leeds was where I had met Allan Schiller and Fanny Waterman, so I invited them round. Allan's progress, and Fanny's quite exceptional gifts for teaching, were very special; so was a Mozart concerto from this tiny child, like a reflection of the composer at the same age. I promised he would play it with us when the right occasion arose, and my long association with Fanny was launched.

Then on the morning of the concert our one and only harp was dropped off the platform during the setting-up of the final rehearsal in the Civic Hall. The pedal mechanism was damaged badly. The harp solo in the *Young Person's Guide* was a major item in the piece, and there was no substitute harp in Leeds. Rushworth & Dreaper in Liverpool promised to put a harp on the train in time for the concert, but in the afternoon they rang up to say that a sudden violent thunderstorm had prevented their getting it to the train on time. The young harpist was in tears, but the show had to go on. John set out to buy a couple of clamps, and somehow fitted them to the harp's mechanism. Miraculously it withstood the solo in the performance triumphantly.

Thus our third term of 1949 ended on a high note in Leeds Civic Hall. It is impossible to describe the warmth and enthusiasm of that Leeds audience, and the way it raised our performance to new heights. If the applause was very prolonged and we had no encore, I used to come on to the platform and thank the audience for their encouragement, and tell them what we hoped to do next. In this case I told them that I had accepted an invitation to Paris in faith, although we hadn't enough money to cross the Channel . . . The gifts poured in, postal orders for 5s., even half a crown. The extra money was vital; the kind messages with which it was sent were deeply moving.

For many years Ernest Bradbury was the leading writer on music for the *Yorkshire Post*, a stern critic. He wrote:

> I was not the only person to be completely taken by surprise when these enthusiastic youngsters opened the programme

> with Dvořák's Carnival Overture. Here was alert, disciplined, and even sensitive playing that set up a magnificent sound and could have put to shame many a professional orchestra.
>
> Perhaps I shall not be believed when I say that in all the music I have heard during the past month nothing has quite excited me so much as the noise of this temporary orchestra; an emotion aroused, no doubt, as much by the genuine feeling behind the playing, as by the playing itself . . . I do not regret having left Edinburgh to hear it.

It was only our fifth concert, yet a critic had come away from the Edinburgh Festival to hear us. Grateful as I always was for encouraging opinions of our work, Bradbury's comment about professional orchestras, perhaps true in 1949, was the kind that set the Musicians' Union out for my blood. Another local paper followed its praise with 'Now what about a youth orchestra for Leeds?', and we glimpsed the problems that might arise when, as we were admired instead of condemned, every town and country would set out to copy our pattern.

At dawn the children left, scattering to all corners of the British Isles. Standing alone on the steps of the empty college, it seemed to me that the founding years were over. The roots were secure, and the shoots growing apace, and we must now be ready to share the flowering of Britain's musical talent in a wider field. Paris in 1950 was my goal.

Nine

Our dark basement office was alight with the happiness that flowed from the children's letters, and there was so much appreciation from Leeds. Plenty of serious work had piled up, so it was a good time for the Executive Committee to meet.

The Committee – including John Newsom, George Sylvester, John Dalby and Douglas Guest – sprang into action, full of ideas. I reported on Leeds, and said I would have to drop the choir: it involved too much time and space – but I hoped to find someone from the many choir trainers I knew to take it over and run it in parallel with the NYO. However, I did want to establish a junior group for eleven- to thirteen-year-olds: they would pay less and not play in concerts, so that the main orchestra did not get any larger. They would be trainees and reserves, with their turn to come in the future. We also had some boarders, though not in a school. These were children who couldn't find an adequate teacher in their area, and were transferred to a school in London where they would live with a family and study with a leading professor. Eventually we did have a small boarding school, under the aegis of the Arts Educational Trust.

Local education authorities had been sending us annual subscriptions, but now Sir John Maud, Permanent Secretary to the Ministry of Education, whose son was in the orchestra, pointed out that this was illegal: money was meant to go to particular individuals. So, sadly, the fees had to be raised slightly now, and applications for a grant had to be made three times a year for each of our 'terms', which we now had to call 'courses' to match the LEAs' terminology. But we made sure that nobody was ever kept away through financial difficulties.

My third all-Britain audition tour was quite different from

the others. There were considerably fewer candidates, due mainly to our growing reputation for a very high standard. And there were still pockets of resistance, including the idea that children would get swollen heads and think they were exceptionally talented. My experience was that a conceited attitude arises where there is one big fish in a small pool. Putting the best together enabled them to appreciate each other, and humility won easily when all the big fish were together. Another idea, promulgated by the Labour Party, was that it was competitive to get in, and all competition was a bad thing. Related to this was the amateur or anti-élitist idea that it was wrong to do something special for the few who merited it: we should all be the same. I often pondered how soon such critics had forgotten where they would be but for 'the few' in 1940 – a carefully chosen, highly trained élite.

The big difference on this tour was that there was interest in the NYO. The local press would write about any local members with pride; when I returned to a school that had a member in the orchestra their appreciation was shown in endless kind hospitality; and the music shops, which had played such an important part at the beginning, now felt they belonged, and gave generous rates for hiring their studios for auditions. The other side of the coin was that the MTA was still working hard to poison us, plotting to pull the carpet from under our feet, and sometimes letters written by its members came into my hands.

But as in 1948, I covered the whole country, this time visiting different small towns and schools, according to the applicants. A grammar school in Grimsby became a centre for a day's work, and when I was leaving the head music teacher asked if I could possibly come back after supper to hear some of her young singers: she was worried about a local operatic singer 'training' their voices. Listening all day was really enough, but I felt I couldn't refuse.

I was given a recital from four fourteen- to sixteen-year-olds, each in turn singing operatic solos – high soprano coloratura arias! – lovely potential voices under great strain. So we had a friendly talk about the gift of a voice, and taking care of it; I mentioned that just as boys' voices break and change, the same happens for girls only it doesn't show so much, and that they might find in a few years that they were not sopranos; forcing now might damage their voices. The best of the four, aged fifteen, looked me straight in the eye and said, 'What do you think I should do?', and I said, 'Stop singing for two years.'

Recently Dame Janet Baker wrote to me:

> I was totally shattered because there was such a lot of musical activity . . . But somehow, I trusted you absolutely and did exactly as you advised which wasn't easy, since the pressures to carry on with my various singing commitments was enormous and I was made to feel extremely uncomfortable . . . However, after about the time you expected my voice emerged, quite changed – from high soprano to what I then thought to be contralto. I made a very nice sound! . . . You actually did me the most marvellous service in giving me such sensible and sound advice . . . If I had not taken your words to heart, I doubt if my voice would have survived the upheaval it was passing through . . . I have never forgotten what you did for me.

Every audition tour discovered unexpected talent, unexpected problems in unexpected places. I travelled on.

We had established a Paris Fund. It amounted to a separate account in the bank and a chart on the office wall (a thermometer with the red fluid aiming to reach £1,000). Every member had a little official card on which he could collect money. They put on concerts, plays or dances for the Paris Fund, and schools in several places did a Christmas concert for us. This spread into carol parties collecting on doorsteps, and two letters of complaint arrived about my members carol-singing to raise their own fare to Paris! As the year ended the red ink on the wall had risen to £650 – mostly via postal orders from 5s. to £10.

In December I chose about forty new members from about eight hundred applicants. I tried to take nobody over sixteen, thus ensuring a minimum of two years' training; I chose about seven for my new junior school, two of them pianists who had not yet chosen an orchestral instrument and one a beautiful boy singer who yearned to play a horn but hadn't got one yet. It was on this tour that I found John Exton, a good violinist at fifteen and later leader of the NYO, but also intellectually interesting. When we last met he was a professor at Perth University in Western Australia. Another keen young man, determined to make a career in music but clearly no performer, went into the percussion department, from which vantage point he could study all the instruments and I could study him. This was Humphrey Burton, who went on to present for BBC1 and 2, retaining his enjoyment of it all, and become BBC Head of Music and Arts and Artistic Adviser to the Barbican Centre. Another highly intelligent cellist I chose, who was not very advanced but sensitive and full of humility, is now Sir Humphrey Maud, our ambassador in Buenos Aires, and tells me he still plays the cello.

In the mean time plans for our Christmas term in Bristol were complete. The remarkable George Sylvester had organised all the accommodation we would need, and enlisted all kinds of support: the Lord Mayor and all the key figures in the city and university, and the heads of many famous schools. We would have the Central Hall for the concert, promoted by the best local impresario. By the time we arrived to make the final arrangements the concert was sold out. A new idea this time was to do two concerts. The neighbouring city of Bath was most anxious for a return visit, and I needed to know how my players would react to two successive nights of excitement, the effect on their concentration. Would a second night be better or worse? Travelling to concerts, and back again in the dark, sounds trivial now, but to most of our children these were all new adventures; and soon we'd be in Paris.

All too soon it was Christmas and on a dark, wet, late-

December evening the whole NYO family reached Bristol's stations, then settled into its new home. By the first supper the crescendo of voices told its own happy story. There was one new housemistress, Barbara Park. She lived in Leeds, and having arrived on the scene to offer help in the summer, she never left us for the next fifteen years. Kind, motherly, experienced, tactful, no impending domestic crisis was not foreseen and forestalled by her, and somehow she'd be on the spot in any emergency – solving it first and reporting it afterwards.

Our work for the week was no longer experimental. We had established a pattern that worked, and each individual had their own programme. Jacques was conducting again: a Russian overture and a big step forward, the Brahms violin concerto. Our soloist Tessa Robbins, who had impressed me with her talent and maturity, turned out to be our secretary's younger sister. We had a Mozart symphony for the chamber orchestra, and this time the English composer was Walton. A new professor was Eric Pritchard, principal trumpet at the BBCSO. Then Bell's Palsy overtook him and, unable to play the trumpet any more, he taught himself to be a timpanist; a few years later he came back to us in that role. His courage was a great example to our members.

Such was the local interest that we allowed a few visitors to sit on the hall platform to listen to the five o'clock rehearsals. These would include local headteachers, and those concerned with music and education in the region. As long as the numbers were small and the visitors understood that neither I nor any of my colleagues could be interrupted in rehearsal, the extra work it entailed could be managed unobtrusively. In fact these silent, absorbed, appreciative guests contributed to the atmosphere and sense of performance in the rehearsals, so our courtesy was rewarded.

We had two quite outstanding evening recitals, by Gareth Morris and Dennis Brain, partnered by a most remarkable pianist, Ivey Dickson, a friend of mine who lived in Bristol. It was our first meeting since the war, and her first glimpse of the NYO in action. All four of us were students together at the RAM; Dennis taught me to play the horn and I did his harmony papers for him. He was a true friend and a fine musician, with a simple style, his own beautiful sound, and personal qualities still remembered years after his tragic death.

We were also invited to another lord mayor's reception, and this time nobody ate anything until they were told. On New Year's Eve we had a party after supper. For this the members organised their own band, dances and games, displaying qualities of leadership and character previously unrevealed.

As the Central Hall had sold out, George Sylvester suggested that we might invite the disappointed to the morning rehearsal. For me the final rehearsal in a strange hall, with highly strung players, requires absolute undisturbed concentration, so I was doubtful, but gave way on strict conditions. I'm glad I did, because to arrive for a morning rehearsal and see a long queue in the road eager to hear you is a very heartening experience. I think everyone paid half a crown, and I know the sum raised covered all our printing costs for the two concerts. The experiment of two concerts, in different cities each night, was a success, the playing and confidence markedly better on the second night. At bedtime one girl sighed, 'If only we could do it every night for a month!'

At about one in the morning I went to bed. It was not long before my telephone woke me: one of the boys had fallen from a top-floor window to the ground below. I expected he was dead . . . somebody else's son in my care . . . I rushed over to the boys' house. Sister was already on the scene and in charge, and with what relief I heard her say, 'I think it's only a broken leg and ankle.' I spoke to the boy while waiting for the ambulance and all he could say was, 'I'm terribly, *terribly* sorry, will I be invited again, or will I be turned out?' His father on the telephone later was much the same: 'Will you give him another chance? The orchestra's his life.'

What had happened was that he and his friends had tied sheets together to swing to the branches of a large tree, hoping thence to reach the windows of the girls' house. He had landed on the grass, within inches of concrete slabs and a rockery. It was our first accident, and I vowed we'd never have another. We didn't. Needless to say, it got into the papers via the hospital, possibly giving our detractors another innings, but relief and gratitude was all I felt.

Back in the cold office (if we kept the fire on, the damp floor steamed), my thoughts turned to Paris. The first to help and advise was the British Council. The cheapest and least time-consuming way to get there was on the night train, and soon I was off to see for myself what we would be undertaking in post-war Paris. Six years of Nazi occupation had changed France; and although de Gaulle had not yet had time to restore dignity and confidence, the mood was very different, much quieter.

The first person I met was Captain Howell, the British Council's man in Paris: a charmer, and faintly surprised at my readiness to bring a hundred children to Paris and actually give concerts. His report to the British Council in London later revealed he had 'expected a large, besuited, bossy secretary, and was faced with a French-speaking, delicate-looking young lady, who was quite clear about the the essentials for a successful performance'. For me, instead of a desk-bound civil servant, I found a naval officer whose ship would never sink. To him, an orchestra was a rather cumbersome animal not met on the high seas. Because of Captain Howell and his excellent contacts I returned to London confident that the trip would work, and that we were really wanted by those concerned.

After much discussion, the Committee gave permission for the whole plan. The Easter term was to be held at Brighton Technical College and Brighton College, a boys' public school, to whose principals we can never be too grateful. There would be a concert in the Dome, Brighton, and two in Paris, the first in the Palais de Chaillot and the next in the famous Salle Pleyel. Finance was the major concern. We had raised £650 and made

£200 profit on the Bristol concerts, but it wasn't enough. At the last minute Sir Frank Willis was able to give us £500 from the South African Aid to Britain Fund (Cultural Section?!), and our first foreign tour was on.

The hardest part of the preparations involved was the choice of whom to take. The reserves and juniors would be left behind, but about ten more had to be excluded because the accommodation we'd been offered was limited. And the passports! Ninety-seven per cent had never had one or even seen one, and we had letters from parents asking if Father's wartime identity card would do instead, or a letter from the priest, or a birth certificate. We sent clear instructions giving the addresses of the passport offices and all the information they could need and why, but it was quite a struggle. One parent wrote, 'I thought we'd just rescued the French from Hitler. Are they trying to label free Englishmen?'

The programme for Paris had to be agreed with my colleagues and of course the conductor – Reginald Jacques – and with the British Council. Ideally a new work was needed, so naturally I asked Malcolm Arnold. With his usual generosity and enthusiasm he responded at once. He thought a divertimento, with different movements to show our various qualities and use the full strength of the orchestra, would be best; and he'd come with us to Paris. Malcolm later gave the full score to John on the boat home; sadly it was never published.

There seemed no end to the arrangements for getting the cheapest yet most reliable luggage vans, buses, boats and trains. At this moment of pressure, Mrs Singer's mother became seriously ill, and so our secretary couldn't come to Paris. With no spare money, how was I to find an experienced, bilingual secretary/manager to look after the conductor, composer, tickets, customs, finance etc., while I took care of performers, rehearsals, concerts and matters diplomatic and social? I sent out an SOS in likely quarters but I will never know quite how it came about that, as I answered a knock on our basement door one afternoon, the unique Mrs Ballingall appeared. She was a gift from Heaven. Very smartly turned out, she graced our only rickety chair, then absorbed at a glance the music, children, Paris Fund chart on the wall, piles of letters ready for the post, and took off her gloves to help stick on stamps . . . Yes, she knew Paris; she was bilingual; she only did temporary work now; she was free on our dates. Was *I* familiar with travelling in France? Hardly. Was *she* accustomed to concert halls and orchestras? Not at all. She was savouring the funny side, but was obviously able, quick, amusing and experienced. The NYO's first foreign venture owed much to her efficiency and tact in our various dilemmas.

On 12 April my colleagues and I were preparing the luxurious Brighton Technical College for what was now known as the 'invasion' of our 120 musicians. We had used some of the money made on the last concert to subsidise the fares of those living north of Sheffield and Manchester, and soon the earlier arrivals were wandering through the grounds – 'Another palace' – to gaze at the sea. It was quite difficult for the staff to herd them in for supper, and I asked a housemaster why they were so slow. He said they were quite dazed and full of wonder and could only say, 'We've seen it on the cinema.' We were no social élite, but even in the '30s there were seaside-holiday excursions from the factories, and so I hadn't realised that so many children, living on an island, would never have seen the sea. In a week they'd be *on* the sea.

That first evening, as was my custom each time we reassembled, I unveiled the whole programme for the week, taking us through ships and seas, foreign trains and language, to Paris, representing our country. They could then absorb the picture of what we would create together in just ten days. I sensed a certain excitement but also a faint apprehension. Going round at bedtime a near-whisper voiced it: 'I've never been on a boat before.'

Our priority, of course, was the music. The overture was difficult, full of colour, with important parts for brass and three timpanists; the romantic Dvořák symphony was new to almost all, but suited the age group; and we had another piano concerto, Beethoven 2, with Nigel Coxe. The excitement for the first day was the new work, unseen, in front of them to read while the composer conducted. It was dedicated to us, and every section had parts suitable for its talent. I noted the astonishing speed of improvement now that some members were in their third year with us. They had such respect for their professors, and their inadequate technique was catching up to serve the musical qualities for which I had chosen them. All of us who taught them became involved in and excited by their progress.

A new member of the team, Elizabeth Beale, had excellent French. She was highly efficient; young but experienced in schools; not musical enough to be distracted by it, almost a foil to its emotion; firm as a rock, she was ideal for adolescents. What great service she gave the NYO, not just in Paris but for some years to come. We also gained one parent, a Brighton police officer with a car, Sergeant Herniman, who gave up a week's holiday to help us locally.

Mealtimes were used for practising French. Fresh air and exercise was walks along the beach, really touching the sea. We had a strict rule of arriving with only one suitcase and no parcels: an instrument in one hand and a suitcase in the other is plenty when getting in and out of trains and boats. They had all been asked to bring two packets of Ryvita and some slabs of plain chocolate, not to be touched until Paris. I had thought of the unfamiliar food, and the lack of an English breakfast, and that they would be hungry, tire more quickly and not play so well. Mostly these provisions survived the week in England uneaten, the house staff telling them that they might not like French snails . . .

In the evenings distinguished people came to tell them about France. One was a friend of John Newsom's who had been in the French underground all through the war. We found our children knew very little of life in occupied Europe, only twenty-five miles away. I wondered if we had been right to keep them in ignorance of so much suffering. As their interest grew they asked, 'Why didn't we know, why aren't we told in school?' Why indeed? Soon they would sail the same English Channel as the Dunkirk boats, but in innocence, bringing good will and music.

I mention these details because people did not realise that we were not a youth group on holiday. We were going as humble representatives of young Britain, which is why appearance, manners and responsibility for each other were so important. The Paris concerts would be wrecked if music was missing, luggage lost, instruments damaged or if some infection knocked them out: we prepared for emergencies. But all the time we concentrated on our purpose: music.

Concert day arrived, and we faced a new audience in the Dome. It had been difficult to fill the hall as we were unknown, but a rumour of a special train coming from London aroused such curiosity that at the last minute we sold out. (The 'special train' was just one reserved carriage for parents.) Without doubt we reached a higher standard than ever before. Yet at bedtime, over mugs of cocoa, all the talk was of whether they would be good enough for Paris, and worthy of representing Britain abroad. There was a new mood: they slept not in the usual sadness that the concert was over, but rather in readiness for a new beginning.

On 20 April 1950 the first non-student youth orchestra ever to perform in Europe had gobbled down its breakfast and was assembling, as rehearsed, in numbered order ready to leave our shores. Each individual was responsible for his passport, instrument and music, at all times of day and night, and his own suitcase when travelling. The numbered order ensured that those whose instruments were not easily portable and who therefore had a free hand were next to cellists, to carry the owner's suitcase. (Almost all our cellos were in canvas bags; wooden boxes were too expensive.) Everything checked, our buses headed through the morning mist for the cliffs of Newhaven.

I had given Mrs Ballingall the hardest tasks: finance, hotel and coping with our famous musicians. Her first shock was the previous evening when she discovered Reginald Jacques had no passport with him. A kind friend drove through the night and delivered it safely to Newhaven. Colonel Liddell had charge of all the travel documents and seventy boys; John Dalby and eight boys checked all the instrumental luggage; Miss Beale spread her strong wings over the thirty girls; and Sister was always to be seen to be free for any emergency. So was I . . .

The buses took us to the docks. On the boat we had a further check of passport, instrument and music, and our party of 110 was safely launched. The fact that a boat in port moves in the tide was a bit of a shock, and one girl was so frightened that she forgot her number and made for the back of the queue, where she ended up holding my hand. Once we were under way excitement overruled fear, and they were on deck in the morning sun. In mid-Channel, when it was a bit rocky, I spotted a group apparently handing round something to swallow, and was instantly proferred this delicacy. It was Kwells. Sister was shocked, because all members had health certificates declaring what medicines they were bringing, which they had to hand in to her; but they thought these were just like sweets and not important. This proved our first minor disaster, in that even by the next morning's rehearsal the wind players were in serious trouble with dry mouths. Into my experience book went 'No Kwells.'

To my amazement, disembarkation at Dieppe was quite efficient and our reserved carriages were in order. Young English people were welcome, and the children began to enjoy the loud voices, the air of apparent panic and the endless gesticulation.

A welcoming party at the station in Paris was a pleasant surprise. Captain Howell was there, with two young guides and

M. Nicolet, head of Jeunesses Musicales.* When all the plans for the next three days had been checked and agreed with M. Nicolet, I was driven to see that all was well in the hostels. They were extremely primitive, with no hot water, but bedtime was in sight, and sheer tiredness would result in sleep. The colonel was just getting things to his liking when a large party of French militia arrived on the premises. They had been demobbed that afternoon, and after a party returned to their former base, only to find it already occupied by young Englishmen. It must have been a good party, as extricating one group from the other took John and the colonel some time and skill.

Concert day in Paris started early. All the performers had for breakfast was cups of cocoa and a roll, but by nine-thirty they were all behind the scenes in the Palais de Chaillot, an enormous building. It certainly held three thousand, if not more, and it quite took their breath away as they settled on to the platform.

An instrument repairer was our first need, and this used up some of our emergency cash. It took time to warm up and get the balance right after the day of travelling, but we were ready to leave just before midday for lunch at a restaurant at half-past twelve. We were late departing, however, because during the rehearsal some press-men had come into the hall, and were so stunned by the standard that they wanted pictures and a chance to meet everybody. After no breakfast, no break and a two-hour rehearsal, the children were hungry. It was a very hot day, and the buses were stifling after waiting in the sun. When we arrived at the restaurant, just in time I thought, a message came that there had been a mistake: they had another party. We had nowhere to go.

For nearly half an hour we had to stay in our parked buses

*An organisation started by one M. Cuvelier in Brussels during the Occupation, to put on concerts for young people. M. Nicolet set up a copy in Paris immediately after the war, and later Jeunesses Musicales expanded into many European countries. The British version was called Youth & Music.

with the boiling sun on the windows. I was in the girls' bus, reassuring and doing what I could to help those who were nearly fainting from heat, thirst and hunger (yet I never heard one complaint). Outside, those responsible for us were gesticulating and coming and going. Even Colonel Liddell had disappeared: he had left his satchel containing all our travel documents beside his chair in the auditorium at morning rehearsal. He writes, 'It was only at this restaurant in the middle of Paris that I missed it. I made my way post-haste back to the Palais de Chaillot, which of course was all locked up. I was able to find somone who let me in and there was the satchel, exactly where I had left it.' During this seemingly eternal delay, how thankful I was to have left our pianist, Nigel Coxe, with Mrs Ballingall, allowing him time for practising and rest, so that at least he would be in form at night. Then, miraculously, Captain Howell drove up. Another restaurant had been found, some way away, but at least we could set off into a slight breeze with the hope of food.

On arrival, we moved in very quickly, filling up every small table. We had failed to notice that in the centre of each was a carafe of wine, and before the food could reach the children every drop had gone. They were so thirsty in the heat, they'd gulped it down like lemonade, and now one after another they were collapsing on to the tables and floor. Excellent French food arrived and many revived, but our buses set off to the hostels more like a fleet of ambulances. Captain Howell surveyed the scene, as from the bridge of his ship. 'I think we'll make it to port,' he murmured. I remember answering, 'A concert is a very active port, a beginning not an end.' I was anxious.

There was no problem over obeying the order for everyone to rest on their beds till five-thirty. Sleep took over, and with the miraculous resilience of the young, by six o'clock, washed and looking smart in uniform, they were lapping up English tea, and by seven o'clock smiling faces greeted me at the Palais de Chaillot. Sister saw everyone and reported only three unfit to play; mercifully these were not key people. Soon our usual preparations were in hand, and by five to eight everyone was tuned and lined up, anticipation mounting, when another blow fell. Nobody had thought of telling us that in pre-de Gaulle France, eight p.m. concerts started at about nine, or whenever the audience came. Down went the instruments and the morale. There were very few chairs, and the behind-stage atmosphere was very stuffy. For nearly an hour they took it in turns to sit down, or get near the only window. At ten to nine Reginald Jacques took over, and just said to the Manager, 'We are going to start *now*, or there will be no concert.' He was right. The musicians each encouraged and retuned their own group, and on to the platform they went, with more determination than inspiration. The 'Marseillaise' rang out as if they'd just escaped from some prison, and during our own anthem the warmth came back.

Our audience, in a barely half-filled hall, was intellectual and cold, but after the sparkling vitality of a great French overture they seemed to sit up. Our young, tasteful pianist impressed; the Malcolm Arnold suite, conducted by the composer, was an immediate success. After the interval our audience had doubled, and as the symphony expanded so did the response of our first foreign audience.

It is hard to explain why the few leading French musicians who were there (out of friendship or duty) were overcome: '*Impossible!* Such technical competence, such musical expression. *Les Anglais! Si jeunes!*' They admitted they had expected a floundering amateur effort from schoolchildren; but now they would come again tomorrow and bring their friends. The press did the rest: 'The more I think of these young islanders, the more I hope that we can follow in our country the example of this discipline, this abnegation which, we have concluded, are not remotely prejudicial to *élan*,' said *Les Nouvelles Littéraires*. *Le Figaro* pronounced: '. . . this army gets thunderous results, thanks to its discipline and to its regiments of brass that Berlioz would no doubt have appreciated; Malcolm

Arnold's Divertimento allowed the latter to show off their warm enthusiasm.'

In England the *Musical Times* summed up:

> Everyone who hears this orchestra for the first time is astonished – and the Paris critics were no exception. This is because people come prepared to judge it by amateur standards. But these players are no amateurs . . . It is difficult to know what to single out for praise: the rich tone . . . the delicate accompaniment . . . the impeccable chording of the woodwind; the crisp attack of the brass – to say nothing of the excellent percussion section. Above all they are an admirable ensemble.

The Salle Pleyel was a beautiful traditional French concert hall, to which I found my way at eight a.m. on Saturday, 22 April. '*Musicienne anglaise*' seemed to conjure up friends from the basement, and soon chairs, my choice of piano, even an extension on the platform became available; our small van of instruments arrived as promised at eight-thirty, the driver clutching a newspaper: '*Très bien, très bien, l'orchestre des élèves!*'

At nine the orchestra arrived, apparently none the worse for yesterday's adventures, if a little tired. A platform rehearsal and sound and balance tests were completed by ten-thirty. In the mean time invitations were pouring in and our hosts were planning trips to the sights of Paris. This hospitality was just what was needed; a change, a treat, imprinting on young memories their first glimpse of Paris in the spring.

Dr Jacques, Malcolm and I had been invited to visit the Mayor. It was important politically to develop Anglo-French relationships and cultural exchanges, especially among the young, but his welcome went far beyond the formal course of duty. We were each created an Ami de Paris and presented with a framed etching of some aspect of the city.

The orchestra were taken sightseeing in buses (Notre-Dame, Sacré Coeur, Sainte-Chappelle), and all turned up in high spirits for lunch (this time plenty to eat and no wine), and returned to the hostels for their customary rest. Later in the afternoon a mobilisation party started in the next-door garden. The bottles of champagne were plenteous, their contents disappeared with fantastic speed, and the future stalwarts of the French Army became both happy and adventurous, some invading the neighbouring hostel. Suddenly upstairs windows opened and the girls called, 'Mr Dalby, save us, please rescue us.' He told me later that he sped in and accosted a crowd of jolly young men with '*Allez, allez, vite!*' in his most military voice, to no avail. But Miss Beale gave vent to a tirade in total command of the language. The happy Frenchmen seemed shocked into silence, scuttling down the stairs and withering humbly away. They had merely expanded into the next building, and were rewarded with a beautiful maiden asleep on every bed! Miss Beale was concerned for her charges and any fright or distress the episode had caused. But after much laughter the peace was restored, and the most serious damage was 'Oh Miss Beale, what *shall* I do? He's sat on my Ryvita!'

This time the concert started almost punctually, the hall was crowded out and the audience were mostly members of Jeunesses Musicales, under thirty. We started with national anthems; by the end of the overture the response was alive, and continued to grow to the interval, Malcolm being recalled several times. This really helped the performers after the various problems and the poor start on the previous evening, and the symphony was the best playing the NYO had achieved so far. This was of the utmost importance as we needed to know for the future what adversities could be overcome.

The evening ended happily, as enthusiastic members of the audience crowded round the buses. We lingered to allow this opportunity for Anglo-French socialising on the pavements until the traffic police said, 'Enough.' This spontaneous event was a fitting farewell to Paris.

All I hoped for now was a safe, uneventful journey home. But with the young nothing is uneventful. In spite of checking everything the day before, we found our seats reserved in two different trains, the second likely to arrive at Dieppe too late for our boat. This meant a lot of quick reorganisation so that those with the longest journeys home from Newhaven were in the first train; yet our heavy-instrument van belonged to the second. At Dieppe my group embarked safely, but some group travel documents pertained to the other half, and the red tape wouldn't allow one of us to go off the boat to rescue the others, who couldn't get on without them. Their train was late, but with barely five minutes to departure time it had heaved into sight. By some miracle Mrs Ballingall found a senior superintendent *de port*, and John Dalby had a card with his title of Superintendent of Music, Aberdeen, on it; the two superintendents were instant friends, and all was arranged.

No fear of the sea this time, but as we neared Newhaven, someone noticed a group of boys leaning against the railings, and apparently playing some game throwing things into the sea. On enquiring it appeared they were tossing their passports into the waves and watching them sink! 'We thought they were just for the Froggies,' was the innocent reply when stopped, and utter amazement that they could be needed to get *into* England.

Our boat was late arriving and the disembarkation and customs areas were hectically crowded. John and I went to the most important-looking 'superintendent' and explained that we were a party of exactly 110 musicians; they had individual passports; they had done no shopping; they had trains to catch to all parts of Britain . . . could we help mutually to save time? A separate gangway was fixed and all passed through, calling their number and being checked from our list. How grateful the official was for our excellent organisation! How grateful we were not to have to explain the missing passports and all it might have involved!

Once home, I thought of all the stories being told in homes all over Britain as they arrived back safe and well from their adventure. For me and my wonderful colleagues, the first foreign tour by the NYO representing Britain was safely completed. It cost little, it left much good will and it was marvellous education for the young. When I reported on the trip to my Chairman and Executive, the British Council and the KGJT, I found they had already heard on their own grapevines that we had made a considerable impression in many circles.

Some important matters were stored in my mind for the future, but I kept a few notes: a performing orchestra must have reasonable accommodation, hot water, enough space and a chance to rest, it is *not* on holiday; details of music and timetable must be adhered to, and transport reliably on *time*; instruments must be equipped for travel. These essentials must be fought for. If performers get ill, the concert could be cancelled. Our performers are not experienced adults, but doing the same hours and concerts as any professional orchestra on tour.

The northernmost city of the British Isles is inhabited by a sturdy, proud, scholarly, deeply Protestant tribe. Staunch to withstand the rough seas of their great fishing trade, Aberdonians are as strong as the granite on which their city is built. The enlightened City of Aberdeen Education Committee had sent representatives to our concerts and then invited us to work there. Although longing to accept, I had to explain that for most of our members Aberdeen was further than Paris, and the fares might prove too expensive; undaunted, they expressed their eagerness to have us by offering a grant of £200 for travel. Since the discovery of North Sea oil much has changed; I am glad that the orchestra's first visit to Scotland was to the Aberdeen of 1950.

The Music Hall in Aberdeen was booked for the concert. Walter Susskind and our remarkable staff of professional musicians were all available. This was especially heartening as the MTA, infuriated that we had succeeded in spite of their opposition, had approached them offering far better fees if they would leave me and work on the MTA summer-holiday course. They remained loyal. There was one important new addition, a friend of Jack Thurston and former principal trumpet at the BBCSO: Ernest Hall. He was a great teacher –

honest, warm-hearted, patient but insistent on the highest standards; he looked for the most beautiful sound from the trumpet and no less. His arrival was a red-letter day for the NYO, and he never left us until old age demanded it.

Accommodation for the girls was in a residential school at Tertowie, and for the boys at Powis Academy, where we would also work. James Thomson, the Headmaster of Powis, was proud of his school, and convinced the NYO would damage it, perhaps wreck it. Pressed by his employer, he grudgingly offered us enough space, with the most stringent instructions as to which doors, passages and staircases were not to be used. He added, 'But of course you won't be able to prevent it.' Some challenge!

So on 17 August John Dalby and I, with a team of local boys, turned Powis into a residential school of music, which involved seventy pillows, 280 blankets, all those mattresses to heave up the stairs. Finally we made a plan to avoid traffic congestion: we walked the building as if we were a thirteen-year-old boy, full of curiosity, then sealed off with stacked forms, chairs or rope where access was not permitted. On the day the orchestra was due to arrive Mr Thomson decided to come over by surprise to survey the horror for himself, but found he was locked out. He then came to the main entrance and, proceeding to his study, found the corridor blocked with forms and the alternative route, another staircase, thickly cordoned off. He came to us at once to say he was impressed. When work started he visited us daily and became more and more interested; he wanted to be helpful and offered to take staff in his car to see the sights of the city; he was almost glowing with pride at the success of the concert on Saturday night. But he still harboured an anxiety: his school, now totally transformed, could not possibly be ready for term to start on Monday morning at ten o'clock . . . Another challenge.

The week at Aberdeen was a particularly happy one. We achieved the highest standard so far, because in Walter we had a conductor who understood the vitality and excitement of the young, yet never lost control. He wanted to come to individual classes, and it was quite difficult to explain that it is easier to practise without performing to an important visitor in the room. He soon grasped the idea that our beginners were doing everything for the first time: our ways were not remotely similar to life with professionals – and the partnership grew. He even joined us one evening for John Dalby's organ recital in St Machar's Cathedral. Another event was our first broadcast on the Third Programme, which in those days represented high-level culture; we felt we'd been invited for the quality of our playing, not just because we were 'youth'.

I had chosen a twelve-year-old cellist of great talent, Carol Sansom, for *Kol Nidrei* by Max Bruch; we were doing a Brahms symphony for the first time, a big step forward; Britten's *Soirées musicales* involved the percussion. Everyone seemed more experienced after Paris, and the happy week showed in an exciting concert. A discerning and astonished audience packed the hall, and gave generous appreciation. The *Scotsman* sent a most poetic music critic, who knew the gold from the glitter, the love from the technique, and was genuinely moved by what he heard:

> This orchestra is as miraculous in achievement as it is incredible to those who have not heard it. The huge body of strings commands a wide range of emotional expression. The woodwind in balance and intonation are unbelievably fine. Richness and perfect control characterise the brass, and the percussion have little to learn of the mysteries of their department. Into one mutual sheaf has this scattered corn been gathered, and an ensemble is found both exhilarating and satisfying . . . The mechanics can hardly be bettered, but in the last issue it is the musicianship of this orchestra that remains on the tablets of our memory. These young people have an insight beyond their years.

On Sunday afternoon we all became furniture removers: down came the barriers and notices, back went the desks according to a diagram we had left on every blackboard. After the evening meal every room was ready except those used as dormitories. At eight o'clock on Monday all the mattresses, pillows and blankets were going into vans. At nine-fifty we had just completed our final inspection when Mr Thomson approached to say that his school was entirely ready for normal use. He was full of congratulation and tribute, and became one of the NYO's most constant and enthusiastic admirers, turning up at all our major events in Britain until his death in 1960. Of course it was terribly important to us to establish our standards of behaviour if we were going to continue to receive invitations. We needed a reputation, and a written reference from each place we inhabited.

There was a positive part to all the work involved. Local members who came to help learnt what was involved in preparing for the marvellous weeks of music we had together, that an orderly plan had a part in the creative work and inspiration that lay ahead. All members learnt that property belonged to somebody and had to be treasured. In later years this was harder to teach, when school property was impersonal and belonged to the state, and work was to be done by somebody else who was paid for it.

Now we embarked on yet another experiment. We had accepted an invitation from the Corporation of Kirkcaldy to give a concert in their Adam Smith Hall, and 110 families would take one member each for the night. To save unpacking and bringing our luggage van from the station, we had accepted Kirkcaldy's offer to lend us their percussion instruments. When we got to the hall they were proudly laid out for us: miniature cymbals and drums lent from the local infant school's percussion band! So it was back to the station for our van, and somehow we made it just in time. Our hosts, the Mayor and other civic dignitaries, came to the concert; the welcome and the crammed hall and the generous hospitality made the whole episode a success. Next to me was a charming retired general. He was greatly taken with the whole idea, and particularly with the young people: their initiative and orderliness, their uniform, all pleased his sense of standard. But what really got him was that all the violin bows went up or down together, perfectly in step. 'If only the Guards could see that,' he muttered, 'that's perfect discipline.' Over the years and for a variety of reasons, from General Wilson of the KGJT to General Delacombe in Berlin, the generals were always on our side.

Kirkcaldy was missionary work, and the letters bore out the fact that most of the audience had never heard a symphony orchestra live. Only one local family overslept, but this meant a fourteen-year-old girl travelling alone all day, with cello and suitcase, and not getting home to the south of England till late at night. Naturally I didn't get to sleep until she was safely home. This anxiety taught me not to risk hospitality unless absolutely necessary.

The NYO's adventurous third year – seven concerts in three countries – was now over. As I was in Scotland, I succumbed to the temptation to move west to my Highland home. Work crumbles unless it is balanced by a desert place apart, the silence of the remote natural world.

Ten

Back in our basement, my first task was to find a new Philippa. Who would want to work on a low wage, in a damp office, for odd hours in odd places, be free to travel and like music too? From the applicants one stood out with obvious enthusiasm and dedication to our cause, Joan Ashton. Recently she wrote:

> I applied for the job while I was occupying a palatial office in Victoria, being secretary to an American efficiency expert. He and I were totally antagonistic, and although I had to give his name to you as a referee, I remember that he refused to recommend me. I applied for other jobs at the same time, but *longed* for the NYO. In fact I turned down a job as Secretary to the Dean of the Medical School at St. Thomas' Hospital in the hope that the NYO job would come my way, and then resumed my holiday permanently praying that you would hire me. And you did! I was appointed by a committee consisting of you, Maurice Jacobson and John Newsom, and joined you in the damp oubliette in Gloucester Place in September 1950.

Quiet and unflurried, she would work all hours at amazing speed; her integrity was unassailable, and her strongest weapon if irritated was her rapier-sharp wit. She made a valuable contribution to this stage of the NYO's history, and forty years later we are still in touch.

But why would so many applicants want to give up salary and security to work all hours in awful conditions, for us? I was too close to the five-year fight for survival to realise that, somehow, in just twelve public concerts and a few broadcasts, we must have made some impression. This very September we had to refuse invitations from Denmark, Germany, Canada, Australia and Vienna. The latter's representative couldn't believe we would refuse three concerts in Vienna because we couldn't afford the fare. 'If *we* had this we would send it round the world,' was his comment. We had to explain that England was different and hadn't noticed us yet. The KGJT grant had already decreased to £500 for this last year, so plans had to be kept small in scale until we could find financial backing for the future.

I talked to Joan about the whole year 1950–51: we had been invited to Hull for Christmas and Manchester for Easter, and had an invitation to perform at the Festival of Britain in May, and most exciting of all to the Edinburgh International Festival. Ian Hunter, the new Director of the festival, had no doubt kept an eye on the progress of the infant NYO he had launched in Bath, and I think the *Scotsman*'s piece on our Aberdeen concert may have helped. It meant a great deal to me to be included on artistic merit in an international event, among great orchestras and performers, no longer ploughing our own furrow from concert to concert.

We were also starting an Ex-Members' Association, as there were already nearly a hundred former students, some taking music professionally and the majority remaining amateurs. They wanted to meet annually, to play as an orchestra and to keep their friendships, and find ways of helping us in return for all they'd been given. This year it performed at the Royal Festival Hall as the British Orchestra, conducted by Susskind. Some were playing in the New Music Series in the Wigmore Hall; some were teaching gifted children who couldn't afford lessons; others helped us at busy periods in the office. They also supplied the majority of the newly resuscitated Royal Amateurs. The RA was founded by the first Duke of Edinburgh, a violinist, and still met weekly. I had been asked to rescue it when it was reduced to only six members. For a season or so I took them over, enlisting over fifty NYO ex-members. We even gave a public concert in the Duke's Hall of the RAM in 1956, and made some money. I then handed over to an ambitious young conductor, Charles (later Sir Charles) McKerras, and some forty years on it is still flourishing as the Royal Orchestral Society, conducted by Arthur Davison.

Joan grasped all the ideas instantly, and silently dug herself into a map of Britain. She wrote recently, 'Planning your audition tour was tremendously hard, and I virtually took over Thomas Cooks at Selfridges. But I was so grateful that you left me alone to get on with it all my own way. These were happy days but not for clock watchers or holiday addicts. I once wrote 87 letters on Good Friday in a marvellous uninterrupted burst!'

The audition tour was for me also the most exhausting part of the year, but what an education! All the dialects, all the different kinds of schools, all the regional temperaments, the darkness of city life, the great beauty of our country towns and traditions. The rapidly changing social scene in which our young were growing up was all laid out before me as I travelled around.

Every tour produced a few 'special' discoveries. This time one was a little girl of eight from Iceland, Dody Trygvason. Her father had sent me a tape of her playing, and after hearing her I invited her to play a Mozart concerto with us at Hull. Soon afterwards the whole family moved to London. Years later, after a student period at the RAM, she went to Moscow for further study, where she met the leading student Vladimir Ashkenazy, whom she married. I have always kept in touch with the family, and in 1984 her eldest son, Vovka, came to stay with me in Dublin, and I could offer him his first recital in the National Concert Hall. Three generations of friendship with a very special family started through the 1950 audition tour.

With my new orchestra for 1951 chosen, and some younger ones for the junior group, we were ready to prepare our Christmas term in Hull. Proud of their music festival and devoted to their choirs and operatic societies, the hospitable people of Hull were very keen to invite the NYO to open their musical programme for the year, and their education department provided splendidly for all our needs.

Reginald Jacques was to have conducted this time, but he

became ill about three weeks before Christmas, leaving little time to find the right conductor to fill such a specialised role. Jack Thurston mentioned a friend, Anthony Collins, a viola player turned conductor who was a specialist in Sibelius. We met, and I was not impressed. Jack promised to train Collins to our ways, and the programme would now include a Sibelius symphony, a very difficult work for us.

Looking back over the first twenty years, the Hull week remains my nightmare. Anthony Collins had expected a lower standard than he found, and this shook him badly. Skating along with a willing professional orchestra is possible, but with students who'd never played any of the works before, disastrous. We took him out of rehearsals, Leonard doing the overture, Ernest Hall and John the Holst, and myself the Mozart with Dody, but he had to tackle the symphony. After a few days, mainly as listener, he fell under the spell of the happy atmosphere and dedicated work, and disappeared one afternoon. He drove miles to visit someone he knew in Yorkshire who made the best cymbals in England. He had noticed our rather small, tinny ones, and he came back with a large pair whose sound he had chosen, and presented them to the orchestra; a little note to me said, 'In gratitude for the experience of being here, and for all I've learnt.'

But our troubles were not over. On the eve of the concert I fell on the snow. It was trivial, but our local doctor for the week pronounced concussion and a few days' rest. Normally on concert day I would be in the hall supervising every detail of the staging: it is so important that an orchestra looks good on the platform; the seating makes a difference to the sound; and for us it was very important to sit as near as possible to the rehearsal plan. This time John and Jack offered to do the platform for me, and as I was still seeing double I gratefully accepted, stressing my worry about the City Hall's platform being too small for us. (It was a great disappointment for younger members not to play in the concert, but occasionally they had to stand down.) Rising late the next morning, and taken by car just in time for the rehearsal, I was greeted by John with, 'It was fantastically easy, plenty of room, I hope you'll approve.' It looked splendid. I started to check . . . Where were the violas? They had been completely omitted! Though we laughed about it, it taught me a lesson: in future, whatever I delegated, it would not be the concert platform. Starting late meant a recording was late, the buses kept late, the cooks upset as lunch was late; all things that are not good on concert day.

The performance itself was made into a great event by the sheer enthusiasm and warm appreciation of the people of Hull. The true simplicity of the Icelandic child, the pure beauty of Mozart, had been the light of the week. The sound of this big orchestra in Sibelius was fine, but would the concentration of the conductor hold? Alas, he lost his way at a key moment. The crisis was averted by the double basses, who had decided not to rely on his cue but keep going their own way; an intuitive timpanist kept a discreet drum-roll going to cover this brief but chaotic mêlée, until somehow everyone climbed back on the basses' foundation. I vowed inwardly that this must *never* happen again. It didn't.

The *Hull Daily Mail* said:

> Merely to attempt the Sibelius is an act of faith and daring. It would be wrong on my part to imply that it was note-perfect, but it was a superb piece of playing. Awkward moments in the obscure slow movement were amply compensated for in many dramatic touches.

Bravo the double basses and the drums!

We had maintained the idea of allowing local people on to the platform for the evening orchestral rehearsals. Joan remembers, 'I have never seen anyone more deeply moved at the evening rehearsal than the then Bishop of Hull.' In fact he became a friend and supporter in the ensuing years.

I also had as our guest, for the whole week, one Dr Leslie Russell, Music Adviser to the London County Council. He had written asking if he could come and study my work, methods and ideas, promising not to be in the way. It was the kind of extra I could have done without, but I tried never to turn away any genuine teacher, and he had in the LCC a vast territory of young music lovers to guide. He was a most courteous and appreciative guest, and Joan was instructed to keep a firm eye on him, as no visitors were allowed into classes and individual lessons, and I didn't want this privacy and concentration interrupted. (So close was her surveillance that, when she was cutting the cake at our New Year's Eve party, Malcolm Arnold thought they were celebrating their engagement.) I took trouble and gave any spare time that week to Dr Russell, and he wrote a letter thanking me warmly for 'the inspiration and instruction' and 'so much kindness in such a busy week', promising 'complete support and co-operation from the LCC'.

In fact it was the kiss of betrayal. From then on no child in his London schools was allowed to come to us, and with a whole week's blueprint in his hand he set out to make a copy, the London Schools Symphony Orchestra, conducted by himself, which he thought with all the might and finance of the LCC would soon outshine us and destroy us. Over the next fifteen years he tried very hard, always including professional students from the royal schools of music, Trinity and Guildhall in an attempt to reach our standard. I bemoan teachers and servants of music behaving like this. Strangely, with all his Goliath power, he failed.

After leaving Hull I pondered on future conductors. I went to talk to Maurice Jacobson, Chairman of the Executive Committee, who had known my work since childhood, and to Sir Adrian Boult, who hadn't and would be objective about what had gone wrong. The NYO's conductor is of vital importance; he becomes the nucleus of the week's work, a lasting influence and memory for members of the first time they played a great work. Sir Adrian was most kind and sympathetic, and offered to come himself for our Easter term in Manchester.

Eleven

Sir Adrian was a man of stature, richly based in the tradition of his training in Germany with Richter and Nikisch, and with endless orchestral experience. Used to his own excellent orchestra (the BBCSO), who knew exactly what he wanted, he had an easy manner. His style was relaxed, almost Edwardian; apart from his daily round in the professional world at the BBC, he was also used to amateur occasions. So it was an important event and a great privilege to have our President with us as conductor.

Owing to our reputation for leaving everywhere in perfect order, we were lent the beautiful new Levenshulme High School for Girls for all our work and meals; we slept in various hostels belonging to Didsbury Training College. We all wore gym shoes, and cellos and basses had special mats to protect the new floors, and wind players carried dribble-cloths to every lesson. Although not resident there, some instinct made me think we should have a fire drill. All instructions were given, written down and memorised, but when tried out by surprise four days later it was a disaster. What should have taken at most four minutes became sixteen, and still there was one missing. A brave housemaster entered the supposedly blazing building to search, when suddenly through the front door our thirteen-year-old fourth bassoon emerged; disobeying all instructions, he was laden with every possession – music case, stand, spare shoes and clothing, bassoon on shoulder – staggering on to the front lawn. He explained that his father was in the Guards and they must never leave any equipment behind! There was a repeat, of course, two days later, which was near-perfect.

Manchester's Free Trade Hall had been destroyed in the war, and a non-conformist church called the Albert Hall was then used for all the city's major concerts. The programme included Sir Adrian's favourite Elgar overture; Smetana's *Vltava*; and two classical arias to be sung by an eighteen-year-old soprano, Mary Hampshire, whom I had heard in Hull's music festival. My colleagues were full of doubt (a girl's voice filling a concert hall?), and I didn't let them hear her until the final rehearsal. Douglas Cameron and Ernest Hall admitted to being deeply moved. A personality of such beauty and spirituality had this gift of a voice, which floated easily through the hall. It was the only occasion in our history when I found a young natural singer ready as a soloist.

I had arranged to have the first four days without Sir Adrian. This was partly to prepare the work for him as thoroughly as time would allow, but also to give added help to our exam students and to cover the extra ground for the Festival of Britain. But the great day was soon upon us, and there was an air of expectancy as our President raised the baton. He was obviously overwhelmed by the vigour and energy, even the volume of sound that emerged. He smiled, enjoyed it, made few comments and went through most of the programme, stopping half an hour early. He told them how impressed and delighted he was, ending with, 'One more rehearsal should do and we'll be ready for the concert.'

This was shattering. Here were students thirsting for instruction, being given just one rehearsal in works new to them. Was Sir Adrian going to leave them adrift on their inexperience? They took considerable reassuring; it was fortunate that there was a recital by Dennis Brain that evening. While the orchestra slept, Leonard Hirsch, Jack Thurston and I went to talk to Sir Adrian: did he really only want one more rehearsal before the concert? He explained that he disliked detailed rehearsing, that in fact sometimes things went better with no rehearsal at all. At the BBC perhaps; but with us? I soon realised that Sir Adrian was of the mind that sport and music were for recreation and relaxation in spare time, purely amateur enjoyment, while we were teaching the talented to strive for

1. John Dalby,
drawn by Ernest Shepard, 1953

2. The first members arriving at Bath, April 1948

3. and 4. Two young members

5. Paris, April 1950

6. Eugene Genin

7. Reginald Jacques

8. Douglas Cameron, Frederick Thurston and Leonard Hirsch in rehearsal

9. Sir Adrian Boult in rehearsal

10. Afternoon rest on mattresses, girls' dormitory. Sketch by Thomas Q. Napper

11. At Abington, 1951

12. The author on the 'wild white horse'

13. Morning break, Abington, sketched by Ernest Shepard, 1953

14. Walter Susskind rehearsing

15. Eugène Cruft with the double basses

perfection. (Perhaps here lay the seeds of much opposition to the NYO.) Together we must adapt so as not to inhibit his special contribution, the floating sound, the Wagnerian sweep, the Edwardian dignity and ease.

Late that night we made a new timetable. We would do all the detailed work, and Sir Adrian would come for shorter rehearsals, and sweep our efforts into one whole in his own way. There was also a technical problem: he used a stick which flopped within the hand, a style long since abandoned. He continually said, 'Watch the *point* of my stick'; after some confusion the young discovered for themselves that in fact you had to follow his wrist, and rhythm was restored. Sir Adrian couldn't get over the daily improvement in the standard, having no idea what work went on in his absence. After the last rehearsal he said, 'See you tomorrow,' but to us in the staff-room: 'I'd been told how good they were, but didn't envisage anything of this standard. I feel overwhelmed.'

Our last evening was spent packing up, cleaning, polishing and making sure everything was as perfect as we had found it. Only the basses, timps, harp and a few cellos were left in the hall to be collected in the morning. In the early dawn John, who had the night-emergency telephone, was woken in the boys' hostel. The school was on fire. The kitchens (never used by us) had burnt out and the smoke and great heat had damaged the floor of the main hall above, where our instruments were. All were rescued but their boxes were extremely hot, and rapidly moved outside to cool in the rain. Far away in the girls' hostel we all slept on. John took over completely, arranging for our morning buses to go straight to the concert hall, and fixing with the caterers a sandwich-and-coffee breakfast to be served down there. Only when everything was safe and new arrangements set did he ring me at about seven a.m. Not a single child knew about it then, and they wouldn't even miss breakfast. John and the housemasters were marvellous. When I arrived with my busload at eight-thirty, everything in the concert hall was going according to plan for our morning rehearsal. Later I expressed privately my disappointment at not being told in the night, on the principle that had the fire involved the students, or even a court case, the absent Director, fast asleep, would not do. The press were arriving for non-existent stories of last night's drama, and soon 120 hungry musicians absorbed five hundred corned-beef sandwiches from the caterers' emergency supply. Then Sir Adrian arrived, and I remember how happily he joined in the picnic breakfast, and enjoyed the inconsequence of a young boy: 'Is that why you made us have a fire drill?' The Hallé Orchestra had been friendly, encouraging and helpful throughout our stay, and some players now turned up offering to lend instruments.

We were not known in Manchester and the hall was not sold out the day before. But the story and pictures in the local papers did the trick: not a seat was left by lunch-time. Loathing publicity as I do, I had much to learn about the importance of the press.

The concert exceeded our expectations, especially Sir Adrian's *Vltava*. The audience was really excited at the end. When I made my appeal, I said that we had survived so far because of help from various sources, and recently £1,000 from a gentleman in Yorkshire, adding, 'Now, I always understood that anything Yorkshire could do would be easily surpassed by Lancashire . . .' The rest didn't matter. Mancunian hearts, moved by the music and the laughter, came round to the buses with pound-notes in hand; the Lord Mayor, Samuel Dawson, brought a personal invitation for a return visit.

To mark the centenary of the Great Exhibition of 1851, there was to be a Festival of Britain, intended to provide 'a shaft of confidence cast forth against the future'. One item was a special Albert Hall concert in May with children's choirs and an orchestra, with Sir Adrian conducting. The organisers thought up the neat idea of inviting the NYO to accompany all these choirs, and thus save the cost of a professional orchestra, wording the invitation as a great honour. I was invited to a meeting in February 1951 and found myself once again too near to the jaws of the Schools Music Association, whose choirs were taking part.

I had to explain that there might well be problems in getting our members out of school in May. Whereas a single school choir involves permission from one school and one education authority for one day, we would have to get permission from over a hundred schools all over the country, and would need at least three days because of travelling and residential accommodation while rehearsing in or near London. Also, orchestrating and copying all the parts would be expensive; who would cover the considerable cost? We could not. Finally, we would be working on our own programmes for a week in April; that, together with scholarship exams for our students, might not leave us enough time to do justice to all the accompaniments. Of course I offered to discuss this kind invitation with my Executive Committee and with Sir Adrian, who was conducting for us in Manchester as well as for this festival.

The problems were formidable, and I thought I was being helpful and realistic. But Mr Trethewy of the SMA rose to his feet and there emerged from his mouth an unrepeatable tirade against me and my 'high-falutin' standards, against highly educated people too grand to 'muck in' with the likes of them . . . Bernard Shore (present as Chief Inspector of Music), normally calm and suave, angrily demanded a complete withdrawal of the insults and an apology to me. To my amazement it was instantly given. (Chief inspectors must have great power.)

Our Executive Committee decided that the NYO should take part in a great national festival. The independent schools kindly boarded our members on receiving letters from Sir Adrian or John Newsom or George Sylvester or Douglas Guest. We compromised on the programme, in that we accompanied the opening choral events and played on our own two items from our Manchester programme. The LPO accompanied the main choral work, *Sons of Light*, specially written for the occasion by Vaughan Williams. Mr McDougall settled the finance for us, in consultation with the festival organisers. My report to the 1951 Council meeting reads:

> The Festival of Britain concert in the Albert Hall was in association with the S.M.A. Students arrived in London on Thursday, and worked throughout Friday and Saturday (May 3rd, 4th and 5th). Hospitality was arranged for every member of the orchestra, and thanks are due to the splendid co-operation by public schools. The L.C.C. was quite unable to help at all in any matter. This occasion was the first time that N.Y.O. members had ever come out of school in term-time.

I have little memory of the concert. What I do remember is that a gentleman from Holland, Mr Van Leer, was there, and so moved by the orchestra's playing that he sent £1,000, offered to repeat it and invited us to Holland. Also that Vaughan Williams drew me aside to tell me how he wished he could support me, but hoped I understood. He had lent his name enthusiastically at the start, but withdrew when he discovered other organisations with which he was associated were opposing us, obviously embarrassing for him.

After Manchester and the Festival of Britain concert, it was time for a Council meeting. The members were impressed by a new pamphlet produced by the Executive Committee giving our aims, achievements and the results in scholarships and entrances to colleges and universities, with a few going directly into professional orchestras. Printing the results made quite a difference to the support from some kinds of schools in some areas. We were still new, and some headteachers were not sure yet whether we were a good thing or some passing stunt. The outstanding results changed the perceptions of such people.

We had a new constitution, which required us to elect new officers every three years and to appoint an honorary secretary (George Sylvester). I also wanted an experienced headmistress on the Council, and we were joined by Rachel Pearse of Mary Datchelor Girls School. She was always a great help to me, and did much to steer us through problems within the system of the LCC, giving many years of loyal service to the NYO.

The grant from the KGJT was almost finished, but we were helped by a wonderful gift of £1,000 a year for three years from Sir Stuart Goodwin of Sheffield, and £1,000 from Mr Van Leer, with more promised. The LEAs had also been supporting members splendidly. We had just enough to live on, and so continued to plan ahead in hope. I even raised the possibility of six concerts on six consecutive nights in Brussels. This seemed quite a shock and produced a lot of discussion. Could our children manage it? What sort of impresario was involved? Who was filling his pocket? How much time would there be for cultural education while there? I was pleased that they all cared so much, and was allowed to pursue the idea further.

Finally, Maurice Jacobson reported that he had arranged a meeting with the MTA at which it was agreed to work happily together in peace in the future. Next day, quite by chance, I met my former professor and friend Ernest Read outside the RAM. He greeted me warmly and invited me to join him for a quick lunch. Referring to the MTA he said, 'You've won. You succeeded for two reasons: the right title and perfect timing. Your ship was under way before the MTA committees could sink it. You had many powerful forces lined up to stop you and you were not afraid of them.' I asked him if he would like to work more closely with us now, but he said, 'Thank you, no. I work very hard and must have peace at home.' His second wife was a leading light of the MTA, organising their summer schools and the Ernest Read student orchestras.

All that remained now was the last great musical event of these first five founding years. And what an event it proved to be.

Twelve

We had accepted the invitation to play at the Edinburgh Festival, but as yet we had nowhere to stay, as no schools or colleges within reach could have us. When we were nearly despairing a friend of John Dalby's, one Henry Ritchie, had an idea. He lived in the village of Biggar, and nearby there was a camp where city children would come for holidays in the country: the Glengonnar Camp School at Abington, Lanarkshire. I was in the next train to Edinburgh, and then forty miles on by bus into the sheep-farming countryside of the Scottish Lowlands. The camp was set in the most beautiful scenery, equidistant from Glasgow and Edinburgh.

The camp Commandant was most welcoming, but somewhat stunned at the thought of 120 musicians and their world-famous teachers inhabiting a riverside camp for small children. I was by now familiar with the expression that comes over a face when its owner is not sure if he's meeting some strange mythomaniac, so I hastened to be entirely practical; we started to explore every inch of the property, armed with my usual tape measure, ruler and pedometer.

Indeed, there were difficulties – particularly no large hall for the symphony orchestra – but as the day went by the co-operation grew, and by the time I left for the night train we had decided to use their dining-room as our hall and bring in a marquee dining-room and kitchens; I was also shown the village station, only half a mile away. The Glengonnar Camp was to play a considerable part in the wider education of our musicians in the ensuing years.

Then my mind turned to transport. Travel to Edinburgh on concert day would be easy, by bus; but how was everybody to get to the tiny village station on the fringe of the camp?

Miraculously, the great LMS Railway from Euston to Glasgow passed through Abington. Of course no main-line express trains would ever stop there . . . unless we could persuade them. A letter would take too long and the answer would be no. So at nine-thirty the next morning I started telephoning the LMS, asking simply to be put through to the person who had the power to stop trains. After a slow start I reached an office that planned timetables. By two-thirty the switchboard became encouraging: 'You're getting warmer!' At quarter-past five however I was about to give up, saying, 'I've been searching *all day* for the person who has the power to stop an express train at a village station,' and a kind voice said, 'Tell me what you want.' Soon I had explained my problem; he warmed to my story: the children, the music, the camp and the Edinburgh Festival. Patiently this man explained that Abington was on a gradient, and for an express to stop for two minutes there would mean arriving twelve minutes late in Glasgow. I needed it to be stopped three times, first with about eighty students on the way up, next the night train with the professors, then back the day after the concert. The next day this kind man rang me again to say he would do it. He had been with the LMS since he left school, at one stage as an engine driver, and he really knew and loved his railway. I've forgotten his name: we never actually met, we never wrote a letter. But exactly what he arranged for us happened, and we owe much to this gentle professional railwayman 'with the power to stop trains'.

Now it was time to prepare our members for our next adventure: life in camp. Instructions were sent for warm clothing for day and night, thick shoes and mackintoshes, and detailed instructions on how to leave the train in two minutes flat – by lining all the corridors and opening all the doors and more or less pouring themselves and their luggage on to the village platform.

But how would our professors react to life in camp? They had followed us loyally to various places in various conditions, but this? They thought I was joking, even when asked to equip themselves for wet weather and to bring torches, yet no one failed to accept. In a last letter enclosing their night-sleeper tickets to Abington, I warned them that the ticket inspectors would tell them that the train didn't stop at Abington and press them to change at Carlisle, but they were to stay in the train and it would. Of course this happened, and some wavered, but Ernest Hall took charge and made them obey my instructions. I'm told he kept muttering, 'You don't know our Ruth Railton' when the officials refused to believe that their train would stop. At Carlisle the engine drivers changed, and to the amazement of the night attendant the Royal Scot stopped at the village to deposit seven world-famous musicians.

I was on the platform to meet them and pointed out the camp on the hillside, the most prominent part being the huge tent that was our dining-room. 'So it wasn't a joke!' said Jack, and their spirits fell. When we arrived, the relief at not having to sleep under canvas brought laughter, followed by a welcoming Scottish breakfast, the view of the hills in the rising sun and the children's happy voices. After just four years musicians of this stature were willing to come with us anywhere; I never took this devotion for granted at the time, and I look back on it now with happiness.

The majority of our members were from big cities, and the first evening was one of quiet wonderment. After supper in the huge tent we all walked through the sunset, along the river and the path through the woods to the forbidden main road.

The beds were too small for our larger young men and conditions were of extreme simplicity. We had expected some trouble, especially with the girls due to beetles, spiders, friendly country mice and even bats. Instead a postcard home said, 'There is a wild white horse in the field by our chalet. He comes as close as he can, and opens his mouth wide, showing heaps of teeth, and makes an extraordinary sound. It's very frightening, but luckily he can't get through the hedge.' (One afternoon I slipped away with sugar and hay to tame the 'wild white horse'. He was very big and lonely, but, taking a young violinist used to horses with me, and mounting with the aid of a gate, we brought him into the camp. How many there were who had never actually stroked a live horse. He joined us daily, preferring the sound of brass, lingering outside their rehearsal-room.)

John wrote to me in a recent letter:

> The austerities were not all that bad; in fact the near primitiveness of it all went towards the NYO's spiritual making; for the sylvan nature of the immediate surroundings and the glory of the unspoiled countryside in general had the effect of making us all feel at one with life.

Refreshed and full of energy, we started work at nine a.m. in preparation for our most important concert so far. We were fortunate to have Susskind again, as his finest qualities would produce an exciting concert. A Wagner overture gave all sections plenty of work; we had a Mozart clarinet concerto with Colin Bradbury, who had been with us from the beginning, as soloist. (Colin later won a scholarship to the RCM, then became principal clarinet of the BBCSO and joined the staff of the NYO; eventually his own twins were members.) A Kabalevsky symphony was new to everyone. The first evening we decided to contend with our greatest problem, the hall. It was too small: we just packed in. We were all a little set back, but it was all we had; we learnt to listen in this very long, very low, very narrow, wooden hut.

We had one new professor this time, Hubert Dawkes. He was quiet, gentle, an exceptionally gifted young pianist, organist and harpsichordist. I needed him mainly to accompany for the evening recitals, but his natural talent fitted in with everything that went on, and he offered to help as needed. It was also love at first sight when he met Joan Ashton; they have now been happily married for nearly forty years.

On Sunday we were invited to the village Presbyterian church. The minister mounted the pulpit and in a voice like Ian Paisley's called out, 'What was it Lucifer missed most when he was turned out of Heaven? . . . The sound of the morning trumpet.' Every head turned to look at the back of the church, where Ernest Hall was sitting. Then our crowd really sang the last hymn, and when we left a very old man in the porch said, 'I'd like to hear music like *that* in Heaven.'

But our local reputation might have been damaged when one evening a conscientious housemaster, Ronald Sturley, spotted three girls in the woods after the bedtime bell. He gave chase, only to discover he had captured three chambermaids from the local hotel, terrified and exhausted by their attempts to escape their would-be attacker. A quick visit to the hotel manager, who luckily had a sense of humour, made amends and a new friend.

Throughout the week musical work was paramount. Tackling the problems seemed to add character to the playing, and Walter, enjoying the challenge, rose to his most outstanding best.

Then came the great day, starting with breakfast at five-forty-five. We were to leave the camp at six-thirty for the morning rehearsal in the Usher Hall, Edinburgh, our concert being at two-thirty. Joan has 'horrendous memories of being fully dressed in afternoon finery (grey georgette and cream lace from Marylebone Road) at 5 a.m., and tramping round the chalets to make sure all the professors and staff were awake'. No buses or van broke down, and at nine-thirty a fully groomed, smartly uniformed, unrecognisably civilised orchestra was on the Edinburgh platform.

And the sound? It took time to adjust after our narrow hut but our anxiety on that score was soon over. During the rehearsal I was interrupted to speak to a few strangers who had crept in to listen. One was the great conductor Mitropoulos. He was fascinated, unable to believe the standard, and wanted the dates for our visit to New York. When I explained that we'd love to be invited but had no money to get there, he seemed baffled. 'You should tour the world,' he said. 'The States would go mad for it.' I went back to work, ensuring the staff were on the lookout for the one person I *had* written to invite, Bruno Walter, one of the great musical minds of the century. He was conducting Beethoven 9 that night so couldn't come to our afternoon concert, but with his generous kindness made time to come in the morning. He crept in and sat near the back to listen. After a while I went to sit beside him and thank him for coming. 'I am stunned,' he said. 'You mean it is the strings who are children, but the wind are all professionals?' He could only see the outside edge of the orchestra – the strings – and thought the rest must be adults. At that moment the music was approaching a climax, and I pointed to a small boy in shorts, Alan Suttie, on the outside edge of the percussion group, his mouth moving as he counted the bars, face alight in excited expectancy; then came his one glorious bang, and a triumphant smile. 'Ah, now I understand,' said Bruno Walter, and the tears poured down his face. At the end of the rehearsal I asked him if he would say a word to the orchestra, and he was hesitant at first because without time to think he might not express his message well enough. He came; and we all remember clearly his first sentence: 'As I am nearly four times your age I think I shall begin by addressing you as my dear children.' Alas, the rest of his prophetic message has been lost, but he certainly told them they had been born into an age when true values would decline, when disorder would increase, yet they had found an anchor to which their souls could cling, and the inner truth of music would enable them to prevail. He thanked them for the 'living quality' he had heard in their playing.

Afterwards, the City of Edinburgh gave us a civic lunch in the City Hall. Manners for formal occasions prevailed, but with breakfast having been at six, that excellent meal was of the utmost importance. Our hosts enjoyed the speed with which the food disappeared, which in itself showed our appreciation and gratitude to the city.

By two o'clock we were behind the scenes of the Usher Hall. There is no experience in the world like the atmosphere of the immediate pre-concert nervous excitement; so much had gone into this, and the great moment was actually here. Walter Susskind was in fine form for the Wagner, and Colin Bradbury was calm and controlled, making a beautiful sound and phrasing with the natural simplicity Mozart demands; then the Malcolm Arnold let everyone off the lead in a burst of confidence, and the symphony produced our best playing. Ian Hunter was especially pleased and immediately invited us back for next year.

Then the festival organisers took us in hand, inviting us to the evening concert of the New York Philharmonic. The children were allowed into their seats in the hall an hour before the performance as there was nowhere to go except our buses; most of them fell asleep. But the percussion players, probably due to John, were off to see Saul Goodman, the NYP's world-renowned timpanist, who showed them his tools, giving advice and encouragement enthusiastically.

Most of our members had never heard Beethoven 9 live and it was a stirring experience to complete the day. But the festival had also offered free tickets for the tattoo at Edinburgh Castle! We thought of sending a busload of the most tired back to Abington, but no, all wanted to stay for this midnight spectacle. What a day. They had given their best but had been given so much – unexpectedly – in return. From six a.m. to our return to camp at two a.m., it had all been new experiences and inspiration.

After the truly great Beethoven, I crept round to the artists' rooms to thank Bruno Walter for his words in the morning and for the performance. There were a few people there, and he asked me to wait. When all had left and the door was firmly shut, he relaxed on a sofa and said, 'Now, come and tell me. What is this miracle I have heard and seen today?' I sat on the floor at his feet, and for the next twenty minutes, until the hall had to shut, we talked . . . how such a concept came to me; the belief that talent shouldn't be wasted; choosing first those with spiritual gifts; the training in work and self-control; the price of dedication to what you love most; all the talent in the world being of no use if the human character fails the growing soul. He said he would write to me, he would always keep in touch, because in my time life would become emptier, more technical and superficial. That evening changed my life: knowing this great, warm, deep personality meant never being artistically alone again. Our letters continued until his last illness.

At the camp, surveying the scene at breakfast I marvelled at the resilience of children, tired, hungry, radiantly happy. The only tears were on the village station as the Royal Scot roared in and bore them all away. With the family gone, Joan and I completed our own work in the awful blank aftermath. After thanking everybody we left for Glasgow, Joan going on to London while I took the train that would wend its way up the west coast and deliver me to my Highland home.

We had a fantastic press: 'a triumph of enthusiasm and ability . . . admirable playing – no face-saving clauses required' from *The Times*; 'buoyant life and proficiency unimaginable in an orchestra of schoolchildren' from the *Telegraph*; 'the highlight of the Festival, the most refreshing event and the most thrilling occurrence' from the *News Chronicle*; 'most of us attended in a spirit of benevolent patronage . . . only to sit up in delighted astonishment . . . technical control not dreamed possible . . . And to skill were added enthusiasm and a sense of wonder, a miracle of music' from the Manchester *Guardian*. All thought we deserved financial support, and most compared us favourably with professional orchestras, unknowingly stoking the fire of fear in the Musicians' Union. The *Scotsman* mentioned Bruno Walter saying that the NYO was 'one of the most inspiring things I have ever heard in my life', and the Lord Provost James Miller congratulating us publicly and expressing the hope that we would come back. In addition they allowed their columns to be used for letters, including one from Dr Herbert Wiseman, Head of Music at BBC Scotland, offering his address to collect money for us; others offered help and wanted to know more about the NYO.

Then came over seventy letters, many with pound-notes enclosed, to be acknowledged. It was very encouraging, but after five years with barely a break I was too tired to enjoy the response. It was not the responsibility, or the fight for survival; but rather that so much work – for every audition tour, every term, every important concert, all the travelling – depended on the strength of just two people, myself and one overworked and underpaid secretary. We were really floating on a sea of faith without the rudder of adequate finance or any permanent port. I needed a little time to get the future into perspective.

Strange as it may seem, my mind wandered into wider fields, the whole of young England in this brave new post-war world. If so much could be done by training the right talent at the right age in music, what about other spheres of activity? Ninette de Valois found talent, struggled in the early years, but look at the Royal Ballet and its schools now – her great and lasting gift to England. What about doing the same for young mathematicians and scientists? We might have the world's best in that area too. What of the speaking of English, the pride in a great language and the confidence that that gives? What of the delinquents? While unearned money was being handed out increasingly, so would their numbers grow, and surely there is a better way than shutting them up in prison? Was Britain so absorbed in political and material change that it was (is?) underestimating all the potential of its native talent?

My father was a man of imagination and vision: he'd been through two world wars and spent much of his life in the big cities. As we walked in the mountains, we talked of this. 'Stay with the young, in whatever line; they are our future,' he said. Finding the right use of talents and the right place to serve was always difficult: sometimes a path unfolded gradually, sometimes a sudden opportunity could be seized.

Then came a letter from Bruno Walter. He believed the orchestra would come to be accepted as an artistic entity in its own right and with its own style, its own sound, its own integrity and its own zeal. 'This comes from *your* choice of child and of teacher, and *your* own perception as a musician . . . indefinable but distinct.' He wanted me to consider that if I moved away from the NYO too soon, before its special quality was secured in tradition, it might crumble.

Gradually I realised that my life in music belonged to the children and all we had created together. I don't know whether it was Bruno Walter's letter and his faith in me, or the lilting lapping of the water on the shore outside my bedroom window, or the noisy nagging of the oyster-catchers, but when I woke up one morning I had decided it was time to go back and fight on for what I believed in.

As I left home my mother said, 'I'm so glad you didn't let your music go.'

Part Two

THE DEVELOPING YEARS

Thirteen

The founding years were over. My belief in our young musical talent had proved true, and the official world had glimpsed it with astonishment, and famous musicians with delight. That the best talent should live and work together proved more right than I'd expected, as the children were so happy to be with others better than themselves, instead of being an exception in their own school or area. Most of all we had learnt together how much real concentration, rest, playing and listening could be planned into each day, and how to time a balanced programme to peak in just seven days, building the climax – the concert. I had underestimated the value of public performance, the sense of achievement, the stimulus of the audience, but it was undoubtedly this that gave our standard a leap forward each time. Now we had to start building the future on this foundation.

I turned my mind to the plans for the whole of 1952: back to Liverpool in January, Bournemouth at Easter, and the lovely invitation to return to the Edinburgh Festival in the summer. Working on this made me realise that it was time to talk to our Treasurer, as the life-saving support of the KGJT grant ended in 1951. It seemed we could survive on our savings for the year, but it was urgent to find some new, regular finance.

One Sunday evening in November, when I was just preparing for another fortnight away on the audition tour, the telephone rang. It was Sydney Harrison, a piano professor at the Guildhall School, inviting me to supper to tell him more about the NYO as he was writing an article about it. We had met recently when we were both adjudicators at the Isle of Wight Music Festival, but had no time then for talk. During the evening I related our story, our purpose and our problems. Suddenly Sydney said, 'I must come clean. I wasn't going to write an article (but I will now); it was just that I needed more information about the NYO.' A friend had told him there might be some finance available for music, and the Harrisons had said, 'Why not give it to Ruth and her orchestra?' So they both wanted me to know that I might be approached by this acquaintance of theirs, one Philip Zec. Months went by and I forgot about it.

In the spring of 1952 I was approached by Mr Zec and invited to lunch with him and Cecil King, the Chairman of the *Daily Mirror*, at the Savoy Grill. I shook hands with a very tall man, with plenty of greying hair, and very blue eyes – partly sad, yet quick to sparkle – but as he sank somewhat heavily on to a chair my first impression was of a man burdened with sorrow. He ate just one course, very quickly, and pushing utensils aside leant on the table to talk to me. I only remember the last question, 'What do you do for money?'

'Earn it, whenever there's time, and people send us gifts. So far we've been saved by the King George's Jubilee Trust, which has kept us afloat.' After he'd left, Phil Zec revealed that the purpose of the lunch was for his Chairman to meet the Director of the NYO, as there was a possibility of finance for it. He surmised our meeting had gone well, but I felt awful at having shown such scant interest in money.

A little later there was a letter from the *Mirror* to the Chairman of the Executive Committee, with a marvellous offer of sponsorship, which was finally discussed at a full Committee meeting on 2 June 1952. Sponsoring was quite different from charitable gifts, both legally and in the ways a newspaper could participate to help us. This could quite easily have damaged our image, with the wrong kind of publicity. When dealing with people from the *Mirror* throughout these months we found them businesslike, intensely interested and keen to get things right. I know I found it a pleasant change, and so peaceful after the toll the opposition had taken over the years.

On 4 July Sir Adrian chaired an important meeting of the full Council; also present were a director of the *Mirror* and Philip Zec. The sole purpose was to discuss this offer of financial assistance. It was a tough meeting. There were those who were whole-heartedly for; those who agreed subject to safeguards; two who thought it too dangerous to contemplate (to stoop so low would finish us); and a few, including me, who fought like mad to be certain that it could never be the Daily Mirror Youth Orchestra, that the programmes and events could not be chosen by them, and that any spotlighting on individuals in our care must be forbidden, and so on. The minutes reveal that I said, 'It's better to close down in poverty than be destroyed in riches.' John Newsom calmed the proceedings by saying that the *Daily Mirror* was likely to become a much better paper under its new chairman and that Cecil King was a highly educated and cultured man with whom all matters of taste and dealings with schools would be understood. Also, for some years the *Mirror*'s sister-paper the *Sunday Pictorial* had run a most successful National Exhibition of Children's Art, and the firm would want to succeed now with music.

But still there was fighting for written control of publicity, and for many details to be made clear. Suddenly and dramatically, the two gentlemen from the *Mirror* rose to their feet: 'We have been amazed and very impressed to hear you all fighting so hard to guard your integrity, and the trust you hold. Make your own terms, and come back to us for a final agreement.' And they left the meeting.

How ungracious we had been! We'd been sent a most generous offer, and we needed it, yet we were afraid of the press and that it might, unintentionally, destroy us. The minutes, above Sir Adrian's signature, conclude: 'It was unanimously resolved to approve the *Daily Mirror*'s offer of financial assistance, and Mr. Newsom and Mr. McDougall be authorised to complete the details.'

And so it was. On 2 August 1952 an agreement was signed, and it was the *Daily Mirror* that saved the NYO from all further financial worries. The final agreement allowed us complete authority over all aspects of music and educational policy. It was most generous financially, and the only publicity they claimed was 'sponsored by the *Daily Mirror*', written very small on our programmes. There were many ways, especially with printing and contacts all over the country, in which they could help. I was still very nervous of the liaison, remembering Bath, where, along with the *Express*, the *Mirror* had behaved in bad taste. But I needn't have worried. Those highly paid Fleet Street journalists, printers, publicity designers and public-relations experts called on us most courteously. Watching us work away in poverty in our damp basement den, in a cause that mattered more to us than all the money on earth, was a mystery; but they tiptoed carefully among us, not trampling on a world they knew little or nothing about.

Soon a journalist, Paul Cave, was sent as a liaison between us and the *Mirror*, and what a nice man he was. He was the first to experience my unfortunate loathing of personal publicity. I had to explain I was trying to create the utmost beauty in music for its own sake, showing the young how to strive for it, and sometimes their fresh faith and love of doing it touched emotional peaks that adults cannot. Promoting *me*, as the *Mirror* expected, was horribly irrelevant and I would have none of it. 'But most people would give anything to have their picture on the front page of the *Daily Mirror*,' sighed Paul.

How difficult I was as I directed promotion of me to promotion of the orchestra and its purpose! How impossible I was to insist on no stories about individual children – no photos that would cheapen our intentions or standards in the eyes of the schools! (The *Sunday Pictorial* had been banned in the Irish Republic for printing a photograph of a nun playing a trombone.) Paul revealed that the *Mirror* wanted a full page-two article and front-page announcement. They got it, entirely due to his gentle persuasion and extreme patience. On 19 August they announced their sponsorship of the NYO with a most generous tribute to our work, and with dignity and good taste.

*

While this saga was taking place, so was a whole year's work with the orchestra. The audition tour had gone well, breaking some new ground, confirming past contacts, and hearing slightly fewer candidates now that the standard and purpose were better understood. As far as possible I was taking nobody for less than two years, and indeed my best students were to be those I had for about six years, though the average time with us was about three. We were never concerned with the orchestral concert alone, but always with a balanced musical training, and the right atmosphere in which all talents could grow.

This year the Christmas term started with a warmly welcomed return to Liverpool, with the great luxury of all our needs for work and residence in one building, the C. F. Mott Training College. Choosing the orchestral programme for each term was quite difficult. Priority was our members' education. I tried not to repeat a work within four years, so that each time we played works new to them. I aimed for one classical work; one English or modern or a first performance; one that would involve the heavy brass and full percussion; and then what the conductor did best.

Once more I invited Reginald Jacques, as his particular gifts put new members at ease in rehearsal, and once more I had asked an English composer for a new work. Benjamin Frankel had heard the orchestra at Edinburgh, and was so impressed that he asked if there was anything he could do to help us. So now I asked for a piece that would give the brass and percussion plenty to do. His response was *Mephistopheles' Serenade and Dance*, a rather rubbishy piece of programme music. It was a considerable study in orchestral playing, and luckily the composer agreed to conduct it. The rest of the programme covered Wagner (*Mastersingers Overture*), Mozart (a piano concerto, with a most poetic twelve-year-old, Frances Holmes) and the *New World Symphony*.

The work this week seemed to be a higher standard than usual with new members at Christmas. The concert was in the

Philharmonic Hall, and it was interesting that A. K. Holland commented in the *Liverpool Post* on the progress since our last visit: 'no longer the staggering novelty of three years ago . . . but the enthusiasm and vitality was as heart-warming as ever . . . altogether a phenomenon.' Two things linger in my mind from Liverpool. When it was all over, our little pianist, who had been so happy with us all the week and played so beautifully at the concert, wept bitterly when her parents came to collect her, and didn't want to go home. The change was too sudden, away from so many friends and so much music, to go back to a country town and school life.

And it was during this week that one night we nearly killed Eugene Genin. The training college we'd been lent was heated by electric radiators. In preparing the rooms for our distinguished musicians I tried to make them look attractive, and had moved the furniture to make more space – the bed went against the wall, and beside the radiator for warmth in a very cold January. One night Genin awoke choking, the room full of thick smoke. He managed to find a light and open the window before collapsing in the corridor. What had happened was that he had put his thick overcoat on his bed like an extra blanket and the sleeve was hanging down and touching the electric radiator. It caught alight, smouldering like a cigarette and emanating a thickish smoke. All was well, and being such a marvellous character he had the whole staff-room laughing as he displayed his one-sleeved coat. But it was so nearly an awful tragedy, and entirely my fault for not knowing about electric radiators.

How often I longed for a building of our own, as every time we met we faced the responsibility of borrowed premises and different circumstances. But if that were so it would be too expensive to travel to give concerts in a different city each term, and travelling would lose us precious teaching days. No, we must remain a mobile school: the same children, same staff, same teachers in one community in a different home each time.

For Easter 1952 we accepted an invitation from Bournemouth.

This was partly due to Noel Hale, the Music Adviser there and a member of our Council, but also to others concerned with the Bournemouth Symphony Orchestra and the Education Authority. Bournemouth School was lent to us for all our work from breakfast to bedtime, and Wentworth School, an independent boarding school some distance away, provided accommodation for the night. Once again this involved all the work of moving 120 mattresses into the day school's gym and some emptying of classrooms, so that everyone could have an afternoon rest and silence. As elsewhere, Bournemouth set about providing all our needs with the utmost courtesy. I remember a whole platoon of boys, volunteer furniture removers, to help Joan and me. They laid the mattresses, set up the rehearsal-rooms and dining-rooms, working all day as if dedicated to some sacred cause, leaving us a list of their names and addresses in case of need in the ensuing week. Never had we felt so fresh for the invasion the next day. We tried to find out what, if anything, we could do in gratitude. It emerged (they didn't *ask*) that passes for our evening (five p.m.) rehearsals or tickets for the concert would be a treat, as in those days the young had much less pocket money.

The great event this term was having Sir Adrian as conductor, and he had agreed to tackle Brahms 1, the biggest work we'd attempted so far. There was an unhurried sweep about Sir Adrian's interpretation, and I wanted them to sense the bigness of Brahms 1 as a whole. A further step forward was that we could now afford extra professors, such as Dennis Brain and Gareth Morris, who came for two days or so.

The Winter Gardens, a very pleasant concert hall, was packed for our concert. I remember a very discerning and responsive audience, one that was used to its own symphony orchestra every week. After the overture, Susan Tunnell played the Saint-Saens G Minor piano concerto and Frankel conducted his *Mephistopheles*. Sir Adrian created a really remarkable sound in the Brahms. He came off the platform muttering, 'Extraordinary . . . I didn't expect that!' He never understood how much teaching and practising went on in his absence, as he just took short rehearsals and as few as possible to cover the ground. On the night the performance that *we* had prepared took off, and he was amazed, but very happy.

After the concert I had to make the usual appeal. The applause had hardly faded before a stranger approached me, deeply moved by the playing, and handed me a cheque for £250. A few days later another cheque for the same amount arrived from his London office. I rang up to explain to his secretary that I'd already had it, and offered to send this one back. 'Oh no,' she said, 'he was so thrilled he told me to send it; you keep it, he'll never miss it!' Of course I wrote and thanked for both, and that £500 was a major help filling the gap left between the KGJT grant ending in 1951 and the start of the *Mirror* sponsorship in April 1952.

By contrast, four children from the same address sent a half-crown postal order each. In those days sixpence a week pocket money would have been quite a lot, so no doubt they were each giving at least all they had for a month. One was Iona Brown, then eleven, now a world-famous violinist. In due course two more Browns got into the NYO, Timothy on the horn and Ian on the bassoon and piano, both now well-known musicians. Iona tells me that I wrote each of them a separate thank-you letter, a different message in each, and she has kept hers to this day.

Bournemouth also forged my link with the Tunnell family from Leeds. The musical parents, wanting their children to be professional musicians, gave them every opportunity to develop. Susan, a pianist of seventeen, played the concerto on this occasion, and quite soon John joined the violins, and later led the orchestra, and a still younger brother, Charles, joined the cellos.* They all did well professionally.

It was at Bournemouth that I first met Charles Groves, the

*Now principal cello in the ECO.

Conductor of the Bournemouth Municipal Orchestra. A most sensitive and kind man, who twenty-five years later became our President and sometimes conducted the NYO.

At this time, it seemed to me that the general attitude to our existence was changing. Those who loved us (the audiences and the real musicians) wouldn't let us die. The profession seemed less frightened of us and was sending us its talented children. More education authorities wanted us to meet in their areas (whether out of curiosity or disbelief). 1952 seemed to be the year of 'If you can't kill it, join it', and a certain amount of imitation was starting. I felt as if we were no longer swimming against the current in a crocodile-infested river, but had reached safer land, with no doubt new kinds of dangers in the forests ahead.

To complete the year we looked forward with joy to the summer at Abington and the Edinburgh Festival. Walter and I had fixed a programme that was right for our students and for his temperament, and not conflicting with other orchestras at the festival. Glinka's *Ruslan and Liudmilla* would be an exciting start that involved all the performers. Walter chose the *Young Person's Guide* and his favourite symphony – his native music, Dvořák. The soloist for the Haydn concerto was a superb oboist of sixteen from Liverpool, Adèle Karp. Working with this age group, a damaged front tooth, a broken finger, a school epidemic of mumps – any such thing can wreck plans, so I would prepare another soloist in reserve.

We also looked into the possibility of our first concert in Glasgow, for the day after Edinburgh. We discovered we were welcome and that the St Andrew's Hall was free on Sunday 31 August; I calculated that what we could make on the concert should cover our transport and extra day in the camp. We could only venture into what we could afford.

An invitation now came from Pathé to make a short news film, partly in the camp but mainly on the platform in the Usher Hall. Pathé's news and short films were shown in every cinema in every town, and I thought parents and teachers who couldn't come to our concerts would enjoy seeing it, and the children enjoy making it. It took some negotiating, due to shortage of space and electricity in the camp. Ian Hunter, co-operative as always, agreed to the only mutually acceptable possibility. We could stay behind after our evening concert, but not later than midnight. This meant a very long day – leaving the camp at six-thirty for a morning rehearsal in the hall, and not being back till about two a.m. I was always careful not to undertake more than the young could manage, but thought that with two or three hours' sleep in the afternoon and enough food all would be well. Once again Edinburgh rallied to our side. A large empty hall was made available; the Red Cross would provide mattresses; the festival would organise lunch and high tea near by; then they could all take the concert and film in their stride.

Meanwhile the incomparable Joan would be leaving us for marriage in the autumn. We needed somebody to overlap and learn her methods and be with the orchestra in action in the summer. We didn't advertise; we let a few people know, and the RCM recommended one of their students. She had won a scholarship there, but realising she would not make a great pianist she wanted to give it up and embark on some new line connected with music. She had done a secretarial course at school, so I invited her to call on us in our underground den. The wrong person would be put off instantly by the conditions.

Diana Scholefield was nineteen, quiet and gentle, intelligent, with wide interests but essentially musical. It was plain to see that she would be kind and sympathetic with children and parents and would understand boarding-school life, having been in one herself for five years. That was a great day for the NYO, because (after an unsettling false start) she gave over ten years of her life to the cause, and a nicer human being and loyal friend could not be found.

We were badly shaken by the advance publicity for the Edinburgh Festival. The NYO was returning having left a 'vivid memory of the sensational impression last year' (*The*

Times), 'after its triumphant success' (the *Scotsman*), being 'one of the most moving concerts in the whole Festival' (the *News Chronicle*), and an article in the *Radio Times* said that we were the first item to sell out. Such an unexpected fanfare of tributes was more than anyone could live up to. We could only hope we wouldn't disappoint this warm welcome.

So it was back to the beauty and seclusion of the camp on the hillside and the Royal Scot stopping in the village. There were about forty new members since last summer, most of them experiencing Scottish scenery and all the adventures of camp-life for the first time. To appear at the festival again was an honour indeed; to make a film for Pathé was an excitement; Glasgow was to be a new experience for us all; but the news of the *Daily Mirror* sponsoring us, announced just four days ago, was the great surprise. One asked, 'Does it mean that we *will* go on next year for *sure*, and you won't have to say, "I *hope* to see you next time"?'

'Yes, it does,' and the reaction, of relief oozing into applause, was very moving. I hadn't realised quite how deeply it worried them that we might have to stop and that I had never been able to promise we'd meet again.

This time the programme was perfect, masses of work and variety, and Walter was in his very best form. Adèle had been in the orchestra for some time and knew us all, and was an exceptionally artistic performer. The Britten took a lot of skill and humour, the Dvořák symphony seemed to fit the countryside, and we also made various recordings for the BBC.

On the evening of the first day one young cellist, Morag Easton, reported to Sister feeling unwell, and was sensibly isolated to our one-room sick bay. On Monday, the high temperature made us call in our local doctor, and on Tuesday she seemed a little better. On Wednesday evening I went to say good-night, and was instantly aware that something serious was wrong. The local doctor thought I was fussing when I asked for a specialist from Edinburgh, and wouldn't help. Who would? I rang a parent, Dr Black, a famous consultant in

Birmingham and father of the oboist Neil.* That wonderful man asked all the right questions then sorted all the etiquette, and late that night a superb physician arrived (alas, name forgotten), having driven forty miles from Edinburgh. Everything took time because of our isolation, but an ambulance eventually arrived, and Sister went with Morag to the nearest hospital, near Glasgow. The miracle was that Morag came from Glasgow, so that her mother got there almost as soon as the ambulance.

By the afternoon we heard how desperately ill she was: it was meningitis and we were all in quarantine and not allowed to leave the camp. I decided not to tell the children. I told my Chairman in London, Paul Cave (in confidence), Ian Hunter in case the health authorities made us cancel the concert, and finally Walter. He panicked and sent his wife and son away from the hotel, but gradually calmed down and agreed to continue conducting us. The children sensed we had a weight on our minds, so in the afternoon I told them that Morag was seriously ill. We were all sad and work suffered, so after supper we decided to have a cricket match, staff versus students. We made our team (minus Walter; they don't play cricket in Prague) and enlisted Paul Cave, a former county cricketer. As we all succumbed at the wicket Paul smashed his sixes, and finally sent our only ball with a victory stroke into the river! The *Daily Mirror* had started well.

Friday was a better day. Morag was out of danger and we were allowed to give both concerts, quarantined in our own buses and the camp. There were no other cases. In all my time with the orchestra the greatest strain was the responsibility I always felt for other people's children. I decided that the NYO must have an honorary physican, a well-known name, commanding respect so that no matter in what area we were staying I could always ensure we had the best advice in any emergency.

Concert day started at five-thirty a.m. Breakfast was at six,

*Principal oboe of the ECO.

and full rehearsal at nine-thirty. After lunch everyone was grateful for those mattresses, and most people slept. There was time for a good walk and a quick glance at the fine city and its castle before a Scottish high tea. We were back in the hall at seven. Both Rafael Kubelík and Hans Oppenheim came to the concert, and the international audience was very responsive. I was told in the interval that the Chairman of the *Mirror* was there, unknown to us. Leaving all *Mirror* arrangements to Paul Cave, I realised I hadn't even invited him . . . 'Don't worry,' said one of the paper's staff, 'our Chairman is a very quiet man. He likes to see and judge everything for himself, but he wouldn't want to be noticed.' At the end an announcement was made about the Pathé film, inviting the audience to stay, and move to the front to be in camera. It was amazing that so many stayed in support, and it was completed by half-past eleven. One last effort was needed: to pack everything and keep our promise to be away by midnight. It was two-thirty when 120 tired and happy musicians fell asleep in the silent camp.

While we slept John had stayed behind in Edinburgh to get the dawn train to Aberdeen. In the Festival Club he met Hans Oppenheim, a musician of great insight. John's diary recalls their conversation:

> 'I was present at the NYO's concert several hours ago. As it happens that overture does not appeal to me at all. Yet to my amazement, half-way through tears of gladness welled up behind my eyes. Can you explain it?' I trotted out all the rational answers I could muster. In fact I gave a potted version of all the NYO's aims and how it tried to fulfil them. I thought I had done well. With a disarming smile he replied, 'Thank you, but I prefer to regard it as a miracle.'

Sunday dawned and after a late breakfast Sister reported that everyone was in good trim for our first concert in Glasgow. The Lord Mayor received us with a kind speech, and we met many new people from the Royal Scottish Academy of Music, the Scottish National Orchestra, the university and the education department, whose genuine interest brought them out on a late-August Sunday afternoon. The hall was not full, but the response warmed as the concert continued. What struck our children was the enormous difference in the personality of the audiences and the people they met in Edinburgh, the dignified capital, and Glasgow, the industrial centre; yet they were only an hour's journey apart.

On Monday morning, the Royal Scot glided in to the village station and bore them all away. And in that desolate aftermath there was an added sadness: Joan's last day with the orchestra she'd served so well for two tough years. But Diana had made a splendid start, the first spell with the *Mirror* had gone well, and so had both concerts. Then the newspapers arrived. In trepidation we scoured them . . . Nobody could want a better press, but I was disturbed. It was no fault of ours that we were favourably compared with professional performers, but I knew at this first glance what a price we'd have to pay: 'the strings executed the rushing passages of the overture with a precision and electric quality of tone that put to shame the weary professionals of the Scottish National Orchestra' (*The Times*). The *Daily Mail* said:

> The orchestra showed again its astonishingly adult power and perception. All the technique essential to the performance of great music is here. Moreover there is a fire in the attack, and informing everything that is done a freshness and a rapture that must make older musicians sigh.

And what of Glasgow? The *Glasgow Herald* wrote, 'We should indeed be proud of this orchestra, and the players certainly have one priceless asset some of our professionals seem to have lost, a tremendous enthusiasm which gives great verve and impetus to their playing.' The *Scotsman*, after a glowing piece, let us stand alone with 'this astounding orchestra is one of the great achievements of our time', and also the *Daily Telegraph*, with 'only a generation ago such a concert would have been unimaginable'.

Fourteen

1952 had been a good year, of musical progress, from Wagner in Liverpool to Brahms with Boult in Bournemouth, to a triumphant concert in Edinburgh with Susskind, and our first film for Pathé News. But most importantly it was a year of financial stability, the one in which we stepped out of the temporarily encouraging arms of the King George's Jubilee Trust and into the permanent reality of sponsorship by a great newspaper. We had thought that if the *Mirror* supported us, all the other papers would avoid us, but the reviews from Edinburgh proved this was not the case. We also thought that some schools or education authorities might withdraw their candidates, but there seemed no sign of that either. There were a few nasty anonymous letters, sometimes funny, sometimes sad. It was usually fear that 'your kids will soon get the best jobs and do us down'.

Soon Diana was struggling with her first audition tour: piles of applications, timetables and invitations for 1953, Coronation year. With the ever-increasing work and just one young secretary, I used to stay very late at night in our basement, drafting letters and plans for Diana to deal with in my absence on the tour. That special character, the London bobby on his beat, seeing my light on, would check by tapping the railings that there was someone in. One night I was looking up as he passed, and he escorted me up the road, in a fatherly manner suggesting I shouldn't stay later than ten p.m. From then on if he saw my light he would tap, and I would pack up quickly. One night he approached the front door, up the steps, and when I came out there he was, flat on the ground, mercifully not too badly hurt. Barbed wire had been tied to the railings across the entrance, about three inches above the steps, unnoticeable if you weren't looking down. It was intended for me, on my way out, and by a million-to-one chance tripped him, on his way in, instead. He was cut and bruised, but his only concern was that he hadn't been able to run after three thugs who had been hiding down the steps of the next-door basement and who had made off at the double.

The police took the matter seriously, and went off with my *Nasty Letters* file. Thereafter if I worked after seven p.m. I reported to them, but as far as possible I took work home. For many months I felt very well protected by the London police; they even asked for my travel schedule, and checked that I was in my flat when I was due home.

It was at an Executive meeting in December 1952 that we thrashed out the plans and hopes for Coronation year, bearing in mind that we could now afford a few essentials: a healthier office, more secretarial help, better printing for the programmes. It was agreed to meet in Sheffield in January, adding a concert in Leeds. Two concerts each time we met were now normal, but ahead lay the opportunity to give six in Brussels in April following our first Royal Festival Hall concert. John convinced those present that given reasonable conditions we could manage this without overtiring our players. We agreed to accept Edinburgh for the third time, and repeat Glasgow as well, in the summer.

I also got permission to prepare a full report on the NYO for an approach to the Queen Mother in the hope of her patronage in time for the Coronation concert.

Our Treasurer, Mr McDougall, explained that the *Mirror* thought better conditions of work were a priority, chiefly a suitable office, and announced that my salary was to be raised to £1,000 a year. There was, obviously, more work than could be managed by one young secretary, and I was to get some experienced help for Brussels.

In fact it was time for a new look at everything, now that we had a little more money. First I engaged two more professors. Our bassoons had been neglected (they had such bad instruments) but I now enlisted a virtuoso bassoonist, Gwydion Brooke. Then I sought out the most artistic timpanist in England, James Bradshaw, Professor at the RAM and timpanist for the Philharmonia. For him, every tap or roll had to be beautiful, shaded and graded and timed to perfection. Through him Britain gained some very fine young timpanists (Seaman, White, Suttie, Brady, Howie, Cumberland) and the NYO's percussion section, already dramatic and exciting, gained an added artistic dimension.

Our printing and publicity needed an overhaul. Here the *Mirror*'s advice was marvellous, and they designed an illustrated brochure-cum-programme for our concerts. It included the names of the Council, professors and staff; every member was listed instrumentally, with the place they came from; there was also a list of scholarship and exam results. Judging from the letters we got, the latter seemed to alert the academic world to the fact that we were educating young musicians, and were not just a performing orchestra. (Some members were going straight into professional symphony orchestras. We didn't encourage this, but a place in the profession could not always be turned down for expensive further training.) The whole programme/brochure, used first in January 1953, cost 6d. and paid for itself. The words 'sponsored by the *Daily Mirror*', in very small italics, appeared once, inside, not even on the front page! I feel ashamed now at how ungrateful and mean we were, fearing this association might damage our support. Would it prevent royal patronage? Astonishingly, the *Mirror* never complained at our lack of generosity or asked for a better deal.

More help in the office was urgently required and Diana welcomed the thought of an experienced colleague, so once again I sought out Mrs Ballingall. She agreed to come after Christmas, see us through the Brussels venture and set about finding us a new office. Soon auditions were complete, thirty-five new members admitted, and on Boxing Day 1952 we set off to prepare the City Training College in Sheffield for our invasion.

The major event this week was another new conductor, our fifth. Hugo Rignold was a Canadian, a violinist-turned-conductor who was currently conductor of the Liverpool Philharmonic Orchestra. He had three great interests in life: violins (he had a Strad.); fast cars (he arrived in a Ferrari); and dogs. He was not an inspiring musician, but an excellent teacher, reliable and orderly in timing his work, conveying a calm, unhurried confidence. He appreciated our standards of courtesy and professional manners, and his thoroughness and easy temperament were major contributions to the NYO.

There was to be an official visit from our benefactor Sir Stuart Goodwin, the leading local industrialist, a great opportunity for us all to thank him. He and his wife were very quiet, retiring people, but they called on us at work and seemed to enjoy the rehearsals. Sir Stuart told us that they wanted to help the young do well in life. They did help, and we owe them much.

We had also been approached by the Professor of Psychiatry at Sheffield University, a Dr Wing. John had known him in the RAF, and his musical wife, Celia Miles, was at school with me. The professor had spent years developing aural IQ tests, and wanted the experimental opportunity of trying them out on a group whose aural responses should be acute. Subject to obvious conditions we agreed and set aside time after supper for us all to be his guinea-pigs. Much importance was given to children's IQ at the time, but all the tests were visual, and could even be taught by good teachers. There are whole groups of people who would score low in visual testing, but be miles out in front if the alternative approach were valued. These include the blind, and Africans I've known, whose listening and intuition reveal a different intelligence. It is a more difficult route for assessors, and we live in a visual age, but Dr Wing was trying.

Our members were delighted to take part in a scientific experiment and did so with their usual energy and enthusiasm. Dr Wing was equally keen and very thorough in assessing his results. He not only gave me a list of all the individual results, from which I remember that Martin Gatt, now an internationally known bassoonist, was top; but he also took averages of the various groups: were violinists more intelligent than woodwind players, or cellos more than brass? All the scores were exceptionally high, which didn't worry him, and we got through all the tests far more quickly than planned. What bewildered him was why the percussion department's average score should be the highest. We were able to soothe the great man, who thought his tests had gone wrong, by explaining that into our percussion department went the very young, highly talented children, who played the piano or organ, or composed, or hadn't yet found the right instrument but whose potential could not be left behind. I always had a group who were called General Musicians, and there are several famous musicians today who started in my GMs. In fact Martin Gatt was one before he started the bassoon, so was Howard Shelley, and Humphrey Burton another. Dr Wing was reassured.

Work went on, but the whole week in Sheffield was overtinged with a great sadness. Jack Thurston had cancer in both lungs. One had been removed in an operation before October, but he would insist on being with us, staying in the sick bay, looked after by Sister. He came to every woodwind rehearsal, asking me to do the rehearsing then go over to his chair to get comments and instructions; his voice was husky and soft and he could only talk a little without getting too short of breath. 'I can't blow my whistle any more, but I can sit here and help.' With courage and dedication he taught on, every comment so intensely precious as the whole class sensed it might be their last week with him.

The main work for the concerts was the Glazunov Sixth Symphony, chosen by Ernest Hall as it had plenty for the brass – unfamiliar to most of us. The overture was the sparkling *Merry Wives* by Nicolai; we had a piano concerto, Beethoven 3 with seventeen-year-old David Wilde;* and I had asked Richard

*Now Professor of Piano at the Hochschule, Hanover.

Arnell for a new work. He suggested we give the first performance in England of *The Black Mountain*, and generously wrote a march specially for us. With him all the parts were ship-shape and arrived in ample time. The platform in the City Hall had two enormous stone lions at each corner facing the performers in devouring attitude, which caused some amusement at rehearsal. (Apparently Sir Thomas Beecham used to bow to each of them.) Hugo was as reliable in performance as in rehearsal, and our standard, even with so many new members, was still rising. The Sheffield audience and press were happy and so was Stuart Goodwin. After we'd thanked him and said goodbye, he handed me a small parcel. We had had a conversation earlier in the week about musicians having short nails, and why it was better to cut than file them. The gift was the most perfect Sheffield-made steel nail scissors in a case, a right-hand and left-hand pair. They were invaluable, and since they were stolen, twenty years later, I've never found another pair of left-hand nail scissors.

Hugo had been exceptionally kind to us in a rather sad week, and we wanted to give him a present, a memento of his first visit. Sending an SOS out to the nearby Yorkshire farms, we found a perfect collie puppy. They took to each other at once. The dog was instantly named Nicolai, and grew to enjoy music and fast cars. It is said that Nic used to go on the platform in Liverpool at rehearsals, and sometimes take a bow at concerts.

The following afternoon there was a second concert, in the music-loving city of Leeds. Yorkshire friendship creates a special audience, which enables the performers to give more with such responsive listeners. In addition we had friends in Leeds, such as Dr Hooper, Jack Lyons, Fanny Waterman and the Yorkshire Symphony Orchestra. It was a very happy return and concert, but hardly had the applause died down when a sense of disaster struck. Important people were talking in small groups, and we were wondering what had gone wrong.

Apparently while we were playing the City Council was having an important meeting. It was to decide whether to continue its funding of the Yorkshire Symphony Orchestra, without which it could not survive. The vote went against it, and the news was spreading through the retreating audience. It seems some music-loving councillors, feeling sure the vote was safe, were at our concert; had they been at the meeting there might still be a YSO. John and I were stunned. Of course it wasn't our fault in any way, but it felt like it. In a recent letter Sir Jack Lyons wrote:

> After the concert it was announced that the YSO would receive no further finance from the Leeds City Council and would consequently have to disband in due course. I remember well how shocked we were, particularly Roslyn [his wife], who being Canadian said, 'To what kind of a city have you brought me . . . what about our children? To what sort of cultural life can they look forward?'

In fact Sir Jack set about trying to save it, but it was too late. It was a very sad day for Yorkshire and its young musicians, who had access to specialist teachers among its members.

Returning to life in our damp basement headquarters, we were hopelessly overcrowded. There were now three of us, and thanks to the *Mirror* we had more essential possessions: some waterproof metal filing cabinets, a portable typewriter, boxes of cymbals and other small percussion needs, piles of hired music for sorting and returning. Looking back I wonder how we managed. Mrs Ballingall decided she should waste no time but set out to find a new office. Diana typed from dawn to dusk, and I dealt with the Executive Committee and the endless musical matters, and we were soon in gear again.

Ahead lay our Easter term, with our first concert in the new Royal Festival Hall, a Coronation concert, and then our most ambitious effort so far, a whole week abroad. We had to find residential accommodation near London, always a problem, and also book all the trains and boats to and from Brussels and make the other arrangements, and 18 April was only three months away.

But for me the priority was to write to the Queen Mother to ask for her patronage. I thought it was time to take up the invitation to 'write again when your plans reach fruition'. It was five years since our first public performance, and now we were financially secure. It took me at least a fortnight of detailed work to present our aims, our achievements so far, all the cities we'd played in, the press reports, the best pictures of the children in action taken for us by the *Mirror* and the financial history, all bound like a small magazine. I took it all to Sir Adrian, presuming he would approve, and expecting he'd want to sign the letter as President. He said he was impressed with the presentation but he seemed a bit hesitant. I asked him if anything was wrong or should be altered, but he declined any criticism. Eventually I asked if he would prefer the Chairman of the Council to sign it? After looking again at the material, he said how pleased he was with the achievements and delighted to sign in full support.

Over three weeks went by without a word. I was in the RFH for a concert conducted by Sir Adrian, and took the opportunity to go behind the scenes to ask if he'd heard anything. Yes, he had, more than a week ago now. He'd been asked questions about whether the children were well looked after, and he was afraid he'd said that he thought not: they worked too hard, and didn't have enough of the holiday spirit. I was shattered, mostly because he hadn't even told me, but also because of this betrayal of trust by our President. I thought it was probably too late, but I had to try to put things right.

I rang our nurse and two parents, one a doctor, and without telling them why asked if I could use their names as referees regarding our members' welfare. Through the night I wrote out a timetable of a day's work, and a typical concert day. It gave the name and qualifications of Nurse Blake and our dietician, and showed that sufficient qualified staff were always on duty. Looking back, I don't know how we could have cared for them any better. I wrote a letter to Sir Arthur Penn, then Treasurer to the Queen Mother, saying that Sir Adrian had told me he had conveyed his anxiety concerning the care of the members of the NYO, so I was enclosing details of their work, rest, diet, relaxation, and early bedtime.

At the first reasonable hour next morning, I rang a friend, the famous physician Lord Evans, for an appointment. 'Come now, I'm here till ten.' I poured out my story and my distress at the idea that we were overworking the children, and showed him my letter and details. I admitted that of course after two concerts and a long journey home they'd be very tired, and how well I remember his reply: 'It never hurts the young to be over-tired, as long as they are doing what they really enjoy.' So I plucked up the courage to ask if he'd be our Hon. Physician. This strong, silent man said nothing, but there was a definite twinkle in his eye; he wrote a letter for me to enclose: 'As the newly appointed Hon. Physician to the NYO . . .' With this enclosure I sealed the envelope containing my night's work and delivered it to Buckingham Palace. It was now 18 February.

On 25 February 1953 came a letter from the Palace. I was afraid to open it, and then sat re-reading it over and over again for a long time.

> Dear Madam
>
> I write to thank you for your letter of February 18th, and to inform you that after studying the information which you have kindly provided, Queen Elizabeth the Queen Mother will be graciously pleased to extend her Patronage to the National Youth Orchestra of Great Britain.
>
> Her Majesty has been greatly interested to read of the striking progress of this undertaking and is happy to support an activity which is remarkable both for its achievement and its promise.
>
> I am returning the photographs you so kindly submitted.
>
> Yours faithfully
>
> Arthur Penn

This was a really great moment in the orchestra's history. It was not just the great honour for us, but for everybody all over the British Isles who had helped. It was an almost personal feeling of belonging, as is the case in England between the Queen and her people. She had encouraged me in 1947, and through the tough, hungry years I was helped by that and by knowing that I had permission to write again if we succeeded.

From 25 February 1953 Her Majesty took a close interest in our events and came in person to our most important concerts in the Royal Festival Hall. She would acknowledge any telegrams of greeting we sent as we toured abroad, representing our country with the banner of her patronage. We were doing this work for Britain but also, always, in devoted love and respect for her.

A Council meeting was arranged for 5 March, with Sir Adrian in the chair, after which the announcement of this great honour was made. But now I sensed a feeling of sabotage, though very slight. Sir Adrian had not wanted us to be granted royal patronage; another member now said our high standards were upsetting professional orchestras; another thought success in Brussels and Edinburgh would give the players swollen heads. Such comments were not from the real musicians but from the music-administrator types. Every time I thought we were moving into smoother waters, there seemed to be rumblings in the deep.

There was, however, good news that week. Mrs Ballingall had found us an office – on the first floor of a seventeenth-century house just off Gloucester Place – but we couldn't move in for three months. There was also bad news, in that my new and very special Diana was not compatible with Mrs Ballingall. Although she knew the latter was only temporary, and necessary for Brussels, she was unhappy and I had to let her go. I was really sad, but I had no choice.

Fifteen

Soon our 120 young musicians would be with us again. This time we had been lent Ashlyns School at Berkhamsted, which was not too far from London for the concert, but quiet enough to leave us undisturbed while we prepared for our first whole week abroad. Just over a fortnight together and the travelling would give us all time to know each other better, and I was looking forward to seeing how the members would manage with concerts every night for a week. We couldn't know.

I was able to get Walter Susskind for the first week and the RFH concert, but he wasn't free for the week in Belgium. I sought out Hugo Rignold, asking him a favour – to take over from another conductor. He was free and, with some coaxing, agreed. We had the same superb team of professors, adding Leon Goossens, in his day the best-known oboist in the world. The programme was fixed to suit both us and Brussels, with *Egmont* overture; a Mendelssohn violin concerto with Ralph Holmes, a very talented sixteen-year-old; a new work, *Coronation Suite* by Rawsthorne; and the César Franck symphony as a compliment to Belgium.

Everything was going splendidly except that the Rawsthorne score and parts, promised in March, had not arrived. At a lunch-hour staff meeting Walter and I asked for suggestions for a short work to replace it. To our amazement several professors said, 'You couldn't possibly do a thing like that – cancel a new work, first performance, programme announced . . .'

'How can you play a work that isn't here? No score, no parts and only four days to learn it in? I'll *have* to cancel.' It would have been best if I had.

But someone went to see Rawsthorne in London, and came back that evening with a thin score and a few parts, ready for *us* to copy by hand. This meant all the staff were up very late copying enough parts for the morning rehearsal. The promised *Coronation Suite* had become just one piece, called *Coronation Overture*. It was a shoddy little work, and the broken commitment was a rotten example to the young composers we were training; a poor reward for encouraging new British music.

Walter, presented with the score, pressed for the presence of the composer, so Genin went to London to fetch him, and the composers' class spent the morning copying. Now we found there were no percussion parts. This was disastrous, because in accepting the work we had explained about our large percussion and harp sections, who had nothing to do in the rest of the programme; worse still, our first major gift from the *Mirror* was our own set of timpani, a superb xylophone, a new side-drum and a glock. Now they could not be used.

When the composer arrived for the first rehearsal John took him to the percussion class, and persuaded him to write a part for the xylophone. By the end of the first full rehearsal Rawsthorne had given John permission to write in parts for everybody. This John did, and they increased daily. At the final rehearsal Walter said, 'Vatever vork you are playing, I do not know; it is not in my score!' I remember replying, 'You just conduct the right number of bars, and I'll guarantee you'll all end together.'

'Ah zo, and if we do not? . . .' But they did. With daily imaginative additions, the composer was delighted, but we had no time to alter his ending, which slowed down and faded out like a damp squib.

However, the rest of the programme was going well. And there were also preparations for Brussels: checking passports, money (all had the same, a minimum sum), concert clothes, strong suitcases and locks, spare strings and reeds, instrument cases in good repair . . . We always had to remember that most of our members had never been outside their own country, let alone crossed the sea in a boat. The excitement and some nervousness were just tingling under the surface all the time.

We thought about how to be the most polite and gracious guests, to respect the different customs of the host country, and we practised speaking French. What wonderful people our house staff were. Unpaid, unhonoured, unsung, they gave about a month of their time each year, often for years on end, to serve the NYO. This time the boys were guided by Donald Leggatt, a housemaster from St Bees, and Ronald Sturley from Launceston. The girls were even luckier, with the remarkable Editha Roupell. She was wise, motherly, full of stories and laughter and partnered with a young charmer, Mary Rose Seldon. Our nursing sister was Dorothy Field. We all had the same aim: to give every individual in the orchestra the confidence that reliability and self-discipline bring.

So all we needed as we completed our preparations were just two rules: (1) Obey orders; (2) Never be without your passport, instrument and music. We returned to our numbered order which worked so well in Paris.

On 18 April they were off in buses, some for their first sight of London, most for their first time in the Royal Festival Hall. We had a beautifully printed new programme, with a picture of the Queen Mother. Everything was perfect in the hall; afternoon sleep was permitted in the auditorium (those seats are the most comfortable in the world); fresh air and a walk on the riverside terraces on a perfect afternoon was a treat. Then it was tea, and behind the scenes to prepare for the concert.

Our preparations for a performance were very important. Physically, everything must be checked – clothes, hair, instruments and parts. Emotionally, there must be enough time for a warm-up, and relaxation to offset the excitement and concert nerves. (Sister would usually be smilingly on the prowl.) Finally we would have a very thorough tuning. We were silent as we assembled for the orderly move on to the platform, then stillness was added. A hundred and twenty people on a platform, completely still but relaxed and thinking, conserving their vital energy, has a powerful effect on the audience and its expectancy.

To do this well depended on perfect timing before the conductor went on. In different halls with different audiences, the timing was always different. But tonight there was a major crisis: we had to put the orchestra on just after eight, but Walter hadn't arrived. Still hoping he'd be there any minute, we sent for Hugo, who was in the audience. Hugo refused to go on, quite reasonably as he hadn't rehearsed with them. Of course, in an emergency the musical director takes over, but this was so sudden. John was preparing an announcement for the audience, and I was somewhat shaken, but trying to think myself into *Egmont*. The silent orchestra becalmed the audience, which became quiet too, when like a hurricane Walter came racing along the back corridor, throwing off his coat, almost knocking John over, enraged by the traffic jam that had delayed him. He stormed on to the rostrum; then followed the most stirring and dramatic performance.

As soon as Walter was on the platform I raced back to my seat in the hall, as I was next to a very special guest, Sir Thomas Beecham, invited by Leonard Hirsch and Douglas Cameron. For me the finest English conductor, a very great artist and fascinating personality, it was indeed an honour for us that he came to listen. After the overture he seemed very moved, and then said, 'That, Miss Railton, was good by any standards.' A little later he added, 'I should like to meet them at closer quarters.' Of course I thanked him and said I'd arrange it any time to suit him. I wanted him for the NYO more than anybody else.

The Mendelssohn concerto went well, Ralph being our best violinist at that time. Sir Thomas left before the Rawsthorne and I was glad, as its feeble ending just before the interval was a bit of a come-down. The symphony brought out the best playing of which they were capable, and everybody was very happy, the audience giving us a splendid send-off for Brussels. The press went as far as '. . . the orchestra's disciplined, unruffled air of expectancy, throughout an unusually long wait on the platform, was as impressive as its playing'.

After a good sleep and a late breakfast, we all assembled with notebooks and pencils, and I explained all the plans for Brussels. First we told them how splendid they had been during the wait on the platform, and what had happened behind the scenes. Also about Sir Thomas, and what he had said. Morale was high, as most boys like trains and boats. But there could be so many opportunities to mislay things, so easy to get separated in a station crowd! They laughed so much when we told them about events in Paris, and understood why we were being so particular about details. We rehearsed our numbered order and our two rules, then there was time for questions: 'Is it true that the Belgians drive on the wrong side of the road?', 'Do we have to eat frogs and snails to be polite, or can we leave them?', and sometimes they'd take me for a ride:

'When the boat is sinking, do we still take our instruments with us into the lifeboats?'

'If your Strad. has a foolproof watertight case, and you know you can swim to Ostend, yes. If not . . .'

'Obey orders!'

In the afternoon we had the experience of changing conductors on the same programme – the same horse with a new jockey. Hugo Rignold was very good about picking up Walter's performance, and changing little. And so to bed. Even when lights were out it seemed as if the whole building vibrated with excitement.

Safely off the boat at Ostend, we were soon on the station platform, lined up away from the edge, as our train to Brussels was not the next one but the one after. As a train pulled in, the porters shouted at the tail end of our 'crocodile' to get in quickly, and obediently they did. From where I was at the crocodile's head, I could see a third of the orchestra disappearing into a train to Bruges! Luckily Mrs Ballingall and Donald Leggatt were very quick and somehow got them all out again just in time. Rule 1 was changed to 'Obey orders *from members of our own staff only*', and it proved invaluable on many future foreign tours.

We were met in Brussels by representatives of various

organisations, including M. Cuvelier, the founder of Jeunesses Musicales, and soon all were settled in hostels or with families. Our most important concert was the next day, and everyone was on the platform of the Palais des Beaux-Arts at ten. All were fit and so pleased to see each other, having been separated since five the previous evening! All the instruments survived the journey, so we were soon playing again. Several important musicians came to the rehearsal, and by one o'clock the radio was proclaiming that the '*jeunes sont très impressionants*', and we were obviously very welcome.

The concert was '*organisé par la Société philharmonique de Bruxelles*', the '*troisième concert symphonique de gala sous le haut patronage de son Excellence Monsieur l'Ambassadeur de Grande-Bretagne, du British Council, et de l'Union belgo-britannique*'. We discovered all this when we asked for a programme. We also discovered that the Rawsthorne programme note was for the *Coronation Suite* we had expected, and not the one small item we had received. Our hosts decided not to make an announcement, but just to play what we'd got and hope for the best.

We started the performance with national anthems, then the Beethoven, then the Mendelssohn, and they loved Ralph Holmes; the audience was warming to us. Then came the Rawsthorne, and at the end of this one meagre item they presumed it was the first of a suite, and didn't applaud. So the first half of our gala concert ended with Hugo leaving the platform in respectful silence. It was entirely my fault for not having the courage to refuse to play an unfinished and unsuitable piece. The Franck symphony made up for everything and was the best playing we could offer, accepted as a gesture by the Belgian audience.

For the next five nights we were in the care of M. Cuvelier, and the audiences were all members of Jeunesses Musicales. They appreciated Ralph's Mendelssohn, but of course each night came the flop of the Rawsthorne. The symphony made up for it, as the Belgians love Franck and showed their enthusiasm. But what was interesting and important for us was the experiment of a week of concerts: by Saturday we'd learnt a lot. The standard improved, with the confidence of knowing it had gone well before; little extra liberties and expressive touches emerged. After three concerts and several sightseeing tours, we detected some tiredness and arranged a quiet day with a little rehearsal for weak spots, and then rest and repairs, with the odd sore throat or tummy ache to be cared for. The next three concerts went into top gear: the last was the best. At bedtime one of the youngest said, 'If only we could play every night for ever . . .'

It was important that '*les Anglais*' leave a good impression, not forgetting to say thank you to anyone who had looked after them. David Butt, our principal flute, later principal flute of the BBCSO, tells me that I'd asked everybody to take a small gift for their hostess. He was staying with a lovely family, who sent him home with a food parcel. They were so grateful for the British in the war, and knew we still had rationing. He remembers how grateful his parents were.

And so to Belgian trains and the boat trip, really enjoyed with no nerves this time, and all the chatting and sharing of adventures, and then the cliffs of Dover loomed, and you could feel the homing instinct rise as they made for the railings, as if to get closer to England. For some there was still a long journey in an English train, for some an all-night one to Scotland. As I said goodbye to every member I was very proud of them. They were well, and had triumphed over problems, and had done more than they'd ever done before.

John and I had a *post mortem* chat on the train to London. We both knew now that we could manage foreign tours, and had already been invited back for 1955. We looked at the press: 'The unity of their performance is the result of a discipline and style which many orchestras might envy,' said *La Libre Belgique*. Another said:

> From the first bars we had no doubt of the worth of the young musicians. The self-confidence of this remarkable orchestra, the homogeneity of each group of instruments, the exemplary

> discipline, roused the admiration of a large public. A stimulating evening which pays tribute to the music-loving youth of Britain.

We all remember vividly the great interest in England's new Queen. After the war's effects on their own royal family, they said how lucky we British were, and they were right. It was now just ten days to the Coronation, and we hoped that in the reign of Queen Elizabeth II we would continue to represent Britain worthily abroad.

The July meetings of the Council and Executive revealed some change of attitude, perhaps due to the new feeling of security. Most members had come to the RFH concert, previously unaware of the standard we'd reached. One head of a royal school of music was honest and outspoken. He realised that they gave a far better performance than his students' first orchestra; he was full of congratulation, but wondered what would happen when they left us and found the student standard lower? There was a faint mood of apprehension at the idea of our being too successful . . . perhaps we shouldn't perform in public? Luckily that idea lacked support. The Council accepted provisional plans up to 1955, including the invitation to return to Brussels.

In order to ensure that our children got grants from their LEAs, we were now to adopt their terminology and call our three terms 'courses'. The three terms were closely linked to the school year, and a 'course' tended to imply a single occasion. Later this meant our members were given a grant for only one 'course' each year. Finally the LEAs agreed to give grants for one course-in-three-parts, and all was well.

Soon it was August and we could move into our new office. We climbed the rickety seventeenth-century stairs to the second floor, and surveyed our room, which had been decorated as cheaply as possible. There was warm red felt on the floors; light walls; an electric fire fixed in the wall under the mantelpiece and two chairs for visitors on either side; my sturdy metal desk, brought from the basement; and – at last – ample shelves for scores, music and box files. Within a week we had a title plate on our newly painted front door. Our first act however was to hang our only treasure – a beautiful signed studio portrait of the Queen Mother – in the central position, catching the light from two big windows overlooking the street. On the wall beside my desk was our large map of the British Isles, with railways and roads clearly marked, so important when planning audition tours, and the rest was empty space . . . marvellous, peaceful space. And what joy to be high up, after four years of three of us in an underground box fourteen feet by seven. The two smaller rooms were warm and quiet; it seemed too good to be true that typewriters and telephones and musical work could at last be in separate rooms, which would be so much less tiring.

No. 90 George Street, London W1, was to become our home for the next ten years; and many were the famous musicians and educators from all over the world who mounted the stairs to discover the nerve centre of what was, for them, the miracle of the NYO.

As we were settling in, a removal van arrived unexpectedly outside. It was delivering a piano, a music cabinet and a parcel, clearly addressed to us, from Derbyshire. Suddenly I remembered that an old lady of eighty had written to me some months earlier, offering to give me her piano and a Victorian cabinet and contents. They had belonged to her late husband, who was very musical and wanted me to have them. Of course I had written accepting with gratitude, but explaining I would have nowhere to put them until August, and heard no more, because she had died. Up the rickety stairs came the piano, a most adequate upright, and a very useful cabinet and a parcel marked PRIVATE. Within was a little marble box and a letter tied on to it with string: 'Dear Miss Railton, I know you will keep this for me near his piano, as he was so musical. I hope it and the piano will bring you happiness always.' I opened the box: it was just her husband's dust and ashes. Feeling a bit queer, I put it on the corner of the mantelpiece with the lid secured with Sellotape, and there it stayed, a perpetual reminder of a kind and generous supporter.

It was a fitting moment for Mrs Ballingall to say farewell. Her 'temporary' help had seen us through Paris in 1950 and Brussels in 1953, and she had stayed on until we were out of the basement, and installed in the place she had found for us. I owe her a lot, and enjoyed our working partnership, and her quick judgement of people and situations. To her, life was mainly amusing; to me, mainly serious; but we both liked getting things done, and done well.

It was soon time to set off for the seventeenth 'course' in the now-familiar atmosphere of Glengonnar Camp. This time our conductor was Sir Adrian, and he brought his wife with him. He wanted to be with us all the time but, remembering his attitude to rehearsing, we compromised on five days, giving me and my team a three-day head start. Lady Boult was an exceedingly nice person and a great help to me. She appreciated what she called our 'style': the importance of good manners and the dignity of a tidy appearance. I gained that week from her store of wisdom, built on long years close to the profession as a musician's wife.

The programme, to suit the festival and Sir Adrian as well as our children, included the *Academic Festival Overture*, and Saint-Saens's A Minor cello concerto with Carol Sansom, a girl of sixteen, in the solo part. Malcolm Arnold chose four of his English Dances; the main work was Sibelius 1, new to the children.

We took the whole ten days rather easily. The exams were over, and the results good; the week in Brussels was successfully behind us; there were the new office and new ideas ahead. Jack Thurston was in Edinburgh, and insisted on coming out to see us – alas, for the last time – and we had recitals from Dennis Brain, Leonard Hirsch and Leon Goossens. Paul Cave was with us most days and brought with him a leading photographer, Bela Zola. He was an excellent man. He usually wore a Muslimtype cap, and was very soon nicknamed 'King Farouk', whom he closely resembled. All the best photographs of the NYO from 1952 to 1965 were his.

But our chief guest for the whole week was the artist Ernest Shepard. He was a close friend of Editha Roupell's, and she asked if she could bring him as he'd expressed an interest. He sketched us unceasingly: in rehearsal, on the swings, Ernest Hall with a cricket bat (the original now hangs in the RCM), Dennis playing his horn, the whole orchestra on the platform in the Usher Hall. Some of these were in an exhibition he was having in London, but many he most generously gave to me, on condition they were not sold. I treasure most the last picture of Jack Thurston, and by far the best portrait of John Dalby.

It was a happy week, and on 29 August we set off for our concert in Glasgow. One thousand seven hundred people packed St Andrew's Hall on the night. The papers record that the applause lasted for five minutes. We rested at Abington on Sunday and sang in the village church, and on Monday were in fine morale for our third appearance in the Edinburgh Festival.

Such a concert is an exceptional event. The mood is festive everywhere in the city, the audience musical and composed of mainly foreign visitors. This time we found Ian Hunter and invited him to meet the orchestra after the morning rehearsal so that they could thank him, not only for the three invitations to Edinburgh but also for the part he played in giving us a start in 1948.

The evening programme, recorded by the Third Programme, had gained confidence after Glasgow. The Arnold dances raised the roof, and quite shook Sir Adrian. Our more-or-less resident composer, friend and brass coach had been zipping things up in class. After the symphony, once again the orchestra remained on the platform to be filmed for a *Come to Britain* feature in colour, and the audience stayed for nearly an hour – a happy ending to the performing part of 1953.

The Times concluded that 'the National Youth Orchestra is an institution of which the whole country may be proud', and Eric

Blom in the *Observer* 'could not help being touched by merely watching these boys and girls . . . a perfection and accuracy hardly to be surpassed by the most seasoned players and fresh enthusiasm does something to add a special atmosphere'. And of course it was the break from this atmosphere that made each August a sad time too, as some who had been with us for three or four years realised it was their last day and they must leave an important part of their life, the friendships of this closely knit musical family. As I sped north to my Highland home I felt that 1953 was an important landmark in our history.

Sixteen

Our urgent need now was to find a new senior secretary to take over the whole administration. Diana's replacement, Shirley Graham, was typing away all day, a splendid person to assist a more experienced organiser. I rang our Treasurer to find out what we could afford, and to get permission to proceed. It then emerged that Mr McDougall, John Newsom and others on the Executive had met and decided that the NYO should now be run by an employee of the Executive, whom they would appoint, and I should remain Musical Director and float about at auditions and courses doing 'music only'. In fairness to them, this idea was partly to save me from overwork, and from 'burning out too early, as my talent was greatly needed'. With the constitution in place, the Council and Executive owned the NYO, and could employ the Musical Director to do their bidding. Mr McDougall knew an experienced secretary who would work for them, in liaison with me, and he would like to bring her to meet me. I wanted to say, 'Shall I resign today?' but thinking of the children said, 'Thank you, how interesting,' instead.

The next day Miss Davy came to see me. She seemed a very pleasant middle-aged spinster, who had run her own commercial business in the past. Did she know the modern educational system? Boarding schools? Concert halls? Had she ever met any musicians? The answer to all those was no. She liked music but didn't go to concerts. I asked if she would survive music going on all day around her, and she thought she wouldn't notice it. The interview didn't go well, and I told Mr McDougall that I didn't think she realised how closely she and I would have to work together. He thought that once she'd taken over the whole management that wouldn't matter, as her responsibility would be to him and the Executive. I was about to start my ten-week audition tour of the whole country, and was in no position to turn down the plan. It might prove a major success, and my doubts were mostly intuitive.

My contacts all over the country, carefully built up over seven years, were essential to the success of my audition tour. I had friends among the music advisers, heads of schools and teachers in every large city. Without the hospitality of their premises and their sincere interest in the achievements of the NYO, I would not have been able to seek out the best talent. They were really part of this national training school. The wrong kind of letter from an administrator in the office could be hurtful. My brief Sundays in London were not enough to catch up with embarrassing discourtesies, and my work, which required extreme concentration and memory, was marred by anxiety as I returned to a pile of letters marked *Personal*.

While I was still finishing auditions in London, a telephone call asked me to go to see Jack Thurston. He was dying; his voice was very weak and he was short of breath. He managed a joke and a smile. Then:

'Listen, my sweet, just listen. They want to take it over, and get you out. Don't go. Do you understand? *Don't go.*'

'Who is "they", Jack?'

'The establishment. It's too good, my sweet, too important to belong to you. They want it. If you go so will the imagination, the originality, the unique atmosphere. Don't go.'

'But Jack, I've given it to "them". I'm only an employee; they can sack me.'

'But don't go; what *you* can do matters. I've never felt such happiness before . . . it matters . . . music matters . . . but remember, my sweet . . . don't go . . .'

He died on 9 December, and we all lost a great friend and teacher and an exceptional musician. In our next programme Sir John Maud wrote:

> In courage, wisdom, and sweetness of character Jack Thurston was as great a master as in his clarinet-playing . . . He was a musician first and last, but he was also a personality of such exceptional simplicity and completeness – so wise, affectionate, and uninterested in himself – that his whole life had a quality to match the beauty of his playing. He set for himself, as an artist and a man, the most exacting standards; and because he was modest as only the greatly talented can be, and his judgement was unspoilt by any touch of envy, he was a devastating critic of the second-rate . . . Indeed it is because he found delight and gave it, in so many different kinds of conversation and companionship, that within and without his own profession there is grief today among innumerable friends.

For 1954 we decided to go to important population centres, cities that would be new to us, and our work new to them. We had been invited by Wolverhampton to give a concert in their new hall, but they had no adequate accommodation, so they enlisted Birmingham. The latter offered Saltley School for sleeping and the George Dixon School for all our work. On Boxing Day 1953 I arrived at George Dixon School. It was a large boys' school, and took a great deal of rearranging, but by 29 December it had been turned into a music school, duly labelled for the orchestra to arrive in time for supper. The Headmaster commented as he surveyed the results that this was the first time his school had had the feminine touch, and was this the effect of music on the soul? With the invasion came thirty-five new members, so we all worked hard to make them feel they belonged before we moved to Saltley School, with luxurious beds instead of mattresses on the floor. For children to settle after a long journey, the first Christmastide away from home, on a dark winter night, was tough.

This year I had started taking younger members, one of eleven and three of twelve, and slightly more reserves, who came for all the classes but didn't yet play in the concert. This opened the opportunity to more people, but did not enlarge the symphony orchestra on the platform.

The great excitement this time was to have Walter Susskind for the first term of the year: normally we could only get him in the summer. Would his patience manage this more elementary stage? Yes, he was excellent with the youngest ones. With the recent death of Jack, I couldn't face anybody new in his place; Leon Goossens continued to take the woodwind ensemble, and we still had Gareth Morris looking after the flutes. I also had one new professor to guide our young bassoonists. I had always wanted the famous Archie Camden in my team, but earlier he had had links with the MTA, so I didn't approach him. Now he responded keenly. He was a man of gentle charm and kindness, with a fund of real-life stories he would tell with childlike simplicity. Everything he played seemed so natural and easy, and he shared his beautiful talent and his rich teaching experience unstintingly. Likewise in the early days we had very few double basses, but now with one good instrument of our own and some very keen young talent, I wanted them to have their own full-time professor. So I went to Eugène Cruft. A totally dedicated person, if he believed in what he was doing his whole being went into it. Even our bass stools, later on, were made to his design, with ledges for shorter or longer legs, and very successful they were. In this week our young bass players ceased to be 'the back of the cellos', and became confident musicians, as important a part of the orchestra as any other group. Eugène stayed with us until old age finally won. I distinctly remember him showing the orchestra that he could stand on his head on his eightieth birthday.

Brought up in Prague, Walter had an excellent Mozartian style, so it was time to do a Haydn symphony. We balanced this with the very dramatic Berlioz overture and the romantic violin concerto, played by Gillian Eastwood; there was something for everybody in Chabrier's *España*. In October Sir Arnold Bax had died. He was one of the first distinguished musicians to lend his support to the idea of the NYO, as early as 1946, so we included *Tintagel* as a tribute to him.

John and I were on the platform of the new Civic Hall, Wolverhampton, at eight-fifteen in the morning. We always asked for an empty stage, just 120 chairs to be available; we would bring our own stands. Now I was furious as nothing we'd been promised was ready. A huge grand piano blocked the chair-covered platform, and seemingly there was no means of getting it off to the side. I visualised the whole day's timetable running late, an irritated conductor, late lunch, hungry children, cross cooks – everything that disturbs concert-day calm. When the chief stage-hand was found I was full of complaint; with true Midland calm, he pressed some buttons and an extra platform rose out of the floor in front of the stage. The grand piano and everything else unneeded was pushed on to it, and the whole lot disappeared into the underworld! I was full of apologies of course, and efficiency of the Wolverhampton kind soon prevailed. The people of this city were very forward-looking, and now that they had built this lovely new hall they were very keen for us to play there. Judging from their press we did not disappoint them.

We had been warned that it was difficult to get through Birmingham's traffic to the Town Hall, where our three buses and van would have to be at nine a.m. and again at six-thirty – rush-hour times. So one evening John, Genin and I set off to check the vital timing. We reached Fiveways, a part of the city full of roundabouts and traffic signals, and asked a bobby on the pavement for the Town Hall. He obviously didn't believe we were going there at that time of night, but gave some instructions. Off we went, only to discover that in ten minutes we were back beside the same bobby. This time John mentioned our concert, and got the reply, 'Where do you *really* want to go?' Alas, our next attempt brought us back to the same spot, and this time we were laughing so much he jumped to the obvious New Year conclusion. We were officially stopped, and asked to get out of the car. Genin explained we were all strangers to the city, but the policeman's notebook was in hand: London, Liverpool . . . Aberdeen was too much. I produced a leaflet about the concert, but was sternly rebuked. Mercifully a sergeant appeared, and we tried a most dignified appeal to get back to a hundred children in Saltley School, I was visualising the local paper: THREE MEMBERS OF ORCHESTRA STAFF MISSING. NIGHT IN POLICE STATION . . .

The reviews of the Birmingham concert show that Rudolf Schwarz, whom I had not yet met, Conductor of the Birmingham Symphony Orchestra, was there, as well as the bishop and all the leading lights in education and our hosts, including Mr Russell, the Chief Education Officer, and Mrs Smith, Chairman of the Education Committee. These people went to great trouble to accommodate us, so an exciting concert was a little reward for their work and faith in us.

The press for our first visit to the Midlands expressed surprise:

> The orchestra has to be heard to be believed. It is the most splendid and inspiriting adventure in the history of executant music . . . Youthful enthusiasm, coupled with a phenomenal degree of technical efficiency and discipline . . . *No sensible purpose is served by pressing comparisons between the NYO and professional orchestras.* [My italics.] J.F.W. (*Birmingham Post*)

I thank J.F.W. very warmly. It was not our fault that these stupid comparisons were made. We didn't think we were in the least like any of the professional orchestras, neither the very good ones nor the bad ones. There was no better way of making enemies for us, or giving the impression our members were conceited. They could never be, with teachers and conductors such as ours.

The *Coventry Evening Telegraph* said:

> It was reported that one of the most moving experiences was to hear the NYO. I found the reports had not exaggerated one whit: the performances were splendid, and the spectacle, the exuberance unforgettable. Indeed discipline, attack and poise are quite exemplary, and a zest which is communicated to the audience.

The trusty *Times Educational Supplement*, under the heading FIREWORKS IN BIRMINGHAM, wrote a glowing piece: 'the dynamics of the brass, their brilliance never raucous, the rhythmic precision of the strings and balance between the parts made this España a flawless performance'.

My desk was piled with letters. I had quite often spoken on BBC recordings for their overseas programmes, including some in French and one in German for Austria. The BBC is heard all over the world, so requests and invitations came in frequently. There was a lovely letter and some press cuttings from a man in Belgium. Inspired by our visit, he had organised a nation-wide sweepstake, and used the money to give concert tickets to children who could not otherwise afford to go.

Meanwhile the National Youth Brass Band was under way, one of the first of many imitators: the leading exponents had visited us at work, and kept in touch, and our brass professor Ernest Hall had given them great help. Our contacts with the world of brass were always enjoyable, and there were never any problems between the NYO and its follower in brass, the NYBB.

This was also the time of Leslie Russell's LSSO concert in London. January 11 saw his children, stiffened by full-time music students up to age twenty-one, spread on the RFH platform. It was difficult at this time to find enough string players, but there was a fine battery of brass and wind and a girls' choir with which they tackled Vaughan Williams's *Job*. I had suggested to Dr Russell, who understood choirs much better than orchestras, that he should run a London youth choir, encouraging the young men to start singing again after their voices broke, but he decided to stick to girls. The very popular Eileen Joyce played the Grieg piano concerto. The whole evening, in fact, interested me greatly, as it was one of the early efforts to raise the sights and opportunities in school music. I wasn't invited but I'm glad I went.

The LCC had a very powerful press department, so after the concert I expected there would be down-with-the-NYO and up-with-the-LSSO reviews. I should not have doubted the integrity of our music critics. *The Times*'s master stroke was to explain that our work and aims were far from identical. The *Times Educational Supplement* was more direct, and critical. In answer a reply was published, under the name of R. Vaughan Williams:

> In your issue of January 15th your music critic compares the playing of the London Schools' Symphony Orchestra very unfavourably with that of the National Youth Orchestra. I have not heard the latter, but if this comparison be correct, then the 'National' players must be super-children almost too good for this world. The London children were good enough for me.

I was sad that such a great musician should want to sneer at what he hadn't heard. Was he pressured? It was not the Vaughan Williams I knew.

To complete the Leslie Russell saga, at our annual Council meeting in January 1955, in answer to a question about members from London, I explained that children in LCC schools were not able to come if invited. This was because Leslie Russell told them that if they joined us he would see they did not get a grant for any later application to a music college. My statement was challenged as untrue by Mervyn Bruxner, the Music Adviser for Kent and a friend of Dr Russell's. I produced two letters from Dr Russell to children whom I had invited, confirming my statement, and handed these to Sir Adrian, who was in the chair, presuming he would ask for an apology. Instead he read one letter, was embarrassed and uneasy, and said, 'Oh dear, this is all very difficult; I think the best thing to do is just to tear up these letters,' and proceeded to do so, putting them in a waste-paper basket (whence they were retrieved immediately after the meeting, and kept in a place of safety to this day). Dr Taylor, Headmaster of Haberdasher's Aske's, and Rachel Pearse, Headmistress of Mary Datchelor Girls School, were both members of the Council and present at that meeting.

At a meeting in 1963 Miss Pearse raised the point that it was sad that LCC children could not join us because of the threat of being denied a grant. The parents of a child in her school had given her a letter from Dr Russell, similar to mine in 1955. When she raised this, Dr Taylor rose to his feet saying that when I had said the same in 1955 I had been called a liar, and the evidence was torn up, and he wished the matter to be rectified, and my name cleared in the minutes.

Bernard Shore wrote to me a month before he died, in 1985, with his recollections of the early years: 'Leslie Russell of the LCC was by far my worst memory of HMI-dom.' So I was not alone.

Soon I had cleared away these outside events that were encroaching on my mind, and was preparing for the Executive and Council meetings. The plan of one Council meeting a year, with the Executive gathering after every course, had been laid. This time, 5 February 1954, we had prepared a display of the Shepard drawings and press critiques, and set up equipment for everyone to watch the travel film. At the Executive meeting, John Newsom was appointed Vice-Chairman. The Finance Committee was disbanded, with thanks to its chairman Sir Robert Mayer, whose great contribution had been the loan of the 'uninhabitable' basement for nearly five years – and where would we have been without it?

Sir Adrian chaired the afternoon Council meeting. The annual report included Brussels, Edinburgh – on which Sir Adrian could comment – and events up to Birmingham. Future plans included a return to Brussels in 1955, Edinburgh again and America was turned down. Leslie Scott always spent time persuading us to expand into a European youth orchestra, or at least to invite one child from each country to join us; but we had to explain we couldn't undertake more work yet.

We were not used to the calm of financial security, so the Treasurer's report was interesting. In 1951 the entire cost of running the NYO was £2,300, in 1952 £2,500 and in 1953

£4,600 including the week in Brussels. We made our concerts pay and cover travel. The relationship with the *Mirror* was going splendidly, as it was happy to regard its sponsorship as a philanthropic activity and was generous about the very small amount of publicity we allowed it.

So for 1954 the Council and Executive were happy, and the *Mirror* was happy. My team of musicians was increasingly devoted, the critics unstintingly proud of us, and we had a new London office. Yet I was very unhappy. Throughout the week in Birmingham I had been without a secretary: Shirley had been commandeered by Miss Davy, who remained in the office. Consequently more work fell on John and the house staff. We noticed in the printed programme that Miss Davy had become General Secretary, with Shirley marked as her Assistant, unknown to me. I found she had the power to sign cheques, and that I even had to ask her permission to have my letters typed! She said her instructions came only from the Executive Committee, namely Mr McDougall. I sought him out.

Firstly I wanted the assurance that I had no responsibility for expenditure I knew nothing about. New office equipment and filing cabinets, much of which seemed unnecessary to me, were piling up in the two small rooms; surely every extra penny from the *Mirror* was needed for our young musicians? Secondly, I was increasingly without secretarial help, and also in the dark concerning the lady's activities. I added that within these few months I had had letters returned to me from important people which started, 'Miss Railton has asked me to take over her work, and to arrange . . .' with notes such as 'You never wrote this! What's happening?' I handed him one from a professor: 'Of course I'll come next time, but do get rid of that ambitious, disloyal, fussacious grosbeak . . .' My position was becoming impossible.

He replied that the intention was that very soon the Executive Committee and this lady would run everything; I would just be in charge of auditions and music during the courses. He would explain to her about a closer liaison for the moment, and hoped

I'd give it a longer try, at least until after the next course. I could have resigned, but thought of letting down the children and the *Mirror*. I agreed, vividly remembering Jack's hazy voice: 'Don't go, my sweet, don't go.' In any case the problem was the wrong person, not the wrong idea.

The greatest asset in the new office was the piano. I wasted no time in inviting young musicians to play, in answer to their letters, and coaching our young soloists. (If musically beautiful the technique might be inadequate; if that was sound, they might be too young for the chosen work.) It was a huge step forward to have space for teacher and child, often a parent too, and plan the best way forward for the child concerned. The General Secretary meanwhile produced an artificial smile and an attitude of enduring condescension.

We had accepted a pressing invitation from Sunderland for Easter 1954. They had no hall for the concert, but we could go to Newcastle for that, as long as we would spend the week as the guests of Sunderland. We had not yet been to the north-east, so I set off to make plans. The LEA offered us the very best of everything they had. Their best school was brand-new, Thorney Close Secondary Modern. The hall was big enough; kitchens, dining-rooms and gym were all modern; and there was just enough space to turn it into a boarding school for a week. When I commented that my back ached at the very thought of all the stacking of desks and heaving of mattresses involved, they promptly offered me six professional furniture removers! At the mention of the problem of baths, they were ready with plans to go by bus to the public baths. I mentioned that I was sorry we couldn't give a concert in Sunderland in return. The Mayor said, 'Never mind the concert; we'll have you every day for a week.' Why so keen? It emerged that life had been terrible in Sunderland between the wars, and now they wanted the best for their young people; they were going to be in front in this new post-war world. Their strength for survival and pride in their town was a moving experience, and all we had to do was want to come to them.

We came, bringing great musicians, our invaluable volunteer staff and our 135 members, seven from the north-east. One new member of staff joined us at Sunderland, and stayed for the next twenty years: Sister Jean Boddy. I had met her during the recent audition tour, at Radley School. With kindly thought she made tea so that we could sit by her fire in the san. and talk. She was a sturdy, rock-like person, quietly spoken, approachable, with a gentle manner. Sympathy, patience and no fuss were her style, and I was impressed by her great experience of adolescent needs – the stomach ache that can be anxiety or an appendix – and with our highly sensitive lot, a dose of TLC could aid the principal flute's sore throat or the violinist's damaged finger as much as the right chemical. In accepting my invitation she asked only if she need wear uniform, as she preferred to be unobtrusive. Sister Boddy would survey her charges from the platform in rehearsals, or in breaks and at mealtimes, and spot their smallest needs in advance of their looking for her. This was so important, as if bad colds or an infection spread, it could easily mean cancelling a concert. From her NYO baptism in Sunderland, this remarkable character never missed a course, which meant she almost never took a holiday. She was older than the rest of us, but travelled in our conditions on all our foreign tours without complaint, and we grew to love her and depend on her. She was our Florence Nightingale of the mattresses, the Russian night trains, the touring buses, planes and concert halls of Europe. Of such quality are English nurses made. In her retirement she still came to our London concerts until she died in December 1990.

After Easter everyone arrived safely in Sunderland, and adapted with the refreshing excitement of the young to life on the floor, longing to get playing together again. Hugo Rignold had helped to choose a most attractive programme: Rossini for the strings; a Beethoven piano concerto with sixteen-year-old Shelagh Stamp; Elgar's *Wand of Youth* to give endless opportunities to the percussion department; and a Dvořák symphony to suit all. As usual we allowed local teachers and musicians on to the platform for evening rehearsals, more this time as there was no concert in the town itself. Particularly memorable was the visit of the newly formed Middlesbrough Youth Orchestra and its Conductor, Mr Grief. They couldn't afford to travel to Newcastle for our concert, so they came for our final rehearsal and were so appreciative.

We were granted a civic reception by the Mayor, Alderman McGregor English. Over the years our students saw the town halls of their own country and it was an education in itself. There would be a speech from our host, usually not a musical person, and self-control in public was important if amusing mistakes occurred. This time the triumphant last sentence ended with '. . . all music is discord, but the conductor is God.' Our conductor was beside the Mayor and facing my lively boys. Hugo's face – immobile, expressionless – saved the day.

The great event of the week was Sunday in Durham Cathedral. We were shown round and told about its history, and then stayed for Choral Evensong. The place itself, and the great language and music of Evensong within it, inspired everybody. As we all strolled out to the buses I noticed one small boy lingering, eyes transfixed on the vaulting, and I waited by the door for him. 'It's funny: your rehearsal yesterday was all about spacing and shaping . . . There'll never be any spacing anywhere to touch *that*,' and he looked back at it longingly. We had wonderful children in our care. Far too many had never been to a cathedral, yet in England there is a great one within reasonable reach of everybody. On the way back to Sunderland I thought out a possible cathedral-concert tour which might replace a foreign one, that they might discover the wonders of their own heritage and contribute their own art within it.

There had been some difficulty in filling the concert hall in Newcastle: we were new to the city and were not resident among its citizens and press, so we let some of the latter in one afternoon. Photographing them all at rest on their mattresses, one asked a boy if he thought the conditions dreadful: 'I wouldn't mind sleeping on bare boards so long as I could come to the Youth Orchestra,' which reply was printed by the astonished but honest journalist.

The concert was full, and the local critics found it a shock,

> of a pleasant and stimulating kind which braces the spirit. It was Dvořák who said, 'The English do not love music – they respect it', but last night there was as much affection as admiration in the large audience's recognition of a uniquely rewarding musical experience. (*Newcastle Journal*)

There was also the ever-faithful BBC Overseas Service recording and the *Light Programme*.

Seventeen

Night after night at the Royal Festival Hall I could study works I didn't know, and hear new soloists and conductors, or ones from abroad. There was at this time a special club in South Audley Street in London – the International Music Association – with a library, a recital-room and an excellent restaurant. It quickly became a centre for musicians; after concerts life would begin in the IMA. I shall always be grateful to whoever made me a member. It was here that my friendship with conductors such as Kletzki, Kubelik, Malcho and above all Guido Cantelli developed. Also at the IMA I first got to know the incomparable Jean Martinon. He was a most attractive personality, highly intelligent, cultured and amusing. Musically he was a superb interpreter, with his vivid imagination, rhythmic clarity and every mood coloured; in excitement he was perhaps too fast, in sadness too tragic. I couldn't wait to get him for my lively young and enjoy the results. I discovered that his great interest was composing, but he earned his living conducting because that was what everybody invited him to do; his great love, however, was climbing mountains, and escaping to his little chalet at the base of Mont Blanc. So I wooed him with the Glengonnar Camp, the Scottish hills and Edinburgh; my friends explained that the NYO could play.

'If they are so young they cannot play,' he said. (In France at that time they couldn't.)

'Will you come and discover for yourself?' That evening captured the most poetic conductor I ever brought to the NYO.

Ian Hunter was waiting for confirmation of our programme for Edinburgh – a much-valued fourth invitation. When he asked me to include a first performance of a new work by Boris

Blacher, a German composer, I demurred somewhat strongly, explaining I couldn't go through the Rawsthorne experience again. He pressed me, however, because there would be a Unesco International Music Council conference in Edinburgh, to discuss 'Music and the Young', and they had commissioned this piece as part of their publicity. It would be an honour for us to have it . . . I agreed to meet Mr Blacher and peruse the work, hoping that Martinon would refuse it, or someone else claim it. Why should Unesco spend their money on a German composer, so soon after the war, rather than a British one, for a British festival with British performers? But patriotic thoughts were out of fashion.

It was arranged for me to go to Paris and there meet Mr Blacher: a very disappointing encounter. I'd brought a detailed plan of the NYO, with particular mention of percussion and harps, beautiful trombones, eight lovely horns and also photographs: nothing altered his expression. So I became practical: I said it was difficult to perform a work unseen, and produced an agreement for us both to sign. This promised me the score and parts by 1 August, gave the maximum duration of the piece and my agreement to play it if suitable at the Edinburgh Festival on 28 August. He brushed it aside. I tried, 'My Executive requires me to have every commitment in writing; so I'm sorry that another orchestra will have the privilege,' and prepared to leave. Out came his pen. I could of course end up with a masterpiece in our repertoire, but intuitively I was unhappy and suspicious. Why was he so cagey? Was he ill?

Fixing a programme for the summer to suit us and Martinon and Ian Hunter was easy: a Weber overture, a Mozart concerto, the Blacher possibility and Tchaikovsky 5 for the second half. Martinon's expressive eyebrows and shoulders were not too happy about the unknown work, but he was a composer himself so didn't complain.

Meanwhile Miss Davy told me she was behind with letters, and couldn't manage without another assistant secretary. My view, of course, was that what two of us managed before three of us should manage now, with better space and help from the *Mirror*. The implication was that it was a pity to delay increasing the staff, which she would need in the future. What future? One without me? A few days later I had a phone call from John Dalby. He had had a letter, which I never saw, looking forward to working closely with him in the future, and another asking him to attend a special Executive meeting in a fortnight, about which I knew nothing. Maurice Jacobson, the Executive Chairman, was away, and didn't yet know about the meeting, which had been called by John Newsom to discuss my lack of co-operation with the Executive's appointee. I resigned.

I wrote to Bruno Walter to tell him about Edinburgh this year, and that I would no longer be there. Strangely, on the morning of the meeting came his reply: '. . . you must not try to work with your enthusiasm quenched, damp wood makes no true fire. It is sad to desert so soon, so individual a creation . . . What do your sponsors think?' Quite suddenly I thought that perhaps I should have told the Chairman of the *Mirror* that I had resigned, at the same time as I had told the NYO Chairman. I rang his secretary to ask for an appointment, presuming I'd have to wait about three weeks, but she rang back and asked if I could come now. I seized a taxi, pondering how to explain the secret takeover bid. I was nervous, but he was easy to talk to. I said I just wanted him to know that I'd resigned, and not hear it second-hand or from a newspaper. The reason wasn't so easy to explain without letting any of my colleagues down. He asked where the meeting was, and wrote a letter while I waited. Then he looked up and said, 'No Musical Director, no *Mirror* money,' and arranged for the letter to be delivered immediately to the meeting by hand.

Nothing could have been more unexpected! I took the day off, anticipating the effect of Cecil King's letter, which I never saw, on the secret meeting. Would they find another sponsor, or return to poverty? Or close down the NYO, and watch me start it up the next morning with *Mirror* support? I had a good laugh with friends and the strain of the last months was over.

There are no minutes of this meeting. John only remembered that he read aloud the letter he'd had from Miss Davy, whereupon John Newsom said, 'That settles it. She leaves at once.' Then Cecil King's letter was read, and Mr McDougall, whose plan it had all been, resigned. I was really sorry about that. He was such a nice person, and wrote me a letter in which he said he had no idea until he met our professors and conductors what was involved in creating the NYO. He was a professional accountant, and really thought that all that was needed to maintain the NYO was money and a good organising secretary. We musicians were advisers to the conductor, who was there to beat time. He was a great loss as Treasurer, and had given so much time to the Finance Committee before the *Mirror* days. His last gesture was to persuade his friend Roland Bird of *The Economist* to take his place.

Roland Bird took over as Treasurer in September, and served the NYO with skill and friendship for the next five years. He was a rock-like personality; a man of few words but sound advice, respected by the *Mirror*. He arranged for us to buy a bass trombone and a horn, which were then transferred to *Mirror* ownership. He also equipped us with a Grundig tape recorder with which to capture some of our concerts. It was a very heavy machine, unlike the present-day models, not easily transportable to halls and rehearsals. I regret that our tape history is so weak. I asked him recently for his memories and he writes:

> There was concern about the NYO keeping its independence and high standards, and about the *Mirror* not using the NYO for brash publicity. Neither was a source of trouble. There was also concern about overseas travel, insurance, health, management, accommodation etc. Big chances were undoubtedly taken, but there were no troubles that I recall, only acclaim for the NYO's performances.

His sound judgement and financial management served the NYO until December 1959. We owe him so much.

*

We could not complete 1954 without finding a new senior secretary. How does one find the faith and loyalty of a Philippa, the shrewd, independent mind of a Joan Ashton and the experience of a Mrs Ballingall all in one person? I can't remember how it happened that suddenly I bumped into Diana Scholefield. She had been working in Boosey & Hawkes since she left us, and it soon emerged that her heart was still with the NYO. She had all the most important qualities: she was gentle, courteous and sympathetic; she understood musicians and sensitive young people; and she had now spent some time as a professional secretary. Life in an overcrowded damp basement, thrown into a foreign tour in a first job, was not a fair start; I invited her back. She came in August 1954 and stayed, gradually taking over the whole NYO organisation until changes in both our lives caused us to part in 1963. Quietly and unpretentiously, she did more for the NYO than any other person after John Dalby.

On 1 August no score or parts had arrived from Boris Blacher, in spite of reminders in July. I asked Ian Hunter if we could now cancel our performance, in view of the written agreement being broken. He pleaded with me for a week's grace, and the score eventually arrived on the 14th – a short and unattractive piece for a small chamber orchestra, in no way suitable for the full symphonic size of the NYO. I felt sure Martinon would refuse to play it. I telephoned Blacher in vain for parts for trombone, harp and percussion. This was my second experience of being ready to play a new work and being let down. I could do no more until my conductor and all the professors had seen the work and we could try it out.

Soon Diana and I were preparing the camp at Abington for the fourth year. On 21 August we stood alone on the village station, listening for the Royal Scot slowing down in the distance. Suddenly one of the most rewarding and exhilarating moments with the NYO was upon us, as over a hundred members leapt out of the train. Then the greetings, the laughter, questions pouring out as we walked across the fields, anticipating another adventure. After a good Scottish supper, enriched by the fact that butter and meat had come off rationing since we last met, the plans for the week and the new conductor were announced. By bedtime any new staff and members had been happily absorbed into our united family.

In the early morning the night train delivered our team of professors, who brought Jean Martinon with them. He was delighted to see the lovely countryside and insisted on walking to the village hotel as if he were on his favourite Mont Blanc. He had asked especially to be with us all the time and take part in all our activities; so by ten on the first day he wanted to see what was going on, and was anxiously and eagerly wondering, as he looked on such young children, what would happen in Tchaikovsky 5. I took him round every classroom, where small groups were warming up – technical exercises here, sight reading there, sorting players and parts for the different works, percussion still unpacking, fingering and slow scales in the violins . . . 'Ah,' he said, 'I see they cannot play . . . imposseeble.'

Suddenly I realised I had made the most ghastly mistake. Never before had I let a conductor near the children in the first three days, and I should have known that with the French system of teaching being so different from our own, he could only be bewildered and shocked. As mid-morning break approached he was depressed and I thought he might leave for Paris. Leaving my colleagues to cheer him up, I changed the timetable instantly to Full Orchestra. I told them all what had happened and that we must convince him immediately that we *could* play: that we'd start on the overture, and whatever happened, whatever the pace, they mustn't stop, they must play to save the day. And they did.

I had to press Martinon to come and try the overture – 'It is no good, they cannot play' – but, glancing at 120 players from wall to wall in our largest hut, he mounted the rostrum sadly. The young took up the challenge, and clung on at this first reading as if in performance. 'Ah goot, so they *can* play.' His smile returned, and everyone relaxed with relief. For the rest of the week he accepted whatever plans we made, treating the orchestra like professionals; everything at first was either 'goot' or ''orreeble', and his marvellous hands and expressive face explained the rest. Those members who were with us on courses with Jean Martinon will have a lifelong memory of his great artistry.

Two days later Allan Schiller, now aged eleven, but still very small in stature, arrived with his mother; this was my choice of soloist for the Mozart piano concerto. I took him to my chalet to meet Martinon, and Allan was a little shy of this vibrant personality and the French accent. Afterwards Jean said to me, 'If you say so, maybe he can play, but he is too small for the sound with orchestra and the large Usher Hall.' After the first rehearsal, he took it all back: 'Maybe it is a miracle.'

Allan's playing was technically secure, musically intelligent and sensitive, and he could stop and start anywhere. At this age there was no thought of nerves, just a longing to play for the joy of it.

Allan writes:

> I remember particularly the great friendliness of the orchestra, who spent their free time playing with me on the swings. The percussion section made me an honorary member, and I sat with them in rehearsals when I was not working.

Faced with the unfinished Blacher score, Jean Martinon was as depressed as we were. John suggested sending a telegram – 'Boris, this is not Godunov' – and kept him laughing. We set about finding out if the composer was coming to visit us, or attending the *accomplissement*, and when we had finally secured a definite no due to illness, things started to happen. 'I intend to remove the bars where the sound is 'orreeble,' and out they came. 'Mr Hall will give the trombones something nice, Mr Genin will give beautiful music to the 'arps, no just pluck-pluck.' The percussion parts increased daily. Of course this was vandalism and very wrong, but so was our predicament. We could not have played this unfinished score in public without letting down the festival, Unesco and the composer, and damaging our reputation. I would have liked to show up the raw deal landed on us, but the course we chose was braver and possibly wiser.

But there was a worse shock to come. I had kept in touch with Ian Hunter, and the day before the concert he sent us the printed programme. The notes informed us that the Blacher work we were to perform was *two* inventions, one allegro molto, one vivace.* We however had only one short piece, of somewhat different tempo. There was no choice but to cut our piece into two parts, and a suitable stopping place was found: 'At bar X we will all stop; and when we go on again we will play faster.'

And so it came about that, after considerable imagination and skilful orchestration, a piece the official programme called *Two Inventions for Symphony Orchestra* by Boris Blacher, commissioned by Unesco for the International Music Council and the Edinburgh International Festival and dedicated by the composer to the National Youth Orchestra, reached the platform of the Usher Hall and was duly given its first (and only) performance.

Our first week with Martinon was memorable and extremely happy. The Bizet was beautifully French, in style and sparkle; the Mozart was the most inspiring, with childlike purity yet technical maturity from this tiny personality. The Tchaikovsky stretched technique and emotion; the Blacher provided much initiative one way and another. We also had some wonderful evenings: Dennis Brain driving out from Edinburgh to help our horns and give a superb recital, and Archie Camden on another evening. One evening Martinon the mountaineer led a walk

*Now published, dedicated to us and mentioning the first performance by us in Edinburgh in 1954. Yet we never saw or played the *Two Inventions* by Boris Blacher.

through woods, across streams and up hills, like a Pied Piper followed by 130 children.

Then the thrill of the concert itself, and afterwards an invitation to the tattoo in the floodlights at the castle. This superbly planned pageant was for them another example of perfect discipline and timing to achieve an artistic result.

The next night was our third Glasgow concert, which was being broadcast on the BBC's Third Programme. I literally prayed that they would leave out the Blacher, and persuaded them without having to say why. I told Myra Hess about Allan, and she listened in, and afterwards wrote to say she was 'entranced by such perception and conviction'. She added, 'For that Mozart alone and the spirit of the Tchaikovsky, it was worth all the struggle you've been through.'

When I went to say goodbye to Martinon, of course I asked him if he'd come again. 'Next time I will not say "impossee-ble".' So 1954 ended triumphantly with one more fine conductor in our team, our standard of performance still improving and our contacts widening. With our special Executive Committee, and with Diana already devotedly embedded in the work, I had new confidence to plan and expand into 1955. But what of the outside world?

We collected the many reviews from the festival. We were now being treated as a serious musical event, with our own style and standards, no longer remarkable because we were 'youth', nor because we were new. Inevitably Allan Schiller captured all the hearts and the headlines, but not just because he was a child: 'The talent, teaching, phrasing and maturity was not just precocity.' The various leading papers acclaimed once more 'the intensity of enthusiasm – the discipline – the pianissimo in the overture – the sensitivity in the Mozart – the warmth of fervour in the Tchaikovsky'. But what would they make of the Blacher? If they had read the programme notes they would know we had not played the *Two Inventions*, nor anything in key or form remotely like them. At least this would show who were the real musicians amongst the critics, and who the jargon writers. *The*

Times came through with flying colours: 'The orchestra was honoured with the first performance of a work by Boris Blacher . . . His Two Inventions are mere cats-cradle . . . the players came through the test safely.' The *Telegraph* dismissed it tidily and wisely: 'The NYO was well up to its usual high standard last night . . . The one mistake of the evening was the inclusion of Boris Blacher's vapid "Inventions".' The *Guardian*, alas, fell into the mire: 'Boris Blacher's Two Inventions show Blacher at his best, original in harmony and truly inventive,' and wallowed into a whole paragraph. At least we had come through it with nobody's reputation harmed.

There was one last surprise in 1955. The Worshipful Company of Musicians gave us a silver medal, in memory of a Wing-Commander Bulgin, to be an annual award to one of our members: an honour for the NYO and for every future winner.

Eighteen

It was towards the end of September that great activity resumed in 90 George Street. Diana soon made herself a cosy den and reorganised the equipment for our needs; and Shirley typed away in the smaller of the rooms, which was also a waiting-room for visitors or pupils. We thought we were very lucky to have such an office, with considerable character *and* in London W1.

Of first importance was the Executive Committee meeting to review our progress and our plans. These remarkable people in the world of education who formed our Executive Committee were all involved in the effect the NYO was having on musical education and high standards generally, and were really concerned with the problem of getting over to the LEAs the real function of the NYO: that it was not just a youth orchestra but a teaching establishment for carefully chosen potential talent over a period of two to six years for each individual. I had not wanted to call our three terms 'courses' because of this confusion. Mr Scott now suggested that we use the original title, the National Junior Music School, under the NYOGB heading in all our printing. This would accent the long-term teaching and also be a good link with the junior departments of the RAM and RCM.

Next came the plans for the whole year: Bradford in January with Susskind, the RFH in April with Sir Malcolm Sargent for the first time and then on to Brussels for a whole week, possibly extending to Amsterdam. The latest invitation was to give a Promenade Concert in the summer, and Sir Adrian was willing to conduct this. This was another big new step, which the Committee decided unanimously should be accepted.

In addition, the BBC asked to televise our next RFH concert.

I thought the Committee would be keen about this, but to my surprise they showed real concern for the children. I was to check how hot it would be for them, and how long in that heat. This attitude pleased me enormously and gave me the authority to refuse unsuitable invitations with 'The Executive Committee would never allow that . . .'

With plans prepared for our most ambitious year so far, it was time to set off on the ninth audition tour. The gift of the piano meant we could hold auditions in my room in the office. It was Diana's first tour, and she was very good at fitting in invitations to listen to choirs or to judge school competitions in the evenings and at weekends. Sometimes I had to remind myself that I was no longer going into battle for a cause, but into many spheres of welcome and tremendous good will.

The final choice was agonising, but fifty-nine new members were invited; the total was about 140, with more younger ones, and extra reserves for a year that included a foreign tour. Only hearts of stone could fail to be moved by the letters of acceptance, not just from the excited children but also from grateful parents and teachers too. It was Christmas Eve, a Friday evening, when we finished packing and locking up, leaving for just Christmas Day with our families, for on Sunday morning we were in the first train for Bradford.

We had been lent Bingley College, just outside the city, and the premises were ideal in every way for work such as ours. It was luxury: separate bedrooms for all and no mattresses to heave around. Eugene Genin and the Liverpool contingent arrived through the snow on Monday to help us, and by six our fleet of buses hove into sight bearing tired but smiling faces, and in our last bus the never-failing John Dalby and the Scottish members. New house staff enlisted on my recent tour were Noel de Jong from Launceston and David Snell from Gordonstoun, and very expert and great fun they were too; and a charming friend, Delphine Starmer, to look after the younger girls. (Within a year the David and Delphine partnership became permanent, to our great loss.)

David writes:

> I loved music before coming to the NYO but was totally ignorant of the practical side. I remember pointing out what I assumed to be self-seeking affectation in a boy playing the kettle-drums who would keep tapping them and listening in every brief interval. I did not know they had to be retuned. I was amazed that hours could be spent on one phrase which was gone in a few seconds in performance. I was very ignorant.
>
> What a galaxy of talent and temperament was assembled there. Of course it was all drama when you were on form, but that had to be experienced to be understood.
>
> I remember once when sitting next to you in the circle of some hall when the orchestra was coming onto the platform, when you suddenly noticed the stool had been left on the conductor's rostrum. 'Go and get it off,' you said. 'He'll simply walk off again if he gets there and sees it.' I rushed down to the front of the stalls, and just managed to grab a leg and edge it off before the Great Man came on.
>
> I am extremely grateful to you for giving me the chance to mix with those marvellous people – the musicians and the house staff too – and to see the fashioning of great performances from the inside.

David Snell's contribution to the NYO was priceless: eighty boys in his care were gratefully out of mine.

Of course all the house staff and the invaluable Sister Boddy were always observant, approachable problem solvers, and every night, while the family slept, we would all meet to share the progress and laughter of each day.

The evening events were usually a surprise; this time we had a New Members' recital evening, which showed the generosity of the seniors about the beginners: 'I couldn't play like that when I was thirteen!' And the New Year's Eve party revealed the latest rock 'n' roll dancing and gave us new insights into the various personalities in our care.

New Year's Day 1955 started with the announcement that John Dalby had been appointed Assistant Musical Director. The orchestra were overjoyed, as they had the greatest respect for this talented, humorous Yorkshireman, who had in fact been born near Bingley. I could not have had a finer partner, and finally now this could be acknowledged in print. Sometime earlier we had both tried to find a title for Eugene Genin, to cover all he did – teaching, repairs, driving, stage-setting, endless voluntary service in a cause he believed in – and John thought of Orchestral Assistant; we added Ivey Dickson as Pianist for Recitals, and the staff list for the newly designed programme was complete.

On Sunday we went to Bradford Cathedral, where the Dean and Organist had prepared the music and the content of the sermon rather specially for us. And the Lord Mayor, Alderman White, gave us an official reception in the Town Hall the day before the concert. As usual we tried to instil a sense of occasion, what was best for the orchestra in public being different from individuals in private, and everyone was absorbed into the growing pride in our traditions. For my part I never asked anything of a student that I didn't believe was best for them and had found of value myself. We always explained the reasons behind any plan we embarked on, and always asked for questions. Sometimes these were practical details we had overlooked, sometimes partly joking: 'If the girl next to me faints and falls on the floor, do I pick her up, or go on playing and put my feet on her?'

The programme suited our Czech conductor, with the *Carnival Overture* by Dvořák, and a Mozart violin concerto with our leader John Tunnell as soloist (his younger brother Charles was a new arrival at the back of the cellos). Malcolm Arnold had written another suite to suit our players, called *Homage to the Queen*, while the heavier orchestra wrestled with *Háry János* by Kodály. For this we needed a zimbalon, but had failed to find one, let alone learn how to play it. But Malcolm discovered that Chappells had arranged the works of an upright piano to make it sound rather like a zimbalon, and we hired this hybrid. It was a great success, in that it certainly didn't sound like a piano, if only faintly resembling the real instrument. That apart, Walter could get more colour and drama from our uninhibited performers in such items as 'The Battle and Defeat of Napoleon' than from normal orchestras. 'It is easy to whip them up, and very exciting, but exceedingly difficult to hold them. If I lost the reins . . .?' But he never did.

Recently I was in the Royal Ballet School and met Philip Gammon, now a pianist with the company. He reminded me that his first course was at Bradford, and I gave him the zimbalon part.

The concert in St George's Hall, which held two thousand people, was extremely well received. Earlier in the week it was not selling, as it was only a week after Christmas, there was heavy snow and we were new to the city. The tide was turned by a letter in the *Yorkshire Post*, with a large heading above it: FILL ST GEORGE'S HALL TONIGHT. It was from S. E. Best of Doncaster Grammar School (the Headmaster, Dr Sidney Best), in which he asked the public not to be misled by the term 'youth orchestra' and miss the concert. For him, hearing it at Edinburgh had been 'one of the greater experiences of my life'. Dr Best was a Bradfordian and I'm sure this helped. Many members of the former Yorkshire Symphony Orchestra came over from Leeds (some had pupils with us), and the loyalty of Yorkshire parents and friends played a part. There wasn't an empty seat.

By the time they all went home from Bradford we seemed to have an integrated team, in spite of so many new members. We could confidently plan to invite our royal patron to our next London concert, with Sir Malcolm Sargent conducting, to spend a week in Brussels and perhaps Amsterdam too, and expect to be in form for the honour of the BBC's invitation for a Promenade Concert in the summer. I could sense as they said goodbye that they were accepting the challenge ahead with eager anticipation.

*

On 28 January we had a very tough Executive Meeting. I was able to report a subscription from Boosey & Hawkes. They had previously been part of the opposition, but their instrumental sales were soaring with the increase of school orchestras and we accepted this conversion gratefully. There were gifts from Pattersons Publications (Malcolm Arnold's publisher) and from Columbia Gramophone Co. for playing for the Edinburgh souvenir record.

All the plans for Easter, including televising the RFH concert, Brussels, the Prom with Sir Adrian conducting, were agreed. I mentioned my difficulty, because of the Children's Act of 1933 and LCC regulations, in proving to the BBC that a nine-year-old soloist could appear on television. The Executive knew someone in the Ministry of Education, who solved the problem a few weeks later. They also supported my suggestion that we might play in Amsterdam after Brussels, thereby covering two capital cities for the expense of one journey. All these matters were reported to the Council meeting in the afternoon, and many members appreciated the quality of our printing and posters designed by the *Mirror*.

The next day I wrote to the leading impresario in Amsterdam, Concertdirecte J. Beek. Madame Beek replied that a concert in Amsterdam was not possible, but suggested we played in Maastricht where she ran a festival which always had a British contribution and they were going to open a new concert hall. It seemed an attractive idea and worth pursuing.

I met Mme Beek in Amsterdam and we drove to Maastricht, a charming place, partly old-world market town and partly new post-war development. To my surprise the new hall was little more than an outline site with scaffolding showing potential shape and size. I asked the builder in charge when it would be finished. He hoped before Christmas, or in early 1956. With no possibility of playing there, we moved to the Dominican church, a most attractive setting for chamber music, but sadly quite inadequate for our large symphony orchestra plus piano. I measured the space, when Mme Beek said the BBCSO had played there last year, and on the way back to Amsterdam I worked hard on how to cut our numbers without wrecking our programme (already fixed for Brussels). Accommodation was going to be hospitality in families, and gradually it emerged that our concert would be in the afternoon, and for children, for whom our programme would be unsuitable. Then it dawned on me that Mme Beek had an entirely erroneous conception of the NYO, namely that of a school orchestra on holiday, entertaining other schoolchildren. I tried to explain our work and that I would willingly play in Amsterdam, but didn't think I could make a success of the Maastricht project with our huge orchestra and Brussels programme. Perhaps another year when the new concert hall was finished? To my amazement she said, 'If you don't come to Maastricht I will see that you *never* play in Amsterdam.' Concertdirecte J. Beek were powerful people, but I don't like threats and I had tried hard to adapt to the Maastricht idea.

Before leaving Amsterdam I went to talk to Mr Van Leer. From the time he first heard us in the Albert Hall in 1951 he had been most generous and very keen for us to come to Amsterdam one day. I told him I'd wanted to come in April but couldn't get a hall. I found this rather sad, Ghetty-like millionaire genuinely fond of children and music. He'd wanted to invite the NYO so that once seen and heard the same idea could be copied for Holland. I suggested 1956 or '57 and left for home, reassured by his welcoming friendship.

On my return I went to see my Executive Chairman, Maurice Jacobson. Sound musician as he was, he thought we should not risk our reputation by cutting the orchestra's size to fit the church; and our programme was unsuitable for a children's concert. However, it soon emerged that John Denison, a member of the Committee, was a close friend of Mme Beek's, and arranged the British contribution to her festival. Anger reared its ugly head. It raged between them; both raged at me. An extraordinary meeting was called, by which time

Maurice had had a telegram confirming that the new hall in Maastricht could not be ready in 1955. John maintained that if we didn't go to Maastricht it would damage Britain's reputation in Amsterdam. If we had been discussing breaking a contract the atmosphere couldn't have been worse, but it was only an invitation. The Committee eventually voted against going and composed a beautiful letter to the Burgemeester of Maastricht.

This simple decision was complicated by the fact that two days earlier Mr Van Leer had sent us a wonderful invitation to give two concerts in the Concertubuow in Amsterdam, the whole orchestra to be his guests for two days. The Chairman decided not to raise this until the Maastricht decision was taken. A sentence was then added to the Burgemeester's letter: '. . . great regret that we cannot present the orchestra in Maastricht on this occasion, but to show our good will to Holland we are now considering an invitation from Mr Van Leer to play in Amsterdam.' Needless to say, in due course this generous offer was accepted. It is always pleasing when threats are unexpectedly overcome, but what mattered was that our children would now experience the honour of playing in the Concertubuow.

Nineteen

With only six weeks to the RFH concert, and by far the biggest undertaking in our history ahead, Diana and I set off to Canterbury, which was going to be our home for the Easter course. We had been offered the Simon Langton School for Girls for our work in the daytime, and Kent College, a boarding school, for accommodation. How good the education authorities and heads of schools were to us! How grateful we were that this wasn't a 'mattress course', and to Canterbury for finding us a home not too far from the RFH, and so convenient for the boat to Belgium.

Leaving Diana to cope with all the travel arrangements, by road, by sea and by rail, I concentrated on matters musical, and went to see Sir Malcolm. He was looking forward to coming, happy about the programme, his stay in Canterbury, and televising the concert. Then he suddenly asked, 'How old is the soloist?'

'Nine.'

'Can she play well enough?'

'Yes.'

'Can I hear her?'

'She is so special I want it to be a surprise.'

'Very well: I trust you.'

It was important to see Hugo Rignold, hoping he could spare the extra days for Amsterdam, to explain I would take two soloists as I didn't want such young children to play every night, and to give him a score of the new British work. This time I had asked Gordon Jacob to write a piece for us. He not only came to a rehearsal and a concert, but created a prelude and toccata scored for everybody. Finished in good time, with all the parts complete and exact, his final touch of generosity was to dedicate it in his own handwriting across the score to me and my orchestra.

My special soloist was Wendy Waterman, who was the pupil and niece of Fanny Waterman. It is one thing for a child to play at a London concert, another to play for a week abroad. Fanny's pupil Allan Schiller had been such a success in Edinburgh, so I put to her the idea of taking them both abroad, playing alternate nights. She was marvellous, suggesting that she would come herself and take full responsibility for both children off my hands, and persuaded Wendy's mother. I'm so grateful to her, as it was a weight off my mind, and enabled Belgium and Holland to hear these two exceptional talents.

In the hope that our royal patron might be able to come to the concert, I thought of having a special fanfare. Who better to compose it than the Master of the Queen's Music? Next day I went to see Sir Arthur Bliss. He was the most charming and friendly person, and even suggested coming down to Canterbury to meet everybody and rehearse it.

And so to the children and their parents. Although the fees for the course were paid in most cases by the LEA, we used our small emergency fund to subsidise those with the most expensive journeys to Canterbury. In 1955 rationing was over, but money was not plentiful and all our parents, including those who paid for their children's education, made sacrifices for them to come to us. So far the new welfare state had not removed independence and responsibility in the family. Passports were less of a problem this time, and soon all Diana's travel plans were complete. Together we made ready the two schools lent to us for our musical life in the great historic and beautiful city of Canterbury.

During the week we made time for everyone to see the great cathedral, attend an organ recital one evening and go to the Sunday choral service there if they wished. In the choir was a small red-haired boy who joined our percussion department the following year.*

Then came the morning when Sir Arthur Bliss was due to arrive, and we'd lined up the brass section to greet him in the entrance hall. Time went by and he didn't come; presuming the train was late, they went back to work. There was a long drive from the school gates to the entrance, and looking out I spotted a lone figure walking determinedly towards us in the rain. It was Sir Arthur. Somehow he had missed our car at the station, and had set out to walk over two miles to get to us on time. He had brought his fanfare and parts, and immediately went into action, rehearsing and conducting our brass players, adding extra ideas on the way. He was a great personality, radiating enjoyment and teaching with authority. He spent the rest of the day with us, moving around the different classes with enthusiasm and encouragement. Nobody present will have forgotten the day the Master of the Queen's Music spent with us.

Excitement mounted in anticipation of our President's arrival. Sir Malcolm was going to take the evening rehearsal: instruments were polished, hair tidied, everything was spick and span in the hall and tuning had started. We were talking in my room.

'I think I should explain how I like things done. I like the orchestra to be ready for me, and tuned before I come in, and my score put on the stand.'

'Yes, of course you do.'

'I wouldn't like them talking to each other or reading while I'm rehearsing some special part.'

'They won't do that: they're very polite and thrilled to have you.'

'Well, are you going now to get them ready for me?'

'No. They can manage. We'll start on the dot of five.' It suddenly dawned on me that conductors coming to us for the

*Christopher Seaman, now a well-known conductor.

first time were nervous, not knowing what to expect or how they would manage such young players. In fact Sir Malcolm took a marvellous rehearsal, not wasting a minute and increasingly enjoying it.

Before he left for the hotel he asked where they all were now, and I said they were eating their supper. He asked if he could go and see, and of course I said he could join us if he liked but it was only sausage and mash. No, he wouldn't stay, but he walked round a few tables, and after we left the room he said, 'Well, they certainly seem to be all right.'

'Of course they're all right. Couldn't you hear the excitement in the voices?'

'Then why didn't they give me a hand?'

Quickly I explained that we didn't usually clap after rehearsals with instruments in hand. 'We stand in respect at the start and in appreciation at the end; and I'd think it a bit condescending for beginners to congratulate you, but it is just a matter of taste and style.'

'Ah yes,' he said. 'Good taste. Very important. I understand.'

From the next morning, through the next two days and the RFH, the TV rehearsal and the concert, he just became part of us; he loved children and established a special rapport. He was very touched one evening by the playing of a small girl on the cor anglais.* She had been given the instrument as a birthday present and had only had it a week, but was going to play the famous solo in the *New World Symphony*. At this last rehearsal he stopped and said, 'Is that all right for you tomorrow, or would you like to do it again?' and she replied, 'Yes please.' Perhaps the tough world of professional music had provided an armour which the keen freshness of a child's first experience had penetrated, but he was very moved. Nor did he hide the emotion he felt when he first heard Wendy play.

On the last evening we revealed all the plans for the great day, sharing out responsibilities and answering all kinds of questions

*Tess Miller.

so that nothing would take them by surprise. Highly strung children can easily be upset by the unexpected – the heat of the lights, cameras very close, different seating. The house staff reported more ironing, hair-washing, trimming and beautification than ever before. In 1955 to be on TV for a whole concert was a great thrill.

It was an early start from Canterbury, but by nine-thirty everyone was in the Festival Hall, some excited to have glimpsed London from the buses for the first time. All who were new since 1953 were amazed by the size and layout of the RFH. The BBC people were marvellous in co-operating with our platform arrangements and adjusting their lighting and cameras accordingly. One cameraman spent twenty minutes finding a way to avoid shine and reflection on the piano keyboard when I told him the pianist was only nine.

Then came the platform rehearsal for both TV lighting and sound-testing, and we were ready for Sir Malcolm and little Wendy and a full rehearsal. It was hard to believe that so small a child had the tone and power of an adult, and the size of the huge hall presented no problems.

After the rehearsal and lunch, there was time for a rest or sleep in the comfortable seats in the empty hall, and later time for an hour in the fresh air. For many, to be in London, looking at the Thames and Westminster from the RFH terraces, was all part of a different and bigger experience than ever before. Watching them relaxing and strolling in the late-afternoon sun, anticipating the excitement to come, you could almost see them growing up as in slow-motion photography.

There wasn't an empty seat in the hall. The Mendelssohn overture, *Ruy Blas*, really sparkled. But the phenomenon of the evening was Wendy Waterman playing the Bach D Minor concerto. She took control of orchestra and conductor – who had started too fast – with absolute conviction, a performance so musical, with such rhythmic power and sensitive delicacy. Shut your eyes and this was no child playing; open them and there was this tiny nine-year-old compelling the entire audience into the truth of Bach. It was stunning, but also a deeply moving and spiritual experience. Looking back over forty years, it remains for me one of the great performances of my lifetime in music.

The new work by Gordon Jacob was well received and the *New World Symphony*, played with the freshness that comes from the first experience of performing a great work, together with Sir Malcolm's own enjoyment of the responsibility in his hands, created a rousing climax. When the applause had finally faded the whole orchestra assembled in a large area near the lifts so that our Chairman Douglas Guest and his wife could bring important guests to walk around the circle, talking to the children and meeting the staff. Then Lord John Hope (now Earl Glendevon), Under-Secretary of State for Foreign Affairs, came round to encourage us as we set off to represent Britain in Belgium and Holland. He spoke briefly and seriously about what it meant to represent your country, and about the suffering of the Belgians, and especially the Dutch, in the war, and to build new friendships for the future. He was able, in about two minutes, to make us all feel that our little effort, if well done, was important. He achieved in mood just what was needed to turn the corner from a triumphant evening towards the adventure that lay ahead.

While the orchestra was sinking into sleep on the night drive back to Canterbury, John and I, still in the hall, were told that the BBC counted the live TV programme a major success. There was a message from Cecil McGivern, Head of Television, expressing his delight, and congratulations from the Head of Music, Kenneth Wright, whose idea it was. Any anxiety about the extra heat and strong light upsetting such young players proved unfounded. It was hot; intonation was difficult; they managed splendidly.

But there was one disaster. After all the *Mirror*'s generosity and their acceptance of minimum publicity, there had been no mention at all on TV of their sponsorship. I don't know who should have looked after that, but I felt responsible, and it took me a long time to get over what was such utter meanness from us to a very generous sponsor.

At breakfast in Canterbury, all was chatter about the hall and the TV. There was the usual eagerness to know if they'd done well: 'How did it go?', 'Was Sir Malcolm pleased?', 'Was the TV OK?' And so to the usual packing, and off to Dover. Although we had many who had never put a foot in a foreign land or heard a foreign tongue, we were more experienced travellers than when we left for Paris in 1950. The sun shone and with no delay we were soon in Ostend, and into our reserved-coach train for Brussels. There was a warm welcome from the officials concerned and about a hundred Belgian parents had come to claim one member each as their guest for the week. Soon all would be sound asleep, scattered through the homes and streets of a European capital city.

Reunited on the platform of the great Palais des Beaux-Arts the following morning, it was as usual amazing how pleased they were to see each other again – they might have been separated or imprisoned for weeks – but no one more pleased than I. Preparing for rehearsal was so much easier this time, when about a third of the orchestra had been with us for three years and so were in Brussels in 1953. Looking round the foyer we discovered we were announced on a huge display of posters as '*l'événement du récent Festival d'Edimbourg au Palais des Beaux-Arts*', with an exhibition of photographs of our work and concerts, which must have been supplied by the *Mirror*. On our last night there would again be a '*concert symphonique de gala placé sous le patronage de son excellence Monsieur l'Ambassadeur de Grande-Bretagne*'. We were pleased that we had four nights to get into a routine, improve the performance to a climax and be at our best for Amsterdam.

I went to find Hugo Rignold, who had once again agreed to take over from Sir Malcolm for the week abroad, so this was a very important rehearsal. How quickly would the orchestra adapt to subtle changes of interpretation? Hugo was most professional in accepting Sir Malcolm's performance, getting the players' confidence and moulding differences of expression through the next four nights. Fanny Waterman's two special pupils were in cheerful form after a comfortable night in a hotel. We all agreed that Allan, now twelve, would play this first night, then Wendy, and one concert each in Amsterdam.

Soon after midday hostesses arrived to claim their guests. How charming and hospitable they were, all making plans to show them the sights of Brussels and the neighbouring countryside. Before they left I heard, 'My hostess says it's St George's Day and Shakespeare's birthday: is that right?' and 'I'm being taken to the Battle of Waterloo. I knew there was a battle but I thought it was in Spain.' Maybe cracks in the brave new English educational system were showing through. 'I'm speaking French but they think it's that funny' – French in a strong Glasgow accent can be. Sister was always available, surveying her charges. My colleagues and I assessed the mood and felt that the RFH and the journey were far away, and with the resilience of the young all minds were on the opening concert tonight.

The Palais des Beaux-Arts, lit up for an evening concert, is a very large and impressive hall, with two balconies like a theatre, so it can seem full to the roof. There was an atmosphere of curiosity and anticipation and excited chatter. Allan, who was very small and looked about ten, played the Haydn D Major like a professional and so artistically, deserving the rousing reception. Wendy created a sense of wonder on her nights. The Dvořák symphony suited players and listeners, growing in confidence and changing here and there as the evenings went by, with Hugo always in control yet stimulating enthusiasm. Recently one of the players wrote, 'I remember vividly the wonderful reception we received every night from those youngish audiences, and how we looked forward to each concert. I think I played better each time, I was so happy.'

One morning there was a surprise: an invitation to Hugo, John and me for lunch with Queen Elizabeth, the Queen Mother of the Belgians. We were driven to Laken Palace, with rooms of such space and peace, a perfection of style. I can still see the design on the lovely damask tablecloth. Of course Her Majesty was a musician, a violinist, and we had some talk about Ysaÿe, with whom my mother had studied, and the Queen Elizabeth Competition, which she founded and which is now world-renowned. When we were about to take our leave she suddenly asked if we could stay and have some music. She produced a violin for Hugo as well as her own fine instrument, and thought Purcell sonatas for two violins and piano would be just right. That afternoon playing Purcell and Handel trios in those surroundings, with so artistic and beautiful a person as the Queen Mother of the Belgians, is a special lifelong memory.

After three days it was time for a morning of real work. To keep the standard, individual practice could be done at 'home', but Hugo found shaky moments in the symphony to tighten up, and I wanted to improve the orchestral accompaniment for the concerti. As we were all together we used the opportunity to check that postcards were being sent home and to announce the arrangements for getting to Amsterdam and back.

The question I was expecting soon came: 'What are our paper bags for?' When Diana was preparing all the travel plans, there was a problem of expense. Buses for us and a small van for the heavy instruments were possible on our budget, but a larger van to include 120 suitcases was too expensive. In a moment of inspiration I suggested leaving them behind in Brussels ready for our train to Ostend, and 'travelling light', as the wartime posters implored, each with a paper bag. On to the inventory went *One large strong paper bag with strong handles*. (There were no plastic bags in 1955.) Now we explained that on Thursday morning each was to contain a sponge-bag, pyjamas, clean shirt, the minimum absolute necessities for Amsterdam. After a huge burst of laughter came a stunned look of utter astonishment: was it a joke? A voice from Glasgow said, 'All the way to Amsterdam in a paper bag!' answered by London: 'We're not going to the moon *yet* yer know.' From Yorkshire came, 'We would'na have brought 'em for nothing,' and from Ireland:

'And what if it should rain?', and so on. Imagination flowed. The concert that night was splendid.

Next day was 27 April, the gala concert. The hall was not completely full, the atmosphere quieter and stiffer to break into, but Queen Elizabeth was present, as was the British Ambassador Sir Christopher Warner and his wife, and other VIPs from the musical and educational establishments of Brussels. Our hosts thought it was our best concert, certainly a festive occasion, and a last night. As it happened it was the last time we ever played in Brussels, as invitations to wider spheres increased. The press and leading musicians were tremendously impressed with the standard achieved. They thought it was far in advance of anything of its kind in Europe, and found it hard to believe these were not college music students. Their attitude to work, discipline and manners was considered a fine example of something that only the British could do so well.

The Queen insisted on coming behind the scenes after the concert, speaking to members individually, and the two small soloists most affectionately. She hoped we would come again. The Ambassador reported her appreciation of 'a very remarkable achievement and one that must make your country proud'.

To have our ambassador with us on foreign tours mattered enormously to us. Knowing sound advice was available in a crisis, or a political problem, was vital; and an objective report would go back to the Foreign Office and to our patron on the impression we'd left behind. Better still, they would come round after concerts, giving the players a chance to meet an ambassador personally. After Sir Christopher had left I overheard, 'What do ambassadors actually *do*?' A boy replied, 'They're there to show you that England never leaves you wherever you go.' They certainly never left us. In the next ten years, in Portugal, Greece, Israel, Russia, they were always there.

As in 1953, the people of Brussels had taken 110 British children into their homes, for most a world unimagined before, giving them a marvellous week and handing them back fit and

16. A Royal Festival Hall concert

17. Ernest Hall

18. Allan Schiller at the Edinburgh Festival, 1951

19. Dody Trygvason (Ashkenazy) in Hull

20. Queen Elizabeth the Queen Mother of the Belgians talking to Wendy Waterman and Allan Schiller, April 1955

21. Sir Malcolm Sargent in rehearsal

22. Hugo Rignold with Nic

23. (*right*) Diana Scholefield

24. Frederick Thurston, rest time, his last course with the NYO, 1952

25. The Promenade Concert with Sir Adrian Boult, August 1955

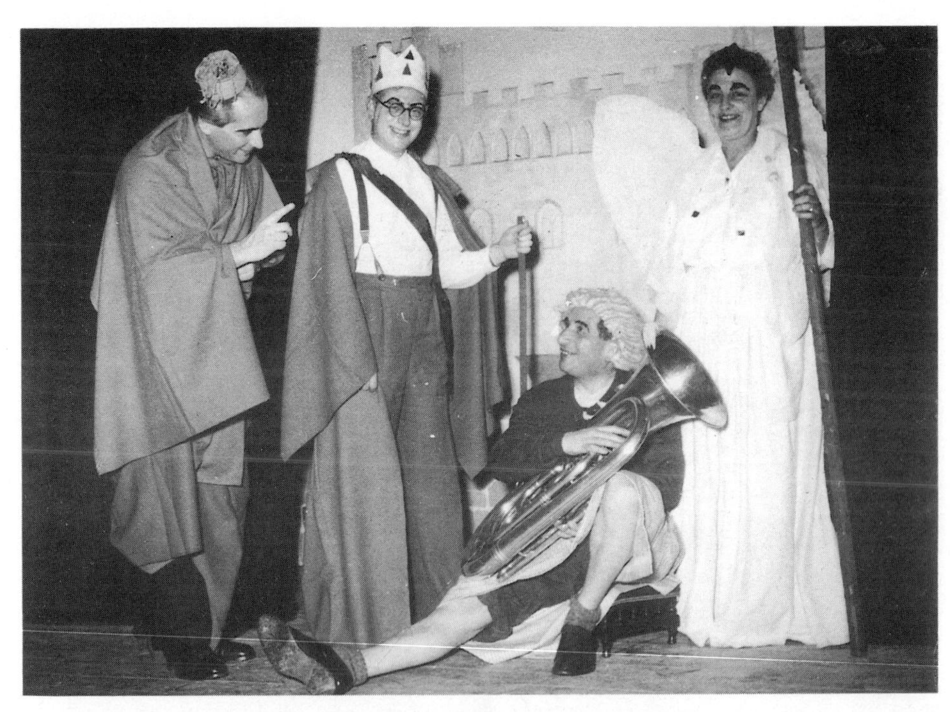

26. The pantomime, Swansea, 1956:
Walter Susskind, Gareth Morris, Leonard Hirsch and Sister Boddy

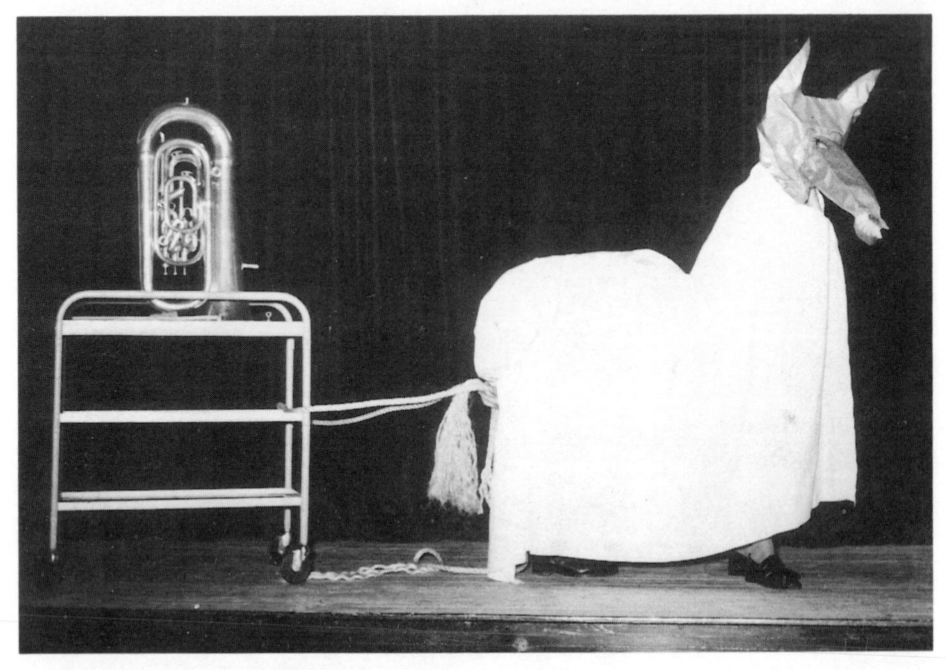

'Beware the back legs, do not hammer on.
They are the legs of Douglas Cameron.'

3
4
НАЦИОНАЛЬНЫЙ
МОЛОДЕЖНЫЙ
СИМФОНИЧЕСКИЙ ОРКЕСТР
ВЕЛИКОБРИТАНИИ
ДИРИЖЕР
ФЬЁЛЬДСТАД
СОЛИСТ—
ЭНТОНИ
ВЕБЕР
МОЦАРТ
МОЦАРТ
БРИТТЕН
СОЛИСТ—
АЛЛАН
ШИЛЛЕР
(ФОРТЕПЬЯНО)

28. A poster announcing the Moscow concerts

29. Derek Bourgeois, later Director of the NYO, and Stephen Baker

30. Moragh McLeod, soloist in Moscow, and Gordon Nelson

31. The Westminster Abbey concert, August 1957

32. The endless queue; the complete photograph was printed across a double spread in the *Daily Mirror*

well, with affectionate farewells at the buses for Amsterdam. Recently one of our then violinists wrote to me:

> I was very lucky with my hosts on both trips to Brussels. With three others you arranged for me to stay with Mme Titeca who was the organiser of the Jeunesses Musicales. Her husband was a psychiatrist with a private clinic in the extensive grounds of his house outside the city. We enjoyed a luxurious standard of hospitality very different from the life-style that any of us were accustomed to in England at that time. I still remember the wonderful smells that wafted up from the kitchen . . . the Waterloo museum containing the vastest painting of the battle . . . buying lace for my mother from a little old lady dressed entirely in black in the cobbled side streets around the Grande Place . . . trying our school French and finding ourselves very inexpert . . . the whole family extremely welcoming . . . and for most of us our first excursion abroad.*

The Belgian parents must have left a hundred such priceless memories on our adolescents. Mme Titeca was a very special person. She is Brussels for me.

It was raining the next morning as I watched everyone assembling beside our coaches with the most astonishing array of (well-labelled) paper bags. A housemaster was checking his charges individually as they climbed in: 'Music, instrument, passport . . .' and into the hold went the somewhat damp paper bags. At least this journey started with laughter, and without the burden of heavy suitcases. Behind our splendiferous coaches followed all our instrumental possessions in our inexpensive little van. Soon we were at the Dutch border, Diana dealing with papers and instruments while a handsome, smartly uniformed official came into the coaches to check our numbers. 'English children very welcome,' he said as we held up our

*Colin Gough, later leader of the NYO, now Professor of Physics at Birmingham University.

passports and didn't have to get out; 'I never see so many before.'

'It's like being in a zoo,' said one small boy.

Almost immediately one could sense a different country, efficient and tidy. The scenery was so flat but the windmills, an occasional tulip field, canals and then the sight of the city and going through some of its narrow streets made the long drive a pleasure. Our destination was an excellent, spotlessly clean hostel. Officials from the Van Leer organisation, a large industrial concern, were there to greet us, and keen to supply our every need. After settling in we all agreed that exercise was the way to spend the early evening; so our hosts arranged groups and took them to a nearby park. A car was at hand so John and I set off with two boys for the famous Concertubuow to check the safe arrival of our instruments; then we planned and timed all the arrangements for the next day. Our devoted staff ironed on through the night, having rescued the best concert-day shirts as they emerged from their damp paper bags.

Amsterdam's generous hospitality provided first-class meals throughout our stay, and one of the most memorable days in our history started early with a Dutch breakfast then quickly off to the rehearsal. The Concertubuow had a special atmosphere, not too big, wonderful for sound, no sign of concrete, and a great sense of tradition. We had been told of damage in the war, but the essential proportions and the old wood in walls and ceiling had been saved. We needed every inch of the platform, which could only be entered from one side; the main artists' rooms were a floor higher so that conductor and soloist came down steps on to the stage – very unusual. I spotted a small window at this level from which you could watch the performance from behind the scenes – where John or I would always be during a concert. It was ten-thirty before we started rehearsal, and it took time to adjust to the sound and balance, so different from the high-ceilinged hall in Brussels. Soon they began to relish the new resonance, and the special blend of musical sound which belongs to the Concertubuow alone.

For the afternoon concert the hall was filled with a mainly young audience, with some teachers, and there was even a queue at the box office hoping for returns. Allan Schiller captivated everybody with an inspiring performance of the Haydn, and the response to the symphony was quite overwhelming. At the buses we learnt that most hadn't ever heard it before; some had never been to a concert – all part of Mr Van Leer's plan to start something like us in Amsterdam. We could not linger, as every minute was needed back at the hostel to relax and refresh and devour an ample meal before getting back to repeat it all. We had never done two concerts on one day before.

There are always little crises before concerts. Every child was responsible for their own music, and tonight our smallest and youngest member, Simon Standage, had mislaid his part of the Bach. 'Never mind,' he said to his tearful partner, 'we can watch the others and pretend!' Simon's trousers were a bit too large and normally kept up by braces. When we were playing without jackets, at concerts, there was usually a call for 'Who's got Simon's safety pins?'

The evening concert was part of a series, and packed to the doors. I was behind the scenes with Wendy, listening to the overture, and after the applause saw her safely on to the platform, and made for the corridor with the little window to view her performance. But others had got there first. As we never had visitors backstage, I quickly asked a stage-hand who was there. 'They made me let them in; they are important people.' It was Mme Beek with her husband and a friend. Not daring to come openly to the concert but devoured by curiosity, they had got in secretly by the artists' door to find out for themselves what they had banned from Amsterdam.

I stayed by the platform exit, listening to the Bach, enthralled by such playing. It was as if some mysterious power was flowing through the small child. It ended. The entire audience stood up. Wendy bowed to silence and came tripping off the platform into my arms. 'They don't clap – didn't they like it?'

'They're clapping now,' I said. The applause was heartfelt through many re-calls.

Afterwards it was explained to us that on very rare occasions, with some great artist or outstanding performance, there is a purely intuitive, inexplicable response in the Concertubuow audience: they just stand, in silence. 'It is our greatest honour for you,' said some of the musicians who came to talk to us. For all of us it was a rare privilege.

The Dutch audience, which was rather quiet and stolid at the beginning, seemed to change in the interval. After the symphony they were so warm, and clearly appreciated Hugo Rignold. Conducting the NYO is a matter of constant concentration, alert for any mishap, and at times emotionally exhausting, as the young give so much, and yet depend so much. He had been splendid, totally reliable since taking over from Sir Malcolm. For the orchestra it was our last concert of the tour, and seemed the best. Next morning the press, *De Telegraaf* (headline: REMARKABLE CONCERT) and *De Volkskrant* (YOUTH ORCHESTRA IS A SUCCESS), explained very thoroughly what we were. To them, this was an unbelievable achievement: professional standard, artistic, exciting, two miraculous soloists of nine and eleven and a fine conductor. Today we had been accepted, not as 'youth' but on artistic merit, in another great capital city.

With great generosity Mr Van Leer had organised a whole day free in Amsterdam as his guests. The first event was a trip round the canals, undoubtedly the best way to get an impression of the character and style of the city and its people in a very short time, which was for us an April morning in the sun. Then we all arrived at the famous Amstil Hotel, and were shown on to a beautiful lawn touching the banks of the Amstil River. As we stood in a semicircle Mr Van Leer came to talk to us. Of course it was our opportunity to thank him publicly, and he seemed moved by the orchestra's appreciation. He knew the concerts had been splendid and now the Dutch would copy our example and have their own youth orchestras in the Netherlands. He then invited us to lunch in this wonderful hotel, which was a great treat.

Later in the afternoon there was an official reception in the Town Hall. After the official welcome and our reply, the Deputy Burgemeester made a very impressive speech in perfect English. Starting with the history of the ancient Town Hall, he referred to the Dutch as a small seafaring people who had founded an empire, as we had done from our own shores: 'The character of the people had strength from always fighting the sea, to reclaim land to live on . . . and fighting wars . . . for independence and freedom at all costs.' He mentioned the British part in the war, including Arnhem, and then told of the struggle for survival of the Dutch under occupation and how thirty thousand people had died of starvation in Amsterdam alone; then looked to the new generations and the new Europe of which we were all part. It was spoken from the heart, and the effect on our young was stunned amazement.

It was back in the hostel at supper when the reaction came. 'Why didn't we know about the war here? What was Arnhem? Dying of *starvation*? Thirty thousand with nothing to eat? The "Occupation" – why aren't we told about it all in school?' Why indeed! Should we shelter our children from their own recent history? Of course British children cannot comprehend occupation, but shouldn't they know what their grandparents' and parents' generation went through? In a lighter vein they commented, 'Our Lord Mayor couldn't talk like that in a foreign language!' and 'Today alone has been worth a whole term in school!'

It had been a wonderful day. They had given the best that was in them, and been so generously rewarded by the people of Amsterdam. Now it was sleep, and packing, and an early start for the long trek home.

On Sunday morning the packing party sent our van on its way; the staff were checking everybody into the coaches: 'Instrument, music, passport,' and the remains of the paper bags, with the odd pyjama leg or shirtsleeve protruding, were safely stacked for their last trip. As we said goodbye one of Mr Van Leer's officials handed me a letter containing an invitation to come back in August. As we set off John summed up: 'It seems we have vindicated the threat of harming Britain's reputation in Holland.'

Then came the first crisis. Six boys helping with packing the van and checking our instruments decided it would be hot in the coaches, and put their jackets in the van also. As it drove away they realised, too late, that their passports were in their jacket pockets. They expected to make contact with the van at the border, not realising it would be at least an hour ahead of us, to allow time to transfer its contents into the Brussels train. This was serious: we could not leave six children behind. We made a plan. We asked the staff member at the front of each bus to collect all the passports together in the hope that border officials might not have time to count them. I spent part of the journey rehearsing in my mind the sad tale of six passports waiting cosily in jacket pockets in Brussels, and brushing up my powers of persuasion in case an individual check was asked for. Luck was on our side: we were late at the border. John found a senior official, and pleaded for urgent help: to get 110 children to a special train at Brussels, and we were short of time. The officer was very experienced, but charmable, and sensed that I was really desperate to get those children to Ostend that night. With paper formalities complete, the piles of passports were not counted and he told the drivers to pull on to a side road and go through ahead of the queue. He seemed to enjoy the thanks, applause and waving from the windows as we glided away.

On this journey I made a decision. For young children who haven't travelled before, journeys in foreign trains and coaches, with a violin in one hand and a heavy suitcase in the other, and four different habitations in ten days, was too much. Our next foreign tour would be by air.

Soon we were in the station at Brussels, facing a night in Ostend. May 1 dawned, and we were on the first boat for England, searching in the sunlight for the first sight of the white cliffs of Dover. The boat was late, missing our reserved-carriage train and van, but somehow everybody squashed into an overcrowded train to Victoria. Of course this was vital as some members had trains to catch to Aberdeen, Leeds, Liverpool or Cornwall, and nowhere to stay in London.

On the journey we arranged for everybody going to Kings Cross to get off first. At Victoria there were no porters in sight, but John found an inspector and explained our urgent need. Suddenly he said, 'Are you the orchestra on TV?' . . . and as by magic porters and trolleys appeared, double basses and cellos were heaved into taxis, and soon all the long-journey members were rushed off to Kings Cross and Euston. The porters had seen our programme too, and stayed to help everybody, muttering, 'It was smashing, when are you on again?' until there were just a few of us left who were going home from Victoria. Just one TV appearance and everybody at the station and docks saw our labels and came up to comment, thank or wish us well. It was my first experience of the power of television.

London, Brussels, Amsterdam: eight concerts in ten days, many new impressions on many young minds, and by midnight all our 110 would be safely in their own homes all over Britain. Only then, with relief and thanksgiving, did I fall asleep.

It was time to report our adventures to the Executive Committee. John Newsom had had many letters from education officers about the RFH concert, saying they were most impressed and moved, and that we should return next April. Invitations had now come in from Germany, Italy and Dublin, and at home from Swansea, Leicester and Bristol again.

Roland Bird didn't seem unduly worried about a £1,000 loss on the recent tour; and so we made immediate plans for the Promenade Concert in August. The urgent problem was that we had nowhere to live for the summer course culminating in the Prom. This time it was the Borough of East Ham that came to our rescue. They lent us the Thomas Lethaby School, and provided every possible help and support. It was, alas, a mattress-on-floor week, but we had enormous help from the engineer resident in the school. He'd been in the Army, so for extra plumbing, furniture-moving or organising rehearsal-rooms, he had the answer. The East End of London then was a community and everybody knew everybody else, and many came to offer help. It was in East Ham that I had discovered John Lill, and got some local-authority support for him so that he could go on to the RCM. There was nowhere in East Ham to give a concert to repay so much kindness, but the Mayor gave a reception in the Town Hall and we met many local people. We had been asked to play in Watford, which was not too far away, and many came to that.

Some months earlier Sir Adrian had asked to see me. He wanted to help a young conductor from America get started in England: would I consider employing this unknown person for part of our course and perhaps the Watford concert? Sir Adrian would come for two whole days after and do the Prom. Only once, in the Hull emergency, had I ever employed anybody whose talent and ability I did not know well, and my colleagues and I did not need another conductor. This was impossible. Sir Adrian was our President, he and his wife had been kind to me, he had a problem, and we needed him for the Prom – and so did the BBC – but what could I do? Against my better judgement I agreed to see George Hurst, a charming personality, and if possible to let him conduct. My only comfort was that he might be some undiscovered genius, and be useful in the future.

On 18 August, 135 members arrived in East Ham. Many had been working since the end of term to help pay their fare and fee: on farms, in restaurants, in offices, one as a lifeguard on Brighton Beach. They were so pleased to be together again as they lugged suitcases and instruments beside mattresses in classrooms and gyms.

Our Prom had sold out as soon as booking opened, and we were all caught out. Parents couldn't get tickets, and we had none for our Council and Committee members. The disappointment eased a little when they heard the whole concert was going out live on the Third Programme.

In those days the Prom concerts were very long, the first half just over an hour. The BBC had asked us to give the first performance of a new work that they had commissioned by Cedric Thorpe Davie, with us in mind. He took endless trouble to keep in touch while composing it, and spent a day with us in East Ham sorting out any problems. Knowing that the new work would take a lot of rehearsal time, we had decided to repeat the Dvořák symphony which we had just done in Brussels and Amsterdam.

Our violin soloist was a young ex-member of eighteen, Ralph Holmes, who had played the Mendelssohn with us in Brussels in 1953. He had been called up, but I managed to get him two days' leave for the Prom, but not for the extra day at Watford. Another ex-member, John Bacon, then a student at the RAM, stepped in at short notice. When work was fully under way we paused one afternoon to attend a reception by the Mayor and Education Department of East Ham, without whom we would have had nowhere to meet.

Not all musicians and conductors are teachers. If something is not right, 'Let's do it again' won't make it so. But George Hurst was always accommodating and with more help from our professors managed the Watford concert successfully. The Mayor spoke to the orchestra on the platform after the concert, and invited them back again. He also sent a telegram on the day of the Prom.

The next two days with Sir Adrian were very important. Changing conductors on a programme is difficult at any time. At the end of the first morning the astonishing contrast with Hurst's style was disturbing. It was looser and freer, and to our players seemed insecure; by lunch-time it was as if the screws and bolts of the orchestral machine were falling apart. In the evening I went with Malcolm Arnold to the back of the orchestra. 'Wait a bit,' he said, 'just wait and listen and you'll hear a new sound grow.' He was right. I had discovered the essence of Sir Adrian's gift as a musician; it lay in the kind of sound he could create, and how it came about.

As time went by it was as if a breath was lifting a skeleton, stretching its limbs and warming its whole orchestral body. The reins were looser, the sweep wider, and in one day the sound was totally different from the concert the night before. It was very difficult for such young players, and I sensed their anxiety. Before they went to bed I could say with conviction, 'Don't worry, I understand. We're creating a new sound to suit the size of the Albert Hall. It will be fine.' It was.

The Royal Albert Hall, completely empty at nine in the morning, is a place of fantastic size. As on previous occasions, the shock, the comments, the startled and excited faces at the first sight of it from the platform made a good start to a great day. How different the atmosphere at night: full to the last seat and with the standing crowd so close to them it was quite frightening, but emotionally thrilling.

Sir Adrian was in his element, really enjoying it all. As the symphony drew to its close I was thinking that my special children had worked hard and had another great experience, and what more can we give our children than that? We were the first amateur orchestra to play at the Proms, and I felt that Sir Henry Wood, my teacher and friend, would have been pleased.

The press, always so encouraging, produced a new headline: WORLD'S MOST *UNUSUAL* TRAINING SCHOOL. At last someone had got us right, instead of presuming we recruited ready-made players. The BBC was very pleased with the broadcast and remembered to mention the *Mirror*. And that was the end of an exceptional year for the National Youth Orchestra of Great Britain.

Twenty

After such an adventurous and expansive year we needed time for steady development on home ground. The Executive decided on Wales at Christmas, England at Easter and Scotland in the summer. So we accepted a very warm invitation from Swansea; the RFH was already booked; we were delighted to be invited back to the Edinburgh Festival after deserting them for the Prom. The BBC had already invited us for another Prom and were very nice about our refusal of the honour, inviting us immediately for 1957.

The Treasurer reported that we had overspent, but everyone agreed not to put up the fees, as together with fares the cost to each student was £30 for the year, and some of them couldn't get grants.

Before throwing myself into the next round of auditions I went to see Sir Thomas Beecham. He was welcoming and amusing, and asked after my family of musicians. I wasted no time in saying they were looking forward to meeting him. Easter in London? Summer in Edinburgh? I produced lovely photographs of the children to entice him.

'I do not need beguiling, Miss Railton. I remember what I saw and heard myself.'

'Then will you come?'

'That will depend on my wife.' Betty Humby was a most sensitive pianist in her day. She had had every opportunity and the best attention herself as a student in the Matthay School. But now she was ill, and wouldn't let him come to us. She thought it *infra dig.* for him to conduct kids.

Walter Susskind was now back in England. When he was conducting in Canada we could have him in the summer; when in Australia, we could only have him at Christmas. Now he could do both. I accepted gratefully as time was short and he was so much part of the NYO. Jean Martinon could do the RFH at Easter.

Meanwhile Diana and her new secretary, Amber Pares, were preparing the annual auditions. This year I would have about fifty vacancies, and on my choice depended the future of the NYO and its ever-increasing standard. With so much talent, it is easy to increase the size, but bigger isn't better, and fine talent needs individual attention. I decided to limit myself to 130 members and not hesitate to take them younger than previously; new members would most likely be aged from eleven to fifteen.

This was the ninth year I had covered the whole country. No longer did I have to face toughs from the SMA hounding me in my hotel, or threats from the Musicians' Union. The complaint now, from some teachers, was that when students came to us I changed their teacher. What happened was that they had such fine teaching with us, and talking to each other would discover that the big city could provide more for them than their locality or school. This was a real problem for good relations. We couldn't show children the best then prevent them searching for it in their area, but professionally it was sometimes an embarrassment, though not really our fault. I tried to teach the children, when we were all together, always to be grateful to the person who gave them their start.

Nine years had brought many changes. The candidates seemed bigger in size for their age, and pubescence earlier. There was still a boy who cycled twenty-five miles to his audition because there was no money at all in the house by Friday: a lovely, self-taught talent for whom we did find a teacher. There was also a coalminer's son, whose father and two brothers went down the mine, and his sister had work in the pit office.

'Could your father afford five guineas a lesson, if I found you a teacher in Manchester?'

'Yes, I think so, as it's getting quite difficult to use up all the money at the weekend.' In 1955 wages were rising, but there were fewer things like washing-machines to use them up. A career as a violinist, saving money for lessons, was a new idea. The boy won an open scholarship to the RCM before he was seventeen.

Sometimes the waiting-room would be near the audition-room, and I would enjoy overhearing the comments.

'How'd you get on? What's she like? Is she *old*?'

'I don't think so.'

'Come on, is she nice?'

'I don't know . . . she just smiles.'

Sometimes I would ask them why they wanted to join and once got the reply, 'I hear you go in as one sort of person and come out as another.'

Once, at the end of a long day in Ripon, parents arrived on the offchance that I would come out to supper in their Yorkshire farmhouse, before taking me to the last train to Leeds.

So many different kinds of people, circumstances, problems, memories. Little did I know that never again would I go to all these highways and byways; never again the night train from Waterloo to my native Cornwall and breakfast in Launceston College; never again the long southern tour of the ancient cathedral cities and the hospitality of so many famous schools; never again to be rescued and refreshed at a winter fireside far out on the Yorkshire moors.

Once our choice had been made, music and all details for travel and the concert would be sent out, only arriving a few days before Christmas. It was on Christmas Eve that one mother rang to ask if there was a mistake; I had sent music marked *Timpani*, but her son had never *seen* a timp. Christopher Seaman was the lively red-haired Canterbury Cathedral chorister I had seen in 1955, who I thought would make a timpanist. He most certainly did, staying with us for six years.

There was a very warm welcome from Swansea, and a special

tribute is due to the Director of Education, Leslie Drew. We needed a lot of space and he found us a superbly run college, and the Bishop Gore School for rehearsals. I expected some Welsh nationalism, and this became apparent in the local paper. We had six Welsh members this time, none of whom had ever played in any Welsh youth orchestra, and one was a double-bass player, actually from Swansea. I hoped our week there would heal geographical barriers through mutual love of music.

The first course of the year was the most important, and nearly sixty new members was a lot. On the second day, the sound of the first full orchestral rehearsal was often quite overwhelming, especially for those who'd never played in one. I've known a player just stop, dazed, muttering, 'What a *wonderful* sound.' Some were nervous, and those I would help and encourage every day; others who were confident would find it difficult to adjust to so many people better than themselves. This kind of shock needed nursing too. With the instrumental mix, the mealtime mix, the dormitory mix and the New Year's Eve party, by the end of the week everybody would know everybody else and become the 1956 NYO.

We kept a special surprise for New Year's Day. I had written to Sibelius for his ninetieth birthday on 8 December and had a beautiful handwritten note in return, enclosing a flower from his garden. This was on display, and the children seemed delighted. One new member said, 'This is marvellous, it's as if you could touch him, and I thought he was dead *long* ago.'

Soon we were ready for Walter Susskind's first rehearsal, and from then on excitement reigned. Other events included Archie Camden, who was teaching the bassoons, giving an evening recital; so did Dennis Brain, after a day with the horns. John Dalby gave an organ recital in St James's Church, open to the public as well as our members. Our soloist was a thirteen-year-old pianist from Blackpool, Ann Pickup.

There was however one evening not filled, and I had said to John early in the week that between us we must produce some surprise event for them. The next day John came back with a hilarious topical version of *Cinderella*, in verse, fully cast by mid-morning in the staff-room. John, who was tall and thin, and Genin, who was short and round, were obvious ugly sisters; Gareth demanded to be the prince; and Leonard was Cinderella in a blond wig with long plaits. From then on all these famous musicians became totally involved, showing much talent for acting. When Walter arrived at tea-time he asked me what on earth was going on, then immediately asked for his part. I explained he couldn't be the prince because Gareth wanted it, and in a flash he said, 'I'll be Gareth's page.'

In the mean time Paul Cave had been working with the local press to help fill the Brangwyn Hall for our concert. He wanted me to come to talk on a radio programme and fixed a recording time after lunch, when I'd normally be free. He was stunned when I said, 'I can't come *then*: it's the only time we can rehearse the pantomime chorus.' His stinging reply was, 'I never thought *you* would put anything before the success of the NYO.' Of course I went; and when we got back Paul joined the chorus.

While the orchestra slept, sewing and pinning and cutting out cardboard went on into the night. Scripts were memorised in the lunch hour. The amazing thing was that the children had not the faintest suspicion of all this activity. I simply told them after supper that the 'surprise evening' involved a company of entertainers who would be half an hour late. They presumed it would be something Welsh, probably singers or harpists. That half-hour was our only rehearsal. Then came the moment, with all assembled as for some serious event.

When have so many world-famous musicians come together on a school stage to play the fool with such style, self-expression and originality, in order to give their young students some fun? Ivey Dickson was in her element, using only themes from the concert programme, to improvise according to whatever might happen on stage. Any gap and the chorus, always with the main theme from *Mastersingers*, would enter from left with 'We must obey orders from our staff only' or from right with 'Never forget your music, mute and instrument.' The glass slipper became a tuba mute that fitted nothing. A great entry was made by our nurse to

'Neath gossamer and tinsel shoddy
Comes our noble Sister Boddy.

And of course there was a pantomime horse:

Beware the back legs, do not hammer on.
They are the legs of Douglas Cameron

and the front legs leapt up to tug the curtain across when it got stuck.

The audience missed nothing, and the actors played to the uninhibited laughter. Everybody from the youngest and newest to the most famous was enriched by an evening of shared enjoyment.

The next morning was work as usual, the last day before the concert. We never knew quite how well a whole programme would pull together until the last evening when it took on a mood of its own: the first concert for so many new members. They were taught everything: packing, setting, order and care of instruments behind the scenes, stage presentation, platform manners; and pride in doing it all well.

On the night the Brangwyn Hall was full. After the national anthem we played 'Land of our fathers' as a good-will gesture. Ann's Mozart had its own beauty and delicacy, then after the interval came the Mendelssohn *Italian Symphony*. The concert ended with the Berlioz 'Hungarian March' reaching the exciting peak that was the art of Walter Susskind. The Welsh audience was exceptionally warm and emotionally responsive – wonderful to play to – and we all thought it was our best Christmas concert so far. I was glad we hadn't run away from Welsh nationalism and had experienced the real people of Swansea.

Sebastian Bell, now Flute Professor at the RAM, was a new member at Swansea. His memory is of my

> insistence that the performance should be rather better than was considered possible in *all* respects and as an introduction to this I recall your statement my first day that in the NYO we did not cough. Consequently in the course of one week over 130 people entirely failed to cough. I was, and still am, most impressed! Works played with the NYO stay in my head in the clearest detail; Brahms 4 and Dvořák 8 particularly. It was also an early and refreshing introduction to the uncompromising standards necessary for artistic and professional success.

As we left Swansea the *South Wales Post* headlined SWANSEA CONCERT WAS A MIRACLE, with a very well written piece.

I paused in Cardiff on my way home. Sitting cross-legged in a taxi, I was suddenly thrown across the floor: a lorry's brakes had failed and it crashed into the back of us. I considered myself undamaged but the local hospital insisted on an X-ray and a night in their care. It was only a cracked pelvis, and I was fully able to walk. I set off for London. I presumed the bruising and stiffness would soon wear off and carried on working. But towards the end of January, I was getting a bit lame and crooked; medical advice made me a very reluctant patient of an orthopaedic specialist in a famous London hospital.

When I came round from the anaesthetic my first thought was how nice it was to be out of pain. Then, as I tried to move an arm, the other one shot up, and I found I had no control of my neck, arms, hands – even fingers. It was very frightening. My legs obeyed no instructions: they didn't move at all. Soothing nurses do not answer questions; 'This sometimes happens after an anaesthetic, just rest,' from a doctor, did not reassure.

Two days later my own physician and friend Lord Evans came to see me. I heard him talking to the specialist in an alcove off my room. He sounded very angry. I heard 'inexcusable', and 'entirely your fault'. Obviously there had been some ghastly mistake and the specialist was leaving Lord Evans to tell me. My first worry was that my brain had gone wrong.

'Your *brain* is all right. The peripheral nervous system is damaged.' He felt sure that soon everything above the waist would recover. But what about the rest of me? In the ensuing pause I remember saying, 'Do you mean a wheelchair for life?' and getting the answer, 'We don't know yet . . .' He still had hope.

He stayed to explain the serious accidental damage to my spine during the operation. Suing doctors in those days was unthinkable so, ironically, truthful explanations were possible. What I remember most is the quiet intensity with which he said, 'Whatever the extent of your recovery it will not be doctors, it will be what you believe is possible, what you overcome, your will-power. The will is stronger than the body.'

Gradually some feeling came back; a genius at the Roehampton Hospital created a steel jacket to keep the sacro-iliac joints in place so that I could stand, and the fight back began. My feet were turned out like Charlie Chaplin's; muscles pulled shoulders and neck backwards to give me a double chin; my face had fallen in. What a sight I was, the perfect cure for vanity! But I was on my feet. My goal: the next course, just eight weeks away.

At the January Executive meeting it was reported that I might only be able to do part-time work – the courses and the musical planning – but no longer the months of travelling for the audition tours. The Committee decided that there would be fewer centres – only in the main cities, and in small towns if there were enough candidates – and that with a little more money about, and the orchestra now well known, people would be prepared to travel. The Committee very kindly suggested I should go by car when able to travel.

The main item of the afternoon Council meeting was the retirement of Reginald Jacques after seven years and the appointment of Douglas Guest as our new Chairman. He was a fine musician, whose own high standards in music and teaching were displayed in his cathedral choirs, Salisbury then Worcester and later Westminster Abbey. Outwardly the strong and silent type, we all valued his absolute integrity and his calm and wise judgement; his natural dignity graced all our formal occasions. He knew the tough early years and this present developing stage, and from this meeting in 1956 he was the guiding hand of the NYO for the next thirty years – a true friend and supporter of all who loved and worked for its cause.

With Roland Bird doing all the financial work, and reporting that the *Mirror* was satisfied, Diana was well able to manage the administration. The kind and generous support at this meeting was more than enough to stimulate the essential will-power for recovery.

Diana was marvellous. We could meet at the hospital or the office and plan and she could organise everything. But the usual problem faced us: we had nowhere to stay for our London course. John Newsom, Director of Education for Hertfordshire, saved the day by persuading Hatfield College and School, one of his best and newest day schools, to have us. The Headmistress was one of those rare people who really wanted to help others. She must have hated her new school being turned upside-down, but she made us feel wanted. She also gave up her own room and insisted I had it for the week, and went out of her way to show us many good-will gestures. With local help the mattresses were installed, one huge gymnasium taking our ninety-two boys. We wore gymshoes all the time, to protect the new floors, especially the main hall. And in twenty-four hours, glorious sound was emerging from every room. The children were extra helpful throughout the week, and I saw more of them individually by sitting in one place, so that they came to me.

The local paper headlined QUIET OCCUPATION OF HATFIELD SCHOOL. Two Hatfield staff members had said, 'The children keep scrupulously to the paths, use a side entrance and generally behave beautifully'; while Mr C. Butterfield, the school caretaker, had said, 'They have other gifts than music, they glide about in rubber shoes, and are angels without wings.' That was a good laugh for my vigorous young men! Once more our reputation was safe for future invitations.

Recently a group of former members reminded me that normally I was always crawling round amongst them in rehearsals and would write little notes and slip them on their stand or the back of the chair. John Braithwaite, principal oboe and now a famous architect, said he thought his section wasn't doing very well, and then found a note on his chair: 'Well done, that solo was beautiful.' But when I could no longer crawl around, someone provided a high chair like a tennis umpire's and there I sat, observing every detail and writing in my notebook. They used to wonder, if I was looking in their direction and then writing, if they were in the notebook.

This time John Addison had written a sinfonietta for us. He was a most charming, efficient person. He had given every corner of the orchestra enough to play, the score and parts arriving in time in perfect order. He spent two days with us helping our composers' class and going through the work in full rehearsal. It was a great pleasure to have him.

Once again, new to so many, we had captured one of my favourite conductors, Jean Martinon, a real artist, a poet, who felt and shaped and brought life to every phrase. The main work was Brahms 4, a first introduction to Brahms for many. It may not have been the most Germanic style, but it was an interpretation they would remember. He was very helpful to our young cellist in the Haydn concerto, Rohan de Seram, and what really sparkled was the Schubert overture, *Rosamunde*, capturing a Gallic spirit.

It was our usual happy day in the Festival Hall, a new event for sixty of them, culminating in the exciting experience of the concert. At the request of Lord Reading, we had invited Bulganin and Khrushchev – presumably the Foreign Office wanted to entertain them and we were honoured to be chosen, together with the showpiece Royal Festival Hall. A box was kept for them, but we never met them.

Diana had taken on more responsibility on this course, and

along with John and all the volunteer staff had managed admirably. In 1989, after John's death, a letter came into my hands that he had written to a friend on 15 April 1956:

> . . . just back from the Easter Course with the NYO, a strangely different one, marred by tragedy, yet together overcoming it. Only those who knew RR before 1956 ever knew her at all. The changed appearance is a shock but the eyes (and ears) miss nothing, and the ideas and imagination are still there. But that torch of vitality that lit up everybody into doing more than they thought they could seems to me somewhat dimmed. What a cruel blow . . . one wonders if she will ever be the same again.

No. I never was. In the next ten years all movement was a painful effort, strapped into my steel jacket each morning. The aching body tires the mind, saps the energy and changes the expression, and therefore the response of others. Will-power had to win, even if progress was slow, and the gradual victory was due to the generous support and understanding of the Executive, and all my musician colleagues and friends.

Wonderful though it was to go back to Glengonnar and the honour of our fifth Edinburgh Festival, we always tried to add something new on each course. So we accepted an invitation to Carlisle. They were very keen to have us even though they had no concert hall; all they could offer in the way of a large hall and platform was the Cattle Market, which would be free (of cattle) on a Saturday. With such sincere pleading, my heart melted. We were to give a first performance of a new work in Edinburgh, this time by Arthur Benjamin, but he was ill, and at very short notice his friend Benjamin Frankel was going to write one instead. At least he knew the orchestra and its size and scope. As usual the BBC were going to take the whole concert for the Third Programme.

On 23 August the Royal Scot duly stopped at Abington village, as was its annual custom, and in two minutes deposited the NYO and its equipment on the village platform. Once more the newer members had their first experience of life in the country. 'So silent in the night, it's quite frightening' and 'What a noise the birds make in the morning' were typical discoveries for the city dweller. It was always a happy week, with its own problems and initiatives; this time moving around with instruments in the rain, or the aftermath of a thunderstorm; but always the hills, the river, the ever-varying sunsets and for some their farewell to the NYO.

Walter started well with great energy and vigour for the Berlioz overture. The new work had no musical or artistic value that we could discover, but it gave everybody plenty to play and difficulties to tackle. Having four ex-members, all of nineteen, as soloists for the Haydn concertante was an entirely new venture: David Stone (violin), reading music at Cambridge, Neil Black (oboe), reading history at Oxford, Penelope Lynex (cello), who won a scholarship to the RAM, and Martin Gatt (bassoon), who had a scholarship to the RCM but was at the time in the Army. And for the first time since our first concert in 1948, we ended with a Beethoven symphony.

The generosity and hospitality of the City of Edinburgh and the festival management were overwhelming. The atmosphere of the concert, and the climax of the tattoo at night, made this day a very special one.

John and I and two boys set off early in Genin's car for Carlisle, a little suspicious of what we might find in the cattle market on a Saturday. Nearing the appointed place, we passed groups of cattle being herded away, and parked at what seemed to be the main entrance to the hall. Inside we encountered a friendly farmer, and explained we were musicians coming to prepare the concert. His smile became a hearty laugh and he disappeared to find a colleague, and in the distance we heard, 'You better come, they're that queer. They want to give a concert in the market.' The smell was rather strong, but we were soon shown to the covered market, and discovered a reasonable-sized platform and about eight hundred chairs for the audience. In a small room off the stage, a man from the BBC was hard at work with his sound apparatus, as the whole concert was to be recorded for the *Music to Remember* programme. Recently Betty Goddard, a housemistress for many years, remembered that while we were tuning she happened to look over to the fence along the side of the market hall, and all along the bottom were faces. The local children were lying on the grass outside with their heads under the fence, to see and hear what was going on.

We were pioneering once more, and as at Bath in 1948, when we had lined up outside the Pavilion in the rain, now the whole orchestra prepared and tuned in the cattle pens. The local paper announced that 'the concert to be given at the Covered Market is unique in Carlisle's musical history, and never before has a Carlisle concert platform presented as many as 120 practised instrumentalists'. Alas it was too small for all of us. In the last drive for publicity the *Mirror* had fixed a small notice to every lamppost in the main part of the city. The people came.

The BBC man was preparing to explain to the audience about the red light for recording. As he came out a beam above the door crashed down, cutting his head quite badly and knocking him out. Sister appeared from nowhere to deal with the casualty, and after a word with Walter we asked the audience if they would mind starting ten minutes late to see if the BBC man was able to do the recording; and indeed, when he was duly bandaged and resuscitated, the show went on. The concert was greatly appreciated, and had been made possible by the local Arts Council but especially Mr Charnley and his staff at the education office. After the concert, we even met people who had travelled from Annan, Dumfries and Kirkcudbright on the other side of the border. For our members to come from the Usher Hall at the peak of a great festival one night to a simple country town the next was a rich experience for them. You play music to *people*, wherever they are.

Noel de Jong was with us in 1956, and recently sent me his memories of life with the NYO:

> . . . the many invaluable lessons I learnt from you about People, Organisation and MUSIC . . . those impromptu evening Recitals, the silences when resting in rehearsal, the stillness when totally relaxed, so beneficial to mind and body. And I remember a slightly hollow feeling in the pit of my stomach at Abington on hearing you announce, 'And now you will all follow Mr de Jong to the top of the hill across the river!'
>
> Gym shoes for all was a brilliant idea in the days when the young wore heavy shoes with steel reinforced heels which could wreck floors and be noisy. And vivid to me . . . about fifty of them sleeping on mattresses on the gym floor and lights out at 10!

As was my habit each September I returned to the peace of the Highlands. There were many uplifting letters and reports, but my own impression was that the year that had started so well in Swansea had not been our best, and that was nobody's fault but mine. I blamed myself for having less energy for teaching, for individual attention to the younger group and for all the priceless detail. Everything was just less than my best. Would my inability to do my best work show in the performances? *The Times*, *Telegraph* and *Sunday Times* had been our most faithful followers and honest critics. They would know.

> Their playing, so remarkable for its technical precision and emotional verve, had always seemed something of a miracle. It was rather a relief when they fell below their own high level, and brought Miss Railton's training once more within the order of nature . . . (*The Times*)

In addition, some didn't like the new works: 'Typical of the enlightened policy of the N.Y.O. that new works are frequently commissioned but in some cases, especially the Frankel overture, were unworthy of them.' On the whole my aim to encourage new British music was not really worthwhile, for the composers or us. Perhaps I could save energy and cut out all that extra work.

I also came across an astonishing idea from Neville Cardus in the *Guardian*:

> This fine orchestra must be heard (and seen) to be believed but had the four soloists . . . not played from memory but used the printed music the audience would have been much more impressed and immediately understood they were capable of reading music.

Music students incapable of reading music? But there was a mood developing at this time against playing from memory. Because not all British soloists had the confidence to perform without the copy, the pretence that it was better when performing a solo recital or concerto to keep the script with you was tolerated. A little slide to the English love of the amateur and a temporary nonsense. Actors learn the words; we learn the music; singers do both. Only when a work has become part of you can the interpretation begin to grow. Another prevailing mood was that there was something sinister about doing anything as well as possible for its own sake; and at the same time there was more money for all, regardless of effort. So far our students had been enormously helped by more money: better instruments, tape recorders, grants for their fees. But I wondered how it would be when a whole generation existed that had never known how to get through by hard work and family sacrifices, one for whom all their needs were 'rights'. The NYO was such a cross-section of the nation that it would be interesting to follow the changes that unearned money may bring in the character of the next generation.

I had used this break to look at all aspects of our work very self-critically; I was ready to hand over to others if it seemed that the standards I believed in were slipping. But now I knew I must go back. The exciting tenth-anniversary year lay ahead, so how could I possibly desert the shared hopes and trust in me of my 130 young friends?

Twenty-One

It was late in September when I slowly, awkwardly climbed the stairs in 90 George Street. Typewriters were clicking away, telephones ringing, maps spread out on my desk. But shafts of sunlight fell on the neat piles of audition papers laid out before me on the floor, and from these would come the sound, the life, the character of the 1957 orchestra.

Diana had worked out a superb new audition system, concentrating on the bigger towns and cities. There was a danger that some talent might be missed, but every year brought its surprises and its rare gems, and the general standard now was unimaginable in 1947.

This September's Committee meeting was particularly important for making the tenth anniversary a special year. Plans were confirmed for Bristol at Christmas, adding an extra concert at Bath to celebrate ten years since our first. 'In accepting, would you ask the promoter, if he makes a lot of money, to give us a little bit of it?' said one. The Committee was getting quite commercial!

Easter was to be the RFH with Sir Malcolm and, we hoped, the Queen Mother for our tenth-anniversary celebration. The Committee hoped we would make a long-playing record as a memento. The summer was to be the Prom followed by Germany, and flying for the first time. Sir Robert Mayer was discussing plans with the German Ambassador.

The Treasurer revealed the good news that the *Mirror* would give us £6,000 for August 1956 to August 1957. We had also saved £2,000 in donations from well-wishers, for any emergency. The Ex-Members' Association must now look after itself, but I reported on its activities. They still helped us at busy periods in the office and on courses. They also supplied many members for the newly resuscitated Royal Amateurs.

Our priority was a new permanent secretary. Wedding bells had just claimed our charming and excellent Amber Pares after only eighteen months, and the temporary, Brenda Stonely, could not stay. We had to employ young ones, who were totally free, strong and able to travel; they must feel at ease with a staff-room full of famous musicians and with children coming to the office for lessons and auditions. Agencies sent all sorts of people; they came and they went.

Then one afternoon a really intelligent girl of nineteen arrived. She had done a year training as a nurse, then decided to be a secretary instead. Her diary records:

> The lady at the agency told me she had sent quite a few applicants along, and none had been offered the job. It was, therefore, with not a little trepidation that I arrived at the N.Y.O. offices. I was ushered into a large pleasant room with framed photographs – signed of course – of famous musicians, and on the floor stacks and stacks of music. Miss Railton was seated behind her desk . . . She had the most piercing blue eyes that could read you like a book, and a most encouraging smile. The interview began. Presently she said 'When could you start?' I replied, 'Whenever you want.' 'Well,' she said, 'you see those piles of music' . . . I stayed straight away to learn how to sort it into different instrumental groups, which would eventually become about 130 envelopes of parts to be posted to members of the orchestra a week before the next course. There was to be a concert in Bristol and Bath and Walter Susskind conducting. I couldn't believe my luck. That afternoon started some of the happiest years of my life.

Thus arrived one of the most special people in the orchestra's story. Mary Shoppee was exceptional: ready to try anything; gentle but full of courage; unspoilt, so everything in the music world was new and exciting; she enjoyed high standards and the importance of detail and accuracy; her nursing training also played a part. Diana was very happy with her new assistant and they quickly became firm friends.

During the audition tour Diana taught her all that the NYO involved. When I came back in December there were three of us who knew all aspects of the work. On the musical side, John Dalby could manage the courses if I wasn't there, but during school terms was not free from his work in Aberdeen. So my mind turned to Ivey Dickson, a first-class musician and marvellous pianist. I took her with me for much of the 1956 audition tour, to play for all the candidates, and in the evenings we could share our views. Although a very experienced teacher of piano and strings, this gave her an insight into woodwind, brass and the repertoire of all instruments and their problems. She was sympathetic and reassuring to nervous candidates, and was a great help in making the tour possible for me.

One Sunday in November came the news of the death of Guido Cantelli in a plane crash. He was returning from Milan, where he had just been appointed the next Director of La Scala – the post he wanted more than all else – to New York, where he was Conductor of the New York Philharmonic Orchestra. Already one of the greatest musicians and most inspiring conductors of the century, he was only thirty-six. We were very good friends and he had introduced me to Toscanini. He had promised that if he got La Scala he would take every summer off to rest and study, and would always give me a week for the NYO, so we had been looking forward to having him for this summer. His sudden death was a bitter blow for Italy, for music, for all musicians who knew him, for his friends and for the NYO.

By mid-December the new orchestra was chosen, with fifty new members including ten reserves. I felt deeply for the disappointed ones, and shared the rejoicing of whole families. In a fortnight Christmas would be over and we would all be together in Bristol.

George Sylvester had arranged everything: the luxurious

Redlands Training College and the new Colston Concert Hall. He also knew all our problems, and had thought about our every need. Leaving Diana to cope with the office and all the organisation, I set off for Bristol early on Boxing Day to initiate Mary Shoppee into the NYO alive, no longer just names on her typewriter. Her diary says:

> I travelled on the train to Bristol with Miss Railton to prepare the college for our purpose. Again I was a little nervous as to what was expected of me, but armed with every conceivable list, telephone numbers and Sellotape there was little to fear. I had no idea how much work was needed before the children arrived. I had no idea how much thought went into compiling dormitory lists, friends, ages, new members, all sorted for happiness.
>
> Each dormitory was arranged and the list of inmates carefully sellotaped to the door. Each rehearsal-room was most carefully and lovingly laid out and labelled. Directions on how to reach every room were placed in strategic positions. Cloakrooms were inspected and labelled, areas not for our use blocked off labelled 'Never go past here' and then the dining-room was made more homely using smaller tables. Only when everything was to her satisfaction did we move to the main hall. This was my initiation into how to set up a whole symphony orchestra. No effort was spared, no detail overlooked, the right spacing for cellos, for bows, for flutes, all tested herself. Some local members had come to help move all the chairs and I was impressed with their quick efficiency. Only when Miss Railton was completely satisfied with the design did she agree to a brief rest, and when daylight faded she checked all the lighting for evening work and recitals.
>
> Next day was a revelation of the importance of good preparation. The staff-room, where so many world-famous musicians would meet, was made as homely as possible, with flowers arranged, and in the dining-room. Then came the work of art of the noticeboard. A huge chart in colour of the seated orchestra with every individual's name on it, so that at one glance members would know where to sit at the first rehearsal and the names of their desk partners. There were attractive posters of the concerts, and various lists to sign, some photographs with every corner pinned, the whole

designed to look attractive. Soon two housemasters arrived, and my task was to show them the way round, thereby testing our labelling, but in addition timing how long it took to get from brass-room to hall, from the furthest dormitory to dining-room and so on. Walking these distances caused several minor adjustments to the timetable, classes ending five minutes earlier, or meals a little later. There was to be no rush when moving with instruments. Only then could the timetable for the week be completed and be duly given its central place by the noticeboards. Soon the cooks and kitchen staff arrived to prepare the evening meal, and we all made friends, good relations with food apparently being of the utmost importance, especially when resident in a girls' school as our young men could eat so much more!

All too soon the trains had arrived and the buses from the station. 'The once-quiet and tranquil college echoed to the chatter of greetings and laughter and a great deal of happiness flowed in. This was for me the most exciting thing, and something I grew to love,' wrote Mary in her diary. Sure enough, there would be John Dalby and the Scottish contingent; the house staff and Sister, our tower of strength; and the last to arrive was the invaluable Genin, all the way from Liverpool in his car. Typical of Mr Sylvester, he joined us for supper to see if all was well, and this gave the orchestra a chance to meet him and to thank him personally. Then, tired from long journeys and anticipating the prospects for the week, they went to bed, new members already knowing they were among friends.

The *Mirror*'s instruments were a great help. We had as good a set as a professional orchestra for the percussion section, so I brought in two extra beginners, and a young trombonist whom I had asked at audition if he would consider moving to the bass trombone if I lent him our instrument. I didn't promise him a place, but he knew he would have a better chance than on a tenor. Three weeks later he'd done splendidly, so I took him.

Work started with great enthusiasm and by New Year's Day we were ready for Walter Susskind. A great conductor is exciting and a little overwhelming at first. Walter's vitality and dramatic style quickly gave us all a chance to see where the weaknesses really were, and the players an idea of what to expect.

While all was going well musically came the first crisis. Our Bristol concert had sold out weeks ago, and a deputation from the city came to ask if we could do an extra lunch-hour concert to avoid so much disappointment. Wisdom told me to say no. At the beginning of the year we didn't know whether two concerts on two nights running plus long journeys might be too much; making it three, with two on the same day, might spoil things. John, Diana and I thought this through. We could leave the youngest out of the extra concert, and cut the concerto; we had some experienced members with us from the days of Brussels and Amsterdam who were familiar with the extra packing of vans and setting. The city of Bristol had done so much for us, so we agreed to do it provided the extra cost was covered.

We also fitted in a lord mayor's reception, at which the orchestra was shown around the new council chambers and entertained to a wonderful tea in the conference hall. We also had a recital from Leonard Hirsch, and of course the New Year's Eve party.

The last full rehearsal of the week would be the whole programme through and the first time everyone would hear our youngest, Stephanie Bamford, play the piano concerto. Although only ten, she had taken everything throughout the week in her stride. Highly intelligent, sensible, unspoilt and very gifted in many ways, she loved music the most. Her own special performance was ready and she glowed with happiness.

Whenever we had a very young soloist there was likely to be talk of 'child prodigies'. One set of people was always going to say how bad it was for them to perform in public, they'd become arrogant and anyway prodigies always fade out; others, new to hearing very young talent, would purr and prophesy a great career ahead. My views conformed to neither group. If a highly intelligent child of considerable musical talent and from a balanced home life develops early, why deprive them of the joy of performance, or the audience of experiencing something beautiful and different? The pre-pubescent child has strong emotion, vivid imagination and no anxious doubts: a message of simplicity and truth all its own. With adolescence the childish trust goes, self-consciousness is born, and with that a different kind of nervousness emerges. Exceptional talent appears only occasionally, and should be treasured and developed wisely.

The two-concert day arrived; once before we had done two on the same day (in Amsterdam), but never in two different cities, so there was the unknown for all of us.

The Colston Hall is very big; we rehearsed until noon. Outside there was a queue lining up for tickets, and this is a very heartening sight to any performer. A new member said, 'Oh look, that's marvellous, they must want to hear us.' A more seasoned player replied, 'It's not *us*. It's the people like us ten years ago who did it. It's called tradition – we mustn't let them down.'

We played the overture, the Bizet and some of the Shostakovich to fill an hour. By the time everything was packed for Bath it was after two-thirty before they had lunch. The head cook had been given tickets and when the children sat down she thanked them, then announced there was a second helping of pudding for everybody – suet roly and it all disappeared.

John and I set off early to Bath. We had some time to spare, so we found a quiet corner for tea in a hotel and had a serious talk. I admitted to him, but to nobody else, that at this stage of a course being always in pain sapped my best work, and I might have to give up. I wanted to last till the end of the year, and then step back or out after Germany. John said I was more mobile, I might get increasingly better, but we shared ideas for a future without me.

We had already prepared the future with Douglas Guest as Chairman, and an excellent Executive Committee; we had just enough money from our sponsor; we had as fine a team of conductors and professors as anyone could wish for; we had the right understanding administrator in Diana with her promising Mary; we had a network for talent-finding. But we were minus an obvious successor for the central artistic direction; John himself could not take over from me full-time, so we resolved to find and train several assistant directors until the right one emerged. Ivey Dickson had all the musical qualities but lacked confidence away from the concert platform. I had my eye on younger performers who could teach – Thea King (Jack Thurston's widow) and Janet Craxton – and two ex-members, younger still.

Our break had been spent on the future of the orchestra, but now it was time to return to the Pavilion for the concert tonight. What was so unexpected was the exceptional enthusiasm of the Bath audience. We had been billed in the local papers with 'the NYO's triumphant return to its birthplace', and before we'd played a note the reception made it clear that they claimed us as their own. This was very heartening; not having been there since 1948, we hadn't realised we belonged in that way.

The performance did not disappoint. Susskind was at his most exhilarating, seeing just how much excitement he could get without losing control. Stephanie's Mozart was a gem of simplicity and beauty, and the Shostakovich had room for drama, the tender cello solo* and a passionate ending. From this first glimpse of the character and sound of this year's orchestra, it seemed it had made a good start.

Outside the artists' entrance was a BBC car to take Walter and me and the soloist to a programme called *Westward Ho*. On no account would I keep Stephanie up late, so I took Raffaele. The programme seemed to be on local events; the item following us was a group of Breton onion sellers and the aroma filled the studio.

We had signed a contract some months ago with the BBC for a recording at Bristol. In the mean time some quite serious trouble had arisen at the Musicians' Union – concerts cancelled,

*Played by Raffaele Altwegg, now in the Swiss Quartet.

talk of a total strike and so on. It was nothing to do with us since our children (of course) were not members, but the union wanted to stop our recording. They threatened, but I explained that we must honour our contract. I assured them that we had no union members, but they refused to believe me and demanded the signature of every child playing in the Bristol concert.

So on our return from Bath, 130 sleepy children had to put their signature to sheets headed *I am* not *a member of the Musicians' Union*. When they'd gone to bed we set about ensuring every player had signed, but we were merely counting scribbles: hardly a signature could be identified. Perhaps because I had said carelessly, 'I'm sorry about this, but the union wouldn't believe me when I said you weren't members so you must sign yourselves,' they didn't like my word being doubted and this was their protest. However, the list was duly delivered to BBC Bristol in the morning.

All seemed well at breakfast, the new members especially longing for this second night, when they would be less nervous and know what to expect and would enjoy it even more. That night the BBC did record the whole concert for the Overseas Service. The evening was best described by D.D.F. of the *Western Daily Press*:

> Bristol welcomed back on Saturday an orchestra that plays for the love of playing and loves every minute of it – the massive National Youth Orchestra of Great Britain. Now in its tenth splendid year, it is without doubt a great musical phenomenon to which this country has given birth.

Of Stephanie he said, 'This little girl with the long golden pigtails is no musical freak, but a serious and highly proficient musician.' Bristol had been very good to the NYO so I was happy they felt they'd had a good concert in return.

It was at this January's Council meeting that Sir Adrian retired as President and was replaced by Sir Malcolm Sargent; Sir

Arthur Bliss and Walter Susskind became vice-presidents. General Wilson, to whose judgement we owed our early survival in 1948, and who was always a wise and kind friend to us, also had to retire.

The Council wanted the RFH anniversary concert to be an international event, we hoped in the presence of our royal patron and with our President conducting, and a reception for foreign ambassadors and government officials. As always they were concerned with the welfare of our children: an invitation to Amsterdam could only be considered if the children were back before Good Friday. (Would that matter today?) BBCTV was interested but had not confirmed, and Independent Television was hovering in the wings. It was interesting that the Council trusted the BBC, but were a little fearful of ITV. They were only to be considered if I was sure 'the presentation would be in our hands'. We had enough material from the Bristol concert for two LPs. We could only sell them at the RFH provided the profits went to us. This was not greed or desperate need, but care about commercial exploitation of the children. Sir Robert Mayer assured us that his plans for our German tour in August were going splendidly. Everyone mourned the loss of Cantelli, but I reported promises from Kubelík, Kletski and Szell.

Mr Bird presented the accounts. It was still thought best not to raise the fees, so that at this time the NYO was managed on £6,000 annually from the *Mirror* and generous treatment by education authorities. Our Easter course was based at Reading University, at the invitation of the Vice-Chancellor Sir John Wolfenden. The superb accommodation was like a tenth-anniversary reward, after some really tough conditions over the previous nine years. There was ample space, a very good hall for the orchestra and welcoming co-operation from all concerned.

At this time of year I would be teaching most days in the office, giving confidence to those trying for scholarships in

April. Our members' successes in major scholarships for universities or colleges had just passed the one-hundred mark in time for this anniversary.

During the week in Reading, many interesting people connected with the university called on us. One outstanding evening was Sir John's talk to the students, mainly on the changing world they would live in. He came to our staff-room on two occasions, full of encouragement to everybody.

After three days' work we were ready for Sir Malcolm. Remembering his elegance and style, our sartorial appearance was spruced up, brass instruments were shining like gold and tuning was complete for the moment of entry at five o'clock. His rehearsals were marvellous: not a minute was wasted, every suggestion was clear, he was patient when there were difficulties, encouraging when things went well. Somehow he identified with their freshness and sheer love of making music, and enjoyed their immediate response: 'Aren't they quick, and so musical. It's a big programme but it's going to be good on Saturday,' he said that evening. He asked what I wanted him to do next day. When I suggested the same work again in the morning, he said, 'Why?' And I said, 'Because it will grow in the night.' He seemed a bit mystified but at the morning rehearsal he turned to me and muttered, 'Some growth! Extraordinary!' He didn't stifle 'growth' but made sure of the security to withstand the unpredictable expanse and emotion that would happen with the inspiration of a great occasion.

Next day we were planning our traditional anniversary party (held every April to commemorate the first NYO concert), at which I always gave each member a small gift. I couldn't think of what to do this time, and in a flash Sir Malcolm said, 'Why not give them all a photograph of me?' He rang up his London office and 150 postcard-size glossy prints were somehow delivered the next day, and he sat down in the staff-room and signed the lot. It was a much-appreciated present at the evening party, and when Sir Malcolm walked in for the rehearsal next morning, a senior member made a little speech thanking him. He was very moved because they were so genuinely delighted.

In one of my imaginative moments I thought there should be some distinctive mark of the tenth year on our uniform and suggested bright red belts for everyone. John Lewis had some quite smart ones in their uniform department, and went to endless trouble to find 130. Tape measures were found and there followed a hilarious session after lunch, listing everybody's waist size. All was well for the girls and the slim young men, but it seemed there would be problems of fitting the torsos of the larger older boys. However, the belts arrived, and ingenious ways of extending them at the back, which wouldn't show on the platform, would have to be devised.

These lighter moments apart, it was a very full week musically. The English work was Britten's *Young Person's Guide*, full of technically difficult solos in all departments; it gave our large percussion section plenty to do. We made extra time this week for the chamber orchestra for the Mozart concerto. Our soloist was Kathleen Jones. Fanny Waterman is the best teacher of young children I have ever met; this was the third time one of her pupils played with us, and I had no doubt of the confidence and enjoyment Kathleen would bring to our anniversary concert.

The most time went to the great C Major Schubert symphony, the most difficult work we'd ever attempted, hard to hold together, and taking fifty minutes' unwavering concentration.

This week Gareth Morris was in charge of the whole woodwind section, not just the flutes, yet generously gave us an evening recital. Ernest Hall was in charge of the brass as usual; 'All I want to do is to pour my years of experience into your young souls,' he would say, and for this huge programme they were eagerly lapping it up. And there was one last treat: Dennis Brain arrived by surprise, went straight to help the horns, then stayed to give a very memorable recital. 'He would speed in, give an exhilarating recital, take a cup of cocoa with us and dash away into the night,' writes one of our horn players.* That night I went to see him into his car and thank him. 'I love coming, the atmosphere breathes excitement,' he said. It was the last time I saw him.

The last rehearsal on the eve of a concert was a very important event, the only time in the week that we could try the whole programme through. Usually there was an audience on the platform, which stimulated the atmosphere. Sir Malcolm was at his happiest, letting his restrained excitement through to give them a glimpse of what might happen tomorrow. For the players it was a chance to discover what a whole programme demands in energy and concentration.

An RFH day was always a special occasion. Over the Thames at Westminster, still new to some, into the morning rehearsal, getting used to feeling like a tiny gnat, listening in this huge space, all were formative experiences and memories. During the afternoon rest each member was given a copy of the newly designed programme. A tenth-anniversary gift from the *Mirror*, it had a very fine eighteenth-century black-and-white design round the edge; our title and conductor were printed in red; centred above these, in gold, was a simple *10th*. There was a full-page formal portrait of the Queen Mother, and the whole back cover was a photograph of the orchestra at the Prom with Sir Adrian. Throughout the information pages were small illustrations of our players to show every instrument. Nothing was spared in the quality of the paper and printing.

It was a great sadness that the Queen Mother was not able to come, and in the event we didn't feel in the mood to wear our new red belts, choosing to keep them for another important occasion. Overcoming a minus with a plus, Diana reported that she'd just checked with the box office and every single seat was sold. It is exciting playing to a packed-out hall, but our members were very aware that they must leave no stone

*Timothy Reynish, now Director of Woodwind, Brass and Percussion at the RNCM.

unturned to deserve this following, and most found it humbling as well as enjoying the thrill. After tea a few of them saw a small queue hoping for returns, and went to talk to them. I asked them what they had said. 'Oh, just how sorry we were that we couldn't have them with us, and that there would be more room at the Prom in the summer . . . and that there were some records on sale upstairs.' The nation of shopkeepers lives on . . .

Then came the moment when Sir Malcolm went on to the platform and into a huge wave of warm applause. It was a programme with something for every musical taste in the audience: the sparkle of the Rossini, the sheer beauty of the Mozart and Kathleen's artistry, the stunning virtuosity of the *Young Person's Guide* played by young persons with such enjoyment, and after the interval the great C Major Symphony. This huge work never lost interest, never flagged in Malcolm's hands, nor did he fail to nurse or bring it to unexpected heights. That evening reached a peak we could not have achieved even the previous year.

The audience was enthusiastic, apparently proud of our native talent; the VIPs were impressed, the foreign ones simply dazed with disbelief. For myself I thought of all the unknown, unsung people from Land's End to John o'Groat's who had helped us so loyally in the early years, and who could now feel some reward as they listened to the radio and read about our achievements in the tenth year.

The evening ended with the orchestra assembling with Sir Malcolm and our Chairman to meet our distinguished guests. Then, elated but tired, they sank into sleep on the long drive back to Reading. Early next morning, as from some living fire, 150 sparks scattered to all corners of the British Isles, leaving us with only the still, quiet embers.

A week later we studied the most encouraging press anyone could wish for. After the early years of opposition and poverty, it seemed that by now we were becoming a valuable national institution, to be defended and protected. Somehow we were no longer a dangerous threat but accepted with pride.

The Times summed it up best under the headline A REMARKABLE CONCERT:

> . . . her struggle and eventual success in forming the orchestra is an example of dogged persistence, even bravery, in pursuing an ideal that we call typically British. Its reward in terms of musical achievement has been incalculable; if, in times to come, British orchestral playing is ever acknowledged as the best in the world a contributory factor will stand out: the existence of the National Youth Orchestra. As always the orchestra amazes with its proficiency and its keen, spontaneous artistry . . .

And, later:

> The most remarkable feature of the whole concert was the account of Mozart's K459 by Miss Kathleen Jones, a pianist of some dozen years old . . . Miss Jones can play with the confidence, accuracy, refinement of tone and stylistic perception that mature international celebrities may seek in vain to command. Everything that she did was so spontaneously right in terms of music that there was no suggestion of a wunderkind. Natural gifts and inspired teaching had simply borne fruit in due season.

I could have hugged the whole newspaper for this, as the Council still worried about such young soloists. God bless the *Times* critic who had ears to hear.

Twenty-Two

The climax of our tenth year was to be the Promenade Concert, and after that going by air to represent Britain in Germany. We explained to Sir Robert Mayer that we could leave for Germany the day after the Prom but we needed information urgently. He assured me that he had agreed concerts in Munich and Stuttgart and possibly Frankfurt too. The German government were financing our stay under their Youth Friendship Scheme, and he should get all the details very soon now.

Our contract with the BBC for the Prom engaged the NYO, with our choice of conductor and soloist, according to our constitution. We would co-operate on the choice of programme (the Prom was longer than normal concerts; some works suggested might be too difficult; a concerto would depend on which instrument and soloist I might have ready; of course works must not be repeated during their season). So off I went to the BBC, and had an excellent meeting exchanging ideas, and came back with a programme to suit us all: a Weber overture, *Der Freischütz*; a first performance of Malcolm Arnold's Divertimento; Bizet's *L'Arlesienne*; Dvořák 4 (now 8). They had suggested the Brahms B Flat piano concerto, very difficult for us, but I said I'd like to discuss it with my colleagues and let them know. It would require a seventeen- or eighteen-year-old able to manage the solo part, someone who would have time to give to it during a school summer term full of exams. That evening I rang John Ogdon, one of my most talented, unusual and lovable young musicians.

'John, do you know the Brahms B Flat?'

'I've read it through.' (John could sight read anything.)

'Do you think you could learn it to perform in August?'

'I think so.'

'Can you come up this weekend? I'll pay your fare.'

'If I came next week instead, I'd know it from memory.'

So a week later, after a Saturday afternoon of Brahms in the office, I could perceive the possibility of a very special performance for the Prom and for Germany. I signed the contract with the BBC confirming the programme, with Hugo Rignold conducting, for 10 August 1957.

The Executive met in early June. All were pleased with the RFH concert. There was no further worry about young soloists, and I could tell them that next time it would be Brahms with an eighteen-year-old. Mr Bird suggested an extra £10 each for the fare to Germany; the BBC were paying us £250 for the Prom. John Newsom thought that was a bit mean when they gained a sold-out Albert Hall from us. He would prepare a letter to Sir Ian Jacob, the Director General. I reported that we were still awaiting definite plans for Germany, and was advised to go there myself.

At the end of June I set off to Munich. I was welcomed by the Chairman and Secretary of the Musikalische Jugend, and two representatives from the British Embassy. I was shown all I asked for, and went on to Stuttgart to see to things there. The Secretary of the Musikalische Jugend then introduced me to a concert agent whom they had asked to run the entire tour. He was able and efficient, as one expects in Germany, and he felt sure Frankfurt would be even more satifactory than the other two cities, so I did not go there. I was not impressed by the Musikalische Jugend, but had confidence in the agent, and left saying, 'See you, with 110 musicians, on 12 August.'

True to his word, the concert agent sent essential details within a week. We were to fly in to Munich and out from Frankfurt. He gave the dates of the three concerts and requested details of programmes and so on.

Meanwhile, to mark our tenth anniversary, the *Daily Mirror* had set up a competition for young brass players under twenty, with a £500 prize. Sir Arthur Bliss was chairman of the judges, and it was an exciting day in the Wigmore Hall. Six of the ten finalists were our members, and the winner was an exceptional trombonist of eighteen, Cliff Jones from Ystalyfera, near Swansea. He was an apprentice clock maker, and the trombone was his hobby. Sir Arthur described his playing as 'absolutely astounding' as he presented the prize, and Cliff replied, 'I'd never dreamt I'd ever be able to afford to study music full-time. Now I can.' His father, a factory charge-hand, said, 'Now he'll have the chance I'd always longed to give him.' So a life was changed through a good idea from a generous newspaper.

One afternoon when we were all very busy organising the tour, the telephone rang. It was the BBC Music Department. They were very friendly and asked whether they could hear my chosen soloist for the Brahms. I said that as it happened he was coming to London to rehearse with me the next day so would they like to come round? I only had an upright piano in the office but it would serve the purpose. The gentleman offered a good piano if we could go round to them.

Only after I'd put down the phone did I think that this was the first time I'd ever let anyone hear one of our soloists before we rehearsed together at the course preceding the concert concerned. I liked to leave the finishing touches until I could discover the mood and style of the conductor, and move the soloist into gear on the last two days. However, I could ask John about it when he came.

John was usually rather sad and quiet, but lit up as soon as he got to the keyboard. We had a marvellous afternoon, getting through the whole work. 'Great music,' muttered John, and I could foresee the birth of a great and rather unusual performance. Mary brought some tea, and I asked John if he'd like to play to the BBC, or was he too tired, rather hoping he'd refuse. But he said, 'That would be nice.' So with plenty of time before his train to Manchester, we walked round to Broadcasting House. I waited for him, asked how he'd got on, and we went our respective ways.

The next morning the BBC rang: in a nutshell, they were

unhappy about John's playing. I asked why, because he was an outstanding young pianist.

'Well, he's got some technique, but that's not enough. He's not musical: not the sort of standard we could consider at a Prom.'

'I'm sorry you got that impression. It's too late now to change the programme, Germany's involved and the orchestra starts work in less than three weeks. I'm sure you'll be happy on the night.'

'I'm afraid we just cannot agree to it. He looks like Billy Bunter, and the whole audience would laugh when he came on.' That was too much. John was round and cuddly, and with his glasses on he looked like Schubert. When I found my voice I said:

'The contract is signed, and the terms quite clear. I must speak to my Committee.'

I knew they couldn't cancel our Prom; but if I fought them there might be no future broadcasts or invitations for the NYO. I sought out Maurice Jacobson, who had very close contacts with the BBC and was on a panel of judges for their auditions. I told him about John, that I was convinced it would be a success, that Barbirolli had now offered him a date with the Hallé with the same work, and that I hadn't anybody else who could touch the Brahms, and only three weeks to the course. Most of all I couldn't let John down. I was desperate. How could I have been so stupid as to let them hear him? Maurice cooled me down, and promised to talk to his friend Julian Herbage and see what could be done.*

It then emerged that the BBC had a professional pianist in mind to whom they wanted to give a Prom date. They presumed if they turned down mine I would accept theirs, not understanding that under our constitution we couldn't employ professionals. Causing bitter disappointment and breaking hope in a young student of undoubted ability didn't seem to

*Formerly Assistant Director of Music at the BBC.

disturb them. They wouldn't climb down over John, so had to agree to change the programme. It was left to me to tell John that the BBC wouldn't have him – the only time in my life that I'd broken a commitment to a child or student, and I've never got over it. John never played a concerto with the NYO as he was a full-time student in Manchester the next year. Five years later he won the Tchaikovsky Prize in Moscow, tied with Ashkenazy. On one of his last visits to Dublin, in 1986 (he died in 1989), I said I was still so upset about that Prom. 'It wasn't your fault,' said John. 'I always understood.' He was a unique personality.

The immediate problem was preparing another concerto for the Prom and Germany. I was preparing soloists for the future – trumpet, horn, flute – but none could be ready in about a fortnight. Then I thought of Allan Schiller, who had plenty of experience with us and who was now fourteen. He could manage Mozart K488 by 10 August and come on the German tour with us. The immediate crisis was over.

Our venue for the approaching summer course was to be East Ham once again, as they had invited us back. On 31 July Mary and I were engrossed in preparations when I was summoned to the telephone for an urgent message. It was Diana. She had just had a telegram from Germany cancelling the tour. (The agent had been brought in rather late, and the tour could not be properly organised in time.) Recovering from the shock, I asked her to check with the German Embassy if it was really true, then tell the Chairman and Executive, keeping it confidential until we could tell every parent ourselves. Such a shock for our members mustn't be heard first from the newspapers. Mary and I hurried back to the office. It took all day and most of the evening to contact the conductor, the staff and every member before we informed the *Mirror* and gave a statement to the press. It was a bitter blow, when all our plans were complete.

On 1 August the cancellation of the tour was widely reported in the papers. No reason for it was given, as we still had no written explanation. The press pointed out that it was to have been the climax to our tenth-anniversary year and that we had turned down offers from other countries in favour of Germany. The Germans themselves had spent a great deal on building contacts and friendships for their young people, the generation that had never known Hitler or personally experienced defeat and world-wide condemnation. So it was a setback for Anglo-German relations that they had let us down so badly and at the eleventh hour too. Their Ambassador, Hans von Herwarth, was apologetic on the phone; he accepted my invitation to visit us in East Ham and explain to the orchestra.

The same day BBCTV rang to offer us a programme on Sunday 11th, the day after the Prom. I was delighted to have this extra event to alleviate the disappointment. I was vividly aware that our members had saved towards their fare and got passports, all but two were going to fly for the first time, none had ever been to Germany. With this whole dream adventure shattered, to arrive in East Ham to mattresses on the floor was a great test of morale.

In the event they were marvellous. We all shared and didn't hide the disappointment, and decided that in any case we were representing our country to a sold-out Albert Hall, and what mattered was ending our tenth year achieving the highest standard in our history. They were cheerful and determined as they set about their work the next morning. On my stand was an envelope addressed to me, and inside a little note. 'We want you to know that even without the exciting trip we are thrilled to be here anyway, with love from Mattress Section 1', with five signatures.

Sir William McKay was Organist and Master of the Choristers of Westminster Abbey – a friend and devotee of the orchestra's work over the years. No sooner had work started on 3 August than he was on the phone: would we like to give a concert in Westminster Abbey instead of Germany? What an honour! Yes please, we would, but with the Prom on Saturday and TV on Sunday we could only manage Monday 12th, subject to yet more changes of plans. The Dean of the Abbey and one Canon Marriot were marvellous, and before the day was out this very great privilege was all fixed up.

It has often happened in my experience that a major blow is followed by a totally unexpected new turning or opportunity. We owe so much to the Abbey Chapter and Sir William for this spontaneous gesture, a heart-warming and inspiring climax to our tenth year.

There was much reorganising done on Sunday, with an extra day at East Ham, different transport plans, and most important a different and more suitable programme for the Abbey. We couldn't know till Monday whether any music we chose would be available on hire, or if we could cover the extra work in the week, and there were only five days left before the Prom.

Our programme for the Albert Hall would do for the TV, in that they could choose what they liked from it. But the Arnold and to some extent the Bizet were not very suitable for the Abbey, and nor was a piano concerto. Two of our horn players were working on the Mozart E Flat concerto and I felt one of them, David Presland, could be ready in time. But removing the Arnold and Bizet would not leave the brass enough to play. Ernest Hall came up with the answer: the Gabrieli Sonata for Brass Instruments. In his care our huge brass section made a wonderful sound, and he was thrilled that this great sixteenth-century music should ring out in the Abbey he loved. (He had played at two coronations.) Hugo Rignold, meanwhile, couldn't have been kinder and more accommodating through all these changes.

Hans von Herwarth was a charming and sensitive person. We polished up our most courteous style of greeting – a fanfare on arrival and his national anthem with the full symphony orchestra (as arranged for the German tour). He had been going to speak to the orchestra immediately, but was too moved by the music, so we went to the platform to listen to the rehearsal until the interval. He told me that through all the Hitler years the anthem was banned, so to hear the young people restoring it with such innocence and emotion was unforgettable.

When he spoke to them he was very sympathetic and apologetic, and promised another visit, to include Berlin, as soon as it could be mutually arranged. He fixed their minds on the future – a new Europe of which we would all be part.

I wrote to him recently. He is now nearly ninety, but he replied in his own hand.

> The visit to East Ham is still vivid in my memory. My wife and I, as well as the Cultural Attaché Brigitte Lohmeyer, were highly impressed by the orchestra at the Promenade Concert, and later by its important role in establishing good relations between England and Germany.

There still remained one unsolved problem: how to fill the Abbey for a concert nobody knew about. We printed some small leaflets with just *Westminster Abbey*, our title, date and time and *Admission Free* on them. Our hope was to distribute them to the Prom audience or enclose them with the BBC official programmes. I went to try what was left of my persuasive power on the Manager of the Albert Hall, a friendly gentleman called Mr Hopper: 'You will have a sold-out Albert Hall tomorrow, but can you imagine an empty Westminster Abbey?'

Mr Hopper listened to my problem, and saved the Abbey concert by his kind understanding: 'Of course it is not normally allowed but perhaps we could make some very unobtrusive plans . . .' We must have had BBC permission too, no doubt organised by Diana. On the night our volunteers very unobtrusively gave away our leaflets to the queue and in the main foyer.

Concert day dawned and the usual routine was enacted in an atmosphere of mounting excitement. About 120 would play; all would be in uniform and take part in the events of the day, but the reserves and GMs would have seats in the audience for the concert.

It was two years since our first Prom. Some remembered last time, but more than half had never seen the Albert Hall. It was fascinating to see the expressions on the young faces as they came on to the platform and got their first glimpse of this vast empty arena, and the great circles mounting up towards the height of the huge dome. Then came the shock of the quite different sound. They felt lonely and exposed, yet enjoyed the thrill of the place, adapting to the consequences with increasing confidence as the rehearsal went on.

We always went through the whole programme as it would be on the night. This was very important if you had never played in such a long concert or performed any of the works before. Allan was in fine form, Malcolm Arnold delighted to hear his work for the first time, and Hugo – steady and reassuring as ever in rehearsal – told them how splendidly they'd worked, and prepared them for the added excitement of the actual performance.

They were each given a programme by the BBC, and in it we found a succinct description of the NYO written by our President Sir Malcolm Sargent as a foreword:

> There can be nothing more stimulating than to take a week with the best of the nation's musical youth, and spend hours every day working with them. This has been my happy lot on several occasions. Miss Ruth Railton founded this orchestra, now celebrating its tenth anniversary, as a school of music for the most talented young musicians in the British Isles. The quality of their work and their achievements are now known throughout the world . . . They work hard under a discipline of practice hours – rest hours – feeding hours – rehearsal hours; a happy band of teenagers existing under St. Cecilia for one purpose only – music-making.

Allan played beautifully and after several bows, when the applause finally faded, he nipped back on to the platform to his place in the percussion section for the Arnold and Bizet. (He was an expert on the bass drum.) At the interval Dame Myra Hess came round to the artists' room to speak to him, as she was very moved by his playing. It was one of her favourite works, and she was so generous in her praise, giving detailed comments and encouragement. Before she left she took me aside and said, 'Uncle Tobs [Tobias Matthay, the great piano teacher] was sorry when you gave up playing, but he wouldn't be now. You haven't let the music go, you've just given it to them.'

The Dvořák symphony suited our players and conductor, and they warmed to the atmosphere. The reception from the huge audience was overwhelming; when eventually they came off the platform, hot and tired, they were obviously exhilarated by the whole experience. It seemed sad to have to cool it all by packing them into buses to drive through the darkness to the mattresses of East Ham.

The BBC officials did come round to say how pleased they were, and the director in charge of the *Light Programme*, who had taken the whole concert live, was very happy about it. So good will with the BBC appeared to be fully restored; and the week that had started shaken by disappointment had ended triumphantly.

Sunday morning was, of course, completely free. Sister remembers that after concerts the young boys were up and eager for breakfast; the girls would come down slowly, talking to relive the night before; the young men, who had thought they didn't need rest, would sleep on . . . But all assembled for Sunday lunch, refilling with energy for the next event, the TV recording. The lights were hot, and concentration was important for the different takes and instructions from different cameras all round and above us. By now many people had access to a TV set at home, but to be in a TV studio, with all that equipment, was another new experience. There were letters in the *Radio Times* asking for a repeat at a better time of the evening. Apparently in the announcer's introduction he mentioned that in the ten years our members had won 236 scholarships and entrances to universities and colleges of music. We'd never counted these up, but checked in the office and found he was right.

*

August 12 was one of the great days in our history. Through opposition and poverty, applause and generous support, triumphs and disappointments, devoted followers and mean destroyers, always with the faith and loyalty of the talented young, we had finally found acceptance in Westminster Abbey.

For such an occasion we could not have had a better group of young people in our care. We were given every possible help with seating plans in the Abbey: no detail was too much trouble to get us all into the available space and still be comfortable and look right. After Evensong we had a sound and balance rehearsal. David had never played a concerto before, so I gave him time alone and with the orchestra to get used to the sound of one solo horn in a very big cathedral. And Sir William, to whom we owed the unexpected honour of the invitation, was there to welcome us and help and advise.

The Abbey had very kindly printed a single sheet with the Abbey crest, the date and time on the front and our programme on the back: the same Weber overture, the sonata for brass, the Mozart horn concerto (K477) and the Dvořák symphony. There was a little note in italics at the bottom saying, *Those who wish to show their gratitude for this performance with be given an opportunity of contributing towards the expenses as they leave the church.* How I hoped the Abbey wouldn't be empty, and that their expenses would be covered.

There was just time for some to take a short walk along the river, past the House of Lords as the sun was setting over Westminster on this warm August evening. When they came back it was with the exciting news, 'It's not going to be empty – there's a queue outside.' Indeed the Abbey doors were kept shut until seven-thirty, by which time the queue was very long indeed, and people poured in until at eight the doors were shut again so that the concert could begin. After the overture they were opened again and more came in to stand. According to the papers, many were turned away. I had warned the players of the rather naked feeling of playing to silence instead of applause, and therefore to be careful between pieces to avoid dropping anything on the stone floor; but after the concerto clapping started, and caught on, and by the end was uninhibited. It just happened, but for myself I would have preferred this huge sound playing to Heaven in a great place to a silent crowd. I leant back against the dark oak of the choirstalls, my work over, just to listen.

My thoughts during the concert were overwhelmingly of thankfulness: that such a small group of schoolchildren should be giving all that was in them for love of playing, for love of music, and no other; that what they created so warmed the hearts of ordinary people that they could fill the Albert Hall one night and Westminster Abbey the next; and that the year in which I had hoped to expand into foreign lands ended instead with this far greater privilege and honour. It was with our own people, in the heart of the nation, of our history and of our faith, that we closed the tenth year.

It was now that, unexpectedly, a change occurred. An objective observer, the *Times Educational Supplement*, had turned us into a respectable national institution. The establishment, having failed to kill us, was suddenly claiming us as their own with pride. In reality, of course, we were still a small private music school, privately financed, without a penny from the state. Although there had been gradual acceptance over the years, I had always sensed a vague cloud of unexpressed disapproval among the powers that be. But this writer had found the courage to end the mystery and expose our secret sin:

> The National Youth Orchestra, in the ten years of its life, has become such an institution that we tend to take it for granted, and ignore the revolutionary nature of its achievement. Recent appearances within three days, at a Promenade Concert, on television and in Westminster Abbey, have raised it to a pinnacle of public fame and respectability. Yet revolutionary it was, and revolutionary it remains. The ideas it stands for, which were dismissed as sentimental moonshine, have been

> vindicated up to the hilt . . . Few people believed it possible that 120 schoolchildren could be found to play remarkably like a professional orchestra: the great service of the orchestra's founder has been to demonstrate that there's no earthly reason why they should not – if adequately led.
>
> One of the splendid things about the orchestra – an amateur body – is that it has struck a mortal blow at the fallacies of English amateurism, the crass muddling-through . . . the jovial tolerance of incompetence. *The cherished notion* that, in making music, working and 'having fun' are antithetical, *has been exploded.* [My italics.] The experience of hundreds of players who have passed through the ranks of the NYO shows that the enjoyment of real work is infinitely more rewarding. The NYO has helped to dispel the old legend of Britain as a cultural wilderness.

I cannot conclude the story of these first ten years without a tribute to the most important and encouraging part played in it by the integrity of the press. The newspapers, mainly *The Times*, *Telegraph* and *Sunday Times*, and their fine music critics – such men as Howes, Cooper, Newman, Cardus – showed genuine interest and appreciation from the start. They didn't join the establishment's opposition, the union's denigration or educational fashions. Their truthful writing was what they heard and saw and thought. They were constructive critics of our ideals, our teaching and our results, the only objective ones. They kept my heart up in the bad times. I'm grateful to them, and of course to the *Mirror* for their genuine partnership and the life-blood of money.

It is with humility that I accept the triumph of survival which was made possible by the selfless work of the wonderful people on our Council and Executive, by the partnership with great musicians, the untiring work of staff and friends, by the devoted following of our audiences, and by the love and loyalty of the musical children of the British Isles.

Part Three

REPRESENTING BRITAIN ABROAD

Twenty-Three

On 1 September, just a fortnight after the Abbey concert, came the tragic news of the death of Dennis Brain. Driving back at night after a concert, in that same car we all knew so well, he came off the empty road into neighbouring fields. He was a rare personality, one of natural simplicity and inner calm, inspiring all who heard that glorious sound and intimate skill. There were many NYO hearts broken that day, and I lost a friend from student days.

Almost as soon as we were back in the office, on 20 September, Sibelius died. We put his special note and flower in the centre of the mantelpiece, realising how honoured we were in having had that personal contact with him.

But life must go on: Dr Herbert Howells, the famous composer and professor, joined the Council now, and the Executive Committee was enriched by Mr T. E. Bean, Manager of the RFH. At this meeting, plans for future foreign tours were discussed. Following Paris in 1950, Brussels in 1953 and Brussels and Amsterdam in 1955, and ahead of invitations from Europe and America, it was to be Ireland for 1958.

We had been invited to Birmingham for the Christmas course, and the city had offered us a superb new training college as our home for the week. There were to be concerts in Leicester on Saturday and Birmingham on Sunday and a live broadcast for Independent Television. The faithful BBC promised to take a recording for *Music to Remember*.

We had one new professor, Frederick Riddle, the famous viola player and teacher. With him the violas took on a new lease of life, and he proved a great contributor to our work in many ways. A new venture was to have Malcolm Arnold as conductor, the main work in the next programme being his

Symphony No. 2. With Malcolm as composer-conductor the course was a very happy and easy one. He had a rich orchestral feeling, and Bernard Shore, who came to one concert, commented on the wonderful sound the orchestra produced.

Mrs Olive Lyell Smith was the moving spirit of the Music Association of Ireland; she had persevered for many years to persuade us to come. She knew we gave a concert in the cities where we were resident for our course, and had persuaded the City of Cork to provide for all our needs; there would be concerts in Cork and Dublin. Normally we only set out for concerts abroad after our work was completed on home shores, but Mrs Smith wanted the best musical training for Ireland, and hoped to learn more of our methods if we spent the whole week there. She hoped to copy the idea for her own country. Her determination had paid off, and we were soon to embark on a new adventure: ten days as guests of the Irish people.

On Monday morning, 7 April 1958, Mary and I flew in to Cork. We were welcomed and taken to the Metropole Hotel, our main base for the week, and to the Imperial, another hotel nearby. Altogether our needs covered four buildings, but mercifully all were reasonably close together. Of first importance was a big enough space for the full orchestra's rehearsals – the Metropole's ballroom would just do – and enough beds for everybody to sleep in. All the boys were to be in one hotel, the professors and the girls in the Metropole. This was luxury for our members – a week in real hotels, and not on the floor – and it seemed the food was going to match. We were just finishing lists for the receptionist in the boys' hotel when we were invited to lunch; used to a quick sandwich, we couldn't do justice to the hospitality before us. 'Irish taties will do you good,' said our host. 'Don't they eat in London?'

When we started arranging rehearsal-rooms, helpers emerged from nowhere. In Ireland, if anything new is happening, there is always curiosity, and readiness to take part. 'What's going on?' we heard every day. We never lacked help and enjoyed the beautiful voices and the endless chatter; they thought we were rather quiet and mysterious.

The next day involved explaining the hours of work in the different parts of the hotels and buildings to the managers and their staff. This seemed an awful shock: 'Working six hours a day – but it's holiday time.' Children here to work, not on holiday, was incomprehensible to them, but they were charmingly ready to fit in with our arrangements. There was time to see Dr Fleischmann, the Professor of Music at University College Cork, whom I knew already; also Mr Curtis, Head of the Cork School of Music, and others involved in this venture. Here was the warm Irish welcome, the curiosity as to what we were up to, the enthusiasm for what was going to take place in their midst. I could see how difficult it would be to control visitors and interruptions when work began.

That evening Mary and I went out for a walk, a breath of the lovely soft Irish air to clear our heads and glimpse our new environment. We thought of our members who had travelled all day from all parts of Britain and were now assembling in Liverpool ready for the night journey to Dublin. (Getting to Cork inexpensively in 1958 was far more difficult than crossing the Channel to Paris or Brussels.) We crossed a bridge in this most attractive small port and, putting up a prayer for a becalmed Irish Sea, we returned to our new home for the week and slept.

A phone call next morning told us that Diana, John, house staff, students, instruments and luggage were all safely disembarked in Dublin. Mary Rose Seldon told me recently that the journey was awful. The members were below deck, overcrowded and cold and with little chance of rest, and it was quite a rough night. However a press photograph shows them all smiling, neat and tidy, on arrival. They were met by Mrs Smith and Mr McCullough of the MAI and experienced at once the Irish welcome and hospitality. The first event was a reception by the Lord Mayor, Mr J. Carroll TD, in the Mansion House, and following that a bus tour of the city. By midday they were in the zoo: the *Evening Mail* comments that 'the visit of this famous orchestra to the Zoo today provided the catering staff with a very busy time. There were 140 of them for lunch but the staff were well able to cope with the situation.' And so to the station for the afternoon train to Cork and another four-hour journey to their destination for the week. We had five Irish members, two from the North – James Beck and Olivia Caffolla – and three from the Republic – Sheila O'Grady, Maeve Broderick and Gillian Smith – who now joined the train.*

Meanwhile the *Cork Examiner* was preparing a welcome. That special newspaper always seemed to me to write so sensitively and artistically; they headlined TALENTED MUSICIANS OF THE FUTURE – AT THE MOMENT THEY ARE TRAINING IN OUR MIDST. The article describes our work and then says:

> What you may not know is that this National Youth Orchestra of Great Britain is a unique venture in the history of music – so unique that invitations keep pouring in to them from countries all over the world – but it has done us the honour of choosing Cork as the venue for this season's training.

With such a welcome, we would have to be at our musical best to live up to expectations. It took time to settle everybody that evening, but an excellent supper in the Metropole found morale was splendid if in very fatigued bodies. It was early bed that night in much-deserved luxury. One young member from Canterbury said, 'I've done the longest journey of my life – a whole day to Liverpool, a night across the ocean to Dublin, and a whole day to get here. Do we stay put now?' I remember saying, 'Yes, for a week. But I'll tell you a secret. In Ireland you can never know what will happen next.'

The first morning, 10 April, started with breakfast at eight o'clock. True to our tradition of punctuality, all were seated in

*All now well-known professional musicians.

the dining-room at eight – but there was no breakfast, not even a cup of tea, in sight, the kitchen totally deserted. At about half-past, two cooks arrived, then some others, and rather nearer nine than eight plenty of breakfast appeared, in stages.

A late start to the first day's work was somewhat inconvenient, so Diana, being responsible for the daily arrangements, sought the Manager to see what went wrong. 'I thought we'd agreed to have breakfast at eight,' she said. 'Yes we did,' he replied, looking mystified, 'but I didn't know you really meant eight o'clock.' This mystification was willingly overcome between them for the rest of the week. In Ireland there were no clocks. Time was not a measurement, merely something elastic, to fit the mood of the person concerned. It was our first, and probably most important lesson of life in Ireland in 1958. Alas now, with the arrival of the modern world and the EEC, glorious clocklessness has left Ireland for ever.

During the next two days work got under way, but it was difficult to manage courteously the endless interruptions. People kept calling, full of ideas and kindness: could they take ten out on a boat; would forty like to come for a free trip in a bus; were they free all Saturday? Our members loved the people; they only had to step outside the hotel to meet friendship and endless, flowing talk. For our professors there were evening invitations and heaps of interesting pubs, and Sister Boddy was in her element. She did like a little flutter on the horses, and there were plenty of people to help her, and plenty of horses.

On Sunday morning there was time to explore the churches and walk around the city. They couldn't accept invitations to lunch because Jean Martinon had arrived and there would be a first rehearsal with him that afternoon. It was fortunate that he was with us this particular week. He had been Conductor of the RTE Orchestra some years ago. He respected and enjoyed the way we worked, but he also understood life in Ireland, and was patient and accommodating to the frequent changes of plan. Some of our professors couldn't come this time, but we had

Leon Goossens in charge of the woodwind, and Christopher Wellington, an ex-member, for the violas.

Monday morning started with all of us determined to stick to routine without interruption. Only four days to go before there were important concerts, and we had a testing programme – including a Borodin symphony, and *Capriccio espagnol* by Rimsky-Korsakov. But at twelve-thirty a charming lady arrived to fetch me for lunch and a talk to the Soroptimists. Mary expressed amazement: 'I'm sorry, we didn't know about this. She's rehearsing now and until one o'clock. I couldn't interrupt a rehearsal.'

'But she's our chief guest and speaker, and we're all waiting for her.'

'Well, I'll go and ask her, but you do understand that she couldn't be with you till after one, and she's teaching again at two.'

Of course I had to go, dashing out in working clothes, only to be met by the most attractive ladies of Cork in the height of beauty and fashion – even hats – and all the elegance of an Irish welcome. These ladies had put in an enormous amount of work in preparation for our visit. I hope I managed to explain how our results were achieved, and said we wanted to give Cork our best concert so far, and dashed away again by two. I could have listened to their lilting voices and interesting questions all day.

By Tuesday we thought we'd established through the Irish grapevine that we weren't being unfriendly, but were *not* on holiday, and 'No visitors' was the way to help us. But by mid-morning a deputation arrived: Mr Curtis with two teachers from the School of Music and one Mr O' Callaghan. When translated, their actual request amounted to whether I could spare the afternoon. They had collected together all the local young people who played instruments and they had some simple music, and could I come and turn them into the Cork Youth Orchestra? – implying that if I would just wave a magic wand over them it would come into existence . . . Such was their touching faith and hope for their pupils. It was impossible to find a way of saying no without discouraging them.

After lunch I collected a few strings players and some brass and percussion reserves to come with me, ready to join in if needed. When we arrived, a small group of very young players was set up orchestrally, looking somewhat bewildered and very nervous. Dr Fleischmann and other leading musicians and educationists had turned up for what the ever-poetic *Cork Examiner* called 'This historic step in the musical life of the city'. According to their reporter I didn't wave my baton immediately, but moved around talking to the children 'about music and the friends one makes as a musician, mingling a handful of her own players with them to give confidence, until the earnest little faces relaxed, and tension disappeared into smiles. Only then did she raise her arms, and the little orchestra rose nobly to the occasion.' In fact this was the launching of the Cork Youth Orchestra, which was carried on by Mr O'Callaghan, and now after thirty years is a youth orchestra of which any city could be proud.

We returned to base and were left in peace for our evening rehearsal with Martinon, and after supper we had a recital from Leon Goossens, to which a few friends and local musicians were invited. I was in no mood for any more changes of plan. Some hope! The professors' new-found friends kept dropping in, full of marvellous stories; Sister's horses seemed to win every race; we were all getting infected with a sense of ever-expanding time into which endless events would fit. Mary's phone conversations ran, 'Thank you, but I'm afraid we're not free on Thursday – you see we're giving a concert then . . .' 'Thank you, but we won't be here next week, we leave *this* Friday . . .'

Wednesday, the last full day before the concert, started firmly: no changes of plan. By mid-morning break Diana faced me with the generous gesture by some local group to take everybody to the Blarney Stone for the afternoon. How could I refuse either the good will or the uniquely Irish event for them all? We couldn't miss work at this stage, but were able to postpone our important final rehearsal due to our ever-patient hotel manager and kitchen staff, who agreed to stay late for supper. John and Eugene, the house staff and Sister and all those without individual lessons were off after lunch to seek their luck – everybody sworn to be back by four. They were: full of fresh air and laughter, one young girl saying, 'It was terrifying . . . they hold you upside-down by your legs – but we're all still alive.'

While they were all away there was quiet and a chance to finalise all the concert-day details for Cork, Dublin and Liverpool. But suddenly yet another deputation arrived. Our concert was sold out and so many people were disappointed. Could we let the public in to our morning rehearsal in the City Hall? I could only say I'd have to discuss it with the conductor and my colleagues, and let them know in time for the evening radio and the morning newspapers. But that was not all! Would it be possible to do a short children's concert in the afternoon, like the Robert Mayer ones in London? They'd never had one in Cork.

I tried to say that it would be best if we just did our one concert as well as we possibly could, and not spoil it by fitting in too much; but such genuine pleading, not for themselves but for their children, and for those left out . . . I promised to consider the possibilities without raising their hopes, and they left. I don't think they realised it was a lot to ask.

Martinon didn't mind about the audience rehearsal. 'If we can work, doors shut at ten, no talk at all, no clap.' He just couldn't do the children's concert as well, but thought I should: 'Irish children very nice.' A view I can now whole-heartedly share. Then we waited for John's return from the Blarney venture to test his reaction. At five we let our friends know that we would fulfil all their requests, but there were very strict conditions, in writing, to which they agreed.

Amazingly, the doors were shut at ten for our rehearsal, and the hall was very full by then. The audience was so quiet that it was possible to work normally as if they weren't there, yet we sensed the quality of an Irish audience. All went well until at the end we rehearsed our respective national anthems in case they were needed – we'd made a special orchestration for the Irish one – and everyone went home for lunch. Before John and I left the hall a group of our hosts surrounded us and said most threateningly, 'You can't play your national anthem here. If you did, the audience would walk out, anything might happen.' Of course we said at once that there was no need to start the concert with anthems: they were not in the printed programme, and we had not realised that our rehearsal could cause offence. We thanked them for the information and assured them there would be no anthems at night.

We fixed a colourful programme for the children's concert in the afternoon: *Oberon* overture; the first movement of the Mozart violin concerto with Sidney Mann; one movement of the Borodin symphony; and *Capriccio espagnol*. Luckily this involved music from four different countries, and thus many opportunities for stories. None of us will ever forget the children of Cork – so many of them, the hall just one sea of lively, beautiful children – and their response: immediate participation in every suggestion, complete silence when we were playing, then the extraordinary sound of many tiny hands clapping at great speed, as children do. That day our representative from the *Mirror* had arrived, and had offered £100 in prizes for essays about the event. So at the end I told them they could write to me about their first concert, and there would be a prize for the best piece. In England there might have been a dozen or so entries, but from Cork came nearly four hundred. I spent a few evenings at home reading them, and some weeks later they were sent five prizes.

In March 1990 the now well-established Cork Youth Orchestra came to give a concert in the National Concert Hall in Dublin. As I live there, of course I went, and was invited to meet them behind the scenes. I reminded them of their first day in 1958, and one member told me that her mother had been in that first group. When I was leaving a gentleman came up and told me he had been at the children's concert, when he was eight. It was his first concert and he wrote about it and won a prize. That started his love of music, and he is now the Administrator of the CYO.

Again, as John and I were leaving the hall we were stopped by a group of our friends, Soroptimists, local musicians, the Bishop and the Deputy Mayor. It was about the anthems. I said quickly, 'Please don't worry, we're not playing anthems,' but that was not the point. They wanted us to play theirs but not ours. John explained about the unofficial nature of our visit not requiring anthems, and that protocol would require both or neither, and we had chosen neither. It was hard to get angry with John, but they tried. Neither of us knew that in Ireland a chance for a fight must never be missed, so we didn't know why this molehill was being turned into a mountain. We couldn't believe this ugly mood – so suddenly following the happy response of the children. Pleading an hour's rest before the main concert, we took our leave.

John, Douglas Cameron and I were the only Council members present, and we took responsibility for playing no anthems. Martinon was in total agreement so when the moment came to start the evening concert, he accepted the applause then went straight into the overture. Nobody moved, nobody walked out. Instead they became immediately one of the most impressive audiences we ever played to: so quiet, so thoughtful, so responsive, by the end positively excited. Recent letters from members of this date all mention the quality of the Cork audience.

After the concert there was a reception, and as suddenly as the threatening and angry voices had been raised, the same people were full of warmth and thanks and speeches and gifts. It had been the most exhausting and the most unusual week of our history, but engraved on the memory for its unique Irishness.

And so into the train for the long journey back to Dublin, where it was an evening off for everybody. The orchestra were in two hotels, and probably made the best of a good night's sleep, knowing the following one would be on 'the ocean'. Then we had a message that John Newsom, our Deputy Chairman, and Cecil King of the *Mirror* were both in Dublin in support, which was really heartening. Mr King asked John, Diana and me out to dinner, and being an Irishman brought up in Dublin took us to a unique restaurant called Jamet. The atmosphere, the food and especially the wine were special and it was just the break we needed.

Early on Saturday morning we were in the Theatre Royal, another exciting venue new to us. A few members were helping me on the platform, harps were tuning, basses finding space, when suddenly two men from the theatre management came up and said threateningly, 'We've heard about the national anthems in Cork, and we want you to know that if you play your anthem here there will be shooting at the stage. We're warning you!' It was a pity some of our members were on the stage – they were quite shocked – but also fortunate that John Newsom and Cecil King were in the hall. The latter rose to his full height of six feet four and said, 'I'm an Irishman, brought up in this city. Are you suggesting Irishmen will shoot children?' The threateners went quickly away.

John Newsom was really worried. He thought the people concerned might bring their friends, and there would be armed men scattered about the hall, and possibly shooting . . . We shouldn't risk the children's lives and must cancel the concert. Cecil King said, 'Nonsense. It will be like last night in Cork. We won't play any anthems, and they'll love the concert.'

While our rehearsal was under way, various checks were made regarding protocol. Our Ambassador, Sir Alexander Clutterbuck, was away; neither the Irish President nor the Taoiseach nor any other government official would be coming; we were in Ireland by the private invitation of the MAI, so anthems were not necessary. By the end of the rehearsal John

Newsom, encouraged by Jean Martinon – 'Ah, they love fight, and they love music, it be OK, like last night, you see' – somewhat nervously agreed the concert should go ahead.

The Theatre Royal was half empty, not surprising on a sunny Saturday afternoon in April in a city where we were unknown. But the *quality* of the audience was staggering, and different again from Cork; enthusiasm broke through even after the overture, and lasted right through the programme. I felt mean that we had no encore prepared to feed their generosity and enjoyment, and had to leave the platform while they were still standing and clapping. After Dublin we never went abroad without an encore fully prepared, just in case.

More packing, more goodbyes, and once more into the night boat for Liverpool. It was far from comfortable for them all, and I just hoped they'd get enough sleep to give Liverpool on Sunday afternoon what Dublin had enjoyed on Saturday. We were not far out on 'the ocean' before I was called to the telephone. It was a Dublin journalist, asking why we hadn't played the national anthems. About seven times during the night the same thing happened, the same question. I suppose the idea was to trick me into saying something that would make a dramatic headline, but all they got was, 'It was not an official occasion' or 'As guests we followed your protocol,' and in fact their reporting proved fair; so what was the purpose of this night-long persecution?

I was sad. Our children felt affection for the Irish people; they appreciated the special quality and depth of feeling in the audiences; they'd responded to the extra concerts with the best that was in them. It seems history was not taught in England after 1945, so they had no idea about 1916 or the Irish people's underlying hatred of the British. It was in no way the fault of the MAI or the exceptional organisation and courtesy of Mrs Smith and her colleagues, whom I cannot praise and thank too highly. In spite of many pressing invitations to return, we never came back.

Musically we were very well received. The *Irish Times* wrote:

> The whole orchestra is instinct with a tremendous vitality and enthusiasm that made all the works thrilling to hear. Technically all sections are magnificent as this testing programme showed . . . But it was in the accompaniment to the concerto that they achieved the highest pitch of sheer beautiful playing . . . I hope that parents and schoolmasters noticed that of this very large orchestra two-thirds were boys, including all the section leaders. – C.A.

(A timely knock at the boys-play-football-and-girls-play-the-piano tradition.) The *Irish Independent* headlined MAGNIFICENT PLAYING BY YOUTH ORCHESTRA.

> In the fundamental matters of tone, intonation and precision things were so excellent that one can only marvel at what has been achieved . . . Sidney Mann (17) played with wonderful ease and beauty of tone . . . this was no amateur concert but one of the most enjoyable and satisfying that we have ever had. – Mary MacGoris.

I don't think we let the MAI down. Mrs Smith eventually succeeded in forming an Irish National Youth Orchestra, in 1984, conducted by the violinist Hugh Maguire.

We were in Liverpool at dawn, trudging a little green and bleary-eyed into buses for our breakfast destination, and on to the excellent Philharmonic Hall. Everything seemed so quiet, so calm, so efficient – so different. The hall was sold out – we were not new here, we had six Liverpool members and others from regions nearby, and of course it was the incomparable Eugene Genin's home too. The Liverpool audience lifted their tiredness, spurring them to a triumphant end to our fourth foreign adventure. We owe to Jean Martinon's inspired conducting the quality and standard achieved in this turbulent week.

The *Liverpool Post* proclaimed:

Strings, woodwind, brass and percussion were of uniform excellence, and the intonation was amazing. One listened, watched and marvelled . . . The NYO is an inspiration and a tonic which leaves one refreshed and confident in the future.

Twenty-Four

After Ireland, we needed a quieter summer at home to complete the year's work. There was the good news that four of our recent members, now students at the RAM, had been chosen as the soloists for Vivaldi's four-violin concerto in a Promenade concert: Kenneth Sillitoe, Andrew McGee, John Georgiadis and Sidney Mann.

The *Daily Mirror* was organising another £500 prize competition, this year for pianists. Their organisation was of the highest standard: the final was held in the Duke's Hall of the RAM, and Moiseiwitsch, Cyril Smith and Denis Matthews were among the judges, whose Chairman was Maurice Jacobson. It was won by one of our GMs, Philip Jenkins.

The British Council had invited us to represent Britain in Brussels at a student orchestral festival, but this was declined. We had the good fortune to be offered Hatfield College for our summer course; we'd accepted an ITV concert and were discussing the possibility of making a film with Herbert Wilcox and Anna Neagle. (Of course the Committee discussed this at length, imposing strict conditions; and we were not to sign any sort of contract and so could withdraw if necessary.)

Because we couldn't go to Brussels in July, and most European countries were sending a group through their Jeunesses Musicales organisations, Sir Robert Mayer, Chairman of Youth & Music, was worried that there was no British contribution. He came to our office and pleaded and *pleaded*. There were six hundred NYO ex-members, the colleges of music would cooperate, he would organise everything – all he wanted me to do was train a (non-existent) orchestra to represent Britain at the festival. It was hard to say no to Sir Robert but, on very tough conditions, including having Diana with me, I agreed to consider it.

Soon Mary found a newspaper cutting referring to the 'Robert Mayer Youth Orchestra', of which I was Musical Director. A young pianist and would-be conductor, later the famous conductor Sir Alexander Gibson, and an all-English programme were mentioned. We were trapped. I sought out Alex, and with an enormous amount of work and a few days' rehearsal, the Students' Orchestra of Great Britain crossed the Channel. In spite of appalling organisational problems we gave a fine concert at the Brussels Exhibition. I pay tribute to Alex as a person, as well as a musician: his qualities of character survived some awful crises, and his musicianship and professional attitude prevailed. Sir Malcolm Sargent found Diana and me after the concert and, horrified to hear we'd been dumped in some hostel sharing a room and hadn't eaten all day, swept us away to dinner with some VIPs. His gesture made up for a lot, after we'd helped a British success on an international occasion.

So with relief 18 August found us preparing the excellent Hatfield College for the invasion. Walter Susskind was coming again, and we were going to include his Nine Slovak Sketches in the programme, fully orchestrated to suit us.

Our first event this week was a live TV concert on Sunday afternoon, relayed from Associated Television's Wood Green Theatre. It was a great treat for lovers of cameras and new technology. Betty Goddard reminded me recently that in these times some cameramen couldn't read scores, and she was roped in to warn them when to focus on brass, or harp, following her score. They were very pleased with the result, and gave us all a wonderful day.

The next day was a public concert in nearby Watford. Our players enjoyed the live audience, and commented on the comparison with performing in a TV studio. But the next two days were to be spent on a film set at Elstree – a quite new adventure, to which they were eagerly looking forward.

The film was called *The Lady is a Square*, and the story involved a famous classical impresario and his wife – played by Anna Neagle – whose daughter falls for a pop star, played by Frankie Vaughan. The drama is finally resolved when at a classical symphony concert – i.e. the NYO and Walter Susskind – the pop star is the soloist and sings Handel, and everyone lives happily ever after.

Some months earlier, before agreeing to take part, I had asked to meet Frankie and hear him sing. I was ignorant as to how pop stars who didn't read music learnt their songs, and didn't know his vocal range. He brought his music adviser with him, and mutual anxieties melted into friendship. I had realised at once that it was going to be difficult for him to sing a straight tune on the beat, rather than syncopated, and extracted a promise from the music director not to teach him the Largo in advance. I would arrange a version in the best key for Frankie, coach him myself and rehearse the orchestra accordingly. I knew this was important, and was very firm.

In due course we had met for the first run-through. Alas, he'd already memorised a version, fully syncopated and decorated, and I knew we were in serious trouble. Frankie was splendid. We worked for an hour, trying to get *on* the beat or on the note, not scooped from below. I went home in despair: it was too late to cancel.

Now we were all assembling at Elstree. It took quite a time to get the orchestra arranged in the film setting. Frankie and I had time for another piano rehearsal, joined by Walter. Then Herbert Wilcox and Anna Neagle came to welcome them all and explain what was going on everywhere, and the time it took to get every detail right. Then came the first rehearsal with Frankie and the orchestra, which revealed some problems. There were so many different cameras, some close-up and some long-shot, not all canned at the same time, but finally a way was found whereby I could beat time for Frankie, quite near him and also in view of Walter . . . and real work began. Frankie was marvellous. Without once showing impatience or temperament he stuck at this straight tune, intolerably difficult and different for him. After thirteen attempts we had a break while Herbert reviewed the takes.

Frankie writes:

> The most memorable moment for me was when we struggled and made the voice and orchestra take. I thought that we had it in the can, and I had to go directly back on to the studio floor to start filming. An hour later Herbert Wilcox and Dame Anna, looking like a ghost, came over and told us that some idiot had wiped the master, and we would have to do the whole thing again. I gather heads rolled on that occasion. It was dreadful after all the trouble we had taken.

I had forgotten this, though I do suffer from shock every time I hear Handel's Largo! What I do remember is that when the orchestra was warming up in the studio, 'Happy Birthday' rang out with great warmth and colour. It was Mary Shoppee's twenty-first birthday.

Then it was back to Hatfield for our last evening of the year together. John Caldwell, who started as a reserve and became our principal flute, won his FRCO and a scholarship to Oxford, we chose for the prized Bulgin Medal.

1958 had taken us from the industrial Midlands cities to the glamorous world of film at Elstree; but it was the Year of Ireland.

The end of the course was not the end of work on the film. There were about fifteen versions of the Largo on tape, but there was no one version I could have passed. One started well, one ended well, one was out of tune in the middle. I found John Hollingsworth, a well-known conductor who also worked in film music. In 1955 he had asked if he could come to a course just as a listener and afterwards wrote, 'What a lovely experience it was – I enjoyed it so much – I learned so much – and everywhere there was that atmosphere – a great love of music and nothing else. It's something I've never experienced before, and surely a privilege for any musician to undergo.'

Now I told him the story. He laughed so much, and teased me about my army really hitting a minefield, then took me out to Elstree, putting in nearly four hours' work on the tapes. Eventually we chose six passages from different tapes, and he cut these up and rejoined the parts with fantastic skill; thanks to him both Frankie's and the NYO's reputations were saved.

The opening performance in London of *The Lady is a Square*, to which all concerned were invited, was in November, and coincided with the last great pea-soup fog in which so many animals in Smithfield cattle-market died; travelling was impossible. But Frankie writes that 'It was a most successful film of that period and one that I could never forget.' He remained a friend of the NYO, calling to see us at work on future occasions. He really cared about opportunities for young people, and gave a great deal of his time and money to projects for them, and was given a much-deserved OBE.

The quiet summer gave us a chance to assess all we'd learnt from the year of Ireland. In future we hoped our foreign tours could be after the summer course, and that travel would be simpler, preferably by air.

For the Christmas course we were the guests of the Manchester Education Authority, who provided the Wythenshawe Technical High Schools – an ideal setting for a happy week. Every possible help was given by the Headmaster and Headmistress of the two schools, and especially by William Pearson, a member of our Council. He had been Music Adviser in Cornwall in the Northcote days, and was now in Manchester, organising all our needs for a mattress-on-floor week. The Manchester department of the *Mirror* was also especially helpful.

The warmth of the Manchester welcome was shown in the support of Frederic Cox, Principal of the Royal Manchester

College of Music; his colleagues at the Hallé; and the Lord Mayor, Alderman James Fitzsimons, who gave us an official reception. We had not been in Manchester since 1951, the time of the fire.

Musically the week had interesting touches. Vaughan Williams had died in August, so we were playing his *London Symphony* in his memory. Ernest Hall, when in the LSO, had played in its first performance, forty-five years ago in 1913. Eugène Cruft, our bass professor, had reached seventy and had to give up his professorship at the RCM, but declared he would never leave his NYO professorship. Hugo Rignold was the conductor. The soloist was Stephen Savage, the runner-up in the Daily Mirror Piano Competition, playing Beethoven's Fourth. I'm amazed that I could have let a boy of sixteen touch a work of such profundity, but I did, as he had moments of exceptional insight for his years. The overture was Nicolai's *Merry Wives of Windsor*; and *The Fountains of Rome* by Respighi suited our huge orchestra of 137. The concert was in the Free Trade Hall, to a memorably enthusiastic audience – one that was used to the Hallé – and the faithful BBC recorded the whole programme. When Sir Stuart Goodwin heard it, he sent us a cheque for £500. What a devoted supporter he was! The Manchester *Guardian* concluded, 'One needs to make no allowances: by any standard this is a superb orchestra.'

When they'd all left, John and I decided that we had a lively new team for what might lie ahead. Among the flourishing talent were David Atherton and Christopher Seaman, now conductors; Derek Bourgeois, composer and later Director of the NYO; Martin Dalby, John's son: Executive Producer, Music, at BBC Scotland and a composer; the oboist Celia Nicklin; Iona Brown, now Director of the St Martin's and Los Angeles Orchestras; and our youngest, Anthony Pay, aged twelve. Martin Gatt was back as our bassoon professor, and two other ex-members, Colin Gough and Rodney Smith, were back as housemasters.

At the Council meeting on 3 February, Professor Ian Parrott, who had come from Wales to the Manchester concert, described the deep impression the performance had made on him. Dr Howells said Council members must not be ornamental: they must visit us at work, and come to concerts. Miss Pearse spoke of her direct experience of the degree to which one of her girls could be inspired as a member. Professor Hadley pointed out that ex-members who went to Cambridge were first-class without exception: they knew how to work and to take part in opportunities with confidence and responsibility. Both John Denison and Leslie Scott were strongly in favour of the educational value of our tours abroad. In fact, the whole Council was participating actively with ideas and advice. Mr Bird reported that we were solvent, and he'd saved enough to get us to Germany.

For our Easter course we had been invited back to the University of Reading, and on 31 March the whole family and staff settled in. There would be a recording for ITV, but the excitement was having Sir Malcolm again. This time he could only spare the last two and a half days, so we worked more thoroughly in smaller groups. Always preparing for the future, I had decided on a young woodwind team: Norman Knight, Janet Craxton, Thea King and an outstanding ex-member, William Waterhouse. I put Ivey Dickson, who had little experience with wind instruments, in charge of the woodwind ensemble, knowing her musicianship would triumph while she gained expertise from the four specialists. An extra treat was having Herbert Howells for the composers' class, as he was so stimulating and interesting in many spheres of our work. There were fewer recitals this week, but one very special one: the pianist Denis Matthews speaking on and playing Beethoven. And in a lighter vein, Frankie Vaughan came to lunch, made a little speech and invited everybody to *The Lady is a Square*, which was on in Reading, but of course we hadn't time to go.

As soon as Sir Malcolm arrived, all the detailed work slotted into place like the pieces of a jigsaw; he really was so happy with children and it brought out of him artistic and emotional qualities the professional orchestras seldom saw. We also had with us a remarkably talented twelve-year-old pianist, Michael Roll. He was another of Fanny Waterman's exceptional pupils, and fully ready with the Schumann concerto. Some years later he was the first winner of the Leeds International Festival. After the exciting concert at the RFH, with Sir Malcolm at his very best, came the time when we all assembled in a circle in a spacious area above the former main entrance, so that our distinguished guests could move round amongst the players, talking to some of our volunteer staff and devoted professors. It was the one occasion when everybody from the Chairman of the Council down to the newest reserve were all together, and could meet each other.

Before they went home I told them I was hoping to go to Germany in the summer by air, and to avoid disappointment warned that I couldn't take more than about 110. But the faithful BBC had offered us another Prom, so we would all be playing in that.

We looked at the press in case it was needed for Germany. In *The Times*, as well as 'For rousing tuttis and general spontaneity and flexibility of response to Sir Malcolm, Dvořák's D Minor symphony was a triumph,' there was a whole paragraph on Michael Roll's performance, temperament, character, assurance, tone and musicianship. Neville Cardus, writing in the *Guardian*, said, 'The playing can only be described as quite marvellous,' and ended with, 'Whatever, one asked at the evening's end, becomes of all this skill, enthusiasm and *love*?' I could tell him now, because they have told me. It remains for ever in the memory, in the soul.

The next Executive meeting was very important. The minutes start with, 'This was the first occasion on which Ruth Railton had not been present at a meeting.' The reason was that the steel jacket I lived in had broken, and without it I couldn't walk. Awaiting emergency repairs made me more vividly aware that I must concentrate my plans for the NYO's future without me. For now, John Dalby took over.

In a recent letter he said how proud he was to have got the Executive's permission, in my absence, for the orchestra to go by air to Germany for a concert in Hamburg and on to one in Berlin. This involved an extra week on our normal course, and Mr Bird suggested that up to eighteen guineas should be asked, including the flight, provided nobody was prevented from coming because of it. £300 from the BBC for the Prom would help. So now we could prepare a new chapter in the NYO's history – travelling by air, to the capitals of the continent of Europe.

Twenty-Five

We had accepted an invitation for our summer course from Mr Bryant, the admirable Director of Education for Tunbridge Wells. He had arranged a PNEU* school for us to sleep in, and Huntleys, a modern day school, to work in all day, with the added advantage of walking distance between buildings, in fine weather.

Since the John Ogdon tragedy there had never been any problem with the BBC. We chose the conductor, Walter Susskind, and soloist – Kathleen Jones again – and co-operated on a programme. This included a Handel overture arranged by Gordon Jacobs, which was a first performance at a Prom; a Mozart piano concerto; Rossini–Britten; Tchaikovsky; and Dvořák – which gave every section of the orchestra plenty to study.

The Prom programmes were long. Our first half lasted about an hour and twenty minutes, with a whole symphony still to come. For such young players it was some achievement, for which we had to prepare carefully. The Prom audience is overpoweringly close, almost touching your feet if you're on the edge of the platform, and behind and above you too. There were also TV cameras adding bright light and extra heat, and every note was being broadcast on the *Light Programme*. But no member will ever forget the night they played at a Prom. The press appreciated Kathleen as a musician, not as a child, and Walter was outstanding. He always said that the NYO needed constant detailed concentration, and took more out of him than professional orchestras.

Sunday was a day of real rest, with all the detailed preparation

*Parents' National Education Union.

for the great event ahead. In the evening they all learnt more about the war, and about the huge efforts the Germans were making as a defeated nation to rebuild friendships for their young people with other countries, and how we might help; but also about the crisis in Berlin, with the Russians threatening to push the Allies out. It was very surprising how little they knew about the war and how few had parents who had fought in it. (We had miners, shipbuilders, fishermen, farmers, doctors, teachers, police among our parents.) Only our Jewish members, two of them refugees from Hitler, knew the history of the last twenty years.

On Monday morning *The Times* honoured us with a large picture, and an appreciative send-off for Germany. As a gesture to Mr Bryant and the people of Tunbridge Wells whose guests we were, we gave a concert on Monday in the Assembly Hall. It was the same programme as the Prom, without the Tchaikovsky, and the last day for Kathleen. She couldn't come to Germany with us, as her parents rightly thought she should have a holiday, so Tuesday and Wednesday were spent preparing a different concerto with Allan Schiller and another overture, and we made a recording for the BBCTV programme *A-Z*.

After supper on the last evening we all met for a final check of individual responsibilities to soothe any anxieties, and to make sure everybody knew their role in the days ahead.

It was a warm August morning as 110 musicians, one conductor, two musical directors, two housemasters, two housemistresses, one nurse and two secretaries set off to Manston Airport. We had chartered two Hermes aircraft, and the firm was very efficient and co-operative, especially concerning the loading and care of our instruments. Our travelling order separated brothers and sisters and mixed those carrying instruments among those without, such as bass and percussion players: this prevented overcrowding in the seats, and embarkation went speedily according to plan. Once airborne, I walked around in the atmosphere of excitement, perhaps a little nervousness – only three of them had ever been in a plane before. They soon settled into a mood of wonderment, enjoying the view, and before long they glimpsed the German coastline and our destination, the city of Hamburg.

Here we were met by the concert agent, several representatives of the musical and educational life of the city, and a mass of TV and press cameras seeking interviews straight away. The youth hostel in which they stayed was spotless, and on this first evening in Germany they were taken on a trip round the docks in boats. There were still signs of wartime devastation, and beside this the impressive structures of the new modern port. They were all very impressed with the efficiency of everything, and the day ended when we were guests at a garden party in the British Consulate.

Our concert in the fine Musikhalle was the opening of the Hamburg season, and sold out; we were well aware of the honour and what was expected of us. The German attitude to musical performance was quickly commented on: they were so understanding of details – a higher stool, a different stand, even the choice of piano – everything needed in the cause of music. We worked hard that morning to get fully up to our best after a whole day off.

In the evening the concert was very warmly received, and enthusiasm increased in the symphony, and they insisted on an encore. Among the musicians present was the famous conductor Schmidt-Iserstedt, who came round to talk to us. Our leader Michael Freyan, whose parents had escaped from Hamburg to England in 1939, was not well, and at the last minute I had moved Iona Brown in to lead. He was very impressed with her playing and spent some time with her, encouragement she has never forgotten. Also present was the leading newspaper proprietor in Germany, Axel Springer, who had put up DM3,000 for the concert, though as it was sold out only DM1,000 were needed.

It had been a marvellous two days – air travel, boats round

Hamburg docks, a garden party meeting German musicians and an important concert in a great hall to a highly discerning audience.

It was an early start next morning for the train to Berlin. Our new-found friends and the agent gave us a send-off and handed us the papers. *Die Welt* said 'the evening had surpassed expectations'; *Bild Zeitung* wrote, 'Walter Susskind gave a brilliant and moving performance. The orchestra didn't just play the Dvořák, they seemed to live it, and the audience rewarded them with storms of applause.' There were other papers too, but England, via *The Times*, had remembered us and reported the NYO being 'given a standing ovation in the Musikhalle in Hamburg last night. It is to play in Berlin tonight.' At the moment all our interest was on the trains, the stations, the uniforms, the scenery; in a few hours we would all be on the platform of the great Hochschule für Musik of Berlin, the former capital city now in a divided and tragically anxious state.

In the mean time our instrument van had been packed after the concert to set off through the night and be in the Berlin hall when we arrived. John had asked our young ex-member housemaster, Rodney Smith, to travel with the van as an extra precaution. While we slept he set off with the van driver. He writes:

> I had been asked to go with the van to Berlin. At the border I had to unlock every box, every timpani and harp, but with patience and good will the paperwork for the *instruments* was declared in perfect order, but not for me! I had to leave the van and walk along the area of no man's land between the West and the East German border. I was well aware that the pillboxes on either side of the road contained guards who may well have been pointing various armaments towards me. That walk in a dark wet dawn will never be forgotten! However, my legs carried me and the East Germans were kind, more friendly than the West, but sorry, my papers were not correct, I would have to leave the van and return to Hamburg . . . so I said farewell to the driver, farewell to the instruments, gave him the keys and caught a bus back into Hamburg. Then with

remarkably little German I managed to get to the rail point to catch a train through to Berlin. Arriving at the hall I was overjoyed to find the keys and all the instruments safe, and a message as to where, like a lost sheep, I would be able to join the fold.

When we arrived in Berlin we were met by the agent and the *Konzertdirektor*, Robert Kollitsch, with the warmest welcome; it was quite overwhelming. The members were taken to a very pleasant youth hostel; Walter, John and me to an army hostel as guests of the British Army.

The afternoon was spent in the Jugendheim an Wannsee Park, where everyone was invited to listen to German choirs and to meet a cross-section of young Germans. For us it was a chance to meet the director of education of Berlin, some teachers and musicians, but especially the exceptional Frau von Wedelstadt, a Prussian lady of great culture, in charge of the British Council in Berlin. She was a personality never to be forgotten by her many British friends over the years. It was also our first chance to meet the remarkable Alan Baker from the Foreign Office, one of the most able, kind and sensitive people I have ever met. He was responsible for everything running smoothly at such a critical time for Berlin, of which we were mainly unaware.

Early next morning we were in buses outside the concert hall when a large crowd collected, blocking our access. My youngest member on the front seat with me said, 'You told us the Germans were very musical, but they haven't even heard us yet!' Little did we know that the crowd had sensed that the British wouldn't send their children in if there was going to be a war, or any giving-in to the Russians. Soon the police cleared a pathway and the crowd watched and clapped as 110 British children in uniform, carrying instruments, walked across the square smiling happily.

Inside, at work, it was a nightmare morning. The media wanted everything – interviews, a recording for RIAS, a television performance. Never have I been so grateful for the training of our students: they took instructions from their own staff, and carried out their unpacking and stage-setting quietly and quickly in spite of all the excitement going on around them. In fact, they were ready on the platform ten minutes early, so we fitted in a few photographs and interviews, and time for sound and light testing. I bargained with the TV people that they could have all they wanted at twelve o'clock if we could have an uninterrupted rehearsal until then. The Germans were wonderful to work with, totally understanding of musical and platform needs, and after photographs with the famous Walter Susskind the bargain was kept.

All was going splendidly until at five to twelve I went to tell Walter about the TV. I knew he'd be pleased, as he loved television, but for some reason he suddenly exploded – 'You didn't tell me, I have wrong clothes . . . I will NEVER conduct this orchestra again!' – and stormed off the platform. The orchestra rose to their feet, as was their custom whenever a conductor entered or left the platform, and sat down looking shocked. John followed Walter and I took his place. I reassured them quickly that it was my fault, and that he would be back for the concert. We would now keep our word, and play for TV. What luck that I'd been so tough about no cameras during rehearsal, or that scene might have gone out all over Germany! As it was, we completed our commitments and returned to the hostel for lunch and an afternoon's rest.

Then came a heart-warming gesture: the Army were giving all the children a meal before the concert. There's a saying that 'An army marches on its stomach': certainly a young orchestra plays well on good food, and this was a great treat. Afterwards a brigadier thanked them for coming to Berlin and 'cheering us all up'.

There was extra nervous excitement behind the scenes. 'The Germans are such an emotional people you feel as if you are in the heartland of music itself,' said one, and this eager response overflowed into the national anthems. Mr Baker writes:

> At the playing of the national anthems there was an electric thrill round the Hochschule für Musik. When you think that they were accustomed to the Berlin Philharmonic this says something for the sound that was produced by a young orchestra on a special occasion.

The concert itself was accepted even more warmly than at Hamburg. They thought Allan's maturity in the Beethoven was staggering, the Britten was exciting, the Dvořák a truly great performance in the hands of a Czech conductor, and they wanted an encore. None of us will ever forget the atmosphere of that night in 1959 with the people of Berlin.

The Commandant of Berlin, General Delacombe, came to the concert and wrote in the orchestra's visitors' book, 'A very great experience – a remarkable concert.' The Foreign Office and the British Council, who had been so supportive, were overjoyed at the success. Mr Baker wrote that 'The people who had sadly referred to England as "*das Land ohne Musik*" immediately sensed that a fundamental change had taken place, and that young England was returning to the golden age of music.'

Berlin had provided a free day as guests of the city. There was a reception by the Mayor, Willy Brandt, who generously gave each member a silver replica of the Brandenburg Gate. They were taken on a tour of East and West Berlin and met Heinrich Albertz, the city's Director of Culture. At a press conference I was asked, 'Do you perhaps ask too much of such young people?' I had replied, 'Wouldn't it be dreadful if I asked too little?' and this made evening-paper headlines and provoked many articles for some weeks ahead. My remark was spontaneous and sincere, but the reaction showed the tendency, as in England, to go easily and spoil our young, to make up for the ghastly tragedy of war the adults had been through. Now, thirty years on, I don't think we expect anything like enough in behaviour or achievement from the young today. The five- to twelve-year-olds give a picture of a nation's future, and comparing ours with the Japanese or Russians should stir us, if we are still a great nation.

While the children slept we had a staff meeting. Diana's plans and paperwork were in perfect order for going through the Russian Zone, but I asked the house staff to take extra care: arriving early at the train and *seeing* every passport, rather than simply reminding the children.

There was plenty of time at the station early the next morning, and many friends, including Mr Baker, had come to see us off. When we were all in the train, one girl, Juliet Stainer, discovered she'd left her passport behind in the hostel. She knew precisely where it was, and Mr Baker fled off, driving through the rush hour to the hostel. John and I stayed on the platform with our distressed Juliet, by the last door of the train, nearest the barrier. We were just planning whether one of us would stay behind with her, or all stay in the train until the Russians checked us at the border, when a young man, one of our members, got out at the front of the train and came running down the platform to us. It was Juliet's brother, Gareth: 'If you're staying behind, may I too? My mother wouldn't like me to leave my sister.'*

We all got in the train as it was time for the doors to shut, but I was hanging out of the window in hope . . . the train started to move and suddenly at the barrier there was Mr Baker, running alongside the train, just handing the passport to me. Our last goodbye to Berlin was a wave with passport in hand, till we were out of sight.

The Russians at the border were extremely fastidious, checking every detail; but at least one fine young housemaster who'd failed to see the passports, thinking I was over-fussy, had learnt for the future that details can matter. At Hamburg, our pilots

*Gareth and Juliet Stainer were the great-grandchildren of Sir John Stainer, composer of *The Crucificion*, Organist of St Paul's Cathedral and Professor of Music at Oxford. Their father was Registrar of the RCM. In 1980, Juliet's son Edward was the youngest member of the NYO, became its leader and is now embarking on a career as a professional violinist.

told us that they'd read about our concerts in English papers and brought us copies.

In all our activities we had not been able to get all the orchestra together to tell them about this year's Bulgin Medal. Our two planes were in radio contact so a simultaneous announcement was made to them all: it was awarded to Iona Brown, who had been in the orchestra for over five years, and had led the concert in Hamburg. It was after much rejoicing in mid-flight that our pilots delivered 110 much more experienced travellers safely to Manston.

A few days later we studied the German press. The music critic of *Bild Zeitung* reported:

> Berliners attend many concerts but they were never so moved as they were last night by the National Youth Orchestra of Great Britain. They gave a performance that was completely beautiful and without affectation . . . compassionate and sensitive interpretation of Dvořák . . . a night which music-loving Berliners will long remember.

Apart from music, a letter from Alan Baker showed we had played our part in building good relations with the new Germany:

> The effect of the visit did not stop with the concert. The friendships set up with young Germans made a lasting effect on a country which still considered itself a pariah.
>
> Adult Germans had grown up in the military discipline of Nazi Germany. What struck me, and more forcibly the Germans, was that here was a large group of young people who came from different backgrounds and were activated by an inner self-discipline because the slim young lady in charge never had to exercise command over them. I think the Germans realised pretty soon that this inner discipline had grown out of your ideals and your teaching.

And perhaps most important is what we now know from General Delacombe, who kindly wrote to me in 1989:

> . . . in 1958/9 the Russians had given an ultimatum to the Western Allies: 'Get out – or else you have six months.' You can well realise the feelings of two and a half million Germans in West Berlin. Will the Allies stand firm or . . .? Thus a visit by the British Youth Orchestra was a clear indication that we would NOT leave . . . the gesture helped to maintain the morale of the West Berliners and also helped to occupy their minds . . . you struck the right note, as the Germans love music and enjoyed your concert.

It was at the Executive meeting of September 1959 that our marvellous Treasurer, Roland Bird, explained he could no longer continue. He had kept our financial affairs in perfect order for five years, and we were deeply grateful to him. His last act was to hand over to a new Honorary Treasurer, Don Ryder,* Managing Director of Associated Iliffe Press, to continue this vital role.

This year's audition tour produced the highest standard in horns and oboe players, and the best string-playing was in Dublin. For sight reading, the weakness everywhere was a rhythmical one. I vowed to overcome this, at least with my own members. Strangely, within a year, the Beatles burst on to the youthful scene, and this effected another change – with its own problems, chiefly that of marking every beat with the foot.

*Now Lord Ryder of Eaton Hastings.

Twenty-Six

Alderman Hyman, Chairman of the West Riding County Council, had a grandson in the orchestra, so we'd received a warm invitation to meet in Yorkshire in January, with a generous offer to occupy the Ilkley College of Housecraft. The Principal was wonderful to us, not just co-operative about our peculiar needs but participating in solving them, almost becoming part of our team for the course.

Hugo Rignold was back as conductor, and a former member, Kenneth Sillitoe, would be the soloist for the violin concerto. One outstanding event was a talk from Dr Howells, with all the charm and Welsh flow of language, on his own early life in music.

The programme was planned to give Mozart to the chamber group, Berlioz for everybody, and I returned to Delius after eleven years, having tried it too soon in 1948, with the *Paradise Garden*. The main work was Sibelius 2. We had hoped to play in York Minster, but the Warsaw Philharmonic was coming in January, and the local population could not fully support two events so close together. But our friend Sir Stuart Goodwin owned a hotel in Harrogate, and hoped we'd play there. The Mayor gave us a reception, and Sir Stuart gave us a wonderful meal in his hotel, crowning it with a gift, a cheque for £500. So our first concert of 1960 broke new ground and was warmly received by a Yorkshire audience in the Royal Hall, Harrogate.

Easter in 1960 was very late, so we had no choice but to meet before Easter. We had been invited to Portsmouth, to include a concert in the cathedral, but the Holy Week dates made this impossible; our friends from former courses in Brighton came to our rescue, the generous and helpful heads of Brighton College and St Mary's Hall lending their premises. There was even no English conductor available, but finally André Vandernoot, whom I had met and seen in action in Holland, came to my rescue.

My latest drive on sight reading and rhythm had caused consternation: our members thought that this time I was expecting the impossible. So bad had rhythmic teaching become all over the country that my clapping and counting tests were genuinely thought too demanding. My senior members prepared a wonderful joke for the anniversary party. Stands were arranged across the platform, on which were copied exceedingly tricky rhythmic patterns from very modern works. All the professors were lined up, and when the beat and tempo was banged out on the percussion whip we were to count aloud and clap. The orchestra expected an amusingly chaotic result, but to their amazement we could all do it. They tried the second piece and we still triumphed. On the last test, Douglas Cameron came in too early, and we broke down into a good laugh. Of course our members went home and told their teachers that to our generation reading rhythm was normal, and I had many letters from teachers in schools, asking for information and methods. By my next audition tour the shock was over and the sight reading better.

Always expanding our repertoire, we now enjoyed a Wagner overture, and a Mozart piano concerto with Evelyn Rix, and embarked on our first Prokofiev, the ballet suite *Le Pas d'acier*, seldom played because it needs such a large orchestra. The concert was in the Dome, Brighton, and André Vandernoot, who like Jean Martinon on his first visit had been a little bewildered by our teaching methods, rose to the occasion with a fine concert.

During the year there had been many invitations to foreign countries – including Denmark, Japan and Australia – but sadly the dates proved impossible, and we decided on Scotland alone for this summer. Many of our members had never been to Scotland and to them it *was* a foreign tour!

This time Aberdeen High School for Girls, with superb

amenities, was our home for the week. John Dalby managed all the arrangements, and the welcome from the city was overwhelming. The Provost, George Stephen, gave a reception for us and took us round the Town Hall himself. The university supported us in many ways and the Principal, Sir Thomas Murray Taylor, visited us at work several times.

We had Walter Susskind back again, with a fully absorbing programme to complete the year's work: Walter's favourite overture, Dvořák's *Carnival*; a Mozart flute concerto with Sebastian Bell, our former principal flute; and for the English work we tackled *The Planets* by Holst for the first time.

A great surprise one morning was a letter from the Rector of the village church in Crathie on the Queen's Balmoral Estate, the Rev. Dr John Lamb CVO, inviting us to the Sunday service. We had all seen pictures on TV of the royal family going to worship there when at Balmoral, but this was reality.

Then somebody pointed out that in Scotland hats were essential in church, and none of us had one. Betty Goddard went to call on John's wife, Louis Dalby, who graciously spread out her entire stock of headgear, and we had an amusing time on Saturday evening matching her collection to the clothes and heads of all the female staff.

Louis Dalby made an enormous contribution to the NYO, accepting life as a grass widow every time we met or went on tour. What is more, she saw little of John in term-time, and when their son Martin joined our viola section she was alone at home. She never once complained though it was a real sacrifice. She was a person of great gentleness, thoughtful, wise and utterly selfless. Recently I asked her about it. 'The NYO meant more to John than anything else: it transformed his life. It was my way of sharing in it.' We all owe her so much.

The Aberdeen concert was upon us. I wanted it to be our best so far, as a small return for Aberdeen's generous hospitality this week, and their faith in us and continued support from the first audition in 1948. Susskind was well known, having formerly been conductor of the Scottish National Orchestra. The audience's enthusiasm created a festive occasion, and the *Scotsman* praised an 'exciting and stunning performance'.

In contrast, early next morning we set off to the quiet peace of Crathie. It is impossible to describe the emotional effect of being in such simplicity and informality at prayer in a tiny village church, with the Queen of England in our midst, a little touch of history and a lasting memory for us all.

Another adventure was breaking new ground in Dundee. The Caird Hall is enormous, and Paul Cave worked energetically to get a half-full audience, but their enthusiasm made the venture fully worthwhile. Then came a return to Glasgow after an absence of five years. The concert in St Andrew's Hall was made possible by Mr W. R. Fell, the General Manager of the SNO, and the enormous help of the YMCA in solving the accommodation problem. We were delighted to read that the concert was felt to be the best of the three, a new peak on which to close the concerts of 1960.

Our steady, hard-working year was rewarded with outstanding exam results. Our members won five university music scholarships, fourteen open scholarships to the RCM, five to the RAM and three to the RMCM, and one each from the RSAM and the Associated Board. Two of my piano pupils were in the RCM list, and they told me that at their final interview the Director, Sir Keith Falkner, asked who taught them. On mentioning my name they heard, 'And to think we never knew that she *taught*!' What did they think I was doing nearly every day of my life?

The Royal Academy lent the Duke's Hall for the final of the Daily Mirror Competition, this time for strings. It was won by Martin Elmitt, one of our cellists, with Iona Brown second. The Chairman of the *Mirror* came to present the prizes, and afterwards asked me if I was pleased with the result. I said I had no quarrel with the judges, but in fact the runner-up probably needed the money more. He immediately pulled out his chequebook and wrote her a cheque for £250. With this she set off to study with her favourite violinist, Henrik Szeryng, and her career took off. To this day she values that spontaneous generosity.

In September we had to say goodbye to Mary. Once again love had stolen a quite exceptional person from us all. She had given us nearly four years of selfless dedicated work, always tactful and courteous, unfailingly reliable in ever-changing circumstances. Diana was losing the perfect secretary, and all of us – staff and members – were losing a real friend.

1961 was a year of change. I was always thinking about the NYO continuing without me and now Douglas Guest, as Chairman of the Council, helped set up a sub-committee to plan the future. The members were Douglas Cameron, John Newsom, George Sylvester, Maurice Jacobson, Herbert Howells and me.

They accepted my idea of final auditions in London. John Dalby and Ivey Dickson – and gradually others – would do the preliminary ones, the best applicants coming to me at a final.

They concluded that eventually I must be replaced by an instrumentalist who understood performance but was also an experienced teacher, able to see potential, on which our results over the years had depended. In addition, the network I had created of good relationships with teachers all over the country must be preserved. They also wanted the original title of National Junior Music School restored, so that the NYO was not considered solely as a concert-giving orchestra. The public only saw and heard the orchestra, unaware of the teaching that created it. So the search was on, not for an orchestral manager but for an artistic performer with judgement who loved teaching.

I put a lot of thought into how to get the best results from the new plan of final auditions. Some candidates would have met me before, but most would be facing strangers in me and the specialist professor I would have with me. Some would know Ivey Dickson, so she must be there to play for them, and I decided that they could each bring one friend, parent or teacher with them, to help make a kind and friendly audience. The atmosphere must be informal. We found a nice warm hall, with a good piano and space at the back for their supporters to listen. The first experimental day was for sixteen cellists, and Douglas Cameron was with me all the time. The candidates played what they liked, then sight read, and could then talk to either or both of us if they had any questions. Most of them brought their teacher and the candidates could all listen to each other. When the actual auditions were over we all had a friendly get-together, from which I learnt that the teachers were so pleased to meet Douglas Cameron, and equally to have heard the standard, of which they were previously unaware. They would say, 'I thought my pupil was outstanding; now I know she's not advanced enough yet,' or 'I don't envy you choosing. I wouldn't have missed hearing that for anything.'

They were also pleased to meet each other, and the students were busy swapping addresses. One said, 'If I don't get in at least I'll understand why, the others were so good.' They knew I only had four or five vacancies and they would get a letter in a week.

So we continued this new idea for over a fortnight, with a different instrument every day. I don't think we lost too much raw potential from the highways and byways I used to visit, and my colleagues agreed that both teachers and parents had a better glimpse of young talent nation-wide. For my part, I had an instrumental specialist with me all the time.

By mid-December I had chosen sixty new members, and was assembling a total of 152 (a hundred boys) with an average age of fifteen. Little did they know as they opened their letters of invitation what territory they would cover, and what marvellous experiences would enrich them through 1961.

I was very fortunate to have five famous conductors, all so different, keen to come regularly, but it wasn't enough for the future. They had to be people of a very special quality, artistically and personally. Janet Craxton, whose artistic sensitivity and judgement were very like my own, introduced me to

Oivin Fjeldstad, a very fine Norwegian musician, and after studying him at work in London I had persuaded him to join me at Christmas.

We had accepted a generous invitation from Portsmouth for the Christmas course. The education authority offered all the amenities in their huge Paulsgrove Modern Schools, and both the Headmaster and the Headmistress gave time to help.

The excitement of the week was the new conductor, due to arrive from Norway on New Year's Day. He was everything we could have hoped for: a gentle person with a reassuring smile, an inspiring musician, a wonderful teacher. He was happy with us, and before the week was over had accepted my invitation to return in the summer for our foreign tour. There were no plans for such yet, but intuitively I knew there would be one. The day Oivin Fjeldstad joined us was a great day for the NYO.

Since Westminster Abbey we had had many invitations to play in cathedrals, and this time we'd accepted the privilege of a concert in Winchester Cathedral. January 4 was a bitterly cold and windy day. At the morning rehearsal cardigans and jackets made playing possible, but for the evening concert, those who couldn't get jumpers on under their uniform white shirts and blouses were really too cold to play. Luckily there was an interval, in which the audience were singing the great Epiphany hymn 'As with gladness men of old'. Paul Cave remembers that I disregarded uniform and everybody put on cardigans, of any colour, for the second half. What most of us will never forget is the sound of the great organ, played by Dr Sumption, and the singing of the huge crowd in that great cathedral. Afterwards they moved quietly back to their places to play the great Brahms C Major symphony, most of them for the first time, in that inspiring atmosphere.

The next day was our concert in the Guildhall, Portsmouth. Although it was a new venue for us it was sold out, and the particularly enthusiastic audience was such a contrast, especially

33. Queen Elizabeth the Queen Mother, escorted by the Chairman and Mrs Guest, talking to Maureen Smith

34. The orchestra's arrival in Dublin, Lord Mayor's reception

35. Jean Martinon

36. The orchestra sightseeing in Berlin:
Walter Susskind, Iona Brown, Michael Freyan (behind Iona's left shoulder)

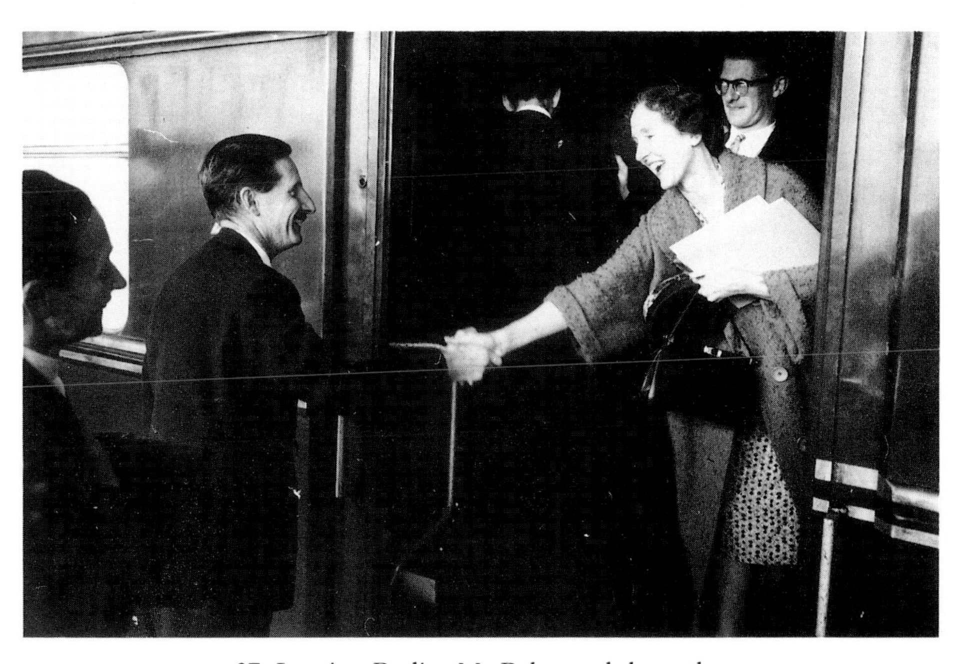

37. Leaving Berlin, Mr Baker and the author

38. The general public listening to the orchestra in the *Daily Mirror* building

39. In Red Square, 1961

40. Returning from the Polish tour, 1963:
Peter McLachlan, the author, John Braithwaite

41. Oivin Fjeldstad, Isle of Man, 1964

42. The 'Anglicised Arabs' in Jerusalem

A. BOGATYR – J. ORI

under the auspices of the Foreign Minister,
Mrs. Golda Meir
proudly present:

The National Youth Orchestra of Great Britain

115 MUSICIANS Conductor: RUDOLF SCHWARTZ
Musical Director: Dr. RUTH RAILTON

TONIGHT — CAESAREA: Roman Theatre, 8.30 p.m.
Special buses will leave from "Egged-Dan," 59 Rehov Ben Yehuda, corner of Rehov Mendele, Tel Aviv, at 6.45 p.m. for Caesarea, and will bring guests back to Tel Aviv.

BEERSHEBA: Keren Hall, **Wednesday, Sept. 2, 8.30 p.m.**
HAIFA: Armon Theatre, **Thursday, Sept. 3, 8.30 p.m.**

TICKETS available at:
TEL AVIV — Rococo and other agencies; JERUSALEM—Cahana; HAIFA — Ginsburg — Yuval; NETANYA—Signal; BEERSHEBA and HADERA.

"... an orchestra with a tone quality of a kind rarely experienced, whose rich and carefully balanced sonorities were compounded of the technical mastery with which these young people handle their individual parts. Their stage behaviour and discipline was exemplary, their dedication and earnestness enviable ... one of those feasts of music that no one should miss."
Yohanan Boehm, *The Jerusalem Post*

43. The new posters bearing Yohanen Boehm's report

44. The Athens Festival, 1964

45. The home of the bats

DAILY MIRROR, Wednesday, September 1, 1965 PAGE 7

One of Britain's finest exports . .

46. Leaving for Portugal, 1965 . . .

47. . . . with Rudolf Schwarz

for our new members, after the silent cathedral the night before. It was important for them to learn that different audiences and different places bring out different performances. As well as the Brahms, we were playing the vivid *Egmont* overture and Mary Gallagher, one of our Irish violinists, was the soloist in the violin concerto; instead of the usual English work we played the Grieg *Symphonic Dances* as a tribute to our conductor.

Portsmouth had been very good to us: the Lord Mayor, Mr Bonnerpink, visited us the first morning to bring an official welcome, and after the concert came round with a written invitation to return whenever possible, and this was much appreciated.

The early-morning goodbyes were always revealing. Two new thirteen-year-olds lingered a little, and came up to me: 'Will we be invited next time? . . . How long will it be before we know? . . . Have we been all right?' Reassurance must always be given when the young are doing their best, and I parted from smiling faces.

The next Executive Committee and the Council passed our plans for Easter in London, and Berlin and Moscow in the summer, for which the British Council would give us £2,000. I expected warnings about anti-Communist opposition but in fact there were none. The political mood at that time must have been to maintain contacts through the Iron Curtain, but I had yet to test the reaction of our parents to the idea.

It was decided that Mr Bean should go with me to Moscow to check the arrangements involved in their invitation for a tour of the Soviet Union. The first Aeroflot line from Heathrow to Moscow direct had recently been inaugurated, operated three days of the week by BOAC, three by Aeroflot. We thought it politic to arrive in a Russian plane, and when the day arrived boldly mounted the steps into this enormous Toupolev, to discover we were the only passengers. It was a lonely moment. There was a staff of twelve stewards and stewardesses, devoid of English, but confidence mounted a little as *four* handsome pilots entered the cockpit. The pressurisation in a Russian plane was disastrous for our ears, and as we crossed the Channel I hoped it wasn't my last glimpse of England. Once fully airborne our sense of humour returned and we got down to work, which filled the ensuing four hours.

Soon two very large plates piled with food arrived, and some vodka, which I refused. We ate plentifully but made little impact on the quantity, which was distressing to our hostesses. With the aid of my Russian dictionary I tried 'Very nice, just too much' – with the result that the dishes disappeared, and back came two plates full of more food. 'Poodin,' said the hostess and disappeared. 'I'll sip the vodka,' said Mr Bean, 'and you'll eat the poodin.'

Once in Moscow there was the warmest welcome. We were shown accommodation in their best hotels, and the Tchaikovsky Hall for two concerts. Musicians and Ministry of Culture representatives were easy to work with; they wanted seven concerts in all – two in Moscow, two in Leningrad and others to be arranged later. We planned a programme – a British work (they wanted Britten) – and a Russian work: could we manage Tchaikovsky 5? I explained that in case of illness there would be three different soloists on different instruments. They were full of questions about how we achieved such a standard, and obviously loved children and enjoyed the photographs we brought. Mr Bean and I returned able to report with confidence that no stone would be left unturned and no request refused to make a success of the first official visit of British children to perform in the Soviet Union.

On 8 March 1961 Sir Thomas Beecham died. He had been one of my early vice-presidents, and always supported me. It was sad that he had never conducted us. (He shared the same birthday as Sir Malcolm, so each year when we greeted our President we also wrote to Sir Thomas. It was interesting to discover, when Rudolf Schwarz joined our team of conductors in 1962, that he too shared this birthday.)

*

The Easter course developed into two major concerts and many exciting minor events. The first was in the RFH, always a peak occasion, with our President conducting and the great honour and excitement of our royal patron the Queen Mother coming for the first time. We had also been asked by the King George's Jubilee Trust to give a concert in Westminster Abbey, as a thanksgiving at the end of their silver-jubilee year.

We needed to meet near London, and once again Mr Bryant arranged everything in Tunbridge Wells. The first evening I revealed the immediate events, but I also told them about Berlin and Moscow, partly because it was going to be announced to the press, and partly because the whole week would be a preparation for a much bigger experience in the summer. Also I needed parental permission both to fly and to go to Russia, and the sooner we knew the position the better.

Work started eagerly on a huge programme; everybody was delighted that Sir Malcolm was going to be with us for the last four days. He was fascinated at what they could do, and it gave him much happiness to be with children. With Sir Malcolm we knew that on the night there would be security, yet the music would sparkle and shine.

During the week Yehudi Menuhin came for most of a day, and wrote to say he was 'very impressed with the atmosphere'. He spoke to the orchestra after a rehearsal and said he hoped one day to have a school like this, but full-time. The Mayor of Tunbridge Wells also honoured us with a visit, and we had one evening off for our thirteenth-anniversary party.

There was an extra full rehearsal for brass and percussion because Christopher Seaman, our principal timpanist, had written a fanfare and linked it cleverly to the national anthem – an offering to our royal patron. I provided a bit more time with Ernest Hall, and sprung it on Sir Malcolm as a surprise.

On the night, the Queen Mother was to receive a bouquet on entering the hall, presented by my little five-year-old niece Diana Railton. Bouquet and curtsy completed, the child remained transfixed by the diamond-glittering vision in front of her. We saw the Queen Mother say something and gently push her aside, and it emerged as we went to the royal box that Diana had said, 'Where is your wand?' and she had replied, 'I left it at home tonight.'

The expectant audience rose as Her Majesty entered the box, and the joyous fanfare burst forth. After the national anthem came the *Academic Festival Overture*; our soloist Maureen Smith, only fourteen, playing Mozart; and the first half closed with Elgar's *Wand of Youth*, in a quite astonishing climax with 'The Wild Bears'. Such was the applause that this commanded a repeat – very unusual to give an encore before the interval.

After the concert everybody, including reserves and GMs, lined up either side of the main lift, instruments still in hand, as Her Majesty, escorted by Douglas Guest, graciously consented to walk among them. She spoke to Maureen and to several others. To one violinist from Ireland she said, 'Will you be going to Russia?' and out came the reply, 'Holy Mary Mother of God I hope so!'

Then a great festive occasion was over and had to be absorbed in talk or sleep in the buses during the dark drive back to Tunbridge Wells.

By six o'clock the next afternoon everyone was in place for rehearsal in Westminster Abbey. The programme was the same except for the festive opening and the Elgar suite. I suppose butterflies and wild bears were not suitable in the Abbey, it being long before the days of environmentalism, and so Brahms, Mozart, Schubert and Smetana it was. This time admission was by programme, which included a request for the audience to refrain from applauding. A short piece then described the work of the King George's Jubilee Trust, which existed to further the physical, mental and spiritual welfare of the young, and quoted the inaugural broadcast by George V in which he trusted that 'many of them may be helped in body, mind and character to become useful citizens'. It would seem to me, working amongst the young in the last fifty years, that we have looked after their bodies, far less so their minds, and neglected the training of character and the power of example.

There was also a short paragraph about our work recalling their grant to us, 'without which it would have been difficult to continue', and acknowledging a jubilee gift to the trust from the *Daily Mirror*, repaying every penny the trust had given to us from 1948 to 1951.

It had been a great week, especially for our newer members: discovering all that goes into creating a concert, and projecting it to a responsive Festival Hall audience: and then the contrast of mood and atmosphere of being in a great church and playing to silent listeners. At dawn – like a puff at a dandelion – they all scattered, carrying their memories into homes all over the British Isles.

Twenty-Seven

The busiest summer in our history was about to begin.

First we had to be sure of our orchestra. The Russian Embassy required complicated forms to be filled out by every member, including the maiden name of their paternal grandmother – not surprisingly, some of them didn't know it or how to find out. After about a month we found we had permission from all the parents except three. Two were Irish: one wouldn't risk losing a visa for America through having been to Russia, and another's priest feared her contamination from wicked Communism; the third child unselfishly thought the anxiety was too much for his widowed mother.

Soon we had a conductor, a programme and the dates (1–12 September) agreed with the Soviet Union, but other invitations – Hamburg and Berlin before Russia, Helsinki and Stockholm after – were slotting into place. An extra Executive meeting was fixed for 20 June to discuss the whole tour and how it would be financed. I produced plans for almost a month, 20 August to 16 September: the summer course would start in Canterbury and end with a concert in Canterbury Cathedral on 28 August. On the 29th we would fly to Hamburg in two planes for a televised concert the next day. By flying to Berlin on the 31st for another major concert and TV broadcast, then flying back to Hamburg, we would have three nights in the same place. All our expenses in Hamburg would be the gift of Axel Springer. On 1 September we would fly in our own two planes to Moscow, where all expenses would be covered by the Soviet government. A contract for six or seven concerts, in Moscow, Leningrad and one other place, had been signed, but no other details were given in writing; to this day Russians never write letters. We would leave Leningrad by train on 12 September for

Helsinki for a concert on the 13th. The accommodation was the responsibility of the British Council and the Anglo-Finnish Society. Then on to Stockholm on 14 September, the flight and hotel accommodation paid for by a Swedish businessman, Alf Evenson. Finally our own planes would bring us back to England on the 15th.

Presented with this outline, I wondered if the Committee might think it was too much. Twelve major concerts, air and train travel, foreign food, strange accommodation and languages – all this was undoubtedly a lot for our young members. They had to be kept well: we couldn't fail to give the promised concerts.

Don Ryder had worked out that we should ask £25 from each member for the whole month. With £2,000 from the British Council to help with the journey to Russia, and accommodation in all four countries being generously provided free, he thought the whole proposition now manageable financially. He was keeping a sum in reserve for any emergency.

Some conditions were stipulated, in particular no flying within the Soviet Union. And we must have extra help to deal with the press before we left: Don Ryder offered to supply someone. So, taking a deep breath, and aware of the huge responsibilities to parents, children, our reputation and that of Britain, we all agreed to undertake the biggest adventure in our history.

By early August our plans were complete; 111 players were fully equipped with passports, visas and above all parental permission to fly and to go beyond the Iron Curtain. It was thought wise to have a press conference to assuage the considerable curiosity about the whole venture. I think this was mostly because the NYO was accepted as an exchange item in the new Anglo-Soviet Cultural Pact; but there was also genuine interest in the details – planes, trains, programmes, conductor, doctor and so on. One journalist summed it up, 'We're very proud of our NYO. We want them back safely.' They seemed pleased that the *Mirror* had appointed a Mr Batchelor to be with us throughout the tour and keep them informed. He was in charge of organising important exhibitions in London, so for going ahead to check or make arrangements he was the perfect choice.

It was a very nervous time politically. At a lunch Christopher Mayhew MP* told me to call it off, because it would be used as Communist propaganda, suggesting that he supposed I was a Communist! And Lord Harewood, Chairman of the British Council's Music Advisory Committee, sent for me. He was very angry and thought I should be ashamed of myself for not playing British music in Moscow. But we were: a major item by Benjamin Britten, at their request. Why had he been so falsely briefed? I was being attacked unreasonably from various quarters. Repeated telephone calls from the Foreign Office made certain I knew we were not to go to Riga, as the British government had never recognised the Soviet annexation of Latvia. We had no intention of going there; but if when in Moscow we were asked to go, would they let me have in writing what I should do? No letter.

Suddenly, on 10 August, disaster struck. Thirty-four London boys and two teachers were missing in a holiday airliner that had crashed off the coast of Norway. Every newspaper had front-page headlines: CROYDON SCHOOL HOLIDAY FLIGHT CRASHES; HOPES FADE FOR LOST VIKING; ANGUISHED PARENTS PLEAD FOR NEWS. I was stunned, realising in a flash what was going through the minds of all our parents and their children, who would be joining us in just ten days' time.

Council and Committee members were ringing constantly: they presumed there would be so many cancellations that our whole tour would be off. We could only wait; we were nervous of every phone call. Days passed. No parent rang.

Then a newspaper-man found one of our parents and asked, 'I suppose you won't let your son go with the NYO?' and got the reply, 'I wouldn't if he was just going on holiday, but it's all

*Now Lord Mayhew of Wimbledon.

right with the Youth Orchestra because they're so well looked after.' Such faith and trust in us was very moving, and even lifted a little the burden of responsibility that had become so heavy. Later a few parents did ring, just to share the anxiety they'd been through, or to give support. Even on 17 August, when all the front pages showed the return of the boys' bodies to their Croydon school, there were no last-minute withdrawals.

We worked calmly on, deeply grateful to one of our parents, Mr Polmear, the Director of Education for Canterbury and father of Jeremy Polmear, our principal oboe, who gave us the use of the Simon Langton Schools. We had also accepted the privilege of a concert in Canterbury Cathedral.

So on 19 August, 152 young musicians set off from all over Britain and by evening were safely in the beautiful historic city of Canterbury. Before bedtime I'd given them an outline of the adventure ahead and one boy said good-night with, 'It's a good city from which to start our pilgrimage.'

The Canterbury course was different from all others. The programme was bigger: the chamber orchestra had three concerti to learn; the *Young Person's Guide* had many difficult solos; and playing a Tchaikovsky symphony to Russians had to be special. All our team of professors came, and our splendid conductor Oivin Fjeldstad.

On the domestic front, there was much for the house staff to teach and to check. One pair of concert trousers or skirt, and two white shirts, to last twelve concerts, plus all the essentials for a month – in one suitcase – could end up a crumpled mess. Betty Goddard and Mary Rose Seldon, James Reid and Rodney Smith had ways of packing and folding; they even repaired suitcases and locks.

Some evenings had to be spent in learning a little about Germany and Russia. About forty had been with us in 1959, but others had no idea of why Berlin was isolated and run by four nations, or why the Wall was going up even as we rehearsed.

There was almost total ignorance of the sufferings of the Russians, the fact that the price of defending their country had been twenty million dead. They could not believe these essential facts of modern history.

The Mayor, Councillor Arthur Wilson, honoured us with an official visit and welcome to Canterbury. After listening to a rehearsal he gave the whole orchestra and staff tickets for a farce at the local Marlow Theatre, just what was needed.

Sunday was our last day of preparation and packing. During the morning we covered the last rehearsals of the chamber group and our three soloists. There was a special invitation to Evensong in the cathedral in the afternoon, at which there was a special prayer and blessing for them. Then after tea the final work on the Britten and the symphony, so they could relax knowing the whole programme was ready for the tour. And as it was the last evening of the summer course, the Bulgin Medal was presented to our most outstanding student, this time Christopher Seaman. He had been in the NYO for six years, was our timpanist and had won a music scholarship to Cambridge, had an organ and a piano diploma, and had composed the fanfare for the Queen Mother at the RFH concert. After a first at Cambridge, he became timpanist at the LPO, and is now a well-known conductor in Britain and America.

After supper we met for a final check: a numbered order for the two planes, with a leader every ten, a luggage party – first out and last in when travelling – and a platform team. All questions were answered in time for the last letters home. Our final responsibility was to impress on them that wherever we went we were guests, so courtesy to our hosts was our priority – they must not cause offence with a careless remark – and to warn that representing our country might mean some little personal sacrifices but we would be judged as a group, and as British, and our country's reputation must come first, every day, all the time. We knew they'd stick together and help each other.

The morning sunlight on Canterbury Cathedral as we arrived

for our rehearsal was so strikingly beautiful we just had to linger a little and absorb the wonder of it. But soon the orchestra was in its appointed area inside, ready to enjoy the sound in such glorious space and height. There was just one verger on duty, and before we left at lunch-time I asked if extra chairs would be available in case of a large audience. I was quickly put in my place: 'You won't need them. We've had the Hallé here, and it wasn't full.'

As was our custom, the orchestra arrived at the cathedral one hour before the concert began. Already there were a lot of people walking around, and some were seated. By seven-fifteen it was more than half full, and people were pouring in at the main door. At half-past, the Archdeacon of Maidstone arrived and had difficulty in getting down the side aisle to reach us in the vestry. Not surprisingly, he was nervous. Ten minutes before the concert the main doors were closed and the queue turned away, including VIPs and people who had travelled from London. It was very hard work cutting a narrow pathway through thickly crammed people to enable the orchestra to get from the vestry to their places, but once there, without a prayer or announcement, the concert began.

After the overture there was tentative clapping; but the sound of the clarinet in the Mozart concerto, so beautifully played by Anthony Pay, brought full applause, and so did the Britten. I managed to force a way to the orchestra at the interval. They had to stay where they were as they couldn't get out. Fjeldstad sat on the base of his stand, and they had about seven minutes just resting, completely relaxed, where they sat. It was very hot. Meanwhile in the audience hassocks were being handed out to people standing in the aisles, and some were taking off jackets to use as cushions on the floor. Our staff had no seats. One violinist whispered to me, 'It's like Berlin: we're completely surrounded by a wall of people . . .' While the players retuned I wormed my way to the very back, and leant against the ancient wall to listen. What a sound . . . and that *enthousiasmos* in playing great music for the first time to such massive support and good will on the eve of flying to Berlin. It was one of the most extraordinary experiences of my life.

When everyone had left I waited with Diana by the main door to say goodbye to the archdeacon. By then I could not contain my tears.

'Whatever's the matter?' he asked.

'Such a wasted opportunity . . . all those people . . . some may never have been in a cathedral before . . . not one greeting . . . not a prayer to join in . . . not a blessing for the children or their parents . . .'

'Oh never mind,' he said. 'We weren't prepared for this.'

By contrast, when we went to thank the verger, who had been under a great strain till the police arrived, he said, 'I'm so sorry about the way I spoke to you this morning. You must have been worried for the children. I was. They were wonderful. I'll never forget this night. God bless you and bring you all safely home.'

The local paper mentions there were over three thousand people in the cathedral, that the police had sent over five hundred away and that it was the biggest crowd anyone could remember on any occasion.

Twenty-Eight

The next morning we all assembled after breakfast. I was able to tell them that every concert on tour would be different, but none would be in conditions like last night. How splendid they had been, and the music had triumphed. Morale was high as with the passport-music-instrument check they prepared for Manston Airport and our two chartered Hermes for Hamburg.

With me on plane One were mainly the younger ones and those most likely to be nervous; in plane Two with John were the percussion and instrument-van party. Walking round after take-off revealed that initial fright was soon forgotten with the first experience of seeing the planet from the air.

There was a warm welcome in Hamburg, including friends from our 1959 visit. The hostel where we would spend three nights was ideal, so clean, so efficient, and the people so kind. That evening our hosts had arranged another boat trip round the docks. The next morning started with a rehearsal in the Musikhalle, a really lovely concert hall, all our needs most understandingly supplied, so Oivin was smiling again after the Canterbury ordeal.

It was the opening concert of the season and the hall was full. There were a lot of young people, and 150 employees of Axel Springer's newspaper. Radio and TV companies and the audience were very appreciative, and that gave everybody confidence for the way ahead.

Next came one of our get-up-in-uniform days, which meant we could travel without luggage and return to base. It was an early start to the airport, where One and Two and our special pilots were waiting for us. It was not a long flight to Berlin, but on the way the pilots had a message to land on the French airfield, the British one being unavailable. It was a time of severe crisis, the Wall still being built, and no doubt extra air traffic in the British Zone. There was great excitement in my plane at seeing Berlin from the air, and as we came in to land I overheard, 'Of course you can't see the Wall, it's not like a skyscraper.'

With German efficiency, transport meeting us had been switched to our French surroundings. There to greet us were our old friends Alan Baker, Frau von Wedelstadt and Herr Kollitsch, and we were soon on our way to the Konzertsaal der Hochschule für Musik. Before we left we were given very firm instructions to take off before midnight, at which moment the electricity, controlled from the Russian Zone, was cut off. If we started the concert punctually we ought to manage to leave by half-past eleven – but I also contemplated a night sleeping in our planes in the dark on a foreign airfield.

The Konzertsaal was new, rather like the RFH, and wonderful for sound. It had been completely sold out, but we were told that some ticket holders would now be behind the Wall, and not able to come. If we would agree to start the concert late, the *Konzertdirektor* would fill up the empty seats without charge from people in the queue outside. We were anxious about the midnight curfew, but left the arrangements to him.

RIAS waited courteously until we were ready for all their radio and TV sound tests, and the press were so polite, obviously appreciative of our visit at such a time. We in England had no idea of what it was like for the 2,500,000 Germans in West Berlin at the 'closing of the East from the West', wondering if the Allies would stand firm. But working among them the tension and emotional strain were very clear. While we were rehearsing Diana was making another desperate attempt to get a reply out of Moscow about the route for our pilots to take from Hamburg, and our place and time of arrival. With Mr Baker's aid she sent a telegram.

That evening the hall was absolutely full. It was our third performance of this programme, getting more confident each time. Tony Pay's clarinet-playing impressed, and the Britten played by young people instead of for them always had an exciting effect. Young David Atherton said, 'The Germans are such an emotional people, they *feel* the music with you. It's different from an English audience.' One paper wrote, 'Was it kind of our young friends to play the national anthem with such emotion at such a time[?], so deeply moving, such a wonderful sound.'

During the symphony a telegram from Moscow was delivered to John behind the scenes: *Proceed to Copenhagen. Four Soviet officers waiting to escort planes.* This was complete news to us; but our immediate concern was getting off the French airfield before midnight. The symphony proceeded and though running a little late we thought we would make it. We didn't count on the prolonged applause; it was impossibly ungracious to refuse an encore, or spoil the memory of such shared musical understanding. Then distinguished visitors came behind the scenes, and General Delacombe spoke to us all. He mentioned the encouragement of our visit, in restoring a day's normality to Berliners. It was sad that we had to rush our packing, with no time to meet all the leading musicians and others from cultural and political fields.

Alan Baker came with us. He seemed to know every road, every traffic light, everybody in charge everywhere. When I reached our planes, One was ready to take off; it was eleven-forty. But there was no sign of Rodney Smith with three boys and the instrument van. I decided to stay with Two in case we couldn't get off in time, and Mary Rose Seldon took my place in One, and we let it go back to Hamburg. It was eleven-fifty when in the rather dim lights our luggage trolley was spotted approaching. John, Rodney and six boys organised the quickest hold-stacking on record, and at eleven-fifty-seven the doors closed and we were on the move. Five minutes later from the air we saw the lights below us switch off; but we were on our way, our mission complete.

The whole event is best summed up in a letter General Delacombe wrote to *The Times* on 5 September:

> Sir, May I express sincere appreciation of the visit of the National Youth Orchestra to Berlin? They were true young ambassadors of our country. This city is going through troubled times, and all of us here, both Berliners and the rest, welcome such signs of Western interest and sympathy. The orchestra's presence made a notable contribution to morale.
>
> Like many others I thoroughly enjoyed their concert programme, and I have heard praise for it on all sides. People here are grateful, too, for the reassuring confidence about West Berlin revealed by the fact that not one parent of the hundred and eleven young musicians showed hesitation over permitting their children to come here at this moment.

Our resilient young were all present at a late breakfast, some a bit bleary-eyed, but there was plenty of talk. Then we were off to the airport, saying warm goodbyes to our Hamburg hosts and friends. Everybody seemed quite pleased to see One and Two again and our pilots and we soon took off for Copenhagen, where according to the telegram four Russian officers would join us. They were tall, handsome and smartly uniformed, and spoke excellent English. Once airborne, I took them on tour, introducing everybody and showing on a map of the British Isles where they came from. The officers were good value throughout the long journey, telling us all about the different republics in the union. Two senior boys came to talk to me: 'Do you know, one has a degree in engineering, and the other is a pilot, and they both speak *three* languages. We're not as well educated as that are we? And what's more they know about music, and one plays the violin.'

Our route was over the Baltic, with a wonderful view of Vilnius, then turning inland to Moscow. All photography was sternly forbidden. Just before landing we all changed our watches, discovering suddenly that it was nine p.m. We were met and welcomed by Mr Shashkin, the head of Gosconcert, two first-class interpreters and four young men variously in charge of us. We passed through a barrier for checking passports, and to our amazement they were kept. This was too much for Oivin Fjeldstad, who'd taken a lot of persuading to come to Russia at all. 'Now I know I will never see my dear wife again, I should not have come.' Tears flowed. Then came John, in as near to a state of anxious distress as I've ever known him. 'I've come to report that all the instruments have gone . . . just gone. We unloaded into a van – no explanation – it's driven away with everything!' Fortunately that was soon explained: it had gone direct to the Tchaikovsky Hall. But I sent a message down the line – 'In *no* circumstances part with your instruments or music' – just in case.

We were given first-class treatment and were soon disembarking at the Hotel Ukrainia, a huge, twenty-six-storey building with an enormous illuminated red star on the top, overlooking the great Moscow River. Of course very few of the children would ever have stayed in a hotel, and as they collected for supper the excitement was intense: 'We have our own bathroom, and a telephone'; 'We have super beds and a view of the river.' Suddenly we had a complaint: the musicians were blocking the hotel's switchboard! Apparently they were so thrilled with their own telephones and so keen to find out which floors their friends were on that they were all ringing each other.

We refused to go in to supper till two lost sheep, both girls of fourteen, were found. The lift to the top floors had broken down, so they found the stairs and proceeded to walk down some twenty-two floors, and eventually found their way to the main dining-room on the ground floor. Somebody identified them by their badges and delivered them safely to us. Tears were soon mopped up, and into our private dining-room we went, standing silently behind the chairs until a housemaster had said grace. Then joyful voices burst out.

This was no supper, but a welcoming banquet of many courses. One interpreter rushed to find out from the housemaster what the 'magic words' were. Why were they silent before they ate? What was 'grace'? What language? He had said a Latin grace and wrote out the Latin and the translation. The evening ended with a little thank-you speech from one of our senior boys, and it was midnight before the day we flew to Moscow closed in sleep.

There was a surprise at breakfast the next morning. Our hosts arrived with flowers, a birthday cake and a gift for Alan Cumberland's fifteenth birthday. They must have gone through all the passports very quickly to discover that it was his birthday, and it was a most charming gesture. Throughout our stay, there was a birthday every day except one, and wherever we were staying, even while we were on the move, the cakes and gifts arrived.

Miraculously, there was no concert this first day, but a sightseeing tour including the Kremlin – the tombs of Lenin and Stalin, the jewels and treasures – and a trip on the underground. It was here that they saw a poster advertising our concert with a big photograph of Moragh McLeod playing the trumpet. This quite upset our soloist, because at home we never had any individual publicity. While all were occupied John went to the hall to find our instruments and see about the platform, and I had a meeting with Mr Shashkin and his assistant, to see if I could find out what the plans for the week were.

What emerged was that the first two concerts would be in Moscow and then it was suggested to go to one of their fine cities, namely Riga. I was half expecting this and had decided to go straight to our ambassador for instructions. But Mr Shashkin was so kind and sensitive that I just looked at him and said, 'Riga,' and drew my hand across my throat. He understood instantly. I hope he didn't think we really had a KGB in England and my fate would be a British Siberia. But he was in difficulties himself: where could he send us instead? I pleaded to go to the ancient capital of Kiev – I knew no other place – but I had no idea how far it was from Moscow or what I was asking for in organisation and expense for them. He promised to let me know after the first Moscow concert, and I left hoping that if he rescued me from Riga he wouldn't be in Siberia himself.

We rehearsed that afternoon to get into practice after the day's travelling and to get the feel of the excellent Tchaikovsky Hall. Oivin had managed to speak to his wife on the telephone and had recovered his smile. The staff at the hall were wonderful, friendly and keen to supply every requirement. The Russians love children; they had never seen any British ones, and the curiosity was intense. The house staff reported that at the hotel the cleaning ladies had a great stage sense and were ready to take over ironing shirts and pressing trousers as if they were behind the scenes at the ballet.

In Moscow, important cultural events are on Sundays. So for us, it was concert day; it had to be our best in every way. For Moragh the posters had added self-consciousness to the normal nervousness, and I never let a child play unless they were eager to do so. I went to find Allan, practising behind the scenes. He was being offered a choice of three Steinway concert grands (in 1961 there was only one in the RFH)! He was delighted to do the first night. After the rehearsal I made sure everyone took their music away with them, though we were pressed very hard indeed to leave it on the stands. I think they wanted to photocopy the Britten, as parts of copyright music were difficult to get.

That evening the atmosphere behind the scenes was electric, and the hall was packed to its capacity of two thousand. The whole programme was broadcast, with the Tchaikovsky live on TV, and Fjeldstad was impressive both as artist and conductor. According to a Reuter report in *The Times*, 'the audience applauded wildly, and crowded down to the stage with shouts of "Bravo" and "Encore." They were unwilling to let the visitors leave the platform even after two encores.'

Alexander Kuznetsov, the Deputy Minister of Culture, summed up the Russian reaction when he went on to the platform to speak to the children. He said he was deeply moved and impressed by the playing, and that he loved them as children as well as fine musicians. 'You have charmed us, delighted us, made us so very happy. Your country should be proud of you.' The British Ambassador, Sir Frank Roberts, was with him and also spoke to them.

There were many distinguished Moscow musicians at the concert, like the conductors Anosov and Rozhdestvensky, Shostakovich, the heads of the Conservatoires and the young pianist Vladimir Ashkenazy, who according to *The Times* said it was 'a highly musical ensemble with excellent creative discipline'. Then behind the scenes came Mstislav Rostropovich, full of enthusiasm, fixing up a time to talk to the cellos the next day. Benjamin Britten had sent us a telegram, which was displayed on a board in the front entrance for all to see.

At breakfast there was delighted chatter. The slow rhythmic hand-clap was a surprise – the children seemed to like it – and so was the difference from an English audience: 'They actually laughed in the amusing bits of the Britten; an English audience would concentrate like mad and think it was supposed to be serious,' said one; 'They really cried in the Tchaikovsky, but in England you mustn't do that in public,' commented another. They were always self-critical too: Were we all right? Was it all right for Britain? This bit or that wasn't good enough was it? They soon knew I was very pleased with them all because it had been such a challenging occasion, and they'd risen to it.

Apparently the concert was such a success that the Ministers of Culture and Education were intent on helping us in every way. Mr Shashkin just said, 'That concert was wonderful . . . you *shall* go to Kiev . . . but it is very difficult to arrange . . . long journeys very tiring for children. I make plan by tomorrow.'

Madame Furtseva was Minister of Culture, the only woman in the Politburo. In a recent letter Sir Frank writes about the original suggestion of our visit:

> [Mme] Furtseva, the friendly and high-powered Minister of Culture, was initially surprised and intrigued, but also a little

> alarmed by what she wrongly expected to be the serious problems of having so many young people to 'look after' . . . but she finally took what the Russians used to call a 'positive attitude'.

Now she was so impressed that she invited John, Diana and me to a special lunch. In her speech she said they were all 'so impressed, both with the serious dedication to the music and with the appearance and attitude of the children themselves'. She wanted me to return to Moscow and show them how to do the same thing. Of course we invited their leading musicians and teachers to visit us at work in Britain. We also met the head of the Conservatoire, and I fixed with him to give Allan Schiller an audition. If successful, he would stay behind to start his training. Everybody present loved the children, and their courtesy. 'They are good simple children' was often said, lovingly, but we never quite grasped the meaning.

That same afternoon our cellists spent an hour with Rostropovich, and Sir Frank and Lady Roberts had a group round to tea in the Embassy. At seven we were all together again behind the scenes of the Tchaikovsky Hall for the second night. Moragh had regained morale, so we were including the trumpet concerto, and an added excitement was a message from Mme Furtseva telling us to expect Mr Khrushchev at the performance.

I was with the violins, everyone was tuned and ready to go on to the platform when I had a message from John with the brass: '*Crisis*, wait.' Derek Bourgeois writes:

> We were getting ready to tune when a trumpet mute fell into my tuba. It lodged so tightly in the hollow nobody could shake, knock, or prise it out. Time went by, stage-hands with tools tried in vain, Mr Khrushchev might arrive at any minute, and we could not play the *Young Person's Guide* without it. It was Rostropovich who suddenly appeared with a tool like a corkscrew, and managed to hook into the mute and pull it out. Tuning was completed and it was one minute to eight when the orchestra went on to the platform.

Although not such a festive occasion as the first night, the response was just as warm, with the rhythmic hand-clapping and the demand for encores, and there was a desire to get close to the English children, to have a good look at them. The comments in the hall were of appreciation; but round the buses they said, 'They all smile – they are good simple children – we love them.'

After breakfast I was able to tell them what we were going to do next: go to the great city of Kiev, leaving in the late afternoon and travelling all night in the train. This was greeted with laughter – an adventure lay ahead – and then a slight nervous reaction – a little pondering of the unknown. It was goodbye to all who had looked after them in the Ukrainia Hotel, especially the cooks. Throughout the tour the food was terrific. We had sent our normal timetable of breakfast, lunch, tea and supper and this had been unfailingly laid on, only with twice the quantity of home, and a birthday cake almost every day as well. Now on our fourth day they were getting used to bortsch at breakfast; 'The Russians like their milk sour; we put sugar in it' (yoghurt); and 'the best ice-cream we've ever tasted'.

I went with Allan to the Conservatoire for his audition: very impressive. He played to five professors, then they had a long discussion and came back to tell me that they had accepted him, and with whom he would study and why. They were very pleased with the concerto at the concert. They thought he should go home with us and come back at the official start of the term, a week later. This he did, and had three very happy years at the Moscow Conservatoire, and from then on a successful career as a pianist and teacher.

The night train had solid wooden bunks, two or four to a compartment: a complete contrast to the luxurious Ukrainia, a splendid education in adaptability to circumstances. There was a restaurant car which could only take forty, but a good hot supper was served in three sessions. There was much hilarity in our female coaches trying to get comfortable for the night, and we wondered how John and his team were managing their seventy young men and their instruments. You can sleep with a flute or violin, but a tuba needs a bed to itself.

At bedtime a little lady came round with glasses of tea. Apparently she had a samovar in a little den at the end of the corridor and (I presumed) plenty of hot water. Not sure whether to sleep on the wooden bunk in or out of my steel jacket, I remembered the two hot-water bottles I never travel without. I took them to her, unscrewed the tops and gestured to her to fill them with hot water. She was obviously amazed, but very willing, and indicated that she would bring them to me later. In due course she came, bringing two very full and boiling hot bottles, which kept me warm and cushioned for the night. When I emptied them out in the morning, I found they were full of tea!

The rather crumpled and dishevelled look next morning was soon cheered with breakfast. Our hosts/interpreters/organisers/guards were quite marvellous; arrangements never failed. Soon everyone was at the windows, absorbing the different scenery, the open farming unlike the hedges and lanes of England. The train was now slowing and stopping at village stations. There were little stalls with women in local costume selling fruit and vegetables. They were obviously unaccustomed to seeing a hundred eager faces, but gradually they came over to shake hands. As the train left they stood, stunned, watching it go as if they'd just seen a load of moon men! Soon in the distance the ancient city of Kiev, the capital of the Ukraine, came into view.

There was a welcoming party on the station: city dignitaries, musicians and children in attractive uniforms, all presenting bunches of flowers. It really was welcoming and very friendly, and we moved into an atmosphere more like that of an English country town.

John and I made straight for the concert hall with Rodney and the luggage following as soon as possible. It was a very nice hall, rather unusual in shape, very wide; the platform was rather small for us, so we quickly decided on no piano concerto. We also decided not to rehearse that afternoon, but give them all time to clean up and unpack, and get some fresh air after the all-night journey. We would be in the hall at six-thirty and have a platform and balance rehearsal before the concert, unless Oivin wanted anything more.

And where was Oivin? He was not too well on the last day in Moscow and our hosts had arranged for him to come by air this morning. Alas, there was something wrong with the early plane, and he was still in Moscow waiting for the next.

While we were discussing this emergency, a charming young lady arrived, introducing herself as the announcer of the programme that night. There were no printed programmes; the hall was sold out but nobody knew what we would play. I told her we started with the national anthems and before I could get any further she said, 'Do you know the national anthem?' I said we'd been playing it in Moscow. 'I meant the *Ukrainian* national anthem. If you play the Soviet one the people will know you are a Communist group from England, here for Soviet propaganda, and the hall will be empty on the second night. I can get some parts from our orchestra.' There were very few parts, for a small orchestra, and no time to copy more or rehearse. So we made an agreement. We would come on the platform, she would announce the overture and we would start at once. We need not mention the matter to anybody else. I also asked her to explain to all concerned that our young musicians were not in any way political.

We were all on the platform ready for rehearsal before I told them we would have to manage that night without Mr Fjeldstad. Then suddenly a message came that the plane had landed and he would be with us in time for the concert.

The Ukrainian people were quite different from those in Moscow. I suppose we had thought of them all as Russians, but they were very keen to tell us that they were a separate nation. They enjoyed the programme, especially the clarinet concerto and the trumpet concerto on the second night; the Britten seemed new to them. They commented on the wonderful sound – very exciting – and the huge size of the orchestra. I was relieved that the Moscow officials in charge of us didn't question why we played no anthems.

The next day our Ukrainian hosts had organised a boat tour on the Dnieper River. There was also a shopping tour, and Mary Rose Seldon remembers that our members were very surprised how little there was to buy. She said the greetings wherever they went were charming, and everybody was very keen to meet English people. The children had a lovely day and saw some part of the old capital city, had time for some rest and were fresh in mind for the second concert.

This time the hall was packed and a queue at the doors had to be turned away. John was behind the scenes, and he told me that during the symphony several people, some quite important citizens, came round asking about life in England. Did people own houses? How many rooms were there in John's house? (He said he felt so ashamed at admitting to seven rooms and that he wasn't compelled to share accommodation.) What were teachers and musicians paid? Do English people like us? And as the last movement neared its end they disappeared quickly to mingle with the applauding crowd.

Kiev was a success in many ways, and a great tribute to Moscow's organisation. They moved such a large group so far at such short notice, looking after everybody very well and filling two concerts without advance publicity. I hope our playing to the people of Kiev deserved all the work and expense they put into bringing us, and getting us now all the way to Leningrad.

Next morning the leader of our team of hosts-organisers-interpreters revealed that we would be leaving Kiev by train after an early lunch for a twenty-six-and-a-half-hour journey to Leningrad. From midday, all night and into the next afternoon with 111 lively teenagers cooped up: quite a challenge for us all. 'Today we will be leaving for Leningrad . . . by train. As you are all now experienced night-train travellers' (much laughter), 'prepare your packing accordingly and brush up your expertise for comfort and entertainment till Saturday evening.' But for us there was a serious side. Sister was very busy with minor running repairs, and two very important concerts lay ahead: they must arrive in good health and morale. Oivin would go by plane, and wanted me to go with him, but accepted that I didn't leave the family, especially on an adventure into unknown territory. A British officer once told me that the general never travels with the troops. I remember saying I was a Monty-type general, staying near my troops when the battle was on. For us travelling was part of the battle.

On the station it was goodbye to city officials; flowers were being handed into train windows; and rows of children waving little flags was our last sight of the kind and friendly Ukrainians and of the famous city of Kiev.

On the journey, time was absorbed by three sessions for breakfast, lunch and supper. Our members were very good at helping with washing up and laying tables. The food was plentiful and celebrating a birthday, with the cake and gifts, was never forgotten. Our last lunch started at noon, and after that there was just an hour left for smartening up for our arrival and important reception in the historic city of Leningrad.

We were given a great welcome here. News of our Moscow success had gone ahead of us, and there was faultless organisation and comfort in the Astoria Hotel. This was quite near the concert hall in which we were going to play, and very convenient for rehearsing and practising.

Leningrad people were different again from Kiev and Moscow: a little more formal. We had to refuse an invitation to tour the city the next morning, explaining that we must put the concert first and we needed all the morning for rehearsal, and a rest in the afternoon, but we would gladly accept such an offer on Monday. It transpired later that they had wanted us to attend a Pioneer propaganda meeting on the Sunday and were very disappointed that we didn't turn up.

It was a big hall, with a large platform and an excellent piano, but not good for sound. Their best hall was closed for redecorating; we worked really hard to make a success of the concert. In the evening it was crowded out. The appreciative audience became increasingly enthusiastic, and we had to give two encores.

The next morning they went to the Hermitage and saw as much of the city and its former glory as was possible to fit in before the preparations for the second concert. This time many of the leading musicians were present, some for the second time ('I couldn't believe it – I had to come back'); and some from orchestras, ballet and opera who had been performing themselves on Sunday, but now had a free evening. But most of the warm response came from the real music-loving people of Leningrad. They crowded round the exit and mobbed the performers as they left to walk across to the hotel. I was among the last to leave, with Oivin, and by then the crowd was chorusing repeatedly, rhythmically, 'Come back again.' We were at the top of some steps and I just said, fairly loudly and clearly, 'We have to be invited.' This was heard near by and passed back through the crowd, and a new chorus started: 'We invite you now.'

Soon the chorusing crowd had moved to outside the Astoria, and already pyjama-clad figures were appearing at the windows. The Russians love children, they love music, this was something new to them and they were rejoicing. For the orchestra it must have been rewarding going to bed in the hotel, hearing 'Come back again' in the night outside, the chant gradually fading away as the crowd dispersed and they fell asleep.

Our next adventure was a train journey from Leningrad to Helsinki. After breakfast our passports were returned. Oivin's face lit up: 'I will never, NEVER part with it again.'

It is sad that none of us can remember the name of the senior officer in charge of us. Unfailingly with us all the time from our arrival in Moscow, he became part of the family. He was a large personality with the warmest of hearts, bearing the burden of responsibility for every detail of our care. He was affectionately nicknamed 'our Russian bear'. We had brought a few presents and gave him the best we had, a gilt-edged leather notecase, but he had to get permission to accept it.

Our departure from Leningrad was moving. The last birthday cake and gift were handed through a train window. We gave our friends NYO badges as mementoes, and also addresses and invitations to visit England, but then we discovered our Russian friends could not give us theirs. I was saying a last thank-you to Russian Bear from the train doorway, and noticed he wasn't wearing his badge. He mopped his eyes and opened his coat to reveal it pinned inside: 'I shall wear it always next to my heart.' As the train started to move he stretched an arm towards it saying, 'This is England for me and I shall never see it again.'

All the time we'd been in Russia we hadn't discussed politics, and had had to watch the children being so impressed with Communist life; but we had to leave them to do their own thinking. It was on the journey into Finland, passing little cottages set among the fir trees and little gardens on the stations, that the mood changed, however. 'Have the Russian guards left?' A feeling of relaxation was perceptible, and as we continued we heard, 'The Russians were so good to us, so kind, but somehow it seems more like home here.' So perhaps they had subconsciously absorbed the tensions of life in a dictatorship and were now sensing freedom – literally, sitting by the open window and breathing the fresh country air.

Mr Batchelor had gone ahead of us, mercifully, as he discovered that the British Council's accommodation plans had failed. He always had with him our list of members' names, ages, sex and instrument, so he contacted the Anglo-Finnish Society, and together they planned hospitality in a Finnish home for every child. When we arrived at Helsinki, to our surprise, on the platform were 111 parents waiting in a group. Mr Batchelor stood between us and called out a name. The child concerned stepped forward, its host did likewise and off they went. This went on until 110 members had been claimed, and only one tall, distinguished-looking gentleman was left. 'Where is my child?' he said.

I explained that the boy who would have been his child was very sick and was still in the railway carriage with Sister, and we were just planning to find a doctor. He walked straight ahead to the carriage, took one look at him, picked him up, carried him off to his car – Sister running behind like a mother hen after a stolen chick – and drove away. This wonderful man turned out to be the leading consultant at a Helsinki hospital. He took the boy there, then nursed him in his own home, and he was well enough to leave with us two days later. This child was our only serious casualty in three weeks of ever-changing circumstances, and was saved by this miraculous chance. The NYO records its gratitude to a great, warm-hearted physician and all the generous parents of Finland.

Early next morning John and I were in the University Hall, a beautiful small concert hall, lovely for sound. After all the unpacking and setting we had a really good rehearsal. We always intended each concert to improve on the last, and this time I think we succeeded. The hall was completely full, the President's wife came and the audience was warm and responsive from the first anthems. As usual the standard of our playing was unexpected, and they became more amazed and enthusiastic as we played on, and at the end they stood and insisted on encores. Sibelius's daughter kindly came on to the platform to speak to them, saying she wished her father had been able to hear them play with such warmth. Our ambassador, Sir Con O'Neill, spoke about a night in which they had learnt about the Finnish people and the Finns had seen with joy a glimpse of young England. We can only thank the people of Finland for the sightseeing fitted into the first evening and all each family did for its adopted child at such short notice. Somewhere there are 111 people who will always remember a home and family in Finland.

Early next morning it was goodbye to Helsinki and off to the airport. There to welcome us were One and Two and our faithful friends the pilots. Soon we had a beautiful view from the air of the Baltic coast, before landing at the capital city of Stockholm.

Our sponsor, a most generous and kind man, Alf Evenson, came to meet us. He was a Norwegian who lived in Stockholm and was very famous in the paper industry. He was delighted to meet Oivin and look after him personally. The organisation was perfect. We were put up in three hotels, and after an early lunch everybody went to the main hall of the Konserthuset, Stora Salem, for our only chance of a rehearsal.

There were problems. The stage was barely big enough for us. The Stockholm Symphony Orchestra had been rehearsing and wanted us to leave their set untouched and just sit amongst it. They hadn't realised we were more than twice their size, with an outsize percussion section for the Britten. Compromise was reached when I promised that our students would put everything back for them after the concert. A group from their orchestra, out of curiosity, stayed for our rehearsal, and were so impressed that they made sure the entire symphony orchestra knew about it.

In the mean time we discovered that the hall was not even half sold for the concert. In August another British youth orchestra, on holiday in Sweden, had given a concert but it had not been a success, so people were not coming to another one. Fortunately news spread from the musicians at our rehearsal, and many leading people in music and education came. Our Swedish sponsor was a little bit sad – 'If only your publicity was as good as your playing' – and a leading conductor said, 'We didn't know an orchestra of school age *could* be like this.'

Large crowds are not everything. For our last concert of the tour we had a small but perfect hall, a discerning audience and a wonderful press. Per-Anders Hellguist in the *Svenska Dagbladet*, under the heading A UNIQUE MUSICAL VISIT, wrote: 'Because of the age, an achievement such as Thursday's concert is utterly amazing . . . It was not the purity and precision, not the vitality and enthusiastic playing, but I have never experienced a more intensive Tchaikovsky performance.' He also mentioned Tony Pay's brilliant playing.

> One expected an amateur ensemble of gifted youngsters . . . but this was a question of an absolutely sensational musical constellation . . . all their playing is instinct with a freshness and a joy in music that makes the listener himself happy

said the *Stockholm-Tidningen.*

For myself I was just deeply thankful that, from Canterbury Cathedral, eleven major concerts and four countries on, the last concert was as good as the first, and that the 111 were all well. And what an education – Berlin: the Wall and political anxiety; Russia: luxurious hospitality, poverty and *love*; Finland: homely simplicity and plenty; Sweden: great riches and generosity – and we had sensed the character of a nation as expressed in its audiences.

Next morning we were in One and Two for the last time. We had set off with nervous inexperienced children and were coming back with confident young adults with a sense of achievement. Our planes glided safely into Manston. Everybody thanked our special pilots and hurried off for the London train. We had booked carriages and a guards van, but when the train came into the station the luggage van hadn't arrived. I found the Station Master and begged for a few minutes' delay, explaining that our members were dependent on this train for their connections all over Britain, with night trains to Scotland and Cornwall and night ferries to Ireland. I promised to write to British Railways and explain – the students were keeping the carriage doors open – and then suddenly our van hove into sight. Everybody helped, and in record time double basses and harps, and all the paraphernalia was aboard: it was a narrow squeeze. What went wrong? The customs men at Manston – documents were in perfect order, we'd left from there and brought the same things back – just decided to be pig-headed and open every box. One thing is certain: Diana will never forgive them. None of us can ever forget that when we finally got home it was our own people who, knowing that train was vital to us, nearly wrecked the last lap of our pilgrimage to serve Britain abroad.

Twenty-Nine

Three days after our return we presented a full report to the Executive Committee, and stressed the part played for over three weeks by our absolutely marvellous voluntary staff – John of course, but also Colin Gough, Betty Goddard and Sister – and we thanked Don Ryder for giving us the remarkable Mr Batchelor, who saved the day in Finland. On the character and professional work of these selfless people would all our future foreign tours depend.

We suggested cancelling the Christmas course. It was a big decision, and might affect future standards. But it was just not possible to clear the aftermath of the tour, undertake all the auditions, plan our next year's work and be in action again in December. So it was agreed to have a quiet year, meeting in Lincolnshire at Easter and Guildford in the summer, looking ahead to a foreign tour in 1963.

As usual I wrote to Bruno Walter, whose encouragement and deep understanding of artistic values I treasure always. It was ten years exactly since he met the NYO at our first Edinburgh Festival. I didn't expect a reply, as I knew he was ill, but a typed letter signed by him came nevertheless.

> It was brave to go to the tragedy of Berlin [his birthplace]. Your visit will have warmed the hearts and encouraged the people there, and in Moscow, in these anxious times.
>
> May you have the strength to continue your spiritual pilgrimage.

It was my last letter. He died four months later.

After Yehudi had visited us in Tunbridge Wells, he set up a committee to help start his school. We had many meetings in his house in Highgate. The intricacies of the English educational system, especially regarding residential schools, were a complete mystery to him. All he wanted was a building full of eight-year-old violinists. In 1962 he asked our Council for two members for a joint committee chaired by Sir Gilmour Jenkins. Dr Taylor and Don Ryder kindly volunteered.

Free from the pressure of the Christmas course, we too were giving much thought to the future. We really needed one school near London in which the orchestra might meet every time, one with enough boarding accommodation or such near by – in fact a permanent base. This would save enormous time and work for every course and include our few full-time boarders. We never had more than half a dozen, and these only because their region could not supply adequate instrumental or academic musical training. This problem was solved for us by Grace Cone, the remarkable founder of the Arts Educational Trust, whom I had known for thirty years. She had a boarding school at Tring, and a day school in Piccadilly, chiefly for young dancers and actors aged from eight to eighteen, fully recognised by the Ministry of Education. She also had a small hostel in London. I always helped her over matters musical, and our boarders were safe in her care.

We also had time to finish all the preliminary auditions before Christmas, leaving the important finals until the spring.

1962 started on 17 January with our annual Council meeting. We had to report with deep regret the death of Dr Boris Ord, who first noticed our work in Bath in 1948, and together with Professor Hadley built a close relationship between our students and Cambridge; and sadly Mr Shields, Chief Inspector of Music in Scotland, a great supporter, was killed in an accident.

The Council had a written report of all the events of 1961, concluding with a letter to our President from Mr Kuznetsov: 'We were so impressed, both with the serious dedication to the music, and with the appearance and attitude of the children themselves.'

Due tribute was paid to Oivin Fjeldstad for his outstanding work. Thanks were expressed to the British Council, to Victor Hochhauser for his introduction to Gosconcert, to Mr Elphick of Reuters, to Mr Batchelor and to British Railways for holding that vital last train.

Don Ryder said that 'the good done by the European tour could not be measured in money'. We were £2,200 down, £1,200 of which was still in Russia and would be reclaimed, so he was not worried. Plans for a quiet 1962 were accepted.

We now had about twelve days of finals in London, a different instrument each day with our professor present. These new candidates were a particularly thoughtful and sensitive group, perhaps with less vitality and individuality than earlier years. Looking to the future, I chose seventy-eight of them, all under sixteen. It was the first time I had a fifty per cent intake, but I thought we could pull together if I gave every present member one new one to look after at the next course.

We had been invited to Gainsborough, a small country town with a mainly farming community, by the West Lindsay Music Festival for our Easter course. Our concert was to be the climax of their jubilee year, followed by one in Lincoln Cathedral. Sadly this had to be cancelled as the dates clashed with Holy Week, but we were invited back to Sheffield instead.

We were fortunate in having Oivin Fjeldstad with us again. Mrs Elwes, the moving spirit in all Gainsborough's musical affairs, offered to have him to stay. 'It is not a house, it is a palace,' he said with his usual smile.

A young composer, Alan Ridout, had written a work specially for us – *Three Pictures of Picasso** – and we had invited as soloist an eighteen-year-old French violinist, Antoine Goulard, whom I had spotted when he won the Carl Flesch Prize.

*Based on 'Guernica', 'Child with a Pigeon' and 'Acrobats'.

The education authority most generously provided the Castle Hill Secondary School, and it was good for the new members to experience the simplicity and toughness of mattresses on the floor. It was a quiet, hard-working week, during which our organist members gave a public recital in the parish church. The final concert was in the State Cinema; the Lord Lieutenant and many distinguished people came, and there was a great sense of occasion for the local jubilee.

The next day we all set off for the City Hall in Sheffield. Between the rehearsal and the concert our generous friend Sir Stuart Goodwin gave the orchestra a wonderful lunch in the Grand Hotel. I remember how he enjoyed watching them tucking in as if they'd been starved for weeks, saying, 'This gives me pleasure! I like seeing young people so happy.' He had given us, and many others, reason to be so.

Listening to the concert from the back of that big hall, I was pleased that such a young and mainly new orchestra did so splendidly in a Berlioz overture and a Brahms symphony. It already had a character of its own, alert and sensitive, so I had no doubt that after one more course this summer I would have a group I could develop and take, with pride, anywhere in the world.

There was one more experiment fitted into this strange year. With our original title restored in our publicity to explain our purpose better, we decided our members would give a recital in the Wigmore Hall in July. The youngest was a flautist of ten, followed by a double-bass soloist aged twelve, and so through different instrumentalists and stages of development, culminating with our best wind players in a quartet. Yehudi Menuhin and many other leading musicians came, along with those from colleges of music and other educational concerns, and it was considered a successful idea.

Then the year of 1962 became even stranger. The Schools Music Association, which had opposed us in every way at the start, was running a summer school in Oxford, on our dates, for our age group, called the 'National Schools Orchestra'. It was as near an outward copy of us as a copy could get. Intentional or not, the title caused a little confusion in some areas.

And the Musicians' Union, who were so frightened of us in 1948, had recently made a new agreement with ITV (probably soon to include the BBC) that only full members of the union could perform. This would prevent any further TV broadcasts of our concerts. We still had the faithful BBC for the moment.

But it was not all setbacks. One day that superb artist and colleague Janet Craxton introduced me to Rudolf Schwarz. I knew he was a man of rare intellect and an authority on Schubert, so I had gone specially to the RFH for his performance of the great C Major symphony. It was masterly, gripping from the first note to the last. Then we met, and I went to two rehearsals at the BBC and then persuaded him to come to us. This turned out to be the best thing that happened for the NYO in 1962. He was from Vienna, but hated the Viennese for the way they treated their musicians: Mozart, Beethoven and his favourite Schubert. He was sent to Auschwitz by the Nazis, but miraculously was just alive at the end of the war. He had been Conductor of the Bournemouth and Birmingham Symphony Orchestras, then the BBC, and now he would come to us.

The orchestra had been invited to give a concert in the newly consecrated Guildford Cathedral. I remember the laying of its foundation stone on a wonderful site outside the city, and all the arguments about it being too far away. I lived in Guildford in my teenage years, and in my school holidays often played at events to raise money for building the cathedral. Due to the wonderful co-operation of the education authority and all the local staff involved, on 14 August the NYO was warmly welcomed to the floors, rooms and halls of the fine George Abbot County Secondary School for the summer course.

There was careful preparation of a big programme before the arrival of our new conductor. This was always a dramatic moment. How would he react to discovering what they could do, or to what they could *not* do until shown? The rather grim opening of *Les Francs Juges* overture was flowing happily on its way when down went the stick: '*No*, not like that . . . Have you never been hungry?' The shock was so good for our newly affluent youth.

After the stunned silence, he told them kindly but firmly what was happening in 1480, and they were aware of his own experience in Auschwitz. When we started again the mood had changed, the sound different; the partnership was made and grew into a musical enrichment over the ensuing years. This time it was not just the Berlioz, but everybody's first experience of the enduring concentration needed through fifty minutes of Schubert's great C Major.

Guildford Cathedral was far from perfect acoustically. We tried various forms of seating, and finally decided the huge sound must just take its own course. Among our distinguished guests was our Council member Dame Diana Reader Harris, Headmistress of Sherborne. One of her old pupils, Rosemary Ellison, was the soloist in *The Lark Ascending*. Dame Diana writes:

> On my left the Chairman of the *Mirror*, Cecil King, was complaining into my left ear that the acoustics were not good enough, while on my right Sir Edward Maufe, the cathedral architect, was muttering, 'It was never meant for this!' My memory is of the atmosphere and quality of the packed-full audience.

This time, as well as a prayer at the beginning and a blessing at the end, the Dean had chosen 'All people that on earth do dwell' arranged for congregation and orchestra by Vaughan Williams, the last verse giving our brass section ample scope for 'praise and glory evermore'.

The music critic of the *Surrey Advertiser*, after saying that 'the orchestra lived up to its reputation of brilliant and enthusiastic playing', was aware that 'the stamina of the orchestra was put to the test in the great C Major. Far from flagging, it seemed to grow in vigour right to the end.' It was a big challenge conquered.

I was touched that the Mayor, Alderman Swayne, wrote to me on behalf of his citizens:

> It seemed to me that having heard such beautiful music in such a wonderful setting it was wrong that people could not express their pleasure and gratitude, applause in the cathedral being inappropriate . . . To put matters right I want to express the appreciation of all who filled the cathedral, as I'm sure that everybody felt the orchestra was deserving of the highest praise.

The course was not over. Next day there was a fifty-five-minute recording for the BBC 'Orchestras of England' series, and another concert on the last day. We had been offered the distinction of giving the first orchestral concert in the new Chichester Festival Theatre, by its Director Sir Laurence Olivier. After the concert Dame Sybil Thorndyke came round to talk to everybody. She loved music, and played the piano. The comments of an actress were so different from those of musicians and music critics: 'It was the *beauty* of the playing that carried me away; that magnificent finale, in response to Mr Schwarz's titanic determination that its splendour should be made plain.' But now it was time for my youngest orchestra to go home, taking with them for always that splendour they had discovered in great music.

Over the years Rudi Schwarz brought us clear thought and judgement, and from the intensity and rather stiff exterior flowed great warmth and kindness. Many of our members now in the profession have found him a wise adviser, and for them and me he remains a wonderful friend. In December 1986, aged eighty-two, he wrote:

> I will never forget meeting you and the NYO for the first time. I thought, to start with, these children will never be able to play a demanding programme. But during the course I soon witnessed the miracle you achieved, to select the talents, to guide and mould and inspire each individual towards such

> devotion to serious music-making that the result was unbelievably exciting and memorable. The lasting memories of musical highlights in my life belong to the NYO.

One morning before this course Diana had come to tell me that she'd decided to leave. She had been with me for ten years – ten years of underpaid, overworked, dedicated service to a cause. She was a very able and exceptionally nice person and friend who deserved career opportunities in a wider sphere. She knew I was planning to leave in 1963, and that we couldn't both leave together. Her secretary, Ann Teviotdale, was engaged and would soon be leaving, so the whole administration needed to be put on a firmer footing before I left. Those members of the Executive who knew her best – John Newson and Herbert Howells who was her professor at the RCM – knew we shouldn't expect her to stay longer. Nobody who has grown up with an organisation in all its stages is replaceable. Diana was so much a part of the life of the NYO, and a friend to all our musicians and staff. Losing her was a very sad day for all of us, but especially for me.

Just when I was feeling this loss as the last straw on a difficult year there came a letter. It was from King's College, Cambridge, to invite me to dinner. The college wanted to show its appreciation of the high musical standard of the many young musicians coming to Cambridge from the NYO. This was a great tribute to the NYO and its professors, and as Cambridge had helped us in 1948 I was glad they felt we had contributed in return. It gave me just the lift I needed to face rebuilding again for 1963 without my special Diana.

Our first task was to find an able young man who could take full responsibility for the administration. Accordingly I put an advertisement in *The Times* twice.

> Rare type of young man required, age about 23 to 28.
> Essential qualities are initiative, a strong sense of urgency, responsibility, tact with people at all levels, ability to organise

> and readiness to carry out a variety of tasks in the service of an important cause. Other valuable assets: an interest in music, a sense of humour, perhaps a university education and the ability to write convincingly and to type. Salary by arrangement. Write Box K276 *The Times* EC4.

I should have added, 'free to travel, and no holidays at Christmas and Easter'.

To my amazement there was a big response. Don Ryder very kindly interviewed and shortlisted, sending me the best three. One was an outstanding young civil servant from the Northern Ireland Office, full of energy and ready to sacrifice security and pension to work in a cause. I chose him – Peter McLachlan – and invited him to visit us at work during the summer, and he came to the Guildford and Chichester concerts. I asked him for his first impressions, and he said, 'Wonderful music, inspiring people, and the right place for me.'

A few weeks later I met Terence O'Neill,* the new Prime Minister of Northern Ireland, and at lunch he said, 'I've got a bone to pick with you: you've stolen my best young civil servant.' A sad loss for him I'm sure, but a red-letter day for the NYO.

October 1 was Peter's first day with the NYO in 90 George Street. London auditions were in progress, so every half-hour a candidate, instrument, and teacher or parent arrived. The only secretary was not well and went home before the day was out. Peter had come from circumstances where there were typists here, filing clerks there, messengers everywhere, meals provided and spacious offices. We had little equipment, and he decided to tackle the broken duplicator, carefully taking it apart and getting absolutely covered in that dreadful blue ink. The last candidate arrived with her own accompanist, who had come straight from hospital with her five-day-old baby, which she immediately placed on Peter's lap. As we left the office that evening I found Peter, undeterred by broken equipment, the

*Now Lord O'Neill of the Maine.

lack of secretary and candidates to look after, but muttering plaintively, 'But I've never held a new-born baby!'

His next initiation was the audition tour, and he came every day to the finals to meet some future members, teachers and parents. This year my chosen few were terrific.

Thirty

Yorkshire folk never forget past friends, and in January the city of Hull gave us a great welcome back after eleven years. The education authority lent us a training college for sleeping, and the Newland High School for working during the day. Diana had very kindly arranged to come back for the week to help Peter on his first course, and we had a new housemistress, Christine Brown, a pianist from Leeds.

Rudolf Schwarz was with us for the second time, knowing much better what to expect, and the programme – with a Verdi overture, Brahms, and Britten's 'Four Sea Interludes' as the English work – was very challenging. We had another very talented pianist of ten, Diana Ostick, for the Haydn concerto.

On 4 January we were on the platform of the City Hall. For many it was their first concert, for everyone the stimulus of a packed hall and Yorkshire enthusiasm and appreciation. The next day came the entirely different experience and great honour of a concert in York Minster, one of the greatest cathedrals in Christendom. The Dean, the Very Reverend Eric Milner-White, had been Dean of King's, Cambridge, and took trouble to help us. He chose the hymn 'O praise ye the Lord' for the interval, and our composers' class had arranged the Parry tune for the orchestra. We set off in buses in the snow. The cathedral was ice-cold; jumpers under blouses and jackets for boys made little difference to blue hands and problems of pitch, and then came an electricity black-out! Somehow determination triumphed over all so that the large frozen audience was not let down.

The Princess Royal, Princess Mary, the Archbishop of York Dr Coggan and a civic party were among the guests. Afterwards in the Chapter House the archbishop made a most appreciative short speech and Princess Mary stayed awhile in spite of the cold, moving round amongst the players, showing genuine interest in them, and of course talking to Rudi Schwarz. In just one week my new orchestra had shown fine new talent, determination, friendliness and humour. They would need it in the years ahead.

At the next Council meeting, there were congratulations for Douglas Guest on his recent appointment as Organist and Master of the Choristers of Westminster Abbey. This was his last summer at Worcester Cathedral, and he invited us to give the opening concert at the Three Choirs' Festival. Sir Robert Mayer and Malcolm Arnold now retired, replaced by John (later Sir John) Manduell, the BBC's Head of Music for the Midlands and East Anglia, and Mr Macklin of the Associated Board. Retiring from the Executive Committee after ten years were Maurice Jacobson, who'd done so much to help in the early years, and John Newsom, who had done more than anyone to enlist the support of LEAs. Dr Taylor became the new Chairman of the Executive.

Don Ryder reported we were solvent again after our loss on the Russian tour, and that the administration had only spent £4 more this year than last. (We were really frugal in the office.) He had also made Derek Page, a member of his staff, available to us for publicity advice and help in any emergency while abroad. He thought we should be able to sustain a foreign tour each summer, given adequate outside support.

Invitations to many important European festivals always had to be refused as they did not fit our school-holiday dates. The immediate choice was between the British week in Zurich, Poland, the Isle of Man, Greece, Japan and Israel. The Council decided we should try to fit in Zurich and Poland this summer.

I reported that we could never appear on ITV again owing to their agreement with the Musicians' Union, and George Sylvester had a bright idea. Perhaps a delegation could go to ITV and the BBC and suggest an extra quota of time for the NYO that would not deprive union members, as it would not be given to them in any case.

There was further discussion on finding a permanent venue in which the orchestra could live and work.

One morning Gerald Moore, the renowned pianist and accompanist and a friend of mine, came to see me. He was President this year of the Incorporated Society of Musicians, of which I was a member. He'd come to tell me that there had been complaints about my 'cruelty to children' at auditions. My immediate reaction was to laugh – but then I realised he was serious, and very embarrassed and apologetic.

'You see we've had such a lot of letters.'

'Do you mean a hundred or so?'

'Oh no, no. Under ten, I'm sure.' I asked him if the postmarks and addresses were from the same area.

'Oh dear. I never thought of that.'

'Were they complaining as teachers or parents?'

'No, it was just your disgraceful and cruel behaviour to children – really dreadful letters. I'm so sorry, it seems so impossible but I had to come.'

There were only ten final-audition days on which anyone from outside could be present, and we kept a list of all who came. Anyway, Peter was at them all, and so was the professor concerned. We gave Gerald Moore the professors' addresses so that he could contact a witness for every occasion; so amid more thanks and apologies to each other, he left.

In the early years of opposition I'd experienced all kinds of character assassinations and physical threats, and kept my *Nasty Letters* file. But nobody had ever thought up 'cruelty to children' before, and I wasn't even allowed to know where or when I committed this crime. I put the matter out of my mind, and prepared for what I hoped would be the best concerts in our history so far.

We had all the ingredients: the Royal Festival Hall with Sir Malcolm conducting and the honour of the Queen Mother's presence; BBCTV; a very promising orchestra; and Jackie du Pré as soloist. Her very talented mother and I were students together at the RAM so I had nursed Jackie as a baby, and watched her grow up. Once again Mr Bryant generously offered us a home in Tunbridge Wells; he was a real friend to the orchestra.

Then things started to happen. Jackie, who was seventeen, rang me from Paris, where she was studying: she had to make changes to her technique, and this had temporarily disturbed her playing. She just couldn't do a concerto now. It was most understandable but very disappointing, and left me very little time to train another soloist on any instrument.

Then the BBC rang. They were going to cancel, although the agreement was signed. Our concert was on 25 April, and there was a royal wedding, Princess Alexandra's, on the 24th. Not only would TV equipment be needed all over Westminster Abbey, but the whole route to the Palace had to be covered. The forty-eight hours before the wedding would involve all their staff and equipment, and to set up in the RFH the next morning was just too much. This was very sad for our parents and teachers all over the country: so many couldn't come to London.

Good news was that Mary Shoppee was coming back as a housemistress, bringing her excellent schoolmaster husband Timothy Boyle to join the team. The strong silent type, with a great sense of humour, he could look quite stern and was soon known to his charges, the forty younger boys, as 'Tough'.

I still had the problem of choosing another soloist. I had eight good horns and three could manage the Mozart E Flat: I chose David Cripps. It was settled just in time for the *Mirror* to change our posters. Sir Malcolm had chosen a joyful programme, with the spirited *Capriccio espagnol*, and the main work was the *New World Symphony*. He was with us for the whole of the last three days.

Soon came our 1963 RFH occasion, its greatest moment with the hall full and the orchestra alert on the platform to sound the fanfare as the Queen Mother entered the box.

The *Capriccio* has one very difficult violin solo, and I had nobody who could manage it technically and also had a good enough violin. Two players together didn't work, but after hours of trial and error I matched four who could manage the solo and whose instruments blended like one. This quartet had their own way of playing exactly together, until in rehearsal Sir Malcolm thought perhaps he should conduct them, and it fell apart. I persuaded him to keep still and ignore them, but just in case he forgot, the little quartet rehearsed with their eyes shut. On the night it was one solo and no critic commented.

But in the front rows were some well-known musicians, including Gina Bachauer and her husband Alec Sherman. They were close enough to see that there were four playing, and Gina was so excited by this that it cemented her close interest in our work, from which we were to benefit later on in Greece.

The players and conductor were as one in their love of the Dvořák symphony, and it was probably the highest standard we had reached in our sixteen years. When the applause faded everyone went with their instruments in hand and lined up for the great moment of meeting the Queen Mother. They were in two lines like a guard of honour, rather far apart, when, escorted by Douglas Guest, she most generously went all down one line and all the way up the other, so that nobody was left out. There was a special word to the horn soloist, and the quartet, and even to a small boy still holding his drumsticks.

When Her Majesty had left, a group of VIPs, musicians and ambassadors joined us, including Edward Heath, Secretary of State for Industry, who made a little speech. We replied by making him an honorary member and giving him a badge. And so to friends at the buses, the glow of success, and tiredness merging into sleep on the long dark night-drive home.

We had not been in London for two years so here was a welcome chance to get the views of the critics. The *Telegraph* – 'In London for the first time for two years, the NYO showed once again that astonishingly high standard of performance, which year after year is an endless source of wonder and admiration' – and *The Times* – 'Dr Ruth Railton's achievement remains an inexplicable mystery . . . their playing still always seems to go just one degree beyond what might be considered the limit of youthful possibility' – were typically supportive. There was a different touch from Neville Cardus in the *Guardian*:

> to see the freedom of the bowing, to see the timpanist at work with gusto, to see and to hear the brave chorus of the brass – all this is a delight to the eye as well as to the ear . . . Such a standard of musical execution and understanding was unheard of and not possible twenty years ago.

I was pleased about the seeing, as I believe that any public performance on a platform should look good. From the beginning we had always taken endless trouble with the platform design. Equally important, if every individual looks their best it gives self-respect and pride in the high standards of their group as a whole. With such support from the leading critics we felt encouraged to represent Britain abroad once again.

The British Council had invited us to take part in the British Week in Zurich, even contributing £4,000, and dates had to be settled. Poland had also invited us for a whole week; could the two be co-ordinated into one summer tour?

It was May when Peter and I set off to fly by Lot to Poland, and then on to Zurich. We were early at the airport, only to discover that the Lot plane had been cancelled. In vain we tried every airline, and our hopes faded. Then we thought of going to Zurich first. All flights to Zurich were full. The thought of depriving the children of the tour because we couldn't confirm dates in time drove us on. A kindly BEA official, having failed to convince me that we couldn't get to Zurich by the next morning, provided a map and timetables of all the airlines and a quiet corner, and left us to it. After about two hours he brought cups of coffee. Eventually we found we could get to Frankfurt –

but not from there to Zurich; we could get from *Stuttgart* to Zurich in the early morning. Then Peter remembered the motorway from Frankfurt to Stuttgart. Tickets were bought, and we were airborne in the late afternoon. We set off from Frankfurt with an excellent car and driver in the rain, which became a thunderstorm, with lightning flashing and the autobahn a river in a gale. It was one of the most frightening experiences of my life, and we owe our lives to that German driver. It was three a.m. when, still in a downpour, we arrived at the Stuttgart hotel, and by seven-thirty we were in the early plane to Zurich. With plenty of coffee and time to repair our jaded appearance, we were punctually with the efficient and professional Swiss managers. The Tonhalle was fine, the platform just big enough; programme suggestions acceptable; accommodation adequate. Two concerts were fixed for 13 and 14 September. As we left for the plane to Warsaw Peter said, 'It was worth the effort – the orchestra will love being here.'

That evening we were in Warsaw: a big contrast in every way but the warmest, kindest welcome, and the bright red flowers of greeting. They wanted at least four concerts in Warsaw and two in Łódz, and everything had to be arranged centrally through the Ministry of Culture and Education and so on – but after two days we returned with sufficient plans to put before our Executive.

The Committee agreed our plans for the summer course in Worcester, with the opening concert at the Three Choirs' Festival on 1 September. After that we would fly to Warsaw in our own BEA Vanguard, give six concerts in Poland, fly to Zurich and give two concerts there. Our plane would bring us safely home on the 15th. Our Treasurer had suggested a total fee of £35 for the whole three weeks.

In May a letter to all the education authorities and the press announced the start of the Yehudi Menuhin School in September, without the prior knowledge of the joint committee; they all resigned immediately. They had suggested he might get started in liaison with the AET, like the NJMS, but

Yehudi wrote to me to say he wanted complete independence. Dr Taylor concluded that we had played a part in getting the school started, and wished him well.

Our NJMS annual solo recital in the Wigmore Hall was on 23 July. There were twenty-six solo performers, ten different instruments, and a composer. One of the youngest, a composer-pianist, was supposed to be playing his own piece, called 'Legal Frolic'. Once on the platform nothing would stop him – on he went, improvising, in a world of his own. I left my seat upstairs, raced down, and behind the scenes one of the staff opened the door on to the stage and called to him to come off. He promptly played two big chords as if to say 'That's that,' and mercifully obeyed. The audience by then had thoroughly enjoyed the unexpected drama and clapped heartily. With the creative young there is always imagination and the unexpected.

Thirty-One

The generous education authority of Worcester had offered us the Girls' Grammar School for all our work, and allowed us to turn the Nunnery Wood High School into dormitories for 150. Oh, those piles of mattresses and blankets! On 24 August the whole family assembled for the course. Ahead of them lay the Three Choirs' Festival concert, representing Britain in Zurich, and a tour of Poland. This time we were going to fly in *one* plane, and the Vanguard's hold and seating was arranged specially to fit 120 of us and our instruments.

Rudolf Schwarz was our conductor, and we were repeating the Elgar overture and the *Capriccio espagnol*, as we had two concerti to prepare, plus a symphony and national anthems and encores. Maureen Smith (now seventeen) was the soloist for Mozart in A (K219), and Helen Powell (fourteen) for the Haydn Oboe Concerto in C. In spare moments we also rehearsed a small choir, memorising a few English songs and madrigals. So often at receptions on tour a young local choir would sing, and without our instruments we couldn't respond.

On 1 September we were rehearsing in Worcester Cathedral. I'd arranged for Richard Deakin, who lived in the area, to lead the orchestra in his home city.* As well as being a violinist, he was an ARCO† and had won a music scholarship to Oxford. Our soloists played in turns, but I chose the oboe concerto for this great event, as the sound was so beautiful in the cathedral. Evelyn Rothwell (Lady Barbirolli), who taught Helen, came over from Manchester to support her.

The next day was spent recording for BBC Radio and on 3

*Now Head of Strings at the RNCM and an NYO professor.

† Associate of the Royal College of Organists.

September we gave a concert in the Winter Gardens, Malvern, with a live TV recording. (The audience was admitted free, but no children under twelve were allowed in.)

There was considerable excitement at early breakfast in Nunnery Wood on the 4th. 'It's goodbye Worcester and Warsaw tonight,' said one experienced chap, and 'I've never flown before' was also heard. Passports, instruments, music and the various responsibilities of the leaders were very important. First we went by train from Worcester to Paddington, then in coaches to Heathrow.

In the sunlight lay our special Vanguard and soon we were all together in this beautiful plane. Peter had all the documents; John was checking the safety of the instruments in the hold; house staff and Sister were surveying their charges; and most important, our conductor was with us.

It was late afternoon with the setting sun lighting up the plane as it made a flawless landing in Warsaw. A large crowd was there to see it land, and after we'd all left the plane the engineers of Warsaw were allowed to visit the scene and talk to our pilots. It was the first Vanguard to land in Poland, and several hundred walked round it, in quiet, awestruck respect for this masterpiece of British invention.

For ourselves there was the warmest reception, the red carnations, a greeting from the City and the Minister of Culture; and a team of four interpreters was to be with us for the whole week. We watched our members set off in buses to the unknown, but at least to sleep in beds again, and devour Polish sausage and cheese and enjoy all other aspects of their hosts' generous hospitality.

Our opening concerts in the Philharmonic Hall were on 5, 6 and 7 September. John and I were on the platform just after eight a.m., to the amazement of our guides, preparing the setting. When the rehearsal began the hall started to fill with quite a scattering of people, curious about our reputation and to see British children. But we worked on uninterrupted.

Any opening night is festive and all-important for a tour. The

British Ambassador, Sir George Clutton, was there, with representatives from the British Council, the Mayor of Warsaw and Mr Zakrzewski, the head of the artistic agency Pagart, and even the Minister of Culture, Mr Galinsky. The press wrote that 'the Polish anthem which opened the concert delighted the audience with the perfection of its performance', and 'the applause reached such a peak that an encore was granted, the Mazur from Moniuszko's opera, and there seemed no end to the cheers from the standing audience'. Sir George came round afterwards, bringing the minister, who was most enthusiastic and admitted he had never expected such a high standard, and 'the talent and the discipline was a revelation, an unforgettable event'. After congratulating Rudi Schwarz he asked him if he had visited Poland before and got the reply, 'This is only my second visit: my first was as a prisoner in Auschwitz.' Such an ovation and warm welcome must have been a very emotional experience for him.

The next night the hall was packed, mainly with children and students. Our programme was not the most suitable for them, but they were extremely enthusiastic, and showered the platform and performers with their red flowers. Here was the usual problem of the word 'youth' in our title. It gave the impression that we would be a rather low-level, amateur school affair. So our first night had been a political courtesy; the second was filled with children and 'youth'. By the third night the news had spread and we had a real audience of the cultured people of Warsaw, their leading musicians and members of their symphony and radio orchestras. Tickets were not expensive in Communist countries, so all levels of society could come for the love of music. There was a queue at the door, and many were turned away. The Warsaw audience showed the warmth and the spirit of enjoyment of the Polish people, as well as their understanding of tragedy. They brought the best out of us, and I can only hope we were good enough to deserve the response they gave us.

It was Sunday, 8 September, and we were about to celebrate

our hundredth major public concert, which would be in Łódz. A welcoming party had assembled to greet us: the Mayor and civic dignitaries, but most important the Chairman of Łódz's Cultural and Musical Society. There was a large hotel very near the concert hall, so after replying to official greetings we set to work on the platform, which was rather small for us. The generous hospitality of the city was expressed in a wonderful lunch, tables decked with red carnations.

The rehearsal went well, leaving time for a walk in the fresh air before the rather early concert. Then things started to happen, and happen so suddenly. Two girls had fainted; then three boys tottered back from their walk and collapsed; Sister started organising chairs in the reception area of our hotel. One of our interpreters went to fetch the chairman who had officially greeted us and, as in Finland, he turned out to be a consultant at the Łódz hospital! He surveyed the scene, and took over the lounge; he asked for coats and blankets, spreading them on the floor to lie the casualties on them in rows. Every few minutes another collapsed; they were not just feeling sick, some were only semi-conscious. With only half an hour to go to the concert, I heard a housemaster announce, 'Will all those still alive go to the hall immediately.' We were twenty-seven short, and the *Capriccio espagnol* had important solo parts. We had two harpists, one was left; fourteen cellos, seven were left; wind and brass sections were organising themselves to cover missing soloists. Maureen seemed fit enough for the concerto, and Rudi agreed with me that 'the show must go on' for as long as there were some players. The harpist finished her solo and collapsed beside her harp, and at the interval about seven more gave up. Somehow the symphony was played, and even a rather weak version of the Mazur encore. I rushed back to the hotel to find our friendly physician and Sister Boddy in charge of an emergency field hospital.

There was a special supper party arranged for after the concert, for which the Minister of Culture had sent a huge chocolate cake with *100th* on the top, a very generous idea as chocolate was short in Poland: I expect the healthy devoured it gratefully. Then one of our buses became an ambulance for the journey to Warsaw. The physician assured me that it was a virus, not as serious as it looked, and in twenty-four hours they would be well again.

While all this was going on Sir George, who had been very impressed at the opening night in Warsaw, decided to come all the way to Łódz, bringing with him Hugh Carleton Greene, Director General of the BBC. What a day for his first impression of our playing and behaviour! I thought, 'No more BBC engagements . . .' How sad that the occasion we hoped to make rather a special one turned out to be quite the worst in our history. But I often think of the physician of Łódz and of the kind, sympathetic hospitality of the people of that city.

There had not been a day off since 24 August, when work started in Worcester. Three concerts there, the flight, three concerts in Warsaw and one in Łódz had been achieved – just. Miraculously the next two days were concert-free: time for the sick to recover, for some exercise and fresh air and to see something of the city and, we hoped, for some domestic repairs. The accommodation was spartan: hot water only twice a week, washing hair and clothes in cold water, and a shortage of irons for pressing trousers and skirts – it was not easy.

With interpreters our members set off round the city. The main street had been completely flattened in the war, and the government had agreed to rebuild it exactly as before, from photographs, but with a much wider road. Even the eleventh-century cathedral had every brick put back as before. This gave the people a feeling of continuity.

Our post-war youth were stunned by what they saw of the effects of war. One group was taken up the highest tower, giving a wide vista of the Polish landscape and the position and size of Warsaw. Another group, walking through the streets, came across a trolley-bus that had come off its track. Everybody got out safely; the driver had a good look and said, 'Kaput.' Our boys went into action at once, pushing and lifting it back on to the track. A bystander took a photograph of this and must have given it to the leading newspaper, which published a big picture with a comment on the example of English initiative and the team spirit of the members of the NYO.

In the mean time Peter, out walking to find museums, suddenly felt someone tug at his coat and guide him firmly along the street. Opening a door in what seemed like an office block, this person shoved him inside. Down some stairs he discovered an enormous room, packed with people, and a Mass in progress. When he came out he was alone; his guide had gone. He shut the door, and there was no sign of a church from the street.

On that day off the sick got well, the tired rested, the energetic saw a great deal of Warsaw, and much domestic activity was fitted in, it being a hot-water day. By late breakfast the next morning resilience had won, and chatter and laughter were back in full swing.

The second free day included a visit to a junior music school, which gave us a short concert; but the main event was a trip to Karolin and the headquarters of the Mazowsze Dancers. I had met and entertained them in London, when Victor Hochhauser brought them over. Their Artistic Director, Mira Ziminska-Sygietynska, and I had much in common: the way we chose talent, the dedication and disciplined training we gave them, the beauty of detail, doing everything as well as possible for the love of it. So here in this lovely house in the country, her folk dancers and singers lived and trained and then toured the world. Her youngest were eighteen, the age of our eldest. They were packing for their next tour, but still danced for us, and showed some of their hand-made and -embroidered wardrobe; the singers sang folk songs in Polish and even one in English. We responded with our amateur effort of an English madrigal, and the afternoon ended with a wonderful tea in the garden. Our members were very appreciative of the quality and standard; the beautiful girls, the handsome young men; the setting in the September colouring. The whole atmosphere was inspiring.

Sir George had kindly invited us to supper in the Embassy. When we arrived, glasses of wine were already on the buffet table, somewhat ahead of the supply of soft drinks, and were rapidly enjoyed . . . but all was well. After I'd thanked the ambassador officially for his hospitality he replied with, 'You deserved it. The concerts were remarkable and you've brought the Poles a breath of England.' And Sister was delighted because the Medical Officer restocked some of her medicines.

Back in action, the morning rehearsal in the Philharmonic Hall was going especially well and happily. Several players remarked, 'Mr Schwarz seems quite different . . . relaxed . . . He smiles more, he moves his arms more.' I just listened to them and said nothing. On our first day off Rudi had asked if I could arrange for him to go to Auschwitz, now a museum; he spent the day there. Next day I went to talk to him, rather nervous in case his visit had upset him. Instead I found him relaxed and talking freely about it, as if an enormous dark burden had been lifted off him. I was very moved by the experience of finding a friend so changed. Now that our sensitive young had commented, Peter thought I should tell them about Rudi's visit. It was common knowledge that he had been a prisoner in that ghastly hell; that he had the courage to come back to Poland for our sakes, and then go back to Auschwitz and return to us without bitterness, seemed something they should know. They were grateful, and it proved a wise move because the concert that night took off into another dimension.

After a whole week in a country the last night is always a moving occasion. It was a wrench from the warmth and kindness of the Polish people, from the participating audiences that could laugh in the *Capriccio* and weep in the Dvořák, from people who through great suffering and poverty could find strength in music and show their love in giving huge baskets of flowers – one taking up the whole podium with a notice across it: COME BACK AGAIN.

Away from all the rejoicing, in a cold dark corner guarding

the artists' entrance, stood a former Polish soldier. He was there for all our concerts, standing on his wooden leg, saluting with his only arm through the anthem; waiting in the hope that we'd play our second encore, the Polish mazur. Of course I spoke to him on each occasion before I left, and on this last night, he ripped the miniature model of the Virtuti Militari medal from his buttonhole and gave it to me. Gripping my hand he said, 'I don't need it any more. I have seen Heaven tonight,' and limped out into the dark street. I put his gift into my evening bag for safety. It is still there.

After affectionate farewells and the red flowers, we walked across the grass fields to the runway. This time we were in two planes of the Polish airline Lot. We were met in Zurich by the officials of the British Week, of the British Council and our agent, and everything went according to plan.

In Poland our members had seen poverty, the grip of a police state and the generosity and unshakeable patriotism of the people. Now the stark contrast hit them: in Zurich everything was efficient, spotless, well-organised and polite: very rich people everywhere and conditions in the hall and hostels so pleasant.

Everyone was fit and looking greatly refreshed at the rehearsal in the Tonhalle the next morning. Maureen Smith played the violin concerto more beautifully than ever before, and Helen Powell the oboe concerto for the second night. Rudi was in great form, and I think these last two concerts were the best of the whole three weeks. A last treat for us all was that George Szell was in the audience and came round to talk to us. It was good to hear him say, 'You've set a standard of which many professional orchestras would be proud,' and he told Maureen how musically she'd played. John spotted Szell at the back of the audience the second night also, and went to offer him his own better seat; Szell said, 'I just couldn't resist coming back. I wouldn't have missed that child on the oboe for anything – what an artist!'

The concerts were really appreciated, and the British Council gave us a free trip on the Zurich See. And on the morning of 15 September, our special Vanguard arrived and carried us all safely back to London.

The Monday-morning newspapers announced, 'HOME IN TRIUMPH'. But there was no time for a rest: we had to report immediately to the Executive Committee to agree plans for the whole of 1964.

It was to be Sunderland and Newcastle in January, the Isle of Man in April; and Israel in the summer, possibly covering Cyprus, Athens and Milan on the way back. The annual audition tour was upon us; the term had begun for our eight boarders; and there was only temporary secretarial help in the office.

Everybody was keen to pursue the idea of a permanent base for the orchestra, near London and preferably in LEA premises with residential accommodation near by. Despite the fact that this new scheme would mean the orchestra losing its impact on many provincial centres, the Executive felt the advantages far outweighed the disadvantages, and we should go all out, with Mr Sylvester's special help through his colleagues in the LEAs, to achieve this in the coming year.

Don Ryder said our finances were still sound. He urged Peter to get a first-class secretary, and any additional help needed, for the huge programme ahead.

Peter set off immediately to Princes Court, the AET hostel where our boarders lived. They had been given a week's holiday after Poland. To his amazement, on the door was a brass plate – THE YEHUDI MENUHIN SCHOOL – and inside about a dozen eight- to ten-year-olds; but all our own rooms seemed intact. Grace Cone was shocked to find we knew nothing about this, as Yehudi had asked her to arrange the same scheme for his children as she'd always done for ours. So here we all were:

different titles, differently financed, different age groups, different teachers, but all living together.

Due to Grace Cone's planning we all got on well. Our members did academic work at the AET in the morning, while the little ones had violin lessons; they then went to school in the afternoons while our noisier instrumental work went on. Our only worry was that our bassoon, pianist or clarinettist might keep the little ones awake in the late evenings. Among our boarders were Susan Drake (seventeen), now a famous harpist; John Bimson (fourteen), now principal horn of the RPO; and Pan Hon Lee (thirteen), now leader of the Hallé. Yehudi was always willing to help Pan Hon, and asked me to help his pianist son when his teacher was ill. Within a year the Menuhin School had found its own premises in Saffron Walden, where it continues to this day.

Thirty-Two

For this year's auditions I wanted to go myself to all the main cities where I had first battled my way some sixteen years ago. I wanted to make sure of the friendships, contacts and support for the future without me. So it was back to the friendly night trains: Edinburgh, Newcastle, Leeds, Liverpool and Manchester. The London candidates came to our office, and the finals were in the Chelsea Old Church Hall.

It was October when I spent a week in Leeds. Candidates came from York, Bradford and Hull, from Harrogate, Halifax and Ripon. On the last afternoon I was with Fanny Waterman: her husband Dr de Keyser kindly offered to drive me to the station for the London train. Main-line trains in those days were comfortable, warm and steamy, but had very high steps to get into the carriages from the platform. When alone I managed by sitting on them and heaving myself up backwards, but this time I asked Dr de Keyser to help me up, explaining that I couldn't lift my legs high enough on my own. Rather astonished, he asked why; as he was a friend and a doctor I put his hands on my thighs to explain. He was shocked: 'But that's in spasm. You *can't* walk about like that,' to which I replied, 'I always do.'

I remember this incident because the sympathy of this kind doctor somehow helped me to keep going, as I knew I must until after Israel. Almost as soon as I got back to London came the announcement of the death of Lord Evans. He was a kind and wise friend, and advised the orchestra on several occasions. When he retired he had introduced me to a Harley Street colleague, Edward McLellan, whom the Council later invited to fill the gap, and he graciously accepted.

The last fortnight of final auditions in London was going

splendidly. Then one afternoon a girl of fifteen, who had come alone, stayed behind to see me. As the others had left, I was able to tell her that she could join us after Christmas, whereupon she burst into tears. What emerged was that the previous year she had come to the final with her father, who was angry when she wasn't chosen. He had then written letters, and asked his friends to write too, saying dreadful things about me. This had made her unhappy all the year, and had upset her schoolwork too. *She* knew she wasn't as good as the others last year, and so worked hard to try again this time, but her father forbade her to come. So she had pretended she was going to school, but caught the train to London instead. I convinced her that the letters didn't matter at all, but she was afraid to go home to father. I lived in nearby Chelsea: a warm fire, some tea; a telephone; then her perfect headmistress took over.

To think that an angry father, out of malice to me, so nearly broke his own child and her career! Later on I was able to tell Gerald Moore that I'd probably traced the instigator of those letters.

While I was heavily involved in matters musical, Don Ryder and Peter had a meeting with Hugh (later Lord) Cudlipp, the new Chairman of the *Mirror*. Costs were rising, and he generously offered an extra £5,000 a year, giving us a total of £11,500 for the adventurous year ahead. This surprise was like a Christmas present for the orchestra. In addition Peter was to have a more reasonable salary. In thanking the Council he wrote: 'To play even a small part in enabling the NYO to continue its magnificent contribution to musical education at the highest level is itself a great reward. In coming here I asked for nothing more.' All the NYO staff asked for nothing, just gave the best that was in them.

One afternoon Peter told me he had advertised for a secretary 'in much the same way as you did for me', and he had three people he'd like me to see. One stood out above the others: young and attractive, with beautiful manners, big brown eyes alive with excitement; I was more aware of an inner self-confidence than the immediate shyness. As we talked I was also struck by the quality of her voice; it is such a help on the telephone, with children and strangers, if a voice sounds welcoming. I tried putting her off: 'There's an awful lot of work, and different every day.'

'I'm not afraid. I can learn about it.'

'Will music going on all day worry you?'

'I'm not supposed to be musical – but I love it.'

'What about boarding school, with our long days and evenings?'

'I've been to boarding school; I know about *that.*' She couldn't contain a little smile.

'Why do you want this job?'

'I want to help people.'

Finally I tried, 'What have you worked in before?'

'This would be my first job . . .' Laughing about diving in at the deep end, I sent her back to Peter. I knew how lucky we'd be to get her, and Peter was of the same mind.

So Jill Wilson, like Philippa, Diana and Mary before her, joined us at nineteen. And like them, by her qualities of character, her warmth, initiative and determination, did the work of several and gave her own special contribution to the life of the NYO.

And so to the Christmas course in Sunderland, where we were received with the same warm welcome as in 1954. The former Director of Education, Dr Thompson, his successor Mr Bridge and the heads of the two Thorney Close Secondary Modern Schools, Mr Nelson and Mr Lowery, were eagerly committed to solving any problems that arose. We had gained a new housemaster, Denis Cocks, Director of Music at Ramsgate College, and it was a tough wintry start for Jill's first course, a nightmare of endless mattresses and pillows. The main work this week was Sibelius 2; and Malcolm Arnold had written four English Dances especially for us, to include every instrument. A new young pianist of thirteen, Paul Roberts, played the concerto.* Once again we had the privilege of Rudolf Schwarz as conductor, and one evening he gave us a talk about music and musicians, his life and career, and Vienna as he had known it. He kept us enthralled for over an hour, a memory to treasure.

On 4 January we were all in the City Hall, Newcastle on Tyne. After the rehearsal came the honour of a mayoral reception given by Alderman Hedley, then it was back to the sold-out hall and the enthusiastic crowd. Audience response affects the performance, and this new orchestra could react and enjoy; I was confident of its growth for the foreign tour ahead.

This time, unlike 1954, Sunderland could have its own concert, in the Empire Theatre. In spite of a very slanting platform, and using our buses as cloakrooms for coats and instrument cases and with only just enough space off-stage to assemble and tune, we overcame the problems in gratitude to our hosts. Then, after one more night on the floor and the dawn farewells to new friendships, it was back to school until Easter.

The *Newcastle Journal* and the *Sunderland Echo* were generous and encouraging, Arthur Milner in the first saying, '. . . their superb training and humility, enthusiasm and *esprit de corps* . . . yielding themselves so utterly to the music . . . The brass in the Wagner and the Malcolm Arnold rose to a virtuoso standard, yet all their efforts, however brilliant, were directed to purely musical ends.' In the *Echo* 'the symphony was most moving . . . the final burst of vitality they managed to inject into the last movement was nothing short of a miracle.'

The annual Council meeting was on 22 January, and started with the good news of a knighthood for John Newsom. If the help he'd given us was repeated in his many spheres of interest, it must have been richly deserved.

Easter would be in the Isle of Man; the summer course would be in a school in Croydon that might become our permanent home, from which we would travel to give concerts, and I had

*Now a professor at the Guildhall School.

already met Dr Beeching* to discuss a special NYO sleeper train. There was residential accommodation near by and the excellent new Fairfield Hall, perfect for our concerts and suited to TV. We proposed accepting an invitation for eight concerts in Israel, after which we might fly to Greece to play in the Athens Festival.

Easter in the Isle of Man was perhaps the most complicated event we ever undertook, yet educationally so worthwhile. None of us had realised quite how distant and isolated the island is. The people hadn't had a live orchestral concert for seventeen years. An orchestra living with them for a whole week was as exciting an idea for them as a course on the island was for all of us.

It was winter when Peter had set out to review the arrangements before we could accept the invitation. The most important person was the Director of Education, Mr C. H. Wilkinson, who had issued the invitation and had the authority to implement our various needs. Harry Pickard was the able and enthusiastic Music Adviser.† Together with Mr J. R. Smith, Headmaster of the Castle Rushen High School, Castletown, they offered the school as our home for the week. Luckily the main hall was big enough, and we would be welcome from after breakfast until nine p.m. for all our work. George Faragher, the Concerts and Entertainments Manager of the Villa Marina Royal Hall in Douglas, wanted two concerts, and finally all was fixed.

That was fine, but where were 150 of us plus professors going to live? The Manx people are good with ideas and full of initiative; of course tourism is their strongest suit. Peter was taken to meet a gathering of the hotel proprietors of Port Erin. These kind, friendly, capable ladies took pride in their fair prices and generous hospitality; they didn't even flinch at the mention

*The new Chairman of British Railways.
†His son Alan had been a member.

of 150 young people and ten staff. In 1964 'youth' from the mainland was beginning to get a reputation for bad behaviour, but all they wanted to know was how many boys and girls and their ages, and they could cope.

Soon the whole project seemed possible, but we would be a bit scattered: professors in the Derbyhaven Bay Hotel, days in Castletown, the concerts in Douglas, and by night we'd be in the care of the ladies of Port Erin. So transport was going to be vital. The Isle of Man Steam Packet Co. came first. Mr Fick the Manager was ready to book us plus our luggage on his steamer on 1 April and back on the 11th, but he was worried about feeding so many for breakfast and lunch, and introduced Peter to Mr Kissack, his Catering Superintendent. Indeed they could only seat eighty, but when Peter explained that our housemaster would arrange the students in relays, and they would help clear and lay the tables, he responded with, 'And your housemaster will not pay for his lunch; he will be our guest.' So it seemed we could cross the ocean. But would the island have enough buses and vans for our daily and concert-day needs? There was nothing the Isle of Man Transport Services couldn't do: they might have to provide 'more than one vehicle, ours being of a smaller capacity than the normal type of pantechnicon used on the mainland'. Buses, taxis, even an airport – they would 'endeavour to satisfy all your needs'.

In England, the twenty years since the war had quickened the pace of life, accenting the commercial side. But this new modernity had not crossed the sea to the Isle of Man, or changed the style of the Manx people. It was not just their 'old-world courtesy' and desire to please: they seemed really to enjoy their many and various efforts to make our visit possible. So we decided to accept this warm invitation from the Isle of Man.

Whenever we were breaking new ground, we had to impress upon our hosts our detailed timetable for work, and gently warn them that adolescents working energetically all day can consume a large quantity of food. We also had to work to a budget, so our suggested menus were simple and filling.

Correspondence with the ladies of Erin was memorable, being so thoughtful and homely. Mrs Murray, proprietor of the Argyll, mentioned that the youngsters might like to bring hot-water bottles. Mrs Faragher of Ard Chreg was taking seventeen and wrote:

> 12/6 B & B is right for me and 5 shillings concert days dinner, and 1/- suppers. I do hope this is alright for you. They won't need Bread and Butter to fill up with when I have finished I hope not, as I usually give them as much as they can eat, leave it to me I will look after them well for you and so will all my friends in P. Erin . . . Still busy this end painting and marmalade making getting ready for you 1st April.

Obviously our members were in for a treat. Peter had allocated Jill and me to a lady who was taking sixteen girls and had two single rooms, and a charming letter arrived:

> I am seeing Dr. Railton has No. 5 for you think she will be alright their. I do too. (Mind you its colder at night in front rooms than back) but let her try it first. She may like the sea air. I will put Electric Blanket in before she arrives we air all beds with one, but by time I get to Bottom its time to go to Top again.

There were letters of welcome, and of hope for our success, coming in all the time. By now the transport company had even collected fifty mattresses and moved them to the Castle Rushen gym for afternoon rest. We had no worries about life in the Isle of Man.

The most difficult part of the whole undertaking was to get everybody in the cheapest way from all parts of Britain to Liverpool by seven a.m. British Railways offered us the twelve-thirty Euston–Liverpool relief sleeper, getting us there at seven in time for the eight o'clock boat. If it was late we'd be stuck in Liverpool for twenty-four hours with a day's work lost.

Finally, on 31 March all was ready for our Easter adventure. Peter was already in the Isle of Man, making final preparations.

Jill was the last to leave the office; she had to get all our luggage to Euston to pack the railway van in a siding by four p.m. Her next task was to meet Oivin Fjeldstad's plane, look after him and bring him by air to the island. Her diary reads: 'My job was to meet the conductor – I only had a photograph of him – and see to VIP treatment for him. He made it very easy for me, saying I reminded him of his daughter. It was my first flight!' John Dalby and Christine Brown were coming from the north, and the senior housemaster was going to be at the boat, so it fell to me to be in charge of the 110 of us on Euston Station at eleven-fifteen p.m. Sister Boddy was the first to join me, and then other members of the house staff, including two ex-members, Gillian Lowe and Christopher Seaman. Smiling cheerful children all arrived, some with parents to cheer us off, but where was the train? From eleven-fifteen to twelve-forty-five we waited on the cold damp platform, sitting on our suitcases or walking up and down to keep warm.

Our special sleeper, coming in five minutes, never came. I thought of singing all the great tunes we knew, but by twelve-thirty everyone was tired and cold. The experienced members, with us in Russia and Poland, were very good with the young ones.

'If the train doesn't come what will happen?'

'We'll still get to the Isle of Man somehow; we have to . . .'

'It will be jolly cold if we're here all night.'

'It's all good practice. If we have to wait in Israel it will be much too hot.'

Eventually the train arrived; the stewards, without their berthing lists, caused further delay. But for Chris Seaman actually checking that our van – packed by the agreed time in the afternoon – was going to be attached to us, I think it would have been left behind. It was the only time in sixteen years that British Railways let us down. We had cigarettes for the engine drivers when they got us to Liverpool at seven a.m.!

Miraculously everybody and their luggage were present at the landing stage to mount the steps into the *Manx Maid*. The tiring night travel was blown away in the sea breezes, and our usual smiling high spirits had returned when we landed at the Douglas Marine Terminal.

We knew nothing of the Isle of Man, but our baptism into local customs was to say 'Hello Fairies' as we crossed the Fairy Bridge, the only main road for our buses going out to Port Erin. We duly took part as if it were some trivial joke, but quickly learnt that even tough lorry drivers do it every time they cross the bridge. At once we were in a world of fantasy – partly faith, partly superstition – a new world for our industrial-city dwellers. In Port Erin at least fifteen lady proprietors were ready to greet us, each claiming their own family from lists Peter had given them. If they were all as well cared for as my group with Mrs Faragher (and I'm sure they were), they were very lucky. At my bedside was a large woolly mat, and in the cold early dawn it was just what was needed on my bed – instead of the floor. Later I learnt that the Port Erin ladies thought my room needed an added touch of luxury, and clubbed together to buy me a mat for my bare feet. I was very touched.

At eight-forty-five a.m. everybody was transported to Castletown for the first sight of their home for the week, the Castle Rushen School. To the Headmaster's surprise, they all came in, read the timetable and labels and notices, and were all in their own classrooms, tuning and ready for work, at nine-thirty. A different building, different music, but life went on as if Sunderland were yesterday. Oivin Fjeldstad and the professors had all arrived safely and were very happy with the Derbyhaven Bay Hotel, its view and its food, so work should flourish.

It was a wonderfully undisturbed week. There was time for extra coaching for the scholarship exams, and with no formal events to fit in and few visitors, a more flexible timetable gave everyone a little more free time to view the island.

In these free moments the horse-drawn trams were of great interest. A trip to the Laxey Wheel, the largest working water-wheel in Europe, was arranged; and one afternoon all were invited to the Witches' Mill. The Chief Witch was reported to be in residence, in what appeared to be a windmill. Some said the witch was a man. I had thought the modern teenager would laugh at such nonsense, but in fact this was not so. A few were afraid to go; some had a thoughtful respect for the occult, and people with good or evil gifts; others were unaffected and gaily set off. 'She never came out of the windmill,' was the report. As the days went by the atmosphere, almost of an earlier century, was absorbed, and it was good for their imaginative development.

The Manx people love beauty and poetry, talk and story-telling. They also love their history, independence and traditions. We had a visit from the Bishop of Sodor and Man and Mrs Pollard. But where was Sodor? None of us knew. Apparently there was once a kingdom of Sudreyjar co-terminous with the Hebrides. Some centuries ago it was conquered, or faded out, and now the Hebrides come under the Crook of Argyll and the Isles, but the spirit of Sodor lives on in the Bishopric of Man.

We were also honoured with a visit from the Lieutenant-Governor, Sir Ronald Garvey. He was to be our chief guest at the concert, but he had to be away and asked if he could hear us play. We used this important moment to try out the Manx national anthem, and then he stayed for most of our rehearsal, and very kindly gave a short talk before leaving. That evening, as ever, some of our members asked me why they weren't taught at school the history of our own islands such as the Orkneys, the Hebrides or the Channel Islands. 'Why don't we value our own history and traditions the way the Manx people do?', 'Mr Fjeldstad knows everything about Norway.' He did, and with pride.

Throughout the week Mr Wilkinson and especially Mr Pickard had to work very hard to get this new event of a symphony-orchestra concert going. As the days went by, news of the huge sound we made and of our hours of hard work increased curiosity; by 8 April every seat was sold. The platform in the Royal Hall had to be extended and a grand piano brought in, but somehow about 110 players squashed on. When I was setting up the stage early in the morning a gentleman introduced himself to me as 'the carpenter in residence'. He would be there throughout our rehearsal and would build or change anything to please us. He was particularly proud of the fact that he had been allowed new wood for rebuilding the platform, and he'd made sure of reinforcement for the weight of the piano so that it would be safe. He had a box of perfect tools – every type of nail and hook – so the delighted percussion section made him an honorary member.

The Deputy Governor, a high court judge, the Deemster S. J. Kneale, was our chief guest so we started the concert with anthems. They enjoyed the Weber overture, Anthony Mott played the piano concerto with style, and the Borodin symphony really raised the roof. The concert was such a new event that there was an air of surprise as well as delight. The BBC made recordings for a programme going out in May, which cheered those who couldn't get tickets.

The *Isle of Man Times* reported that there were over a thousand children at our second concert who had never seen or heard an orchestra before. So of course I told them how it worked, getting different instrumentalists to stand up and show the instrument and then play it. We put care into doing this well and were rewarded with huge applause, and laughter at various items, but the brass section doing a Bliss fanfare won the day. 'The children were electrified,' said the *Times*. We shortened the programme, but the intensity of their concentration after just a brief explanation was exceptional. The *Times* concludes:

> the general public were amazed that they could take so easily this difficult music. It is obvious that they respond naturally when they are offered high standards of professional music-making. We must see that more is given to them in the years to come.

If they have, it will have made all the effort and expense of our visit worthwhile.

Early next morning, after affectionate farewells, it was into buses, over the bridge with 'Goodbye Fairies,' and soon the *Manx Maid* carried us away. Back to railways, back to school, to O and A levels we went – but refreshed from a spell with the very different and staunch outlook of the inhabitants of the unique Isle of Man.

Then came the letters. Mr Smith the headmaster said, 'I only hope that you will come back soon.' The Isle of Man Transport Services, sending their account well below the estimate, wrote, 'Your visit to the Island was a cultural one, so accordingly we have provided the transport at a reduced cost.'

Mr Wilkinson, for the governing bodies of the authority's schools, was

> aware that the renown of the orchestra is such that praise from us may seem superfluous . . . our gratitude . . . is deep and sincere. Will you, then, pass on to all concerned our thankfulness and our happiness that you should have chosen to be with us for your Easter Training Week. It was for me, personally, an experience both moving and indeed thrilling in the best sense of that word.

Mrs Murray thought, 'I suppose for you Port Erin is just a memory, but the general opinion here is that you are grand people, and we . . . want you back.' And we close the story of Easter 1964 with Mrs Faragher: 'And may you always be as happy as we saw you in Port Erin.'

Thirty-Three

During the usual *post mortem* after a course – the thanking and the accounts – Peter thought British Railways had not been reliable enough, and wrote to complain. What is interesting is the style of an official apology in 1964:

> To be quite candid, I find it very difficult to put a good case on our performance . . . I will now explain matters, but this is for your information, and not to be taken as excusing us for these failures . . . due to error all stations did not receive instructions about your special tickets. This arose through a misunderstanding between headquarters and the station . . . Arrangements were duly made for the van to be available at 4 p.m., but with the rebuilding work which is going on at Euston just now there did arise some confusion as to its exact location . . . The empty sleeper coaches were unfortunately delayed *en route* to Euston, and therefore arose the mistakes concerning berthing lists . . . and I do agree this was most upsetting for your party . . . Extremely sorry for these failures . . . sincerely apologise for all that happened . . . hope this will not prevent you from having confidence in us in the future . . .

Peter replied, 'Thank you for the full explanation of the rather catastrophic journey . . . I am hoping that, in due course, it will prove possible to persuade our Musical Director who was at Euston to put her trust in British Railways once more.' Of course we did. We needed them, and they were determined to sin no more.

By contrast, in October 1990, I set out in a British Rail first-class sleeper to Cornwall: an all-mod-con, thermostatically sealed compartment, adequate – if gadgets worked. Alas the heating system did not. The courteous steward had no emergency equipment such as a hot-water bottle; he struggled in vain with the machinery. No heat was bad enough, but an ice-cold draught persisted in its place . . . I suppose without this air machine I would have suffocated. An expensive journey became a sleepless night of torture.

After some weeks, my note of complaint was acknowledged: 'It is very unusual that our system does not work. Perhaps you did not understand the levers on the wall. Always ask the steward for assistance in the future . . .' In 1990 it is the customer who is such a nincompoop she can't read, turn a knob or talk to a steward. My reaction: I will never travel long distances or by night on British Rail again. Public relations as a profession does not seem to include courtesy or sympathy.

I have known the railways of my country since childhood, the pride of the drivers in their engines, working in the heat and the coal; and of all the staff in their particular railway. Then the individuality was swept into one mass nationalised heap; then came Dr Beeching to try to give it back some shape. Now it is modern, uncomfortable, and *very* expensive. Why not go back to four smaller privatised groups, and those whose livelihood is in railways could work with pride again.

From 1947 to 1965 British Railways played a very important part in the life of the NYO. The special arrangements for us were a form of sponsorship for our cause, but they had no public credit for it. We can only thank them now.

Sir Isaac and Lady Wolfson were both extremely keen for us to undertake a tour of Israel, and invited Peter and me to lunch. We left with the promise of £5,000, and perhaps more later, and introductions to meet those concerned in Israel. Our next appointment was to call on General Chaim Hertzog, then at the Israeli Bank in London. He was a very distinguished, able personality of great importance in Israel, and gave me the impression that such a tour was a big undertaking; were we aware of the problems involved – the climate, the travelling in Israel, the customs of the Jews, and so on? Gradually his keen military mind decided we were not afraid of battling with problems. He decided to introduce us to the leading impresario, Mr Godik, and quite soon the latter asked us to come to Israel to review his plans for six or eight concerts.

El Al delivered us to Lod Airport – for both of us our first visit to the Holy Land and an inspiring moment for Christians – and we quickly sensed the admirable efficiency of the Israelis. We were carried off by Mr Godik to his office.

The Mann Auditorium in Tel Aviv would be closed in August, so we were shown the huge basketball stadium instead. Accommodation in Ramat Gan, at the Maccabiah Olympic village, was entirely satisfactory. The Jerusalem hall was perfect. The Roman theatre at Caesarea had plenty of space for our large numbers, but no covering from the sun. Of course concerts don't start till eight-thirty or later, but the wind and the sand getting into instruments as well as the sun when preparing would be problems. We didn't go to Haifa – just saw pictures of a very good hall and took the platform measurements – but there were still Beersheba and Eilat far south on the Red Sea.

So next day we separated. Peter set off to Beersheba by bus. He remembers

> the journey in a very small and stiflingly hot vehicle, conveying villagers and their produce and animals from village to village, and finally a farmer with about 10 chickens which hopped on and off the seats. In my clothes I'd never felt so out of place! Finally at Beersheba – it was like Old Testament pictures – shepherds with crooks and heads covered, sheep on the hillside, and even two camels as I approached the kibbutz where I was to be met.

He was taken to the Keren Cinema, and decided it was just big enough.

In the mean time I had flown to Eilat. The marvellous people were determined we'd give them a concert – being so hot and far away Eilat was often left out. But all too soon it was plain that, apart from the extra flight and packing, it could not be wise to bring instruments or children into that heat. It was only early June and already too hot for me.

Next morning we returned to Mr Godik. He was most understanding about Eilat; we accepted all the other cities, and added a kibbutz in Galilee. We explained that we would have to leave on 5 September if we were to accept the Athens Festival invitation, and he agreed to adjust the six concerts, with the Sabbath free, and write soon with a total plan. As soon as this arrived, with the travelling date of 26 August, we mapped out our summer course in Croydon to end on the 25th, and gave a provisional acceptance to Athens for two concerts on 7 and 8 September.

While we were away, George Sylvester had been pursuing plans for a permanent base. He introduced us to a most inspired person, Keith Revell, the Director of Education for Croydon. He was imaginative and keen to have us, and cared deeply about the part music can play in education. He had a gentle and serious manner with a twinkle of humour always breaking through. For the immediate summer course he offered us a very fine day school, the Shirley Secondary School, for all our courses, with boarding accommodation in the Royal Russell School nearby. We would travel to give our usual concerts at the end of each course. Ultimately a new school was going to be needed in Croydon, and so this could be planned very much with us in mind. It was a marvellous offer. Croydon also had the excellent new Fairfield concert hall. We would start our first course in Croydon this summer, and work to develop a permanent plan for the future. I didn't want to leave until I was sure of a sound and well-secured base for the NYO, to save my successor the huge task of finding and preparing three different homes each year.

Our plans for the summer course were now set, and Rudolf Schwarz was able to come, including the foreign dates. Our Croydon concert would be in the Fairfield Hall on 24 August, with a BBCTV recording in Wembley Town Hall on the 25th. We would fly to Israel in an El Al Boeing on the 26th to give at least six concerts there, and fly to Greece on 5 September to give two concerts in the Athens Festival, and return on the 9th. The efficient Mr Godik had even agreed our programme, having asked for the Britten *Young Person's Guide*, and Athens made the same request. Unfortunately the cost of hiring the parts from Boosey & Hawkes was prohibitive, especially as our large orchestra needed a double set, and there would also be performing-rights fees for ten concerts, so we could only oblige both countries if we could find a way round this expense.

All these plans had to be agreed by the Executive, and depended on the Treasurer's report. As expected we had overspent last summer in Poland and Zurich, and now had a deficit on the Isle of Man venture. Fortunately, there was the extra £5,000 a year from the *Mirror* and £5,000 from Sir Isaac with an intimation of further help. So Mr Ryder optimistically pronounced the orchestra's finances to be basically sound, and said he was continually amazed that so much was achieved for so little. Don Ryder was the most remarkably encouraging treasurer, and we owe him so much for the time he gave us, and his genuine enthusiasm for our work.

The Committee were adamant that we obtain essential health guidance from our Hon. Physician, especially concerning the climate in Israel and Greece.

The mood now was one of urgency: only eight weeks till the flight to Israel – if we could find a way of affording it. But first, above all, would we have an orchestra?

A special letter went at once to every parent, with a confidential form to return. It was a difficult time for family holidays, so could their child be with us for three weeks, 16 August to 9 September (which included the Jewish New Year)? Had they passports, medical certificates and the readiness to contribute £35 for everything: the course, the concerts, the travel and the educational experience of two foreign countries? There was more money about than in 1948, but it was still a lot for some. One Grimsby parent who owned a trawler wrote,

'Thank you for what you have done for my son – it's worth double the money – use the enclosed for someone else's son who can't afford it,' and always sent double fees.

In the mean time I worked on matters musical: the professors, the programme, two sets of soloists for the Bach double, and two for another solo work in reserve, all to be agreed with Israel, Athens and the BBC. Peter set to work on the planes, the buses, the vans, the costs of everything from Croydon to Jerusalem and back, plus all the usual course organisation. And Jill's typewriter never stopped, except when she picked up the telephone or slipped out to fetch sandwiches as we worked on.

By mid-July we had our orchestra, 150 for the course, 110 for the tour, and reserves available for every instrument, all hoping they'd be needed. Most important of all, Rudolf Schwarz had once more agreed to come with us for the Croydon course and the whole tour. I had chosen two sisters, Maureen and Hazel Smith, for the Bach: their sound, style and rapport were so close and so musical, and they could rehearse together at home. The reserve couple were our leader Roger Garland and Anne Parkin, both from Bristol: they were with the same teacher and so able to meet frequently. And when visiting our boarders in Princes Court I suddenly thought of the Handel Harp Concerto, which Susan Drake could manage, and she and I could work together too. So I had three soloists. Somehow all the music we had to hire became available, at a price we could afford – perhaps it was help from our friend and supporter Benjamin Britten. So Israel and Athens were granted their request for the *Young Person's Guide* and our programme could go to print.

On 21 July we had the NJMS annual recital in the Wigmore Hall. The second half opened with the twelve-cello *Hymnus* by Klengel, prepared by Douglas Cameron on the Isle of Man course. The twelve players included some now well-known cellists: Christopher van Kampen, Clive Gillinson (now Managing Director of the LSO), Moray Welsh, Stephen Orton, Timothy Mason and Thomas Igloe. Three of our boarders were included: Susan Drake, Pan Hon Lee and John Bimson. Perhaps outstanding was Tony Pay playing Stravinsky. He won the 1963 Bulgin Medal and a scholarship to Cambridge.

During the last week of July we met the Israeli Ambassador and Cultural Attaché, and influential people both Jewish and Greek. The British Council gave helpful advice about Athens – we were the only British contribution to the festival – but couldn't help us financially this time. The Foreign Office was vaguely disapproving of our foreign ventures. I once asked a diplomat at dinner if it was the safety of the children that worried him, and he said, 'Not in the least.' It seemed to be a matter of 'suitability', from which I gathered that being youth and amateur we were too inferior to represent Britain, even if it was only music. Our ambassadors never took this view, and sent back excellent reports.

Then suddenly came a crisis. Mr Godik had resigned, and without him our tour would have to be cancelled. Then we remembered Mr Batchelor of Iliffe Press, who had gone ahead of us to check everything in Russia and Finland. Don Ryder agreed to let him go to Israel immediately to try to save the day. The next few days were awful: no rumour must escape, no Israel meant no Greece . . . so huge a disappointment for our children . . . waiting, waiting. Then came the telephone call from Israel: the remarkable Mr Batchelor had found a Mr Jacob Ory, who had agreed to take over all the plans.

The arrangements in Croydon were entirely suitable for us. Just seven days to prepare a huge programme and three concerti, but we had an undisturbed and peaceful week. There was a sense of great privilege to come, an inner excitement, and intense concentration to be fully prepared. In the evenings we had various events: a rabbi on modern Israel and kosher foods; a Christian scholar on some historical aspects; an authority on Greece, particularly its drama and the Herodes Atticus theatre; and one evening we had a chance to thank Mr Revell for his vision and work to make this week the start of our permanent home.

We had one new colleague: I had enlisted my cousin Christabel Bielenberg to help look after the girls. She was such a warm and motherly person, with an Irish sense of humour, and the perfect partner for Betty Goddard on this long and difficult tour. Dr Taylor was also coming with us as a housemaster.

There was one domestic evening. Their inventory had stated, *Bring one yard of white material (washable), linen or thick cotton; a one-foot-square piece of strong cardboard; and a yard of white tape or elastic.* There was much curiosity as to what it could be for, and the answer was always 'Wait and see.' Mr McLellan had been firm about keeping the sun off their heads and the backs of their necks, so now they threaded the tape through two holes in the square and tied it on to the head. This kept the sun out of their eyes, and was then covered with the white material, with some hanging down at the back covering the neck. Scissors, needles, cotton, girls much in demand – many producing hidden talent for design – and then a parade past Sister ('You've got to *wear* them; you can't play with sunstroke') of 110 Anglicised Arabs. An evening of laughter played its part.

The concert in the Fairfield Hall was one of the best in our sixteen years. The inner quality of our two Jewish girls, Maureen and Hazel, touched a level of such love and beauty – like Wendy Waterman years earlier – beyond all words. The overture suited the orchestra, the Britten was challenging and enjoyable, and a Dvořák symphony is perfect emotionally for this age group. The Israeli and Greek Ambassadors were both present, and after their kind words we felt encouraged to take the best that was in us to Jerusalem.

The faithful *Times* came to Croydon: 'It is a perennial astonishment to hear how consistently the orchestra confirms the exacting standards it unfailingly sets itself. Last night was no exception.'

Next day we were all in Wembley Town Hall for the BBCTV recording. Walter Todds, who used to do radio recordings in our Abington days, was now presenting the programme.* Engineers and electricians were everywhere, fixing lighting and cameras. It was a hot August day, hot lights; it took longer than usual to get the sound right, but Rudi Schwarz was on familiar ground and everybody worked splendidly to the producer's satisfaction.

One incident was refreshing. Hazel Smith, just waiting to go on to play the concerto, had broken a strap on her shoe, and couldn't keep it on. Betty Goddard, needle and cotton to the rescue, was trying to secure it. 'Don't bother,' said Hazel, 'I can manage with one shoe. I only want to play better than I've ever played before.' Such total absence of self-consciousness was a delight – not a thought of how a soloist with only one shoe might look on TV.

That evening I asked my youngest group if they were excited, and one said, 'Yes, but I've got a crescendo and diminuendo going on at the same time in my tummy.' Mostly it was a confident 'Good-night, see you at Heathrow.'

*Walter Todds kept a close association with us, following my audition tours and the *Daily Mirror* competitions. Later he played a part in the BBC Young Musician of the Year competition.

Thirty-Four

The courtesy and efficiency of El Al at the airport gave us a good start to the tour. It was not long before checking was complete and I watched the long thin line of our 120 walk out across the tarmac, most of them clutching their instruments, to mount the steps of this huge plane shining white in the sun. It was an enjoyable non-stop flight, for some their first. They were soon absorbed in the beauty of the sky or studying a map. Then the first kosher meal, a little doze, a game of chess, and Israel was in sight.

At Lod Airport we were greeted by our new impresario Jacob Ory and a group of young musicians with a banner of welcome from their music school. The first reaction of our members was to the heat. They could not believe such a temperature in late afternoon, such dry air, such hot sun. Soon we were off to our home for the week. The Director of the village, Danny Ben-Av, whom Peter and I had met before, was most welcoming. He made a little speech, and explained that as we were working he had given us the quietest section of the village. There were groups from many countries staying, some just on holiday and up very late at night. Indeed, some of the groups liked staying up through the night, dancing and singing in the open, so it was difficult to get enough sleep. Later in the week Mr Ben-Av was able to tell us that the noisiest parties had agreed to stop at midnight. That was a great help.

The dining-room at meals became our meeting place; at other free times we could never find each other. That first evening we made a few decisions, since Danny Ben-Av had been very firm about the sun: 'You must believe me, it is not like English sun. I tell you. You get burnt. Very sore. Your fault.' So we decided on swimming before breakfast only; heads must be covered in the daytime and long-sleeved shirts worn; nobody was to leave the village without permission; they were told where to find Sister by day or night. They were marvellous the way they entered into such a new experience with enjoyment, and yet looked after each other so well.

Thursday, 27 August 1964, was to be a great day in all our lives. We would be in Jerusalem, actually giving a concert in that most sacred of cities. The Binyanei Hauma concert hall was large, good for the rich sound of our vast orchestra: no fear of too much brass and having to balance down, as in over-resonant places. It took time to get used to playing and tuning in the very different climate, but we really worked for the next two hours.

We were perfecting the Israeli national anthem, with which the concert would start, when a small boy in the audience went to Mr Schwarz and very politely said we played it solemnly and with dignity, but he thought it should be quite different in mood, a joyful triumphant return of the Jews to Israel. 'Very well, we'll try.' And with instructions from this small boy we changed the interpretation, and built up the scoring in the brass. At the concert it was an enormous success and even mentioned by the critics.

Their only chance to go to the Wailing Wall, the Weitzmann Institute or to see the Dead Sea Scrolls was sometime that afternoon, risking the midday sun. They kept a promise to stick to our special headgear and long sleeves, but at one stage around the wall area some trouble started to develop, which seemed due to their being mistaken for Arabs! They were all told to speak English clearly, point to their badges and stick together, and gradually this very young Arab army went peaceably on its way. Meals and rest and time to change into concert uniform fitted in somewhere, and all were back behind the scenes in the concert hall an hour before the performance.

The visit and especially this opening concert was under the auspices of the Foreign Minister Mrs Golda Meir, and I was privileged to sit next to her. She was so interesting, as were her comments in between items. There was a large body from the

Diplomatic Corps, including the British Chargé d'Affaires, and General Hertzog, who was partly responsible for bringing us; he was 'surprised but very impressed' at the response and success. The Bach with our two Jewish girls was especially appreciated and the *Young Person's Guide* justified their request: they were astonished. Having Rudolf Schwarz as our conductor was greatly appreciated too. The orchestra had a chance to meet Mrs Meir, the general and other VIPs and diplomats after the concert, and can now look back on the evening they met both the future Prime Minister and the President-to-be of Israel.

The *Jerusalem Post* had a famous music critic, Yohanen Boehm. On him the response to our next five concerts would depend. The Jewish people have music in their soul, and such enormous talent that we just hoped we hadn't let the side down. We were all very moved and humbled at the way he wrote about us:

> From the way the anthems were played it was clear that we had here an orchestra with a tone quality of a kind rarely experienced, whose rich and carefully balanced sonorities were compounded of the technical mastery with which these young people handle their individual parts.
>
> Their stage behaviour and discipline were exemplary, their dedication and earnestness enviable, and it remained flexible music-making of the highest order. Our enjoyment and pleasure increased with every offering. Our respect for the fine conductor turned into open admiration . . . It was one of those rare feasts of music that no one should miss.

Part of this was quoted on some new posters advertising our next five concerts, to show we were a serious musical event, not a youth group on holiday.

The next day, Friday, was free because the Sabbath began at six in the evening, so there was no concert. Nor could there be any music until after six on Saturday, and therefore no concert that night. One day off was splendid; two days off and a journey to the Sunday concert was too long with no practice, and Susan hadn't played the harp since Croydon. Peter went to Danny

Ben-Av. There was a large unused hall on the edge of the village; Peter asked if we could work very quietly there. Danny Ben-Av listened sympathetically to the problem, and then said, 'I haven't heard the question.' So on Saturday afternoon those who really needed some practice and extra help escaped with me to this secret place. Nobody came near us; nobody was about. Then at about five o'clock a caretaker came in, then found two friends, who expressed horror. Of course we stopped at once and apologised, and heard no more that day.

The next morning we were summoned to appear before a committee including a rabbi. John and Peter went with Danny: we thought we might be sent home. To their amazement the rabbi said he'd sent for them because he wanted to apologise. It was not in any way our fault that this breach of the Sabbath took place. We couldn't know, and it hadn't been explained to us that on the Sabbath there is no work of any kind. He had heard about our concert, and wished us well, and hoped we would accept his apology. No doubt John, with his tact and charm, apologised for our ignorance and any unwitting distress we might have caused. In the mean time we were all getting ready in buses and van to drive some distance for a concert that night in Galilee – mercifully not to the airport.

On the way we passed Nazareth, and had time for the carpenter's shop and a short walk through the streets. Our destination was Tsemah on the Sea of Galilee, where a large kibbutz had been developed, incuding an amphitheatre, with terraced grass slopes for a big audience. The platform was big enough for most of the orchestra and it had a roof from which hung electric lights. The back of the stage was open to the water, and the front to the hillside. It was a most beautiful setting: the lake, hillsides golden with the sun shining on dried grass, a few shepherds and sheep and an occasional fishing boat. In the late afternoon we set the stage and rehearsed diligently.

After a meal in the kibbutz, we watched the huge red sun go down behind the hills, and quite suddenly a ripple appeared on the lake, and the evening breeze we had been warned about began. All the music ready on the stands was safely clothes-pegged, but it became quite windy and we were able to see how quickly a storm could arise; the waves on the shore at the back of the platform were flapping too noisily for playing. Darkness came rather suddenly, and by eight-thirty the audience started to collect on the grass; as we waited the wind gradually ceased, the lights came on, and it was like night in a garden when we started to play. As they played the moon was rising. John and I were at the back of the stage, almost on the shore, and by the middle of the symphony the moon was up, shining on the black water of the dead-calm sea. Compelled by such beauty, we just stood, looking, aware of the musical offering behind us but drinking in life here two thousand years ago.

I thought our performers should not miss this silent peace, so when the applause faded and they filed off the steps at the back of the platform, they followed John silently in single file along the shore, instruments in hand, absorbing the peace in the still night of the Sea of Galilee. Just a little while . . . and back to our tasks. Recently Moray Welsh wrote: 'Those ten minutes on the shore still live with me.' And with me too.

By contrast, our Tel Aviv concert was in the Municipal Basketball Stadium, Yad Elinhue. We remember the size, the expressions on the faces as they arrived to rehearse, the strange sound in this empty arena open to the sky. At least we were big, and could play out; the brass felt uninhibited that night.

On 1 September we travelled up the coast to Caesarea. Here it was quite different: less hot, with a breeze blowing sand into the instruments, and there was no shelter from the direct sun. I was impressed by the skill of the electricians, arranging the few lights at different angles and heights, not being used to such a big orchestra, though we couldn't test them until the sun went down. The wind was still a bit difficult to manage as late as eight-thirty. Anne Parkin, one of the Bach soloists, said, 'The wind kept blowing my bow off the strings.' The audience seemed mainly tourists. Hearing English behind where I sat, we discovered one group who'd heard us in Edinburgh, another at a Prom, so they had come to support us. It was the most difficult concert to manage, but a very interesting place historically.

We had started centrally in Jerusalem, gone north to Galilee and out to the west coast to Caesarea, and now it was south into the desert for Beersheba. It was our hottest day, but the buses were air-conditioned. It was fascinating that the Negev desert was planted with eucalyptus trees, and we also passed small settlements of shepherds tending flocks or leading camels. Near Negev the buses stopped to see a Bedouin village, and Betty Goddard remembers that they were told the chief had twenty wives, three of them English. She says our boys were very impressed! Eventually we arrived at a completely new, modern city literally cut out of the desert and built on its reddish sand.

Peter had been here before, and there was a warm welcome. We were shown an indoor cinema for the concert. Rudolf Schwarz arrived by car in the early evening. The place was packed and two encores were needed to satisfy the enthusiasm. After the long journey home we were especially grateful for the midnight curfew on noise at the village, and we were allowed a special late breakfast.

Danny Ben-Av came to us with a problem: some of his visiting groups were very untidy in the dormitories, and there was going to be an official inspection in the camp that morning with a prize for the best-organised and tidiest country. The house staff were rather pleased, as it was our last concert day and this would be a chance to get clean shirts ready for Greece and some of the packing and sorting done. I added a little stimulus by offering an extra NYO prize for the most artistically designed room. I thought they might think this a bit of a chore on a free morning, but to my surprise there was an energetic and imaginative response to the challenge. We won the tidiness prize for Great Britain, a framed print of Jerusalem presented by the Minister for Tourism. I must admit that after all those mattress years, and weeks of life in a suitcase, I had expected them to do well. The most artistic NYO room was created by four or five of our young men who had designed a restful study. The tasteful arrangement – a few beds as sofas, books arranged with suitcases as book-ends, a trumpet on a corner shelf as an *objet d'art*, a music stand with suitable score on it in a corner – somehow became a living, imaginative room. The occupants included Mark Elder (now Music Director of the ENO), Tony Pay (now principal clarinet of the Sinfonietta), the Maries twins Alan and Keith and David Pountney (now Director of Productions at the ENO). All were working for Cambridge, and all got there: all that intelligence and talent in one little room, exploding so whole-heartedly into this little ploy. I also gave a booby prize to our four youngest boys, who included Pan Hon Lee and John Bimson. They were very tidy – as long as you didn't look *in* a suitcase – and full of humour: a very realistic dead body in full uniform lay on a bed, with a violin-case body and football head. Their prize was an enormous watermelon: the juice was disastrous for clean shirts.

Back to serious work, we set off on the lovely drive up the coast to Haifa, an attractive town overlooking the sea. The Armon Hall was quite large, enclosed all round to a considerable height with tiered seats, but open to the sky above. There was some roofing over the stage, very high up, which no doubt helped project the sound. There was no great problem of balance: just a matter of getting used to the size and sound of a half-enclosed, half-open hall. The platform had been extended for us so that everyone could play on our last night in Israel.

We had experienced five audiences: the formal and well-informed in Jerusalem; the refugee kibbutz community in Tsemah; the popular crowd in the Tel Aviv stadium; the tourist mixture at Caesarea; and the new-town enthusiasm in the Beersheba cinema. But Haifa provided one of those exceptional audiences. The people were almost all from Germany, steeped in the music of the country they'd left behind, conveying all the Jewish warmth, and with high expectations because of Mr Boehm and the press after Jerusalem. There was not a seat in the place, and they were involved from the first note. It was Maureen and Hazel that night in the Bach, playing for their own people. The audience were staggered by the Britten, which became rather over-excited that night. They stayed clapping even when the orchestra left the stage for the interval.

During the symphony, when the second movement was just about to start (much of it is pianissimo), a plane could be heard approaching, and the conductor waited. He waited until it had flown right over above us and its sound had faded over the sea. Not one person moved: they were still in the music, just as if the noise and sight of the plane above weren't there, until the music slid softly into the silence and on to the rest of the symphony. Then came the warmth, the appreciation, the encores – the sheer love of music shared by players and listeners.

I'm still grateful that the orchestra had such a treat, because we worked hard to give everything in us to audiences, and this time it was so richly returned; the players have often told me that it remains engraved in the memory. In my concert-giving life three audiences remain alive for me: the Concertubuow in Amsterdam, when the audience stood in silence before clapping; the Berlin Hochschule during the Wall crisis in 1961; and Haifa in 1964.

These nine days in Israel were great education: the climate and how to manage it, the diet, the newness of a growing country, the characteristics of Jewish people and their customs, their love of music. They did manage to see Nazareth, Galilee, Mount Zion, the Mount of Olives, Caesarea, the Wailing Wall, the Weitzmann Institute, camels in their natural environment and some excavations, as well as all the travelling and six concerts. Throughout our stay in Israel the organisation never failed, the hospitality was overwhelming and the audiences marvellous. We can never be thankful enough.

Although the British Ambassador was on holiday, the Chargé d'Affaires was very supportive throughout. He invited everybody to a party in a beautiful sheltered garden, and served an endless supply of delicious cold tea. Even more important, he also sent a very complimentary report to the Foreign Office, a copy of which later reached our Chairman and was read at the next meeting. Before we left there was a meeting at which we could officially thank Mr Ory, General Hertzog and Sir Isaac.

But now it was time to make another new start, flying off to Greece, where we would be the only representative from Britain in the tenth Athens Festival. At this time the British Army in Cyprus had been replaced by a United Nations peacekeeping force, and it was a tense time politically. In the plane I had to remind them that we were not popular in Greece, and that we might get rudely treated. They knew they must keep together and never answer back or get into an argument. The reminder was timely, because even at the airport, when our labels on the suitcases and instruments were spotted, there were some unwelcome comments about 'Brits'. When eventually our buses arrived at the appointed hostel and everyone was getting out, a group of youths went by throwing handfuls of gravel at us and running away. The orchestra was very quick to sense the situation – some of the girls were already a little nervous – but it was good for them to experience hostility after so much adulation. Our housemasters, Dr Taylor and Norman Knight, were very firm: until further notice we stayed in groups and always with a staff member if there was any free time.

Our hostel was on the corner of a very nice square. In the cool of the evening there seemed to be nobody about so Betty Goddard took a group of about twenty girls for a walk round the square before bed. She writes:

> All was well at first, and we were enjoying our first glimpse of Athens when out of the blue a group of Greek Romeos appeared. Intent on their very attractive prey, I decided to make for home before reinforcements arrived. I felt like a St. Trinians schoolmistress shepherding my 'crocodile' safely round the square and back behind closed doors.

After an early breakfast John and I and the percussion and platform group were off to the Herodes Atticus theatre to survey the scene for our next two concerts. What an amazing setting – we were quite overcome. We set to work quickly to be ready for an early rehearsal before the sun was too hot. We could find no officials or staff, but our instruments were there, still safe and sound. The platform was not wide enough for us, and very long from the back to the conductor, not really right for good ensemble. Eventually a handyman with hammer and chisel appeared, and explained that the extra extension on the front was only screwed on there for another performance, and really belonged to both sides. That would make the platform the right shape and give us an extra sixteen feet in width so that everyone could play. Alas, nothing would persuade him, even with our boys to help, to do the essential job now. We found chairs and set them up as if the front part were already gone; those who would be on the sides couldn't rehearse now. Maddening . . . nobody from the festival . . . nobody in charge . . . we couldn't speak Greek . . . left alone, we did what we could.

Soon the buses with the orchestra arrived. Morale was high, and so was the sense of wonder as they came on to the platform and just stood and stared. Around them was this vast area of the ancient Herodes Atticus amphitheatre, overlooked by the miraculous Parthenon in the sunlight on the Acropolis. Rudi had never been to Greece before, so we all spent some minutes just looking and getting bearings: the rising terraces in front, the endless blue sky.

Then we tuned, and experienced the sound: no echo, not too dry, just blended tone. From the farthest distance, or the extreme sides, or the front row, the sound was balanced and clear. I went to the highest part at the back, and as I spoke quietly from there everybody on the stage could hear every word. After an hour or two of real practice and work, they went back to the hostel for food and rest. Later Dr Taylor, who really knew Athens, was going to take them to the Parthenon and whatever could be managed before tea and preparation for the concert. Sister was on the warpath, as there were a few tummy upsets. With two concerts to go, if Sister said rest, that was it.

John and Jill had left after the rehearsal to be with the orchestra until all returned for the concert. Peter and I thought we would finish the platform and all the behind-scenes arrangements, hoping to find someone from the festival management to ask for an interpreter. It was siesta-time, not a soul in sight. Left on the floor were the hefty hammer and a long strong chisel. It seemed sensible to raise those front boards and move them back to their normal place on the sides, to be able to finish the platform setting before leaving. We were getting on splendidly when very suddenly three tough-looking men emerged out of the stonework at the back. They approached Peter – possibly wanting cash – and he tried his rather shaky Modern Greek on them. This didn't work: they got rough and one hit out at Peter's head. Seeing him fall to the floor, I came over and instinctively picked up the tools beside him, and just stood there, glaring at them. Peter remembers coming round, and through a haze seeing me standing facing them, the chisel raised in my right hand like a dagger! They turned round and went away; Peter recovered and we went in search of shade and refreshment.

When we arrived in Athens we had parted with Maureen and Hazel, whose parents had arranged for them to be guests with a Greek Jewish family for the Rosh Hashana New Year. So it was the harp concerto with Susan Drake for our opening concert here.

I'd promised her a special rehearsal, and we were soon at work on the platform, going through and refreshing the performance. We wanted to get exactly the right tempo and accent for projection in such a huge space, so I went to the terraces in the middle, then right to the top circle, from where she was just a distant golden speck. From that distance I said, 'Can you hear me?' and she could, but an English voice further away beneath the Parthenon called out, 'If it's any help we've heard every word you've said and every note.' So we didn't worry any more, just worked awhile to polish up every detail.

In the mean time Peter, fully recovered, had gone to the festival offices. He found the manager responsible for us and got some programmes, and some tickets for our staff. He also secured instant attention to the platform, and discovered when an eight o'clock concert in Greece actually begins.

Behind the scenes, the artists' rooms were underground; but near the entry to the platform were two long trenches dug in the rocky sand. The orchestra lined up in these, fifty or so per trench, to wait before going on stage. Suddenly the Director and Manager of the festival came up to me in a panic, saying we would be starting a bit late – 'We hadn't expected such a large audience, we've run out of programmes and tickets' – as if it was all our fault, and pushed their way through one of the occupied trenches. Somehow a violin bow caught against a brick on the corner and as they pushed by it broke. A broken bow is a broken heart. The family's life savings were in that instrument and bow. Once I'd got the child to believe my promise that she'd get another bow, the tears and sobbing slowed. A message went along the line to see if anyone had a spare bow they were prepared to lend, and one who had went back to the underground artists' rooms to get it. We tried the borrowed bow and, confidence restored, she could still play in the concert. In such a sensitive group, one upset child upsets everybody. Susan Drake, in tears for her friend, suddenly didn't want to play the concerto. We could have changed the programme and put on our reserve pair – more delay – but after some calm reassurance she was happy to go on.

While I was thus involved the message came for us to start. I heard the unhelpful manager saying, 'Why don't they go on?' and Jill replying firmly, 'You caused a serious accident. You must wait until Dr Railton is ready.' We retuned, morale returned, and everyone mounted the platform calmly.

This concert was a unique experience: the audience in the increasing darkness, the Parthenon superbly floodlit against the sky and the moon rising. And in the centre, 110 little humans were sending out thought and energy in beautiful sound. Behind them the inhabitants of the ancient walls came out in the darkness with their own contribution, a secret competition. The woodwind soloists found it very difficult to keep in tune against the chorus of this army of bats.

We had been ignored as far as possible by the festival that invited us; but now a few officials came round to express their amazement at the unexpected standard. They were surprised too that a mere youth orchestra could draw the biggest audience of their festival so far – about four thousand, they said. Were they pleased? It seemed yes, 'but we did not know it could be very fine orchestra'. Mrs Bielenberg remembers that the response was overwhelming, and the bad attitude to us as 'Brits' and as an orchestra changed completely. Anyway, Rudolf Schwarz was pleased and we all had an unforgettable evening.

Next morning there was a surprise phone call from Gina Bachauer. She was in a hurry, but asked me to tell the Festival Director that Princess Irene, the King's sister, would be coming tonight. I must be certain to tell him because of the protocol. Of course I did so at the first opportunity, and got the reply, 'That is ridiculous, it is nonsense; no member of the royal family has been to the festival this year, and the King is away.' I was just delivering a message.

Tonight would be our last concert of the whole of 1964, and for at least thirty their last concert with the NYO. I spent a little time with my leaving members, some of whom had been with us for four or five years, as there would not be much time to say goodbye at Heathrow. Among them was Anne Parkin, our deputy leader, who had won two scholarships to the RCM, one for violin and one for piano, and was now awarded the Bulgin Medal.

That evening there seemed to be a mood of panic and excitement: officials were very busy, and indeed the princess was coming to the concert. On the first night we hadn't played national anthems, since there was no official need, and some people might be upset by ours. Now it was different; it felt quite like home. The playing had that little extra that a special occasion or last night brings out, and we all felt how lucky we were to be playing in such a place.

As they left the platform after the last encore, there was a message – the princess was coming round. We slipped quickly into our Queen Mother routine and lined up ready for the honour. The princess was very musical, a pianist and a pupil of Gina Bachauer. She was so charming, so interested, and spent time with them asking questions, and then had a special talk with Mr Schwarz. None of this could have happened but for Gina's friendship, kindness and belief in our work.

Then came the final gesture from the princess, an invitation to John and me to dine with her and Gina. To be in historical Athens as the guest of the Greek royal family, sharing musical ideas, was a totally unexpected privilege, a final blessing on the now safely completed tour.

In the sun at Athens Airport lay our special Vanguard. Enriched in mind and memory, a big challenge fulfilled, everyone relaxed happily on the last lap bringing them safely back to England.

Thirty-Five

The experience of Israel and Athens was vividly in our minds when we reported to the usual September Executive Committee. From Foreign Office reports, letters and press, the tour seemed to have been counted a major success, both as music and as good will. There had been no serious health problems, and thanks to the recent extra grant from the *Mirror* we would soon be solvent again.

But while we were away, there were three pleasant surprises. At long last the LCC had agreed to give grants to NYO members, after trying to prevent local children joining us for over twelve years. Secondly, Dr Taylor had generously established an annual prize for an outstanding member, to be used for books and music and known as the Chairman's Prize. Finally, Victor Hochhauser had donated five hundred seats at the opening performance in London of the Mazowsze Dancers, to create a scholarship for one of our boarders, and Paul Crosfield gave £500 for a boarder who was a pianist.

Then we discussed the whole of 1965, always with my retirement in mind. Summer 1965 would definitely be my last course and tour with the NYO. This year all three courses would be in Croydon, our new permanent home, and we would travel for concerts elsewhere. At Christmas these would be in London and Bristol. Our biennial RFH event at Easter would be our 120th concert, and the Queen Mother had graciously agreed to be present. It would also be our President's seventieth birthday and he would conduct. The Committee hoped the summer could include a European tour, preferably to countries we had not yet visited, and returning in time to give a concert in the Commonwealth Arts Festival in the RFH on 17 September, at the invitation of Ian Hunter. He had given me the first concert in Bath in 1948, and it seemed suitable that my last concert should be at his invitation, and in a place of memories and importance in the NYO's history. I had been able to get three conductors who knew us well – Rignold at Christmas, Sargent at Easter and Schwarz for the summer and possible tour.

The Committee gave me every support in agreeing to my request that no mention be made of my leaving, and their confidentiality prevailed.

At the end of September the lease on our office expired, and we needed accommodation until such time as we could move to Croydon. Once again the *Mirror* came to our rescue, providing two large rooms in a former newspaper office. Our special London headquarters, familiar to so many members and visitors over the last ten years, together with the whole row of early-eighteenth-century houses, was going to be rased to the ground to make room for an enormous concrete block, the new headquarters of Metal Box.

It was a sad day as we packed – packing away all the memories of the work and music of ten years. In the late afternoon the faithful Pickfords men arrived, and down the two floors of rickety stairs went all our history and worldly possessions in boxes – and lastly the piano went too.

I was just collecting my personal belongings when a heavy tread on the stairs revealed the arrival of our friendly bobby, a remarkable character of the George St. beat. 'Going for good,' he said, 'I can't believe it. All them children and all them instruments going in and out – the place was alive. All gone,' he muttered sadly. My last act before leaving was to take down my treasured signed portrait of the Queen Mother. He stood to attention as I did so. 'Now all the tone has gone from the street,' he announced, and wiped a tear from his eye. Yet the wrench from all those memories as we locked the door for the last time was shared with a friend who loved his street and his work as we loved ours.

Everything I did this year was with continuity in mind.

Auditions were the most important, and I needed to leave a team who had sensitivity and intuition, as on them would depend the future of the NYO. For the last time I would do all the finals myself; a last goodbye to a life of discovering and teaching such special children.

Some years earlier, a newly appointed music master at the Manchester Grammar School had come to see me. The school excelled on many fronts but not on instrumental music and had nobody of NYO standard. He thought this should be rectified. What should he do to achieve it? The years went by, and this time he presented three highly intelligent, well taught, very musical candidates. I was able to take two, one horn and one clarinet, Roger Fallows and John Butterworth – the first ever from Manchester Grammar, to the delight of the master and the school. Anyone can improve standards if they have a goal, and will learn how and persevere. These days, where standards in many schools are too low, we hear it is the fault of the buildings, the equipment, the lack of money – anything but the lack of will in the teachers, to find a way and achieve their goal. (I have met teachers who no longer expect six-year-olds to read easily.) One can get used to low standards of achievement and think they're normal.

With auditions complete I chose from a wealth of young talent about forty new members, bringing the total to 160, thinking of the future. I was also lucky that the leader of the orchestra the previous year, Roger Garland, now just eighteen, could be with us throughout the year, before going to Cambridge.* It was his sixth year with us, and what an asset he was as leader, helping the youngest ones, imperturbable at difficult times, and always able to laugh.

Christmas came, and on a wet and wintry Boxing Day we were preparing in Croydon. The only available venue this time was

*Later a member of the Academy of St Martin-in-the-Fields and now leading the Gagliano Trio and the Park Lane Sextet.

the Fairfield Schools, one for work and one for sleep, so it was once again all those rows of mattresses on the floor. The invasion seemed to bring an especially lively lot – a good omen for all that lay ahead.

On the musical front, we had Hugo Rignold back again; our principal clarinet Tony Pay would play the Mozart concerto and we were tackling a really big main work, the *Symphonie fantastique* by Berlioz – an ambitious start to the year. I was particularly pleased with the attitude and enthusiasm of the new members. In the first full rehearsal my youngest violinist whispered to me, 'I can't hear myself but I hope I'm helping!' With people like these there was no worry about the future.

After a week they were all getting their first glimpse of the Albert Hall, first outside, then with gasps of amazement at the size within. The concert was being given primarily for the employees of the International Publishing Corporation, of which the *Mirror* was a part, and it gave us a chance to show gratitude for their continuing support. It was our only Christmas concert in London in seventeen years, and I didn't expect such a good and responsive audience.

Immediately it was over, it was packing and off to Paddington Station for the night train to Bristol. To our surprise there was quite a big crowd waiting on the station and at the entry to our platform. Our parents and followers were very supportive, but hardly in such numbers at a station in the middle of the night . . . We soon discovered these were no worshippers of St Cecilia: their goddess was a railway engine.

British Railways were determined to make a success of our night journey this time, and to keep us warm a special steam engine was brought into action. This was in fact the last steam engine ever to leave Paddington. When we were all aboard, the railway buffs were allowed to crowd around it, and have one last look at every detail as it started to warm up and hiss and puff. I felt really sorry for them as we set off, taking a little piece of engineering history away with us for ever.

Welcomed back to Bristol after seven years, John and I were

soon on the Colston Hall platform. The local paper says we spent over two hours getting it ready, and expressed amazement at all the detail involved. There was a big percussion section for the Berlioz, and extra instruments like the E Flat clarinet.

After our new members' baptism in the Albert Hall, this Bristol concert was more confident, and quite different in audience contact, to which the players responded. Our leader was from Bristol and there was a West Country contingent of supporters. The Glinka overture went with excitement; Tony Pay's Mozart Clarinet Concerto was calm and sensitive; and our large orchestra helped the colourful orchestration of the Berlioz, which really took off in the 'Witches' Sabbath'. The night journey seemed to have done no harm, and everyone seemed very happy as they left for home. John wrote from Aberdeen:

> I hate to mention your last year, but I think this orchestra may be your best . . . fantastic talent, spirited and so young . . . you have certainly looked to the future. But now, while we have you, do plan another tour this summer.

His judgement was always sound, so I did.

At the Executive meeting on 27 January, we discussed a remarkable offer of a site in Croydon for their new school, in which we could collaborate in the design, especially the size of the hall, the teaching-rooms and residential accommodation for the full orchestra. Our office would be included too. Sir Basil Spence had offered his services to design and build it.

But to my surprise and real shock, another idea was raised. It was said that the NYO – its spirit, its methods, its results – was so unique that it would be much better to close it down after a triumphal tour in the summer. No such possibility had ever crossed my mind, and I remember pointing out that if we closed, someone would immediately pinch the title and carry on something quite different using our reputation; that would really break my heart.

After a long discussion there was considerable support for the Croydon-school idea; and nobody objected to closing the boarding school. The closing-down idea was to be pursued further at another meeting on 10 March.

The afternoon was to be my last annual Council meeting. How grateful I was that Douglas Guest was in the chair: he had watched and guarded the NYO from the time we first met; now he would guide the established NYO through my retirement into undisturbed continuity. I announced my unavoidable departure in September, and the need to keep this strictly confidential; and the Chairman assured everybody that the Executive had plans for the future in hand.

I was very moved by the kindness of the Council. Yehudi Menuhin was the first to express his regret that I should have to give up, and asked that his thanks for all my help with his own school be recorded. Keith Falkner expressed thanks on behalf of the principals of all the music colleges for the help our work had always been to them, and its influence on their students.

The ensuing discussion of foreign invitations resulted in putting America first, which if we could raise the money to get there would certainly pay its way; Europe came second, to include countries not yet visited; and third was Japan.

Don Ryder reported we were in good health financially, and the Council suggested that a special letter should go from our President to the directors of IPC, to express our debt of gratitude.

I was still shocked by the Executive meeting in the morning. For me closing down was unthinkable. Surely a new musical director, continued *Mirror* support and always meeting in Croydon would ensure our continuity. I already had two assistant musical directors and an excellent administrator.

Ideally, John Dalby would just take over from me, but of course his work was in Aberdeen, his home was there, he was Organist of St Machar's Cathedral, and he was too young to leave such a post without damaging his pension. But he could be the over-all director of the NYO, responsible for policy and in charge of courses and tours. Ivey Dickson was an outstanding musician and teacher, and had worked with John and me for the last ten years. Away from the concert platform any sense of time or place left her, but she was the perfect colleague and assistant to a good leader. If John held the senior position and she was the musical director, responsible for the choice of members, programmes, conductors and the standards of performance, she could do marvellous work. All the burden of administration would be most ably carried for her by Peter. This way I was distributing all my work among three colleagues, using the experience and talent of each to the full.

I felt sure that after ten years of gradually increasing work with the NYO, and knowing that without a successor the Council might close it down, Ivey would accept. I was wrong: she never liked being fully committed to one objective. I explained that my triangular plan would relieve her of organising and responsibility; I really tried everything, but failed to instil in her enough dedication to the cause to overcome her lack of social confidence. 'No, I don't want to be a pale shadow of you.' It was hard to believe she would run away at such a critical time, and that self-esteem was more important than the future of the NYO.

Herbert Howells, Neil Black and I discussed other fine musicians, but they would not be able to give up their performing careers; and the younger ones, our ex-members, were not yet experienced enough. However, I did now seek out Janet Craxton. She was such a superb artist, an internationally famous oboist and outstanding teacher that I had previously thought it wrong to contemplate taking her from full-time performance. A few days later she wrote to me:

> I consider the founding and running of the NYO was and is the most important achievement in our musical lives and one which has had such far-reaching effects as to make any possibility of it coming to an end an equally great tragedy . . . I would feel an enormous weight of guilt on my conscience for the rest of my life if I allowed such a miraculous

> organisation to disappear merely because I was not prepared to sacrifice something and at least make a whole-hearted effort to carry on . . . I cannot put into words how much I admire what you have done, and how enormously honoured I was to feel that you might be prepared to hand on your 'masterpiece' to me . . . and above all to know that if the Council should approach me that I would have your complete encouragement, spiritual and material, so as to make the task possible.

Meanwhile Douglas Guest and I had a meeting with Reginald Prentice at the Department of Education and Science to explore possible financial backing for the future, as we were totally dependent for survival on the generous charity of a newspaper. But government departments must never do anything they haven't done before: that's called setting a precedent, so we didn't get far.

March 10 came and the Executive met as planned. After a thorough discussion it was Ernest Hall, who dearly loved the orchestra, who proposed, seconded by Don Ryder, 'to close the NJMS, better known as the National Youth Orchestra, at the end of 1965, realising what it had achieved over the previous twenty years, and to end with a large-scale tour of Europe'. This decision would be put before a special Council meeting on 22 July and if accepted remain confidential until a press conference at the end of that month.

I remember a feeling of numbed disbelief at what we'd done. So it would all stop, just stop. Part of me knew it wouldn't happen, and if it did the public and the love I'd seen light up in my students would bring it back. In just a month they would be in the RFH with the Queen Mother, celebrating our 120th concert. At a time of such distress, I went out from our new office on to Waterloo Bridge in the March sun, and pondered how much I could give to my special students, and what lasting memories I could plan into my last few months with them.

After the weeks of anxiety about the future, it was with relief that we returned to our Croydon benefactors, preparing the

Whitgift and the Royal Russell Schools for our Easter course. Now we could concentrate single-mindedly on music, and on what we could create together for a festive royal occasion. The news that Maureen Smith had won the BBC's Under-25 Violin Competition at only eighteen was a fine start to the week. (She had left now but Hazel was still with us.)

The programme had *Carnival Overture*, *L'Arlésienne*, a Sibelius symphony, and the Mozart Oboe Concerto with Helen Powell. Everything about it was happy, and perfectly suited to Sir Malcolm. Having him was the event of the week, especially for those who were not with us in 1963.

Normal work was under way next day when the shocking news came that Sir Malcolm was ill and couldn't come. Would we get anybody else at such short notice? As we never had a conductor for the first four days, we could keep the dreadful disappointment secret from the orchestra while we searched the globe for another. I chased Oivin Fjeldstad. He was in Norway, and free. Yes, he would get on the next plane. Once more Jill was off to Heathrow to meet him. How lucky we were. Only then did I tell the children about Sir Malcolm but kept who was replacing him as a surprise.

That evening we had our annual party commemorating the first concert in Bath in 1948, our seventeenth anniversary. They were just lighting seventeen candles and about to cut the cake when I was told Oivin had arrived. I brought him straight in to perform the ceremony, to the cheers and delight of everyone. All the 1964 members knew him, and the crisis was over. What a wonderful man he was. He started work the next day, and the programme suited him too, especially the Sibelius.

We had with us our perfect team of volunteer staff: Norman Smith and Denis Cocks; Betty Goddard and Mrs Freyan;* and two ex-members, Howard Gough and his wife Celia Nicklin;† and of course Sister. They and others like them played an

*She had two sons in the NYO.

† Their three children have all been in the NYO.

enormous part in the style and happiness of the NYO. I feel great warmth and gratitude to them all.

Soon came the lovely day at the Royal Festival Hall. Each time, seeing London was new to some. After the last rehearsal came lunch in the restaurant, the rest in the seats, the walk beside the Thames. Then preparing behind the scenes – lining up for the moment of entering the platform, awaiting the arrival of the Queen Mother in the royal box, starting the fanfare and the national anthem. And the moment the concert was over, still with instruments in hand, they lined up as arranged, and Her Majesty most graciously moved round talking to them and asking questions, and especially to my team of professors and staff. The Queen Mother is more to the NYO than the great honour of her patronage: it was as Queen of England that she wrote with encouragement in the struggling early years.

Next day we repeated the programme in the Fairfield Hall. Having offered us a permanent home, it seemed Croydon was beginning to adopt us as its own orchestra, so a concert was the least we could do to repay their generosity.

Six weeks later, in time for an Executive meeting on 31 May, Peter and I could present the outline of a European tour in the summer. It would include representing Britain at the Sintra Festival in Portugal, three concerts in Italy, two in Switzerland, three in Germany and one in Holland, ending in the RFH for the Commonwealth Arts Festival on 17 September. We had plans to make the whole tour self-supporting, and to travel by air with our special Vanguard to Portugal and Italy and back from Holland. The summer course would be in Croydon, with a concert there and one in Guildford. We would cut down to just 112 members for the tour. After much discussion the whole project was agreed.

But our urgent work concerned finance. It was simply that there was no sufficient and permanent financial security on which to build the future. Grateful as we were to the *Mirror* for its continued sponsorship, it might not always be available; yet it was our only income apart from a few gifts. We hoped the government – the Ministry of Education or of the Arts – proud to ask us to represent Britain at important events in Europe, would contribute some small security. At present the orchestra existed on just three underpaid, overworked people, underpaid professors and voluntary helpers as needed. We could not make new professional appointments, musical or administrative, without long-term security. Without this, the March decision to close would be put before the Council in July.

Peter and I set off for Europe to check all the concert halls, platforms, hostels, coach firms, distances and costs.

Portugal was very welcoming. The Mother Superior of a convent near Lisbon where all the children would stay was a most impressive character. The rooms in her girls' boarding school were perfection: small canopied beds, hand-embroidered coverings, linen sheets, everything spotless with total tidiness. There was beauty everywhere, yet absolute simplicity. '*Nada superfua*,' she said. We were going to hurry away to Sintra and Estoril, but she insisted we walk down the garden with her as she had something special to show us. She was lame, so we went slowly until, at the end of a long path, spread out before us was the sunlit Portuguese countryside, and blue sky as far as the eye could see: miles of silence and calm. We waited. 'This is peace,' she said. 'You will need it in the weeks ahead: that's why I brought you here.' Sometimes, even now, in moments of tension, I recall that view, her vision of peace. The musicians and officials we met also made us feel that we really *must* come to Portugal.

And so to Italy. In Milan we separated. I was taken to the Conservatorio Hall, checking platform space for the grand piano and 112 performers. 'Impossible, so many,' said the Manager. 'Such a big orchestra would need the La Scala hall.' Then to Brescia, to the opera house. Here we would go without a piano, and cut the numbers. I had no time to see another at Lecco before returning to join Peter. He had found excellent air-conditioned coaches and had the timing and maps to Zurich, but the accommodation had to be altered. To save time we flew to Zurich, where we were most warmly welcomed: the same hostel, the same concert manager as in 1963: total efficiency meant no problems there. Frankfurt was more difficult: they (politely) gave the impression that mere 'youth' would be best on a Saturday afternoon, and I explained our programme would not be suitable for an audience of children. The accommodation was rather rough too, but Frankfurt is an important European city, and was on our route home. Then to Hamburg, where we were well known, coming first in 1959 and again in 1961. The impresario wanted four concerts, but we could only do two if we were to include Holland and get home for 17 September; so we chose Bremen and Hamburg. We were invited eagerly to play again in Holland; we could not get my favourite place, Amsterdam, but were welcome in Scheveningen.

Back in the office came the really hard work, detailed work. We drew up a schedule in which we were expecting our young members to give fourteen concerts in twenty days, travelling through six countries, and a last concert for the Commonwealth, in the Festival Hall of our own capital city, had to be the best. Were we expecting too much of them? I talked to Rudi Schwarz to see if he was prepared to do so much. He laughed as I unfolded the plan and then said thoughtfully, 'If I didn't know you and the orchestra I would refuse. But if *you* decide that it's possible, and that they'll still be fit and well for the Festival Hall after three weeks on tour, I'll be with you.'

All of us finally thought we could accept the challenge of more than we'd ever done before, and end triumphantly. The Executive agreed our decision.

The special Council meeting was in July. Dr Taylor, as Chairman of the Executive, summed up previous deliberations, namely that there was 'no satisfactory and stable future for the organisation unless a place can be found for it within the educational system'.

He reported that the Director of Education for Croydon had approached Sir William Alexander, Secretary of the Association of Education Committees, who said the responsibility lay with the Ministry of Education. We had conveyed to the Croydon Borough Council our gratitude for the magnificent gift of the Pitts Place site, which present circumstances made it impossible for us to accept. Dr Guest and I had discussed our future with Jennie Lee, an under-secretary with responsibility for education, and the Secretary of State for Education Tony Crosland. Lord Annan, Provost of King's College, Cambridge, had also spoken to him and was under the impression that, as the matter was 'not of immediate national significance', this first approach had not yet received full consideration.

Lord Annan put forward the final resolution:

> that the operations of the National Youth Orchestra of Great Britain – sometimes known as the National Junior Music School – be suspended with effect from September 18th, and that the Executive Committee of the Council be requested to explore with the Department of Education and Science and other interested bodies various possibilities for the continuance of the orchestra such as would ensure the maintenance of the present standard and its present national reputation.

John Dalby, who knew us best, and Neil Black, an ex-member, proposed and seconded this, and it was unanimously adopted.

As it was my last meeting, of course I placed on record my heartfelt gratitude to so many individuals covering the difficult days eighteen years ago until now, especially George Sylvester, John Newsom and our Deputy Director John Dalby. He had given eighteen years' work as our percussion professor, his pupils now leading timpanists in five famous orchestras, and had been on every course, every tour – all voluntary work – and his qualities of character had enriched us all. The NYO had only survived because of the support in the world of education from headteachers like Dame Diana Reader Harris, Rachel Pearse, Dr Taylor and Mr Scott, directors of music in counties or schools like William Pearson and Christopher Cowan, and representatives of music in the BBC and the universities like Professor Hadley, Herbert Howells and especially our Chairman. The minutes record that I concluded, 'I do want to tell you how wonderful I think it is that, starting alone on one little idea, so many distinguished and remarkable people in such varied organisations had come in to help. Thank you all so much.'

Even now, re-reading the minutes more than twenty-five years later, I feel unworthy, but deeply grateful to the Council for their generous tribute:

> Dr Guest for the Council thanked Dr Railton for imparting her genius to the world. 'Other words do not exist; I feel quite sure the whole Council feels the tremendous debt of gratitude for what she has done. It is a good thing that the country now realises just exactly what the size of the work is. I can think of no other way but to say a very deep heartfelt thank-you to her.' He coupled this with a resolve that no stone should be left unturned to see that this great venture she had founded should in some way remain as a permanent memorial to her and her incredibly hard and devoted work.

I was not distressed after that meeting. The word 'suspended' had a purely temporary feel. I knew I had left everything in readiness to continue except for permanent finance, and that the mood to overcome that problem was very strong. I knew Douglas Guest, with his sound judgement and artistic understanding, would 'leave no stone unturned' and all would be well.

On 29 July there was a very well-attended press conference in the Café Royal to announce our coming tour, my resignation and the future of the orchestra. Douglas Guest was in the chair and a statement had been issued:

> As further time is still needed to explore various ways of putting the orchestra on a sound and permanent footing, within the educational system of the country, it has been

> decided to suspend operations at the end of the summer tour. The Governors will announce their future plans as soon as possible.

Almost the first question was, 'What we all want to know is what is Dr Railton going to do next?' So perhaps I was still dangerous! It quite cheered me up. I nearly told them some of the things I would like to get my teeth into next, but according to *The Times* I settled for 'I care about the continuance of the orchestra more than anyone, but after nineteen years of unremitting work I cannot carry so big a burden any longer'.

The *Telegraph* commented that 'this call for help has come at a bad moment. The NYO, such a shining example for Britain, will be at the back of the queue.' It was in fact a gloomy week in which Mr Callaghan, the Chancellor, had announced a 'big squeeze'.

There was as always genuine interest and support from the press; I hope we thanked them. The situation was best summed up by the *Times Educational Supplement*:

> This great orchestra, which must be the finest of its kind in the world, has for some 15 years, on its international tours, been one of our most welcomed ambassadors. And yet, although it carries the national flag, has inspired many changes in music in schools, and raised standards in the profession, it is still privately run. So Dr Ruth Railton and her Council have decided that it is about time it was known how fragile are the supports that raise it aloft. For years they have negotiated quietly for the orchestra to be put on 'a sound and permanent footing'. As nothing has happened they have boldly played their two strongest cards – the resignation of its phenomenally overworked Dr Railton, and the suspension of activities. If a government which has pledged its support for the arts plays deaf to their cries, let it be forced to listen and take action by an opposition which fields an organ scholar as its leader, and a lifelong musical enthusiast among its spokesmen on educational affairs. The Royal Academy had a £1 million Leonardo with which to go to the nation. The NYO has only the outstanding musical talents of our children.

In fact Edward Heath spoke in the House on our behalf, urging the government to support '*our* National Youth Orchestra'. I was also invited by Robin Chichester-Clark MP and Betty Anderson MP to address the Conservative Party's Arts Committee in the House of Commons. Robin Chichester-Clark wrote, 'There is a very great feeling of sympathy for the National Youth Orchestra and this has been increased by your talk . . . I have a Question down to the Government . . . we will do all we can to help.'

In spite of the press conference explaining that we were only suspended, after my last concert a malicious rumour was started that because I was too ill to carry on myself I wanted to kill my own orchestra! Sir Malcolm was very angry, and did a great deal to stifle such nonsense. It was hurtful that a few of my special ex-members believed it. But it was also marvellous for me to see them getting together and fighting with all that was in them to save what I'd given them, something that mattered so much to them that they wanted it for others and for their children.

I had no doubts for the future.

Thirty-Six

It was in Croydon, where Mr Revell had provided the Shirley Secondary School for all our work and the Royal Russell School for sleeping, that Jill and I were completing all the detailed arrangements on which so much of the quality of the orchestra's work depended: for me the fifty-second course, for me the last time. On 21 August we were all ready for the joyful invasion. Instead, they came in as if in a state of shock, talking quietly in groups. We had not expected this. Our members had read the papers, but now reality had set in: 'Are you really leaving us?' and 'Will the orchestra stop?'

So that very evening I explained that we were only *suspending* matters for a short time, to find out if the government believed in our quality of work and training, and if it could provide a safer, more secure future. Twenty years of the welfare state had taught them to take security for granted: they had not realised that we existed by people *giving* their time and their skills, and that authorities *lent* us their property to work in. I had to be firm. They must understand that the NYO owned nothing material, no property, no money except what we were given or what we earned. All our assets were human – ourselves, our staff, our work, our talent, our music. 'So let us start, and make sure that in my last weeks with you, we will do more, do it better, and enjoy it more than ever before.'

We were going to be together for a whole month. With so much to do morale returned. Apart from rehearsal time, the evenings included experts coming to tell us about Italy and Portugal's historic links with England. We soon discovered we needed a large well-displayed map of Europe. Day by day they got to grips with the whole plan of fourteen concerts through six countries in twenty days, and we kept rubbing in that the last concert was the most important, and that was after we got home. If reaction set in on our return to England, we would never get up to peak again for the RFH.

With such a heavy schedule I had decided to repeat the Berlioz overture and the Bizet suite from the last course, and add by request from Italy and Germany the Tchaikovsky symphony. There were six national anthems, and we specialised in orchestrating and interpreting these with dignity and style. In addition, to avoid any strain or in case of illness, we had three soloists: Helen Powell, oboe; John Wallace, trumpet;* and Nichola Gebolys, piano.

One morning before breakfast Nichola fainted, and in falling broke a front tooth. In no time she was on her way to our Hon. Physician Edward McLellan, and the dental department of the hospital where he was a consultant. A perfect matching tooth was made, followed by a check-up with him to be sure of her fitness for the tour. The only treatment seemed to be a bowl of cornflakes with sugar first thing in the morning. There were no more worries about her or the piano concerto thanks to Mr McLellan, and he was able to come to the RFH for our last concert to hear her.

Everything was going splendidly – Rudi Schwarz and all the professors thought it was the best orchestra in our history – when bad news broke on a totally different front: a financial crisis. The Foreign Office was concerned about the amount of currency we would have with us; they were warning us about customs and exchange problems, going as we were through so many borders. Peter explained that we knew no member had more than £5 because they signed a paper, countersigned by a parent, promising not to bring more. It was one of our normal procedures. Officialdom was doubtful, so that evening we made a plan: Peter would travel with enough money for everything, and everyone else would travel without any at all.

*He played the same concerto at the wedding of the Prince of Wales.

We would have no time for shopping anyway, and this would save delays and problems at borders if the crisis got worse when we were away.

Next day was Sunday and the first of our fourteen concerts. We had been invited back to Guildford, this time to the Civic Hall. We extended the platform so that as many as possible of those not coming on tour could play; it was also John Wallace's first performance as a soloist. It was a bank-holiday weekend, and the hall was full. The Lord Mayor was so delighted that he came on to the platform at the end to say thank you and wish us well for the tour.

On Monday we gave Croydon a Fairfield Hall concert as a thank-you to them. It was a fine hall to play in: room for a piano as well as all our players, and this time Nichola's first performance with us. Our chief guests were the Portuguese Ambassador, the German Ambassador and the Mayor of the new Croydon Borough. The audience gave us a wonderful send-off, and thereby a chance to try out one of our encores.

Early next morning all except the 112 coming on tour left for home; with about fifty of the liveliest and youngest gone from us, the place seemed quite lonely. We were flying to Lisbon in the afternoon, and had just the morning for final packing and checking before they all assembled in a circle in the main hall for a last passport and money inspection. It was then that Peter told them about the financial crisis, and why we had to be so particular about the amount of money we were carrying and that to save any problems we had decided to travel without any. They would be given stamped postcards every day to send home, but leave their money behind. Everybody was given a strong brown envelope by an official from Barclays. All they had to do was write their name and the amount on the envelope, put in all their worldly wealth, seal it up and hand it to the official to put in his special box and take it to his van outside the main door. They would get their envelope back unopened the day we got home.

This seemed a simple operation, causing some amusement

with everybody unpacking pockets and handbags, but as I was about to leave for the airport I sensed a sudden change in atmosphere, and decided to walk round the circle. Some were looking quite pale and anxious. I spoke to my youngest boy: 'Will this be your first flight? Are you looking forward to it?'

'I *was*, but not now.'

'Why? What's happened?'

'Well I don't feel very well now that my money's gone.'

'Why? You won't need it.'

'Well you *are* what's in your pocket. Now I'm nothing at all. I'm nobody.'

'You're very important to me. I chose *you*, not your money.'

I was quite shocked. I just spoke to them cheerfully about the pleasure of travelling through five countries without needing a penny, and that I understood the Queen of England never carried any money when travelling, ending with a heartening 'See you at the airport . . .'

But worse was to come. Peter had been checking the envelopes for the bank receipt. Although every member and every parent had signed a paper saying their child only had £5 with them, some had £100, some more – one had £330 in German marks – so some of the anxiety was due to a bad conscience. What luck we'd taken this course: if stopped at a border we would have announced £5 per student, and been found to be lying.

I was really shattered. On the way to the airport all I could hear was 'you *are* what's in your pocket'. My mind wandered back to the early years, when people seized opportunity, not money. Was this new era one in which everything could be bought? Even a parental signature was now a meaningless scribble endorsing a lie. It was the right time for me to leave what I'd created, without money, for the love of things money can't touch.

On the runway at Heathrow lay our special Vanguard. Using every seat and every inch of space in the hold, we could fit in exactly. A perfect flight conquered first-time nerves, and soon we were in Lisbon. The convent seemed even more beautiful in the late-summer light. Beauty lay in every room: embroidery on every bed, and a gift for everybody. The same style was maintained for meals. The whole visit was rare perfection of hospitality, and just the peace and calm we needed. John Wallace wrote recently, 'You could never forget that convent. Most of us had never seen linen sheets, let alone slept in them, and the gifts were all hand-made.'

Next morning, refreshed and happy, we were soon in coaches for Sintra, advertised as 'a little hill station outside Lisbon whose beauties were sung by Byron and Southey'. We were to give the last concert in the ninth Sintra Festival, in the Carlos Manuel Theatre. It was small, but courteous help was available, and by choosing the oboe concerto there was just enough space for everyone. The British Ambassador, Sir Archibald Ross, was there and, no doubt due to his influence, leading figures in the political, educational and artistic fields of Portuguese life turned up for the event. At the end the President of the republic, Admiral Thomaz, unveiled a tablet in the hall in honour of our visit.

As usual when breaking new ground, the quality and professional standard of our playing was unexpected. But it made a deep impression, and the press was excited by this 'miraculous performance'.

Next morning we were about to prepare calmly for our Estoril concert when some officials arrived to explain it was cancelled. Mercifully, it turned out to be only the hall. We had to be on TV for the whole concert – by order of the dictator Salazar – and so move to another place where sufficient power could be supplied. John and I were taken to a school hall where massive improvisation was already under way at nine a.m.: cables everywhere, lights going up on ceilings and a small stage open from one side on to a big yard, already full of vans and equipment. All the TV programmes that evening were to be cancelled for our concert! Looking at the tiny platform I ventured to ask where we were to play. 'Too small? Ah, we build you another platform . . . Chairs? Stands? We find.'

Rudi Schwarz was wonderful; not many conductors would adventure with us as he did. It was late afternoon, and under very hot lights, before we could actually rehearse in the weird circumstances. Somehow at eight the concert started. There was a brief interval in which the performers couldn't leave the platform, but the side exit was opened to get a draught of air. Suddenly into this area swept some motor cycles with sirens wailing. A telegram was being delivered – into my hand alone – from Salazar. Alas the original is lost, but he thanked the players for magnificent music, and mentioned our example and cementing the friendship of our two nations. We completed the concert, and were told next day that it was watched by four million people.

Recently I wrote to Sir Archibald, who had been so encouraging to us, and he replied:

> I well remember the impact your Youth Orchestra made in Portugal. This would have been considerable at any time but when, as in 1965, our official relations swung from bad to very bad, a cultural event like yours was a tremendous boost to morale and brought to the surface all the latent admiration and affection for our country in the hearts of the Portuguese people and even its establishment – hence Salazar's telegram.

In October the Sintra Municipal Council sent a special message that 'this house should show the deepest gratitude for the distinction granted to us, and also the fullest admiration for the National Youth Orchestra, and for the interest awarded to the Sintra Festival'. The proposal had been accepted unanimously, and the letter signed by the Mayor, António Asseca.

After one more night with the peaceful nuns, and postcards supplied and sent home, we all returned to the airport and our friend the Vanguard. Unexpectedly, there was a delay, apparently due to our being overweight. Everybody had been given a bag with a bottle of wine and presents, and sadly all these had to be left behind. Perhaps the plane was carrying more fuel this time for a longer journey. Soon the problem was solved somehow, and we embarked for the flight to Italy, our work for Britain in Portugal complete.

It was then that the pilot explained that we were following a special direct flightpath, across Spain and the Mediterranean and turning north into Milan. It was perfect weather, our young travellers gaining confidence and following maps as the time passed. But as we neared Milan we met a thunderstorm through which, after considerable time circling round, we had to land. A storm in flight is a frightening experience, but our numbered order meant that older and younger members were interspersed, and fears disappeared into relief once we landed.

We were met, but the first impression of Italy was still one of delay and confusion, and much panic everywhere. Eventually buses and van were located and the children were off for four nights in hostels in Milan: gone was the luxury of Lisbon, but a good smell of coffee and ample supply of spaghetti was the introduction to Italy.

It was Saturday, and our first concert was to be in the Teatra Grande di Brescia that evening. I set off to prepare the way with John, two strong members of the percussion department and an Italian secretary. Once out of Milan it was main road all the way to Brescia, but some pleasant landscape in the September sun for the orchestra to enjoy in the afternoon. The little eighteenth-century opera house was beautifully proportioned and decorated; the platform was too small for all to play, and with no space for a piano we could very suitably have Mozart with Helen. Our first anxiety was to locate all our worldly wealth in the van, supposed to have come here direct from the airport. No van: no concert. The secretary disappeared in panic. Our stage work complete, we went in search of some lunch, and in a nearby *trattoria* enjoyed the local chatter. Symphony concerts were rare, as they always had opera. Every seat had sold long ago: 'We like children; we like music; we like British.' The wine flowed. After siesta-time the van came out of hiding, just before the orchestra's coaches came into view, so all was well.

Our first concert in Italy was given to this country-town audience – serious musically, very enthusiastic, happy to stay all night if we would just play on. We had a wonderful press the next day, which cheered our agent, who needed to fill the main concert in Milan. Our second concert, next day, gave us the most beautiful drive through the mountains to Lake Como, and the small opera house of Lecco. I had not had time to see it on our previous visit: if I had, I would have said, 'Impossible!' We made a workable orchestra with about seventy-five to eighty players, with just enough room for John to stand for the trumpet concerto. This concert had been organised by Jeunesses Musicales, and the audience were mainly 'youth' and country people from a farming area. In spite of such difficult circumstances for us, it was greatly appreciated, a very happy Sunday-evening event.

Then came the most important day – the privilege of playing in the world-famous Conservatorio Milan, where Toscanini and all the great conductors and soloists have played, and to an informed and cultured audience. At last, enough space behind the scenes, a large enough platform with room for a grand piano and a lovely auditorium in which we could enjoy our huge sound. There was a sense of occasion as everyone settled comfortably on the platform, and for Rudolf Schwarz too a more familiar environment. There was even a piano in an artists' room so that Nichola could practise – she hadn't seen a piano since the Croydon concert. When the rehearsal had started I went down the hall to test the sound as they warmed up on the national anthem, as orchestrated by us. An official came up to me, radiant with delight at the sound in the empty hall: 'Wonderful music, magnificent, but *not* our anthem . . . no, not our anthem.' This was serious. I rushed to Peter: 'Where did we check the anthem? Where did you get the parts?'

'Ricordi.'

'The Floor Manager says it's not their anthem. What are we playing? It may be some Fascist tune! Go and find out.'

Peter soon came back, laughing: we had the right anthem. The Manager was trying to pay us a compliment; he meant our musical performance of it was so wonderful it was unrecognisable. Anyway, cleaners and staff were collecting in the hall out of curiosity, and spontaneously applauded, so that crisis was over. The piano concerto came back freshly, and was given the most time; and Mr Schwarz stiffened up any weak passages in the symphony. We had to be at our best for Milan.

There being no British ambassador in Milan, the Consul General and several members of his staff came in support. They came round after the concert with words of encouragement and obvious appreciation. But none of us will forget the Milan audience: cool and critical at the start, appreciative of Nichola's Mozart, warming up in the Bizet. After the interval we had become accepted as musicians, not as youth, and through the symphony the response grew, and the '*Bravo*'s, the standing applause and encores raised the whole evening to a memorable peak.

Next morning a friend from the British Consulate brought us all the press, saying that we had impressed the critics as much as the audience. The *Corriere della Sera* headlined DEFINITO: UN MIRACOLO; *Il Giorno* and *La Notte* just headlined ORCHESTRA MIRACOLO, and all seemed to mention '*applauso entusiasta*'. Two rather different comments struck us: 'I have tried to overcome my own fear of superlatives, but this must be the best non-professional orchestra in the world' and 'so musical, so dedicated, they had a sense of disciplined yet lively teamwork which is perhaps only possible in Great Britain'. Perhaps, to foreigners, England had a reputation of pulling together to achieve results. I hope we still have it.

Our Milan impresario, Signor Moltrasio, was so excited that he produced 112 postcards and stamps for them to post home from Italy before we left. We'd brought the best that was in us, and the audiences had enjoyed it; we could leave today feeling that together we had upheld Britain in Italy.

With seven concerts behind us, we had reached the half-way mark. Sister reported no serious casualties, but they were tired and fully deserved a relaxing day without music. We were soon to set off in three coaches to drive through the Alps to Zurich, and it proved to be the treat of a lifetime: 160 miles of mountains and lakes in perfect summer weather, another world for most of our members, who had never left England before. We went from Milan to Como, across Lake Lugano to Bellinzona, and gradually closer to the high mountains at St Gotthard. We noticed how sensitive the children were to light and shade, to sights and scenery of such wonder. Sitting behind me were two who evidently had Bunyan in the school syllabus; I heard, 'Now we really are like pilgrims arriving at the Delectable Mountains,' answered by, 'I hope that doesn't mean we're going to die yet.' This made me even more acutely aware of how easily a whole busload of us could disappear over a precipice! I was glad to reach the St Gotthard Tunnel, which we had made our half-way stage, and where we had to disembark anyway. Everybody had a packet of sandwiches and a bottle of water with them, so a picnic, a walk-about and photography all fitted into the break.

In 1965 the road through the tunnel was not finished. There was a special railway, and our buses were mounted on huge wheeled platforms; we re-embarked and went through. Then on we drove through the highest mountains to Andermatt, gradually down along the shores of the Urner See to Schwyz, and finally following the full length of the Zurich See into the city itself.

In Zurich we returned to the same hostel where we had been two years ago. The manager gave them a good evening dinner after the long journey, and our agent and some leading musicians came round to welcome our return. It was heart-warming, because although our actual conditions were of the simplest and the cheapest, 'We're being treated like royalty' was the comment of thirteen-year-old Ian Laing from Buckie. A happy welcome and an early night marked the half-way point.

September 8 was a routine day. The morning rehearsal was in the excellent Grosser Saal of the Tonhalle. The stage was rather small for us, and they had asked for the trumpet concerto, so it was John once more. It took time to warm up after the day in the buses, but with an afternoon's sleep and the packed hall in the evening, full energy returned. Like Milan, it was one of our best and most appreciated concerts. To us, the Swiss did not seem as excitable as the Italians nor as emotional as the Germans. Their appreciation showed with 'We don't know how such a standard is possible . . . but will you come again next year?'

The next day was supposed to be completely free; but early in the morning an administrator from the Pestalozzi Orphanage at Trogen called to see us. He would supply transport and all expenses, but wanted an afternoon concert in the open air for his several hundred orphans. This was a really hard decision. It meant the total loss of a free day, and one without buses. I wanted to say no, but the members would have read about Pestalozzi, and this was a request to give to people who had so much less than themselves. So after talking to the staff, we decided to tell them what had happened and let them vote. I made it very clear that it was all right to say no, not selfish. A substantial majority said yes.

The Pestalozzi Village had at least a dozen houses, each for a different nation, each one home for about fifty orphans. There was an English home, an Indian, a Greek, Hungarian, Tibetan, American, and others. They had their own staff, of their own religion, language and customs.

So that afternoon we set up the orchestra at one end of a lawn, and in front of us, in their own groups, cross-legged on the grass, were these very young children, none of whom had ever seen an orchestra before. I chose a short programme: the overture, one movement of the trumpet concerto, a bit of Bizet with plenty of percussion and the Waltz from the Tchaikovsky. I didn't expect Rudolf Schwarz to come – he deserved a day off – but he insisted on joining us.

It was fascinating to watch the reaction of each infant-nation. One laughed and clapped excitedly; the Americans were rather fidgety; the Germans concentrated; most impressive of all was the absolute stillness of the Tibetans. At one point a very loud tractor started up on the hillside nearby, but somebody ran up the field and called out to him to stop; he waved at us, then sat on his tractor to listen to the rest of the concert. At the end a child from each group came forward to hand a little gift to the players. Then I took a group of the tiny Tibetans to handle and look at some of the instruments. One wanted to hold a cymbal, but it was too heavy for him to lift!

The village had laid on a wonderful tea party and many interesting people involved in the whole Pestalozzi idea joined in. Sadly we couldn't stay very long as there was much packing and preparation and rest needed before travelling to Germany the next day.

Leaving Switzerland for our three concerts in Germany meant another long day of travel – about four hundred kilometres in coaches to Frankfurt. Educationally it is a good way of getting an idea of the landscape of another country, and a rest from concentrated listening and playing; but it is also tiring. We went on the main motorway from Basle up the Rhine, pausing at a suitable stopping place for an hour's break at about halfway, then journeyed another hundred miles, arriving at youth hostels in Frankfurt in time for a good supper.

Morale was good next morning at early breakfast. Everybody was in the Opera House by nine-thirty for a morning rehearsal: all was German efficiency. I looked about for the grand piano; at my mention of it, it came up through the floor. It was Nichola's turn; some time was needed to get the balance right, and likewise for our heavy brass.

The Manager was still under the impression that we were

some youth exchange-scheme on holiday, and surprised that we were working. Then he started listening, then gradually a few local musicians dropped in out of curiosity. Peter gave them the Italian reviews, and they were asking why they didn't know about our visit.

Our concert was at two-thirty, and indeed the main area of the Opera House was full of young people, students and secondary-school pupils. They were a most appreciative audience, but in the balcony there were hardly any professional musicians or informed adults. At the interval came a request to extend it by an extra ten minutes or so. After the concerto two leading musicians had rushed out to telephone the head of the music school and the leading conductors to tell them to come quickly. It was Saturday afternoon and they lived near by, and in time for the symphony the audience upstairs had increased.

But for all of us in education, the most important person in the hall was Kurt Hahn. He was eighty, and had come a long way to hear us. He came on to the platform to talk to them all and it was worth going to Frankfurt for them to meet and listen to him. I remember he quoted Keats – 'I have seen a stoat today, the creature has a purpose, its eyes are alive with it' – and said that the audience was moved by their dedicated and selfless service to a cause. After spending some time with us all informally he went all the way back to Baden. From there he wrote me a letter which I shall treasure all my days.

> My life's work had been founded on the belief that a child's strength can be kept alive through adolescence if on the threshold of puberty a 'grande passion' is kindled and subsequently maintained. There are many and various healthy passions which can serve as guardian angels of adolescence. There is no more powerful one than music . . . I have never seen better faces than the faces of the 112 youths who had gathered in the Frankfurt Opera last Saturday. The example you have created constitutes an obligation which people cannot ignore who are concerned with the destiny of youth.

The Germans, always keen to build friendships for their young people, put on a party for the orchestra and young musicians and others from Frankfurt: a little social life was just what was needed, and they really enjoyed it. The directors of education and the youth services came and made little speeches. Mrs Bielenberg was told they were unaware of the quality of the NYO, and were embarrassed to have treated it as a touring holiday-group.

In the mean time the Principal of the School of Music, with two conductors and a few professors (the pianist very impressed with Nichola), invited John and me to dinner in his home. They had been deeply affected and moved by the performance: 'It was unimaginable . . .' Three of them had only heard the symphony, and were distressed that such an experience was lost to the mainstream of musical life in the city. 'We want to apologise: we have insulted you. We did not know.' I asked what else we could do: we had supplied the comments of great musicians, the list of great festivals we'd played in and the press – even the Berlin reviews – but we just had to accept that nobody would believe until they had heard for themselves. I said that our orchestra had had a great experience in playing in the Frankfurt Opera House to the future musicians of the city, and how honoured we were to spend an evening with them. We were warmly invited to return next year.

It was Sunday, for us a day of rest – seven hours in coaches! It should have been a simple journey all the way to Hamburg on the autobahn. We had arranged to bring light refreshments for a pause after two hours, and have a really good lunch after about four hours, near Hanover, before the last lap into Hamburg.

In Frankfurt the girls' hostel was some distance from the central one with all the boys. It was simplest to arrange for two of our three coaches to collect the seventy-five boys, and the third to collect the thirty-seven girls, Sister Boddy and our two superb housemistresses Betty Goddard and Mrs Bielenberg. The latter really knew Germany and the autobahn stops from memory. We had a good map and agreed the stopping place for our first break.

Coach One and coach Two, a housemaster in each, set off in style, kept in reasonably close contact, and duly arrived at the agreed stop. We had solemnly promised that whoever got there first would wait for the others. Time went by, and there was no sign of Mrs Bielenberg's coach and all my precious girls. All the refreshments were in the back of their bus too! After forty minutes I started to fret. After an hour I insisted on making some police contact.

There was a footbridge over the motorway to the traffic-police office, and Peter set off to find out if they could locate our missing bus: it had our NYO labels on the windows. Yes indeed, they'd had a report that a coach containing British children had gone off the autobahn. No, they couldn't say yet how many were injured. No, they had no more information yet. Poor Peter. Later he said:

> My heart was pounding as I climbed back over the bridge. My legs felt like lead. How was I to break this terrible news to Ruth and John? Providentially as I was half-way down the steps off the bridge, our third coach came sailing by underneath. I was speechless when I got back to you, and still pretty shocked that evening when Sister forced a sleeping tablet into me for the first and only time in my life.

Coach Three had kept their promise to wait if they reached the stopping point first. But when they set off from the hostel the coach got entangled in some overhead scaffolding and could not break free. In fact the local fire engine with lifting gear was called – a most exciting start to the day. And it was unfortunate that when they finally got moving they stopped at the wrong place. After nearly an hour they had decided to move on. They were quite cheerful, and had eaten their refreshments. We were in a state of reaction from anxiety and relief. All was well now, but we'd lost an hour, and it was in fact three p.m. when we got to the planned Sunday lunch. In the whole of my seventeen years this was the only time I saw a few signs of morale cracking under strain. It is surprising what a good meal can do. We also changed the coach seating to a more sociable mix before we set off on the last hundred miles to Hamburg.

The welcome at Hamburg was just what was needed. We had stayed in the hostel twice before, in 1959 and '61. Such splendid hospitality, like a welcome home, turned the corner for our tired travellers. The director of the hostel and our agent made little speeches of welcome, and read a greeting from the Mayor. Everybody felt safe and happy as they went off to bed.

It was plain at breakfast that the resilience of youth had won. Once again we mounted buses, for the trip to Bremen. A good hall, Helen's concerto, Rudi in fine form after a day off and a very appreciative audience restored us to happy normality.

As strangers, in 1959, Hamburg had welcomed us for our first concert in Germany; now, as friends, we would give them our last. We were all stimulated to make it our best, and they asked for the trumpet concerto. For us they were the perfect audience, so keenly intelligent to play to, so rapt in musical understanding. That night I felt new life had come to sustain the rest of our tour, and there will always be a warm place in my heart for Hamburg.

A leading critic wrote:

> We in Hamburg have vivid memories of the astonishing standard of this orchestra. Its members change – only three including the leader were here in 1959 – new younger members joining each year. What remains the same is its spirit, its silent concentration, its exciting energy, its love of playing – all its own miracle.

No time yet to relax. There was an early start to the airport, where lay our special Vanguard and our friends the pilot and his staff. Soon we were in Schiphol Airport, warmly greeted with efficient arrangements to take us to the Kurlzaal at Scheveningen. It was always a relief to find a large enough platform and space behind the scenes. There was also an excellent piano for Nichola, her last opportunity to play before the RFH concert. Our whole day was spent in the hall and its environs. Of course there was a rehearsal for sound and balance, and time for Nichola to practise. A wonderful lunch was provided, then after a rest and a walk there was just time left to get the last foreign stamps for postcards home.

I asked our agent if at this difficult holiday time there would be a full hall, and got the reply, 'Of course, the Dutch people do not forget.' And so it was. (We had not played in Holland since 1955.)

The British Ambassador was away but a Mr Burrows from the Embassy came in support. He told us the large audience included all the senior Dutch music critics, and that the response, showing special appreciation by standing, was unusually enthusiastic. It is very moving when a whole audience suddenly stands up; after much applause, all sat down again, completely still at the sign of an encore. This last concert in Holland, our sixth country, left us with the happiest of memories as we left the platform straight to Schiphol.

There, lit up in the darkness, the friendly Vanguard was waiting for us. Soon each was safely strapped into his narrow bed, taking one last look at the lights of the continent of Europe, and with the lull of the engines fell fast asleep. When they woke we were in England, all safely home.

Mr Burrows very kindly sent us all the Dutch reviews in translation, saying it was rare to see such a uniformly cordial press: 'a luminous example . . . serious study and a true love of music' (*Haagsche Courant*); 'the orchestra has a beautiful sound – a unique concert. The Mozart Piano Concerto was flawless and crystal clear' (*Nieuwe Haagsche Courant*); 'excellent ensemble, yet the programme was rehearsed in one week; (*Nieuwe Rotterdamse Courant*); 'not a weak spot in the orchestra. It is unlikely that the violinists possess priceless instruments; yet one could not tell this for certain' (*Alg. Dagblad*).

*

After the journey from Heathrow it was two a.m. on 16 September when everyone was finally settled in Dr Taylor's marvellous new premises at Haberdasher's Aske's, which he had lent to us for these last two days. Many slept on until a meeting at twelve noon followed by lunch. It was to be a completely free day, my only rule that there was not to be one note of music.

We were all tired, including the staff, from the oldest (Sister Boddy) to the youngest (Jill), and we were all very proud of the splendid way the orchestra had survived all the varying conditions and the long hours of travelling, never failing at a concert. They were all so different – in age, in strength, in character – but the whole had pulled together and succeeded. It was time for well-deserved praise, not just for the performances but for the children themselves. My special 112 were as fine a group of young people as could be found anywhere. I loved them. Today was my last day with them, and we talked quietly together, with some sadness, for they too had close friendships and would soon be parted. Tomorrow we would go to the very heart of England and play joyously together for the last time.

I decided to return to London that evening, to be early in the RFH next morning. We all had supper together and I was just leaving the dining-room when John stopped me. Knowing my love of choirs, a few of our best singers had, with his help, secretly defied the rule and in a faraway corner had prepared a farewell to me. They had chosen 'The Silver Swan' by Orlando Gibbons to sing for me before I left. To this day I cannot hear that tune without remembering all my members, from 1947 to '65, scattered around the world as they now are.

The RFH has many memories for me, from the opening night in 1952 through Toscanini's last concerts, the great days of the Philharmonia with Cantelli, the countless rehearsals I'd slipped into over the years studying new works and unknown conductors, our own first concert there in 1953 and now my last. September 17 must be a great memory for them, the triumphant climax of the tour and the culmination of nineteen years.

Ian Hunter was with us; so were our Chairman Douglas Guest and other members of the Council; the Chairman and other representatives of the *Mirror* who had so generously financed us; and representatives of the government who hadn't contributed a penny; and all the assemblage that a Commonwealth Arts Festival brings.

I was always behind the scenes before the concert, and beside the entrance to the platform where everyone passed me as they moved on to the stage. When the overture was under way I would stay with the soloist, until she in turn was on the platform, and be there to share her happiness after her performance. John would take over at the interval while I listened in the audience, but tonight I stayed with him.

Rudi Schwarz had been the genius of the tour. He had nurtured unfailingly the growth and change through thirteen very different concerts, yet tonight found new inspiration for the last time. After two encores he said, 'They won't stop until you go on.' Our last encore was a piece of great music, English music, with a special meaning for me, Elgar's *Nimrod*. I conducted it; then, with my orchestra, left the platform . . . and my life in music . . . out into the dark night . . . but I was sure of the light burning in thousands of young hearts who would never let the music go in an England no longer *das Land ohne Musik*.

APPENDIX A

The Concert Programmes

The Assembly Rooms, Bath; April 1948

Weber. Overture. Oberon
Mozart. Piano Concerto in A K488.
Soloist: Elizabeth Powell
Malcolm Arnold. Suite for Youth Opus 1 (first performance)
Beethoven. Symphony No. 2 in D
Elgar. Pomp and Circumstance No. 4

The Guildhall, Cambridge; August 1948

Beethoven. Overture. Fidelio
Grieg. Piano Concerto in A Minor.
Soloist: Nigel Coxe
Delius. On Hearing the First Cuckoo in Spring
Schubert. Symphony No. 8 in B Minor (The Unfinished)
Tchaikovsky. Nutcracker Suite

Philharmonic Hall, Liverpool; January 1949

Glinka. Overture. Ruslan and Liudmilla
Schumann. Piano Concerto in A Minor.
Soloist: Sheila Randall
Elgar. Suite No. 2. The Wand of Youth
Tchaikovsky. Suite. Swan Lake
Beethoven. Symphony No. 5 in C Minor

Central Hall, Westminster; April 1949

Weber. Overture. Oberon
Beethoven. Piano Concerto No. 4 in G.
Soloist: Robin Wood
Elgar. Suite No. 2. The Wand of Youth
Dvořák. Symphony No. 8 in G

The Town Hall, Leeds; August 1949

Dvořák. Overture. Carnival
Mendelssohn. Violin Concerto in E Minor.
Soloist: Beryl Kimber
Haydn. Symphony No. 100 (The Military)
Britten. The Young Person's Guide to the Orchestra

The Central Hall, Bristol; The Pavilion, Bath; January 1950

Borodin. Overture. Prince Igor
Brahms. Violin Concerto in D.
Soloist: Tessa Robbins
Mozart. Symphony No. 39 in E Flat
Walton. Suite. Façade

The Dome, Brighton; Palais de Chaillot, Paris; Salle Pleyel, Paris; April 1950

Berlioz. Overture. Benvenuto Cellini
Beethoven. Piano Concerto No. 2 in B Flat.
Soloist: Nigel Coxe
Malcolm Arnold. Divertimento (first performance)
Fanfare, Tango, Chaconne
Dvořák. Symphony No. 8 in G

The Music Hall, Aberdeen; The Adam Smith Hall, Kirkcaldy; August 1950

Rossini. Overture. Semiramide
Bruch. Kol Nidrei.
Soloist: Carol Sansom
Gordon Jacobs. Passacaglia on a Well Known Theme
Rossini–Britten. Soirées musicales
Brahms. Symphony No. 4 in E Minor

The City Hall, Hull; January 1951

Schubert. Overture. Rosamunde
Mozart. Piano Concerto in F. K459.
Soloist: Dody Trygvason
Holst. The Perfect Fool
Sibelius. Symphony No. 2 in D

The Albert Hall, Manchester; April 1951

Elgar. Overture. Cockaigne
Mozart. Aria. Deh Vieni
Handel. Aria. Lusinghe piu Care.
Soloist: Mary Hampshire
Bizet. Suite No. 1. L'Arlesienne. Farndole from Suite No. 2
Schubert. Symphony No. 8 in B Minor (The Unfinished)
Smetana. Symphonic Poem. Vltava

The Usher Hall, Edinburgh International Festival; August 1951

Wagner. Overture. Rienzi
Mozart. Clarinet Concerto in A.
Soloist: Colin Bradbury
Malcolm Arnold. Divertimento No. 2 (first performance)
Kabalevsky. Symphony No. 2
Smetana. Symphonic Poem. Vltava

The Philharmonic Hall, Liverpool; January 1952

Wagner. Overture. Die Meistersingers
Mozart. Piano Concerto in C Minor. K491.
Soloist: Frances Holmes
Benjamin Frankel. Mephistopheles' Serenade and Dance (first performance)
Dvořák. Symphony No. 9 in E Minor (The New World)

The Winter Gardens, Bournemouth; April 1952

Weber. Overture. Euryanthe
Saint-Saens. Piano Concerto No. 2 in G Minor.
Soloist: Susan Tunnell
Benjamin Frankel. Mephistopheles' Serenade and Dance
Brahms. Symphony No. 1 in C Minor

The Usher Hall, Edinburgh International Festival; St Andrew's Hall, Glasgow; August 1952

Glinka. Overture. Ruslan and Liudmilla
Haydn. Oboe Concerto.
Soloist: Adèle Karp
Britten. The Young Person's Guide to the Orchestra
Dvořák. Symphony No. 8 in G

The Town Hall, Leeds; The City Hall, Sheffield; January 1953

Nicolai. Overture. The Merry Wives of Windsor
Beethoven. Piano Concerto No. 3 in C Minor.
  Soloist: David Wilde
Arnell. Prelude. The Black Mountain (first performance in England). Assembly March (first performance)
Glazunov. Symphony No. 6 in C Minor

The Royal Festival Hall, London; Palais des Beaux-Arts, Brussels; April 1953

Beethoven. Overture. Egmont
Mendelssohn. Violin Concerto in E Minor.
  Soloist: Ralph Holmes
Rawsthorne. Coronation Suite (first performance)
Franck. Symphony in D Minor

The Usher Hall, Edinburgh International Festival; St Andrew's Hall, Glasgow; August 1953

Brahms. Overture. Academic Festival
Saint-Saens. Cello Concerto in A Minor.
  Soloist: Carol Sansom
Malcolm Arnold. English Dances (first performance)
Sibelius. Symphony No. 1 in E Minor

The Town Hall, Birmingham; The Civic Hall, Wolverhampton; January 1954

Berlioz. Overture. Benvenuto Cellini
Bruch. Violin Concerto in G Minor.
  Soloist: Gillian Eastwood
Bax. Tintagel
Haydn. Symphony No. 100 (The Military)
Chabrier. España

The City Hall, Newcastle upon Tyne; April 1954

Rossini. Overture. Semiramide
Beethoven. Piano Concerto No. 1 in C Major.
  Soloist: Shelagh Stamp
Elgar. Suite No. 2. Wand of Youth
Dvořák. Symphony No. 7 in D Minor

The Usher Hall, Edinburgh International Festival; St Andrew's Hall, Glasgow; August 1954

Weber. Overture. Euryanthe
Mozart. Piano Concerto in G. K453.
Soloist: Allan Schiller
Boris Blacher. New work (first performance)
Tchaikovsky. Symphony No. 5 in E Minor

St George's Hall, Bradford; January 1955

Dvořák. Overture. Carnival
Mozart. Violin Concerto in D. K218.
Soloist: John Tunnell
Malcolm Arnold. Homage to the Queen
Haydn. Symphony No. 102 in B Flat
Kodály. Suite. Háry János

The Royal Festival Hall, London; Palais des Beaux-Arts, Brussels; Concertubuow, Amsterdam; April 1955

Bliss. Birthday Greetings to Her Majesty
Mendelssohn. Overture. Ruy Blas
Bach. Klavier Concerto in D Minor.
Soloist: Wendy Waterman
Gordon Jacob. Prelude and Toccata
Dvořák. Symphony No. 9 in E Minor

The Town Hall, Watford; Promenade Concert, The Royal Albert Hall, London; August 1955

Borodin. Overture. Prince Igor
Cedric Thorpe Davie. Diversions on a Tune by Dr Arne (first performance)
Bruch. Violin Concerto in G Minor.
Soloists: Ralph Holmes, John Bacon
Tchaikovsky. Marche slave
Dvořák. Symphony No. 9 in E Minor

The Brangwyn Hall, Swansea; January 1956

Wagner. Overture. Die Meistersingers
Mozart. Piano Concerto in F. K459.
Soloist: Ann Pickup
Walton. Suite. Façade
Mendelssohn. Symphony No. 4 in A (The Italian)
Berlioz. Hungarian March from the Damnation of Faust

The Royal Festival Hall, London; April 1956

Schubert. Overture. Rosamunde
Haydn. Cello Concerto in D.
Soloist: Rohan de Seram
John Addison. Sinfonietta (first performance)
Brahms. Symphony No. 4 in E Minor

The Usher Hall, Edinburgh International Festival; The Market Hall, Carlisle; August 1956

Berlioz. Overture. Le Corsair
Haydn. Symphonia Concertante Op. 84 for Oboe, Bassoon, Violin and Cello.
Soloists: Neil Black, Martin Gatt, David Stone, Penelope Lynex
Benjamin Frankel. A Shakespeare Overture Op. 29 (first performance)
Beethoven. Symphony No. 5 in C Minor

The Colston Hall, Bristol; The Pavilion, Bath; January 1957

Elgar. Overture. Cockaigne
Mozart. Piano Concerto in D. K537.
Soloist: Stephanie Bamford
Bizet. Suite. L'Arlesienne
Shostakovich. Symphony No. 1

The Royal Festival Hall, London; April 1957

Rossini. Overture. Journey to Rheims
Mozart. Piano Concerto in F. K459.
Soloist: Kathleen Jones
Britten. The Young Person's Guide to the Orchestra
Schubert. Symphony No. 9 in C

Promenade Concert, The Royal Albert Hall, London; August 1957

Weber. Overture. Der Freischütz
Mozart. Piano Concerto in A. K488.
Soloist: Allan Schiller
Malcolm Arnold. Divertimento
Bizet. Suite. L'Arlesienne
Dvořák. Symphony No. 8 in G

Westminster Abbey, London; August 1957

Weber. Overture. Der Freischütz
Gabrieli. Sonata Pian e Forte, for Brass Instruments
Mozart. Horn Concerto in E Flat. K447.
Soloist: David Presland
Dvořak. Symphony No. 8 in G

The Town Hall, Birmingham; The De Montfort Hall, Leicester; January 1958

Beethoven. Overture. Leonore No. 3
Bach. Concerto for Two Violins
Soloists: Francis Mason, Margaret Roose
Tchaikovsky. Overture. Romeo and Juliet
Arnold. Symphony No. 2 Op. 40

The City Hall, Cork; The Theatre Royal, Dublin; The Philharmonic Hall, Liverpool; April 1958

Weber. Overture. Oberon
Mozart. Violin Concerto in A. K219.
Soloist: Sidney Mann
Hamilton Harty. The Fair Day from an Irish Symphony
Borodin. Symphony No. 2 in B Minor
Rimsky-Korsakov. Capriccio espagnol

The Town Hall, Watford; August 1958

Berlioz. Overture. Carnival Romain
Beethoven. Piano Concerto No. 2 in B Flat.
Soloist: Jonquil Glenton
Susskind. Nine Slovak Sketches
Franck. Symphony in D Minor

The Free Trade Hall, Manchester; January 1959

Nicolai. Overture. The Merry Wives of Windsor
Beethoven. Piano Concerto No. 4 in G.
Soloist: Stephen Savage
Respighi. The Fountains of Rome
Vaughan Williams. Symphony No. 2 in A (The London)

The Royal Festival Hall, London; April 1959

Handel–Elgar. Overture in D Minor
Schumann. Piano Concerto in A Minor.
Soloist: Michael Roll
Rossini–Respighi. La Boutique fantasque
Dvořák. Symphony No. 7 in D Minor

The Assembly Hall, Tunbridge Wells; August 1959

Handel–Elgar. Overture in D Minor
Mozart. Piano Concerto in D Minor. K466.
Soloist: Kathleen Jones
Rossini–Britten. Suite. Soirées musicales
Dvořák. Symphony No. 7 in D Minor

Promenade Concert, The Royal Albert Hall, London; The Musikhalle, Hamburg; The Hochschule für Musik, Berlin; August 1959

Handel–Jacob. Overture. Theadora
Rossini–Britten. Suite. Soirées musicales
Mozart. Piano Concerto in D Minor. K466.
Soloist: Allan Schiller
Tchaikovsky. Suite. Casse-noisette
Dvořák. Symphony No. 7 in D Minor

The Royal Hall, Harrogate; January 1960

Berlioz. Overture. Benvenuto Cellini
Mozart. Violin Concerto No. 3 in G.
Soloist: Kenneth Sillitoe
Delius. A Walk to the Paradise Garden
Sibelius. Symphony No. 2 in D

The Dome, Brighton; April 1960

Wagner. Overture. Rienzi
Mozart. Piano Concerto in C Minor. K491.
Soloist: Evelyn Rix
Prokofiev. Suite. Le Pas d'acier
Dvořák. Symphony No. 9 in E Minor (The New World)

St Andrew's Hall, Glasgow; The Music Hall, Aberdeen; The Caird Hall, Dundee; August 1960

Dvořák. Overture. Carnival
Mozart. Flute Concerto in G.
Soloist: Sebastian Bell
Holst. The Planets *Jupiter, Saturn, Uranus*
Sibelius. Symphony No. 1 in E Minor

The Guildhall, Portsmouth; Winchester Cathedral; January 1961

Beethoven. Overture. Egmont
Spohr. Violin Concerto No. 8 in A Minor.
Soloist: Mary Gallagher
Grieg. Symphonic Dances
Brahms. Symphony No. 1 in C Minor

The Royal Festival Hall, London; Westminster Abbey, London; April 1961

Brahms. Overture. Academic Festival
Mozart. Violin Concerto in A. K219.
Soloist: Maureen Smith
Elgar. Suite No. 2. Wand of Youth
Schubert. Symphony No. 8 in B Minor (The Unfinished)
Smetana. Blanik (No. 6 from Ma Vlast)

Canterbury Cathedral; The Musikhalle, Hamburg; The Hochschule für Musik, Berlin; The Tchaikovsky Hall, Moscow; Kiev; Leningrad; The University Hall, Helsinki; Stockholm; August 1961

Weber. Overture. Oberon
Mozart. Clarinet Concerto in A.
Soloist: Antony Pay
Mozart Piano Concerto in G. K453.
Soloist: Allan Schiller
Haydn. Trumpet Concerto.
Soloist: Moragh McLeod
Britten. The Young Person's Guide to the Orchestra
Tchaikovsky. Symphony No. 5 in E Minor

The State Cinema, Gainsborough; The City Hall, Sheffield; April 1962

Berlioz. Overture. Le Corsair
Mendelssohn. Violin Concerto in E Minor.
Soloist: Antoine Goulard
Ridout. Three Pictures of Picasso (first performance)
Brahms. Symphony No. 4 in E Minor

The Chichester Festival Theatre; Guildford Cathedral; August 1962

Berlioz. Overture. Les Francs Juges
Vaughan Williams. The Lark Ascending.
Soloist: Rosemary Ellison
Dvořák. Rhapsody No. 3 in A Flat
arr. Vaughan Williams. The Old Hundredth for Orchestra and Congregation
Schubert. Symphony No. 7 in C

The City Hall, Hull; York Minster; January 1963

Verdi. Overture. The Force of Destiny
Haydn. Piano Concerto in D.
Soloist: Diana Ostick
Britten. Four Sea Interludes from Peter Grimes
Brahms. Symphony No. 2 in D

The Royal Festival Hall, London; April 1963

Bliss. Fanfare
Elgar. Overture. Cockaigne
Mozart. Horn Concerto No. 4 in E Flat. K495.
  Soloist: David Cripps
Rimsky-Korsakov. Capriccio espagnol
Dvořák. Symphony No. 9 in E Minor (The New World)

Worcester Cathedral; The Philharmonic Hall, Warsaw; The Concert Hall, Łódz; The Tonhalle, Zurich; August 1963

Elgar. Overture. Cockaigne
Haydn. Concerto for Oboe.
  Soloist: Helen Powell
Mozart. Concerto for Violin in A. K 219.
  Soloist: Maureen Smith
Rimsky-Korsakov. Capriccio espagnol
Dvořák. Symphony No. 8 in G

The City Hall, Newcastle upon Tyne; The Empire Theatre, Sunderland; January 1964

Wagner. Overture. Die Meistersingers
Beethoven. Piano Concerto No. 1 in C.
  Soloist: Paul Roberts
Malcolm Arnold: English Dances
Sibelius. Symphony No. 2 in D

The Villa Marina Royal Hall, Douglas; April 1964

Weber. Overture. Der Freischütz
Mozart. Piano Concerto in A. K414.
  Soloist: Anthony Mott
Bliss. Prologue and Five Dances from Checkmate
Borodin. Symphony No. 2 in B Minor

The Fairfield Hall, Croydon; Jerusalem; The Tsemah Amphitheatre, Galilee; Caesarea; The Municipal Basketball Stadium, Tel Aviv; The Keren Cinema, Beersheba; The Armon Hall, Haifa; The Odeon of Herodes Atticus, Athens Festival; August 1964

Berlioz. Overture. Benvenuto Cellini
Bach. Concerto for Two Violins in D Minor.
Soloists: Maureen and Hazel Smith; Roger Garland and Anne Parkin
Handel. Concerto for Harp.
Soloist: Susan Drake
Britten. The Young Person's Guide to the Orchestra
Dvořák. Symphony No. 7 in D Minor

The Royal Albert Hall, London; The Colston Hall, Bristol; January 1965

Glinka. Overture. Ruslan and Liudmilla
Mozart. Clarinet Concerto in A.
Soloist: Antony Pay
Dvořák. Scherzo Capriccioso
Berlioz. Symphonie fantastique

The Royal Festival Hall, London; April 1965

Walton. Fanfare for the Queen Mother
Dvořák. Overture. Carnival
Mozart. Oboe Concerto in C. K314.
Soloist: Helen Powell
Bizet. Suite. L'Arlesienne
Sibelius. Symphony No. 1 in E Minor

The Civic Hall, Guildford; The Fairfield Hall, Croydon; The Carlos Manuel Theatre, Sintra; Estoril; The Teatra Grande, Brescia; The Opera House, Lecco; The Conservatorio Hall, Milan; The Pestalozzi Orphanage; The Tonhalle, Zurich; The Opera House, Frankfurt; The Musikhalle, Hamburg; The Grosser Glockensaal, Bremen; The Kurlzaal, Scheveningen; The Royal Festival Hall, London; August–September 1965

Berlioz. Overture. Carnival romain
Haydn. Trumpet Concerto.
  Soloist: John Wallace
Mozart. Oboe Concerto in C. K314.
  Soloist: Helen Powell
Mozart. Piano Concerto in B Flat.
  Soloist: Nichola Gebolys
Bizet. Suite. L'Arlesienne
Tchaikovsky. Symphony No. 5 in E Minor

APPENDIX B

Council Members and Staff

The Council, 1949

President: Sir Adrian Boult

Vice Presidents:

Mr John Barbirolli — Dr Reginald Jacques — Sir Malcolm Sargent

Chairman: Sir Adrian Boult

Vice Chairman: Dr Reginald Jacques

Treasurer: Mr Walter Hutchinson

Assistant Treasurer: Mr R. S. McDougall

Sir Arnold Bax	Master of the King's Musick
Mr Mervyn Bruxner	Music Adviser, Kent
Mr Douglas Cameron	Fellow and Professor, Royal Academy of Music
Mr John Dalby	Music Adviser, Aberdeen
Mr John Denison	Director of Music, Arts Council
Sir George Dyson	Director, Royal College of Music
Dr C. Edmunds	Principal, Birmingham Midland Institute
Mrs Walter Elliott:	Chairman, National Association of Girls' Clubs
Mr R. J. Forbes	Principal, Royal Manchester College of Music
Mr Arnold Foster	Director of Music, Westminster School
Dr Greenhouse Allt	Principal, Trinity College of Music
Mr Douglas Guest	Director of Music, Uppingham School
Dr P. A. S. Hadley	Professor of Music, Cambridge University
Dr Charles Hooper	Inspector of Schools, Leeds
Miss Mary Ibberson	Director, Rural Music Schools Association
Mr Maurice Jacobson	
Mr Hector McCurrach	Director of Music, Harrow School
Mr John Newsom	County Education Officer, Hertfordshire
Mr William Pearson	Music Adviser, Cornwall
Mr Leslie Scott	Headmaster, City of Bath Boys' School
Mr Bernard Shore	HMI (Assessor)
Mr George Sylvester	Chief Education Officer, Bristol
Mr Sydney Twemlow	Music Adviser, Norfolk
General T. F. Wilson	King George's Jubilee Trust
Mr Cyril Winn	

Director: Miss Ruth Railton

Secretary: Miss Philippa Ramsden

Appendix B

The officers of the NYO

President:	Sir Adrian Boult (1949–58)
	Sir Malcolm Sargent (1958–)
Vice President:	Mr John Barbirolli
	Dr Reginald Jacques
	Sir Malcolm Sargent (1949–58)
	Sir Adrian Boult
	Mr Walter Susskind (1958–)
Chairman of the Council:	Sir Adrian Boult (1949–55)
	Dr Douglas Guest (1955–)
Chairman of the Executive Committee:	Mr Maurice Jacobson (1949–64),
	Dr Taylor (1964–)
Vice-Chairman of the Executive Committee:	Mr John Newsom (1949–64)
Honorary Secretary:	Mr George Sylvester (1949–65)
Treasurer:	Mr Walter Hutchinson (1948)
	Mr R. S. McDougall (1949–55)
	Mr Roland Bird (1955–60)
	Mr T. S. Ryder (1960–)
Honorary Physician:	Lord Evans

The following served on the Council in ensuing years

1949	Dr R. S. Thatcher
1950	Mr Arnold McShields, HMI, Scotland
1951	Mr J. G. Barr, Superintendent of Music, Glasgow
	Mr Roland Bird, Deputy Editor, *The Economist*
	Mr Noel Hale, Organiser of Music, Bournemouth
	Mr Ronald Harding, Director, Sussex Rural Music School
	Miss Diana Reader Harris, Headmistress, Sherborne School for Girls
	Sir Robert Mayer
	Mr Boris Ord, King's College, Cambridge
	Miss Rachel Pearse, Headmistress, Mary Datchelor Girls School
	Dr Taylor, Headmaster, Haberdasher's Aske's
1954	Sir Ernest Bullock, Royal College of Music
1955	Mr Malcolm Arnold
	Sir Arthur Bliss, Master of the Queen's Music
	Mr J. H. Bruce Lockhart, Headmaster, Sedbergh School
	Mr Frederic Cox, Principal, Royal Manchester College of Music
	Dr Edric Cundell, Principal, Guildhall School
	Mr Arnold Foster, Director of Music, Westminster School
	Mr Henry Havergal, Principal, Royal Scottish Academy of Music
	Mr Ian Hunter

	Dr Herbert Wiseman
1956	Dr Thomas Armstrong, Principal, Royal Academy of Music
1958	Professor J. A. Westrupp, Professor of Music, Oxford University
	Professor Ian Parrott, University College of Wales
	Mr T. E. Bean, General Manager, Royal Festival Hall
1959	Mr J. W. Horton, HMI (Assessor)
1960	Mr Ernest Hall, Professor, Royal College of Music
	Mr Gordon Thorne, Principal, Guildhall School
	Mr M. Thornely, Headmaster, Sedbergh School
	Miss Watkins, Headmistress, Bedford High School
	Mr T. S. Ryder, Managing Director, Kelly Iliffe Holdings
1961	Mr Keith Falkner, Director, Royal College of Music
	Mr B. W. Appleby, Music Organiser, Doncaster
	Mr Stewart Mason, Director of Education, Leicestershire
	Mr Neil Black
	Mr Victor Gollancz
	Mr Yehudi Menuhin
	Mr Eric Simm, Headmaster, Salford Grammar School
	Mr David Willcocks, King's College, Cambridge
1962	Mr Christopher Cowan, Director of Music, Winchester College
	Mr John Rust, Deputy Principal, Birmingham School of Music
	Miss J. A. Tredgold, Headmistress, Cheltenham Ladies' College
	Mr L. D. Stewart, County Music Adviser, Cambridgeshire
	Dr Bernard Rose, Magdalen College, Oxford
	Mr J. Rankin, HMI, Scotland (Assessor)
1964	Mr L. H. Macklin, Secretary, Associated Board of the Royal Schools of Music
	Mr John Manduell, Head of Music, BBC Midland
	Mr Harold Magnay, formerly Director of Education, Liverpool
	Lady Ogilvy, Principal, St Anne's College, Oxford
	Mr Lionel Salter, Head of Opera, BBC
1965	Mr Peter Davies, Organiser of Music, Southampton
	Mr Alec Sherman
	Mr Chevenix Trench, Headmaster, Eton College
	Mr Robert Stobie, Organiser of Music, Midlothian
	Mr Walter Hart, Music Adviser, Kent
	Mr Watson Forbes, Head of Music, BBC Scotland
	Mr Eugène Cruft, Treasurer, Royal Society of Musicians
	Lord Annan, Provost, King's College, Cambridge

Appendix B

Professorial Staff

Musical Director: Dr Ruth Railton

Assistant Musical Director: John Dalby, Ivey Dickson

Conductors:

Sir Adrian Boult
Dr Reginald Jacques
Walter Susskind
Hugo Rignold
Sir Malcolm Sargent
Dr Rudolf Schwarz
Jean Martinon
Oivin Fjeldstad

Strings

Leonard Hirsch
Douglas Cameron
Keith Cummings
Eugène Cruft
Frederick Riddle
Eugene Genin

Woodwind

Frederick Thurston
Leon Goossens
Gwydion Brooke
Gareth Morris
Janet Craxton
William Waterhouse
Norman Knight
Thea King
Archie Camden

Brass

Ernest Hall
Malcolm Arnold
Dennis Brain

Percussion
John Dalby
James Bradshaw

Harp
Gwendolyn Mason
Marisa Robles

Other distinguished musicians who taught for the NYO

Richard Adeney
Leonard Brain
Victor Brightmore
Jack Brymer
John Cruft
Ambrose Gauntlet
Max Gilbert
Ronald Harding
Arthur Hedges
Henry Holst
George Hurst
Aubrey Johnson
James Merrett
Arthur Milner
Manoug Parikian
Gervaise de Peyer
Eric Pritchard
Frank Probyn
Max Salpeter
Sydney Sutcliffe
Lionel Tertis
André Vandernoot
John Walton
Roy Watson
Christopher Wellington
Eric Whittaker
Stephen Whittaker

Administrative Staff

1947–48	Secretary:	Philippa Ramsden
1949	Secretary:	Mrs Singer
1950	Secretary:	Mrs Ballingall
1951–52	Secretary:	Joan Ashton
1953	Administrative Assistant:	Mrs Ballingall
	Secretary:	Shirley Graham
1954	General Secretary:	Vera Maynard Davy
	Assistant:	Shirley Graham
1955–63	Secretary:	Diana Scholefield
	Assistants:	Amber Pares, Brenda Stonely, Mary Shoppee, Ann Teviotdale, Martha Burghard
1964	Administrator:	Peter McLachlan
	Secretaries:	Jill Wilson, Nigel King

Voluntary Staff

Housemasters:
Timothy Boyle
Andrew Clark
Denis Cocks
Noel de Jong
Hubert Dawkes
Thomas Dennis
Peter Francis
Colin Gough
Howard Gough
John Hind
Harold Last
Donald Leggatt
Colonel Liddell
Roy McCornish
James Reid
Norman Smith
Rodney Smith
David Snell
Ronald Sturley
Rex Thompsett
Christopher Wellington

Medical:
Doctor: Dr Jose Payan
Sisters: Miss M. L. Barnes
Miss C. M. Blake
Jean Boddy
Dorothy Field
Bunty Neave

Housemistresses:
Mary Boyle
Elizabeth Beale
Christabel Bielenberg
Christine Brown
Mrs Freyan
Diana Fryer
Betty Goddard
Mrs Howard Gough
Barbara Park
Editha Roupell
Mary Selby-Biggs
Mary Rose Seldon
Delphine Starmer

Social Affairs:
Shirley Barraclough
Jill Braybrook
Marion Brodie
Mrs Chalmers Park
Winifred Forselius
Mrs Johnston
Gillian Lowe
Helen McDougall
Elizabeth Morgan
Miss O'Dwyer
Nancy Strudwick

Index

Index

INDEX